SUNDAY WORSHIP

A Planning
Guide
to Celebration

Kevin W. Irwin

SUNDAY WORSHIP

A Planning
Guide
to Celebration

PUEBLO PUBLISHING COMPANY

New York

Design: Frank Kacmarcik

ISBN: 0-916134-52-0

Printed in the United States of America.

To Gabriel O'Donnell, O.P.

Contents

Introduction xi

Introduction

The publication of the Roman Missal in 1969 ushered in a new era of eucharistic and sacramental practice in the Church. The pastoral tone and import of the *General Instruction on the Missal* ends a rubrical, or *direction-oriented*, emphasis in eucharistic worship. The *Instruction* is profoundly pastoral in tone and the result of much historical, liturgical, and theological investigation. Yet, like all the revised rituals from the Second Vatican Council, the liturgy of the eucharist needs careful planning and preparation to achieve its full effectiveness as a celebration in memory and in hope of Christ's paschal mystery. "The pastoral effectiveness of a celebration depends in great measure on choosing readings, prayers, and songs which correspond to the needs, spiritual preparation, and attitude of the participants. This will be achieved by an intelligent use of the options. . . ." (*General Instruction on the Roman Missal*, no. 313). The document indicates that the task of liturgy planning is not an option, for it clearly states that "the choice of texts is to be made in consultation with the ministers and others who have a function in the celebration, including the faithful. . . ." This section of the *Instruction* concludes: "Since a variety of options is provided, it is necessary for the deacon, readers, commentator, and choir to know beforehand the texts for which they are responsible, so that nothing shall mar the celebration. Careful planning and execution will help dispose the people to take part in the eucharist."

Liturgical celebration should take into account the nature and circumstances of each assembly and should be "planned to bring about conscious, active, and full participation of the people. . . . Such participation of mind and body is desired by the Church, is demanded by the nature of the celebration, and is the right and duty of Christians by reason of their baptism" (*Instruction*, no. 3).

The purpose of books such as this one is to help liturgy planning groups choose options from the Sacramentary which accord with the scripture readings of a given eucharistic liturgy, in the light of the needs and capabilities of the worshiping assembly. Planning groups function best when they give pride of place to the scripture readings, see to it that planning reflects the particular occasion and congregation, aim at achieving a balance and proportion between the liturgy of the word and the eucharist, and see a particular liturgy in its context within a liturgical season. In practice, such groups fulfill their task when they select the appropriate introductory rite, preface and eucharistic prayer, and final blessing from the texts of the Sacramentary which reflect the scriptures. In addition, to aid the involvement of the community, they may in some instances compose suitable comments on parts of the liturgy such as the introduction to the liturgy, before the readings, the general intercessions, before the eucharistic prayer, before the Lord's Prayer, and before the dismissal (*General Instruction on the Roman Missal*, no. 11). Yet, these selections and comments should not be the only elements of liturgical planning. The choice of music and the adaptation of the worship environment are extremely important nonverbal parts of planning and of liturgical celebration. The liturgical *experience* of faith is primary—an experience which is communicated through signs, symbols, and gestures as well as music, art, and the activity of the celebrating community.

This book is a new edition of the author's three-volume work, *A Celebrant's Guide to the New Sacramentary*. It is intended to help direct the planning of the Sunday liturgy and of those celebrations which replace the Sunday observance. In the Fall of 1973 Mr. Bernard C. Benziger spoke with me about editing a commentary on the "new" Sacramentary. I suggested that more important was a work on how to best use the Sacramentary's options, particularly as its use depends on the Lectionary. The result of our conversation was his invitation to write the three volumes that appeared from 1975 to 1977. The scheduling of this new edition is opportune since some of the suggestions in the first edition are less appropriate now, and the wordings of suggested comments during the liturgy are not needed, since their use has become more common. Remaining are revised introductions to the liturgical seasons as well as reflections on all the Sundays of the three-year Lectionary cycle and those celebrations which replace Sunday observance. A thorough study of these introductory essays would be very helpful in giving planning groups some background on the feasts and seasons for which they are preparing. (In 1981, a second edition of the Lectionary for Mass was published containing an expanded introduction on the importance of the proclaimed word and relatively few optional scripture texts to be used at the eucharist should these be deemed appropriate for pastoral use by national episcopal conferences. Since the Bishop's Committee on the Liturgy is presently engaged in a study of this second edition, and an action on its implementation in the United States is not expected for some time, this work contains commentary and suggestions based on the original edition of the Lectionary and its cycle of scripture readings.)

I wish to thank Mr. Benziger for his invitation to revise my work for a new publication, and Mr. William C. Smith of the Pueblo Publishing Company for his patient and helpful work, especially on those volumes which were written during my sojourn in Rome.

The initial inspiration for this work came from my experience as an associate pastor in parishes in the Archdiocese of New York. Then, after completing a doctorate at San Anselmo in Rome, I served as the Director of Liturgy at the North American College (Rome) where I worked in a liturgical setting which was unique. I wish to acknowledge and thank those faculty members and students with whom I collaborated during those years. In such settings the asceticism and humility needed by those who make liturgy a stock-in-trade is learned, however slow that process may be. At present I teach liturgy full-time at the Graduate School of Religion and Religious Education at Fordham University (Bronx, N.Y.) and am in residence in the parish of the Immaculate Heart of Mary, Scarsdale, N.Y. At times the responsibilities of these two diverse ministries become heavy. Yet, the challenge of both keeps me honest, lest the teaching of liturgy become divorced from the daily prayer of a community of Christians that is varied and challenging. I am deeply indebted to those at both Fordham and Immaculate Heart of Mary who have inspired much of what is contained in this book.

Finally, this work is dedicated to a friend with whom I first studied liturgy at Notre Dame, and who has been an inspiration and guide ever since. It is appropriate that the work I dedicate to him is a revision, for he has seen the revision of many of my thoughts, ideals, and aspirations over the years. He has even been the gentle cause of some of them!

Kevin W. Irwin
Feast of St. Benedict, Abbot, 1981

Chapter One

Season of Advent—"As We Wait In Joyful Hope"

TWO COMINGS OF CHRIST

It has been a frequent homiletic device of preachers to inform congregations that "advent" means "coming" and that the season of Advent is a four-week preparation for the feast of Christmas, the commemoration of the birth of Jesus, the day when Christ came once in human history in innocence and infancy. Penitential practices are stressed even to the point of paralleling Lenten observances, and the season of Advent is seen as a four-week penance before the feast of Christmas at which point all the preparation is ended and Christmas excitement takes over.

In reality, however, this is not the case, either liturgically or theologically. The Babe of Bethlehem was born once and for all time and cannot be born again, and so 2,000 years after his birth Jesus is still with us and will remain until the end of time, Emmanuel, God-with-us. His presence has not come to an end, and his concern for us is no less real and evident now than it was at his Incarnation and through his earthly life. "Advent" still means "coming," but the coming we prepare for is not primarily the event of Christ's Birth. The coming we look forward to is that of the end of time—Christ will *come again*—Lord Jesus, *come* in glory. Advent is the season of waiting, of watchfulness, of hope and expectation for the day when Christ's return in glory will bring time to an end. Advent is not the season of erasing or redoing events of history as though the Incarnation had not happened. It is the season when we await and prepare for Christ's coming in glory to call the elect into the kingdom forever.

Advent is a season of eschatological hope and expectation. It is a time to concentrate on this essential aspect of all Christian liturgy—that it looks to the future as much as it does to the past. Christians gather in the name of the Lord in the present age, not only to recall the saving events of the past, but also to look forward to the final age to come, when all will be completed and the faithful will take their place at the Lord's right hand. Liturgy is the celebration in time (the present) which recalls and relies on God's acts of salvation (the past) and which looks forward as well to the time "when sacraments will cease" and the Lord will come again (the future). It is then that the blessed will join in the eternal banquet of the Lamb of God. Liturgy is the present commemoration of past deeds of Christ—a commemoration which looks forward to the future coming of Christ. Celebrations of Advent which look only to the past event of Jesus' birth are inadequate and imbalanced.

During the embolism after the Lord's Prayer at the eucharist the celebrant leads into the doxology by praying "as we wait in joyful hope for the coming of our Savior, Jesus Christ." The memorial prayers of the third and fourth eucharistic prayers contain variations on this theme by stating that the present community recalls the death, resurrection, and ascension of Jesus and is "ready to greet him when he comes again" and looks "forward to his coming in glory." The nature of this prayer, taken from the Jewish liturgy, reflects the nature of all worship—that it looks to the future as well as to the past. Christian liturgy continually points beyond the present celebration to the reality of the hoped for salvation accomplished when Christ returns in glory. All Christian liturgy is a plea that such celebrations may come to their culmination in the Father's kingdom. Present celebrations of worship are a glimpse of and a share in the reality that will only be complete when Christ will come again to draw the just into the peace of the Father's kingdom forever. All Christian liturgy cries out "Come, Lord Jesus." But until that final coming and granting of the fullness of salvation, the Christian community gathers in the meantime to share a common vision and experience of what is as yet to be accomplished.

The season of Advent is the liturgical season that invites reflection on such things as the nature of the present celebration, the fact of coming judgment, and the invitation to election in the kingdom. In this season more than any other we look to the future. In this season more than any other we reflect on how well we as the church now live and wait "that we may find our lasting joy in the coming of our Savior Jesus Christ."

Advent is the liturgical season that commemorates the two comings of Christ. He came once from the womb of the Virgin and will come again as the Lord of power and might. The first part of the season commemorates the second coming, for we pray in Advent preface 1 "now we watch for the day, hoping that the salvation promised us will be ours, when Christ our Lord will come again in glory." In the latter part of the season we pray in Advent preface 2 that "in his love Christ has filled us with joy as we prepare to celebrate his birth." The solemn blessing of Advent speaks of the Son of God who once came to us and who will come again; of the Redeemer who came to live with us as a man and who will come again in glory to reward the faithful with endless life. In the Introduction to the Sacramentary, Advent is defined as a time of preparation for Christmas when the first coming of the Son of God is recalled, and also as a season of preparation for Christ's second coming. "It is thus a season of joyful and spiritual expectation" (General Norms for the Liturgical Year and Calendar, no. 39).

ADVENT IN HISTORY AND THE CONTEMPORARY REFORM

Just as it was centuries before the liturgical year as a whole evolved and took a somewhat final form, so also it was hundreds of years before the season of Advent became fixed as a four-week period before the feast of Christmas. Originally, it had been variously calculated to cover three, four, or six weeks. It was initially thematically connected to the Epiphany of the Lord and only later was it joined to the feast of the Nativity. In Gaul, for example, it was a three-week preparation for Epiphany. (While the classic night for the celebration of initiation was the Easter Vigil, the feasts of Pentecost and Epiphany were important times for the administration of baptism as well.) In fourth-century Spain, Advent began on December 17, a day that is still important in our liturgy since from December 17 to 24 the emphasis in the readings and prayers of the liturgy is on the first coming of Jesus at the Incarnation, and the antiphons for the Magnificat of Evening Prayer are the traditional "O" antiphons. By the late fifth century the season in Gaul had lost its orientation toward Epiphany (on January 6), and instead, became a preparation time before Christmas (on December 25). In Rome, at this same time, Advent was not a preparation for baptism and did not have the short-lived penitential aspects which it had in Gaul, such as some fasting in preparation for baptism. There is evidence at Rome that five Advent Sundays were celebrated. Despite the obvious structural parallels between Advent and Lent, specifically a season of preparation for baptism in Gaul, Advent at Rome was never associated with the other aspects of Lent that included the solemn reconciliation of penitents, and strict discipline for all. Rather it was, and is now restored to be, a season of heightened awareness of Christ's presence now and of his second coming in the future. Thus this season could be called one of changed disposition rather than one of strict discipline.

When Advent came to be conceived of as a season of strict discipline, it is not surprising to find catechesis centering on its penitential aspects. The absence of the Gloria and the use of violet vestments are perfect examples. Both of these Advent practices are Lenten practices and so the understanding of Advent easily became confused with that of Lent.

However, the absence of the Gloria in Advent has the advantage of having attention drawn to it when it is used at Christmas, at which time its incarnation themes are put in clear focus: the announcement of peace through Christ, and praise of him, "the only Son of the Father." And the use of violet vestments reflects the tone of the season by encouraging a simple and reflective attitude in our common prayer. Again, the shift to white at Christmas is all the more dramatic by way of contrast. While the season is understood in terms of spiritual and hopeful expectation, nevertheless the joy is quiet and the rejoicing is restrained in Advent. It is the verdict of liturgical history and theology that Advent is quite different in theme, content, and attitude from the season of Lent.

Another element that has been customarily stressed regarding Advent and which can be clarified in the light of history and theology is the emphasis on Advent as the beginning of the "church year." While the origins of Advent can be traced to the fourth century, it was only when Advent texts were placed at the beginning of liturgical books that this season came to be associated with a beginning of the church year. The placement of Advent at the beginning of such books came about in the eighth and ninth centuries. Furthermore, *the* culmination of the church year has always been Easter—indeed a natural time for beginnings, both spiritual and seasonal. The solemnity of Pentecost and the commemoration of the sending of the Spirit "to renew the face of the earth" could also be regarded theologically as a day of beginnings. Also, the fact that the civil year begins on January 1 and is the cultural commemoration of new beginnings and resolutions, makes any emphasis on Advent as the beginning of the church year problematic. Furthermore, another instance of beginnings could be seen in the now suppressed time before Lent beginning with Septuagesima Sunday. On this day the reading at Matins began with Genesis 1, the biblical book of beginnings. Hence, this could have been regarded as a time of new beginnings.

While liturgical books still begin with the Advent season, to isolate this season as the beginning of the Church year is an unnecessary and imprecise emphasis. What is far more important to note is the continuity in the liturgical year with its cyclical and eschatological character, especially where the liturgies of the last Sundays of the year, most especially the Solemnity of Christ the King, have close thematic unity with the first Sunday and first days of the season of Advent. Furthermore, what is equally important to note is the continuity and unity that runs through the Advent-Christmas-Epiphany season. The theology of this entire cycle is a preparation for the coming of the Lord and his many manifestations. Advent should be seen in continuity with the Christmas-Epiphany season until the feast of the Baptism of the Lord. In this way the whole sweep of the season can be understood. In this time we celebrate Christ's manifestation to the nations as well as his incarnation, his mediatorship as well as his childhood, his redemption as well as his birth, his being seen by those powerful in the eyes of the world, as well as by unlearned shepherds.

From the first Sunday of Advent to the Baptism of the Lord, the celebrating community is progressively incorporated into the life and ministry of Christ among us. As is stated in Sunday Preface 4: "By his birth we are reborn. In his suffering we are freed from sin.

By his rising from the dead we rise to everlasting life. In his return to you in glory we enter into your heavenly kingdom." Advent is that time of watchfulness and the banishing of preoccupations so that we may enter more fully into the mystery of the Incarnation. The incarnation feasts make us aware of God's love for us and our being incorporated into that love in life with each other. The manifestation of Christ to the nations at Epiphany is the commemoration of the universality of redemption and God's unbounded love for all peoples. The feast of the Baptism of the Lord is the memorial of the inauguration of Christ's ministry and the renewal of our share in that ministry begun at our own baptism. The eschatological force of the season of Advent reminds us continually of our vocation to live in Christ's love and to love each other in him unselfishly so that when Christ comes again we will join him in his Father's kingdom.

THE SUNDAYS OF ADVENT: AN OVERVIEW

Taken together the Sundays of Advent are a progression from reflection on the end of time when Christ will return, to his incarnation when a new era of time was begun for mankind. The first Sunday is decidedly eschatological where the scripture reading and the prayers of the Sacramentary speak of our being called to Christ's side in the kingdom, of the promise of eternal life, and of our eternal communion in heaven. On the second and third Sundays the figure of John the Baptizer emerges as the proclaimer of the nearness of the kingdom, and the one who calls us to prepare the way of the Lord. The baptism John administers is one of preparation for the baptism that will come with Jesus in the power of the Spirit. John stands as a self-effacing figure whose vocation was to announce the ministry of Jesus. John's vocation was to stand aside when the Lord would come as the Savior. The Baptizer comes as one who points beyond his own life and career to the life and ministry of Jesus. In the liturgy of Advent John stands for us as the prophet summoning us to repentance, preparation, and reform of our lives now so that one day we may join the elect in the kingdom of the Father. The Baptizer calls on contemporary congregations who live between the first and second comings of Christ to self-examination and communal scrutiny on the ways in which we live as those who bear the Christian message in our own time. The liturgy of the fourth Sunday of Advent is the clearest example of a celebration which prepares for the feast of the Nativity. The readings reflect the humanity of Jesus and his human birth as Messiah. The intensity of the season reaches its high point here for this is the immediate preparation for the feast of the Incarnation at Christmas.

While there is an inherent logic and structure to the season of Advent, it should also be borne in mind that the season is part of the larger time up to the Epiphany, and that even within the season itself certain themes continue to emerge throughout the whole season. The notion of the second coming of Christ and its importance in the life of the Church, for example, is not eliminated once the second and third Sundays of Advent arrive, nor does the celebration of the manifestation of the Lord to the nations at Epiphany leave out all traces of the human birth of Christ. While the eschatological note is struck most clearly in the beginning of Advent, it is found again in the second Christmas preface ("he has come to lift up all things to himself, to restore unity to creation, and to lead mankind from exile into your heavenly glory") as well as in the opening prayer for Epiphany ("lead us to your glory in heaven"). Similarly, while John the Baptizer is the preacher of repentance and personal reform, the exhortation to right conduct is found in the reading from the letter to Titus used as the second lesson for Midnight Mass ("to reject godless ways and worldly desires, and live temperately, justly, and devoutly in this age as we await our blessed hope, the appearing of the glory of the great God and of our Savior Christ Jesus").

The point at issue here is that while we can come to a deeper appreciation of a given liturgical cycle by understanding its theological emphasis, it is equally important to discover nuances and degrees of differences throughout a given cycle so that the richness of the scriptural and liturgical texts may be appreciated. The progress of the liturgical year is not from one logical step to the next; rather it is better appreciated as one mystery celebrated with varying nuances and aspects. The variety and diversity inherent in the liturgy serve to indicate again that there is no one theme for a given liturgical celebration; there are, in fact, many themes which may be drawn from the texts of a given liturgical celebration. Once the nature and theology of a season is understood, and the intention of the editors of the Sacramentary and Lectionary is respected, then a wealth of images, symbols, and perspectives on the central mystery of faith emerges for the planning and celebration of the liturgy.

PASTORAL PLANNING FOR ADVENT

One suggestion that the planning committee may consider to enable the community to appreciate the eschatological as well as the incarnational emphasis of Advent and to understand the place of the figures of Isaiah, John the Baptizer, and Mary as those who call us to conversion and prayer in this season, would be to schedule and publicize homily topics and the names of the preachers for the Sunday eucharists of this season. The committee may wish to invite a guest preacher for "the parish Mass each Sunday," or they may arrange the Mass schedule so that the same member of the parish clergy would preside at the same eucharist for the Sundays of the season. Then a central theme for all the Sundays could be selected and developed over the four weeks. One such theme could be the "Two Comings of Christ"—a theme which needs special development on the part of the homilist lest he leave his hearers confused by its complexity. Another could be the "Personages of Advent" centering on the prophets, especially Isaiah, and John and Mary. Or the theme could be directed to underscore the various facets of Christology developed during Advent based on the titles of Jesus taken from the Sunday gospels—Messiah, Lord, Jesus, the Christ, Son of God, Son of the Most High.

If one of the above plans is not feasible for the celebration of the eucharist, one of the themes might be suitable for an Evening Prayer on each Sunday of Advent. This would include an opening hymn, psalmody, psalm prayers, a New Testament canticle, scripture readings, homily, Magnificat canticle, intercessions, final prayer and blessing—all chosen to reflect the theme of the particular Sunday. The same format could be used for all four weeks with variations provided weekly for the prayers of the celebrant, the readings and homily, and final blessing. Another advantage of scheduling such a noneucharistic service would be to reintroduce into the parish worship schedule a form of devotion and piety that is solid in its biblical foundation, theology, and liturgy, and which would aptly supplement the celebration of the eucharist. Despite the elimination of strictly penitential aspects from the season of Advent, the mood of the liturgy is still reflective, watchful, and oriented to the glory of God known in His Son Jesus. Purple vestments are worn and other sanctuary appointments may be added to carry out the mood of reflection and meditation. A cloth of basic violet and perhaps a contrasting color or two may be used as an altar frontal. It should be left plain with no words or slogans attached since the altar as the symbol of Christ needs no further elaboration. Banners or hangings can also serve to highlight the mood of the season but these should match or at least contrast well with the altar frontal and should be of a size which serves, but does not dominate, the already existing church architecture and art. Again, it is the colors and their arrangement which express and communicate a mood. Any or all of these suggestions may help to convey the impression that this season has special characteristics of watchfulness and hope.

The placing of an Advent wreath in the sanctuary is another useful addition to the seasonal decor. What should be kept in mind here is that this wreath should be of such a size and prominence as to be obvious to all in the church. The committee could think of making one which is larger and more elaborate than those designed for use in homes. When decorating the wreath with the appropriate candles, the unity of the season with four Sundays of a common emphasis should be underscored by having candles of the same color. The insertion of a pink candle, matching the formerly prescribed pink vesture for the third Sunday, interjects a discordant element into a season whose unity and integrity is to be reemphasized. The use of four violet candles is to associate an entire season with a common theme and purpose.

A more ambitious, but nonetheless significant, addition to the church decor is the Jesse tree. This is a fir or other evergreen decorated with different images and symbols of the Advent season. These can be made by children in educational programs, or by members of other parish groups, and some new symbols can be added weekly. The signs of the history of salvation may include the serpent and fruit for Adam and Eve, a slain lamb for Abel's death, the ark for Noah, the ladder and star for Jacob's vision, the scepter for the promise given to Judah, the tables of the Law for the promise given to Moses, the star of David for the prophecy made to him, the hand with a burning coal for the prophesy of Isaiah, the whale for the prophet Jonah, the outline of the city of Bethlehem for the prophecy of Micah, the lamb for John's confession of faith in Jesus as Messiah, the tools of the carpentry trade for Joseph, a crown for the Blessed Virgin, and a chi-rho for Christ the Savior. These all help to illustrate the prophecies and readings of the Advent season and can help create an atmosphere of reflection.

The communal celebration of the sacrament of penance during Advent is presupposed in the revised Rite of Penance, and while the same is true for Lent, the proposed services in the Appendix to the Penance Ritual underscore the differences between these two seasons. The Lenten service is consciously one of renewing the commitment and conversion of baptism; the Advent service is clearly one of preparation for the commemoration of the incarnation in a season of watchfulness and hope for Christ's second advent. The intensity of expectation is noted by reference to St. Paul's exhortation in Romans 13:11–12 "to wake from sleep, for our salvation is nearer to us than when we first believed." The readings concern the coming of the Lord (the prophet Malachi), the plea for the return of the Lord "Come, Lord Jesus" (Revelation), and the ministry of John the Baptizer to prepare the community in repentance for the Lord's coming (Matthew). It would be important to keep in mind the sample introduction to the service since it clearly points to the appropriate theology of Advent:

"My brothers and sisters, Advent is a time of preparation, when we make ready to celebrate the mystery of our Lord's coming as man, the beginning of our redemption. Advent also moves us to look forward with renewed hope to the second coming of Christ, when God's plan of salvation will be brought to fulfillment. We are reminded too of our Lord's coming to each one of us at the hour of death. We must make sure he will find us prepared for his coming, as the gospel tells us: 'Blessed are those servants who are found awake when the Lord comes' (Luke 12:37). This service of penance is meant to make us ready in mind and heart for the coming of Christ, which we are soon to celebrate in the Mass of Christmas."

The season of Advent is indeed a time of joyful and spiritual expectation. Such an orientation is found in some of the hymnody for Advent where we "rejoice" because Emmanuel is to come to Israel; we wake for our light has come; we hear the Baptist announcing glad tidings of the King of Kings; and we greet the coming Bridegroom with songs of joy. The seventh-century chant *Creator Alme Siderum* summarizes the theology of Advent by praying to the Lord of light who created all things, who came in lowliness, who shared our mortal cares, whose task it was to suffer the cross, who reigns now as the King of Kings, and who will judge all people on the final day. In the familiar "O Come, O Come, Emmanuel" the titles of Jesus are filled with Advent theology—King of all the nations, Dayspring, Key of David, Rod of Jesse, Lord of Might, and Wisdom from heaven's height.

What is involved in the season of Advent is profound meditation on the coming of the Lord as savior, redeemer, mediator—the One who was born a child and reigns as Lord. Of all liturgical seasons, Advent helps us take time seriously, for in our celebrations in the name of the Lord we recall the past when he came among us to share our very human life, and we summon the future when he will come in glory. And in the meantime we seek to live as he would have us live. "Deliver us Lord, from every evil, and grant us peace in our day. In your mercy keep us free from sin and protect us from all anxiety as we wait in joyful hope for the coming of our Savior, Jesus Christ."

SUNDAYS OF ADVENT "A" CYCLE

FIRST SUNDAY OF ADVENT

The readings for this Sunday provide the keynote to the entire season. The prophecy of Isaiah speaks of the coming of the Lord as a judge and says that those who await his coming must live according to his ways and in his light. The perspective here is eschatological, of the end time when God will lead all nations together into one assembly. This will happen by God's design and at his direction, not ours. The reading from Romans is a traditional reading for this day and stresses the theme of the season, which refers continually to the coming of the Lord "already" but "not yet" in history, and of his coming again at the end time. Our conduct is to be guided by the baptism we have been privileged to receive, for from it we are given God's power to live his gospel. We are dependent, therefore, on God's presence and grace to live our human lives, not on our own sometimes almost Pelagian moral determination and character formation. While none of the "signs and wonders" have yet occurred ushering in the end times, nevertheless the gospel reading invites us in the here and now to act as if the end were very soon. We are to be watchful for the Lord's return. The mistake of Noah's generation should not be our own—to be oblivious that the demands of the Lord are always upon us.

The prayers of the Sacramentary reflect well the themes of the scripture readings. The opening prayer speaks of our will for doing good; the reward of having done the Lord's work will be to be joined with his elect in the kingdom. Those found worthy to be among the chosen and elect at the judgment will be called to the right side of the Lord, as noted in the opening prayer. The left side is the realm of those rejected because of their wicked conduct. At the time of judgment, one's social or financial status in this life will make no difference—what will count is the love and faith with which we have approached Christ and our sisters and brothers during this life. The alternative form of the opening prayer is preferable if the liturgy centers on the expectation, watchfulness, longing, and the coming of Christ as the theme of the day.

For the introductory rite, the blessing and sprinkling with holy water could be used and an introduction composed to reflect the idea that Advent is a time to intensify our living of the Christian life, a life in Christ first begun at baptism. Should the third form of the penitential rite be used, the celebrant could profitably use the second set of sample invocations referring to the two comings of Christ ("you came to gather the nations" and "you will come in glory"). These invocations might profitably be sung ending in *Kyrie, eleison*, with the congregation repeating this acclamation. This ancient usage refers to the "Lord" who is merciful and reflects the biblical notion that the Lord will judge his people justly, but with mercy. The prescribed preface for this Sunday is the first Advent preface which speaks of the two comings of Christ, in humility as a man, and in glory at his return.

Either the second or third memorial acclamation would serve to reiterate the second coming of Christ "Lord Jesus, come in glory," and "we proclaim your death, Lord Jesus, until you come in glory."

To introduce the Lord's Prayer, the celebrant might choose the fourth invitation to prayer since it speaks of prayer "for the coming of the kingdom." The solemn blessing for the Advent season is provided as the blessing of the day and mentions both themes of Christ's incarnation and return, and our need in the present to act according to his commands. Two prayers over the people which would be appropriate for a simpler form of blessing would be number 1 which speaks of being led to everlasting life, and number 16 which speaks about consolation in this life and being brought to the life to come. One way of underscoring the unity of the season of Advent would be to use a variety of these options for all four Sundays.

SECOND SUNDAY OF ADVENT

While the incarnational emphasis of Advent does not properly begin until December 17, some traces in the liturgy of this Sunday show such an incarnational orientation. The readings speak more directly of the coming of the Messiah with the messianic prophecy of Isaiah so splendidly stated in the first reading, and in the gospel which deals with the ministry of John the Baptizer.

Most probably the lesson from Isaiah was originally intended to express the hope and expectation of the ruler of David's line and hence first served as a model for the earthly king of the period. Later on, however, the prophecy came to be interpreted in a messianic way. The genealogy from the root of Jesse and the endowment with the Spirit of the Lord make of this Messiah a link between the human and the divine. His gifts are decidedly "charismatic," with wisdom and understanding at the head of the list. In his role as judge, he will treat his people with justice and faithfulness, with mercy and love.

The second reading from Romans more clearly reflects the eschatological orientation of Advent since its message is the hope the Christian has even though Christ has yet to come again.

Completion and perfection of our faith awaits those who already believe that Christ has come.

The gospel message speaks of the life and work of John the Baptizer. The message of the gospel is that while the ministry of John is to prepare for the coming of Christ, it is not the infant Jesus for whom we need preparation. It is for the whole mystery of Christ and for the entirety of his message that we prepare. The implication for the season of Advent is that we are not playacting at Bethlehem, and basking in nostalgia and memories of serene events. Rather we need preparation for the taxing and demanding words and deeds of Jesus. He comes as the "more powerful" one endowed with the Holy Spirit, whose words demand much and whose example causes each of us to reflect more deeply on our response to Jesus.

The third form of the penitential rite could be used as a suitable introduction to the liturgy, for the invocations in the second set of sample invocations refer to the two comings of Christ ("you came to gather the nations," and "you will come in glory"). The use of *Kyrie, eleison* would be an appropriate response. The opening prayer of this Sunday speaks of receiving Christ when he comes in glory, and the alternative prayer establishes waiting and watchfulness as necessary prerequisites to receiving his wisdom. Waiting is not merely a passive exercise, for the allurements of this world are to be purged to prepare the way of the Lord. The preface of the day is the first Advent preface continuing the eschatological orientation of the season. As in last week's celebration, the use of either the second or third of the memorial acclamations would be helpful to reiterate this eschatological orientation. This is also the reason for repeating the suggestion that the celebrant use the fourth introduction to the Lord's Prayer. The prayer after communion speaks again of the wisdom of God and the things of heaven, the reception of which demands a new attitude toward worldly wisdom and the things that pass away.

For the final blessing, number 1 of the prayers over the people is presented as an appropriate choice. In its place, however, the celebrant could add to the solemnity of the Sundays of the Advent season by concluding the liturgy with the solemn blessing of the season. Other options from among the prayers over the people would be number 2, concerning love for one another as a suitable preparation for the Lord's coming, or number 18, which prays for new life and the reforming of our lives in accordance with the words of John in the gospel.

THIRD SUNDAY OF ADVENT

Formerly called "Gaudete" Sunday to distinguish it from the mournful, somber Sundays which were considered the essence of the Advent Sundays, this third Sunday no longer stands in such stark contrast to the rest of the season. The penitential practices of the entire season have been dropped in favor of a season of joyful expectation rather than a time to do penance. The four Sundays of Advent now present a unity that is not broken, as previously, by one Sunday with a different theme. While the entrance antiphon is still "Rejoice in the Lord always" (Philippians 4:4) this theme is to be understood as central to the theology of the whole season. It would be appropriate not to use rose-colored vestments this Sunday in order to keep the continuity with the other Advent Sundays.

The tension between the final coming of the Lord and the mystery of the incarnation which was part of the liturgy of the second Sunday of Advent continues this Sunday. The Old Testament and gospel readings speak of the healing and strengthening that characterizes God's favor. This is made manifest in the ministry of Jesus. In the book of Isaiah the return of exiles was to parallel in joy the first Exodus of this people from bondage into freedom, from slavery to liberty. The eyes of the blind will be opened, as will the ears of the deaf; the lame will walk and the tongues of the dumb will be loosened. The New Testament authors used much of this language in their own descriptions of the healing worked by Jesus. The point in the New Testament miracles is that the power of God, at work in the Exodus and in the return of the exiles mentioned in today's first reading, was at work in Jesus. Therefore, the miracles can be seen as signs of the Father's love present in Jesus.

The gospel clearly aligns itself with the Old Testament lesson since the question of John is really the question we ourselves ask. Are we looking for another Messiah? Are we not satisfied in the coming of Jesus and the incarnation of God's love in and through Jesus?

The more eschatological Advent theme is seen in the second reading from the Letter of James. Here the coming of the Lord, to which the author points, is the last judgment. The second coming of the Lord may still need reemphasis and exploration. And so, using this as the theme even in this third week could be valuable for the congregation whose immediate association of Advent has been only with the birth of Jesus as the coming of the Lord.

The third form of the penitential rite could serve as an appropriate introduction to the liturgy this Sunday, and using the second or third set of sample invocations would be an appropriate way to underscore Advent themes. The third set stresses names of Jesus which are used through this season: "mighty God and Prince of peace," "Son of God and Son of Mary," "Word made flesh and splendor of the Father."

The opening prayer of the liturgy speaks of the birth of Christ and so refers to the more incarnational notion of the Advent season. The alternative form contains more explicit reference to hope, longing, and the return of the Lord at the end of time, and so would be a very appropriate choice to underscore the eschatological aspects of Advent.

The preface for this Sunday may be either the first or second Advent preface with the use of the first still preferable because of the eschatological orientation still present at this point in the season.

Once again, the use of the second or third memorial acclamation and the fourth sample introduction to the Lord's Prayer would be effective ways of reiterating the themes of this season.

The prayer after communion requests divine help for us in this season of preparation and is a helpful reminder that our own initiatives and our own self-determined preparation can become too easily the major theme of this season. The solemn form of the blessing for Advent is presented here and its use suitably underscores the unity of the four Advent Sundays. As alternatives, the celebrant may substitute solemn blessing number 3 in Ordinary Time or number 5 of the prayers over the people, which speaks of rejoicing in God's mercy, still a theme of Advent, but not so obviously seen in this Sunday's liturgy.

With the liturgy of this Sunday the cycle of Advent preparation comes full circle. From the beginning of the season with its orientation to the end times and the eschatological expectation of the coming Lord, to the second and third Sundays with the eschatological and incarnational comings of the Lord mingled, the awaiting of the Messiah in the incarnation was clearly a secondary theme. This fourth Sunday is the final stage of preparation since its emphasis is on the incarnation of Jesus, born of the Virgin and conceived by the power of the Holy Spirit. The vesture used this Sunday is still violet and Advent themes are still very much in evidence, yet the mood is one of almost imminent completion and fulfillment.

The readings no longer speak of the challenge of the Baptist and the need for patience until the Second Coming. Rather, each of them relates to the incarnation of the Son of God. The first, from the Book of Isaiah, may be understood on two levels. It relates to the historical situation in which Isaiah gives a sign to Ahaz that the Davidic dynasty will survive despite present difficulties. The other level deals more directly with the messianic hope to be fulfilled paradoxically in the birth of a son to a virgin mother. The reading is chosen to harmonize with the gospel in which Matthew cites the prophecy explicitly. The Matthean text is of the supernatural conception of Jesus in the womb of a virgin who assented to God's plan being worked through her. Emmanuel is thus born in time to be forever with his people.

The reading from Romans speaks of the birth of a man from the line of David according to the flesh, yet adds the dimension that the incarnation leads to redemption since this man becomes the Son of God in power by his passion, death, and resurrection. The theme here of the relationship between the incarnation and the redemption is an alternative theme for the homilist on this Sunday.

The introductory rite of this liturgy could quite suitably be that of the third form of the penitential rite with the third sample set of invocations. While these titles of Christ are appropriate throughout the season, the second ("Son of God and Son of Mary") is especially appropriate this week. In addition, the second set of invocations remains very useful because of the understanding it gives of Christ's two comings.

The opening prayer of the liturgy expresses the theme of the Pauline reading since it proposes for our reflection the suffering, death, and resurrection of Jesus, even though the mood of this day concentrates on the incarnation. The alternative prayer, however, speaks explicitly of Mary's part in the incarnation since she placed herself at the service of God's plan. The prayer also makes mention of the watchful hope which characterizes Advent. The prayer over the gifts also mentions the power of the Spirit at work in Mary, and begs that this same power might sanctify the gifts of bread and wine.

The second preface of Advent is prescribed for proclamation on this last Sunday, and fittingly so since the focus of attention is on the Virgin Mother bearing the child in her womb, the ministry of John the Baptizer in being Jesus' herald, and the need of waiting and watching, since the time of expectation has not yet ended.

As has been suggested for the other Sundays of this season, the use of the second or third of the memorial acclamations would serve to underscore the eschatological theme of Advent, as would the use of the fourth of the sample invitations to pray the Lord's Prayer.

The prayer after communion makes mention of the coming feast, yet it does so in such a way that the emphasis in the prayer is rather on our growth in faith and love as preparation for Christmas.

Number 3 of the prayers over the people is presented for use at the conclusion of the liturgy. Once again, the solemn blessing of the Advent season is still very appropriate to complete the four Sundays of the Advent season.

SUNDAYS OF ADVENT "B" CYCLE

FIRST SUNDAY OF ADVENT

The scripture readings for this first Sunday of Advent in all three cycles of the Lectionary provide a fitting climax to the eschatological note struck in the last Sundays of the year, most especially in last week's liturgy on the Solemnity of Christ the King. These texts all speak of vigilance and preparation for God's final act of redemption. For all three cycles of the Lectionary, the gospel readings for this first Advent Sunday are taken from the concluding portion of the apocalyptic sections of the synoptics. This Sunday it is the doorkeeper who is urged to be on guard constantly for the return of the master of the house. The theme enunciated in the Old Testament reading for this Sunday, taken from Isaiah 63, is also one of watching, but the prophet's cry is for a dramatic act of God since the intervention so longed for is pictured as the opening of the heavens, whereby God would bring to an end the era of evil and oppression and usher in a new era with its longed-for salvation. The notation over this reading in the Lectionary is, "Oh, that you would *tear* the heavens apart and come down," showing again the forceful imagery of this reading in the context of its original setting. The responsorial psalm continues this notion of the inbreaking of the kingdom of the power of God with the text "Lord, make us turn to you, let us see your face and we shall be saved." It is by looking to the Lord alone, says the psalmist, that salvation will come to us, that we will be sure he will take care of his people (the vine) and that he will give them new life. Expectation of a final revelation of God forms part of the second reading from first Corinthians as Paul encourages this community to wait for the final coming and revelation of our Lord Jesus Christ.

We are faced in these readings with a number of theologically profound Advent themes. The Christian Church lives between the times of what has been revealed and accomplished in the life, death, and resurrection of Jesus and of what is still to be accomplished at his second coming. There is an urgency in these readings that the Lord achieve his plan now and that the still unfulfilled promise of the complete extension of the reign of God may now come to pass. The Christian Church is indeed the pilgrim church on earth since it prays at every liturgy, but especially on this Sunday, for the coming of the kingdom. Living between the times of Christ's incarnation and second coming, the Church prays in the meantime that the Lord will come again in glory and waits with vigilance because the Christ event has yet to be fulfilled totally in the kingdom of God. We pray at this liturgy that we may be faithful to the reign of God that has come, and we pray that it will come to its promised fulfillment. The liturgy challenges us to turn from the false securities of this life and to pray earnestly for the coming of the kingdom.

For the greeting at the opening of the celebration the celebrant may wish to underscore the text of the second reading from first Corinthians by using the second greeting: "The grace and peace of God our Father and the Lord Jesus Christ be with you." For the introductory rite the third form of the penitential rite could be used with invocations of Christ taken from the second or third sample forms in the Sacramentary. These refer to the two comings of Christ (second set), and titles of Jesus used in this season (third set). The response to these is: "Lord, have mercy" but during this season the option of using *Kyrie, eleison* would be useful as a way of emphasizing that the Lord whom we worship and who will come again is the merciful judge of the living and dead. The opening prayer has many references which are very appropriate to underscore the eschatological mood of this liturgy.

The first Advent preface is prescribed for use this Sunday for it emphasizes the eschatological nature of this first part of the season. This understanding can be reiterated in the selection of either the second or third of the memorial acclamations: "Lord Jesus, come in glory," "until you come in glory." A fitting introduction to the Lord's Prayer is the fourth of the examples in the Sacramentary since it invites the community to pray "for the coming of the kingdom."

At the conclusion of the eucharist, the solemn blessing for Advent is provided in the mass formula for the day and is especially appropriate because of its many references to the theology of the season. Of the prayers over the people, number 1, about anticipating the everlasting life which the Lord prepares, and number 4, about the fulfillment of our longing, are both suitable choices.

In order to underscore the unity of the season of Advent, it would be appropriate on all four Sundays to use some of the options selected for this Sunday.

SECOND SUNDAY OF ADVENT

While the design of the revised Lectionary for Advent presents the figure of John the Baptizer as the center of attention on the second and third Sundays of this season, thereby giving these Sundays some incarnational emphases, there are still strong eschatological notes in the liturgy for this day. The second reading from the second letter of Peter, a late New Testament book, was originally addressed to a community which looked more to the present rather than to the second coming of Christ when he would return in glory. Hence the author underscores the eschatological component of the Christian profession of faith in Christ who has died, is risen and who will come again.

The selection from Deutero-Isaiah was obviously chosen for the first reading to coincide with the preaching of John the Baptizer in the gospel. Although the primary reference is to Isaiah, the passage may also be applied to the Baptizer, and so it may quite suitably be used to describe the ministry of proclaiming the word in our own day. The message is to prepare for the intervention of Yahweh; the prophet of the word is to speak out, to cry out, even at the top of his voice, since he heralds good news. The preacher, whether Isaiah, the Baptizer, or the contemporary minister, is engaged in the task of making the word of God active, vibrant, and urgent, since the meaning of the word "gospel" is not merely a written account of the words and deeds of Jesus. Rather, it is much more the active recounting now and announcement again of God's word to his people. As applied to the Baptizer, the main figure in the liturgy this Sunday, this means that he is still proclaiming the word through contemporary communities who in this season look for the coming of the Lord. In the gospel of Mark, John stands at the juncture of the Old and New Covenants, and the author explicitly makes him the messenger, the herald, the precursor of Jesus because of the citation of the text of the prophet Malachi (3:1) in the second verse of the gospel text. While Matthew and Luke, along with Mark, cite Isaiah 40 to describe John's work, Mark's use of Malachi underscores his understanding that John's preaching and baptizing marks the beginning of the mission and work of Jesus. It is also part of Mark's editorial plan that the Baptizer opens his gospel, thus heightening the connection between the preaching and message of the prophets, and the preaching and message of John.

In Matthew and Luke their gospel accounts begin with two chapters which contain the annunciation to Mary, the birth of Jesus and his infancy. Such details do not belong to Mark's purpose for he wishes to stress, from the beginning, the ministry of Jesus. As the first written gospel, Mark shows that "gospel" means the account concerning Jesus Christ in the apostolic Church, not merely the words of Jesus. Furthermore, for Mark, the Baptizer is different from the other prophets since his mission includes the external rite of baptism to signify the repentance he asks of his hearers. But just as John was different from his Old Testament types, so is Jesus different from John, for the precursor states clearly that a mightier one is coming, whose sandal straps he is unworthy to loose. John's message in this gospel concerns a "baptism of repentance which led to the forgiveness of sins" (Luke 3:3), as well as the announcement of the Mighty One in Jesus. During the season of Advent we concentrate on the actions of coming and meeting, not merely Christ's coming and meeting us, but our coming to and meeting him. The cutting edge of the season is how much we are willing to prepare our lives for his message and way. It is not so much that we "build the kingdom" but we allow it to be built by God by removing those dispositions which hinder its growth in us.

In planning the liturgy for this Sunday the committee should look to the following Sunday as well and consider how much emphasis it wants to place on the ministry of John the Baptizer, for his role is central in the gospels proclaimed on these two Sundays. On these Sundays the blessing and sprinkling with holy water would be a fitting introduction to the liturgy as the completion of the baptism preached by John. Should the planning committee wish to reiterate the note struck in last week's introductory rite, it could select the third form of penitential rite with the second or third set of invocations with their obvious Advent themes.

While both of the opening prayers underscore our task of removing whatever hinders us from welcoming Christ into our hearts, the invitation to pray and the shorter text (the first) is well phrased, while the alternative prayer is certainly more poetic in its description of light and darkness, the glory of Christ and the vision of his wisdom. Advent preface number 1 is prescribed for use this Sunday and it underscores the eschatological tone of the season. Using the second or third of the memorial acclamations would underscore this eschatological orientation, as would the use of the fourth invitation to the Lord's Prayer.

The first of the prayers over the people can be used to conclude the liturgy for it fittingly refers to the everlasting life prepared for those who believe in Christ. Should the committee wish to reinforce the general themes of this season with greater solemnity it could appropriately choose the solemn blessing for Advent to conclude the liturgy.

THIRD SUNDAY OF ADVENT

Formerly called "Gaudete" Sunday to distinguish it from the mournful, somber Sundays which were considered the essence of the Advent Sundays, this third Sunday no longer stands in such stark contrast to the rest of the season. The penitential practices of the entire season have been dropped in favor of a season of joyful expectation. The four Sundays of Advent now present a unity that is not broken, as previously, by one Sunday with a different theme. It would be more appropriate not to use rose colored vestments this Sunday in order to keep the continuity with the other Advent Sundays.

There are three themes clearly enunciated in the readings for this Sunday: the note of joy and rejoicing that the Lord is near, the ministry of John the Baptizer, and the eschatological emphasis that we await the final revelation of the Lord. The first two are predominant in the readings and the other is secondary. The theme of joy and rejoicing is unmistakable as it is the entrance antiphon: "rejoice in the Lord always; again I say rejoice! The Lord is near" from Philippians 4:4–5, and it is found in the second Advent preface which may be used on this Sunday, "in his love Christ has filled us with joy." It is certainly the clearest theme of the readings, and is now understood again to be part of the theology of the entire season, rather than just a part of "Gaudete" Sunday.

The second theme is a reiteration of the preaching and challenge of John the Baptizer enunciated in last week's liturgy. In the reading from the fourth gospel the Baptizer is firm in stating again and again that he is not the Messiah; he testifies to the coming of the light in Christ, but he himself is not that light. The author of the gospel repeats the synoptic citation of Isaiah when he describes John as a voice crying in the desert, "prepare the way of the Lord." He also repeats what was emphasized in the second part of last week's gospel, that the one still to come is mightier than John, "the straps of whose sandal I am not worthy to unfasten." The Old Testament reading most clearly coincides with this gospel in that it relates to the Christology in the gospel for the day. John renounces the titles of Messiah, Elijah, and the prophet, and defers to Christ. The text of this servant song in Isaiah has profoundly influenced the Christology of the New Testament and the understanding of Jesus's ministry.

While this Sunday falls within the time of the incarnational emphasis of Advent (from December 17 to 24), it nonetheless still reiterates the eschatological note of Advent in the second reading where the Thessalonian community is called to be blameless in conduct and to be perfect in holiness until the coming of the Lord Jesus Christ.

If the planning committee has chosen to do so, the liturgy this Sunday could be appropriately centered on John the Baptizer, whose ministry was emphasized last week. In addition, the theme of joy is dominant this week, and there are many eschatological references this Sunday as well.

The introductory rite may be the rite of blessing and sprinkling with holy water, especially since the administration of the Baptizer's baptism is mentioned in the gospel. Or the committee may wish to continue the unity of the season by using the same penitential rite as last week, with the invocations of Christ taken from the second or third samples in the Sacramentary.

The incarnational note of Advent is struck in the opening prayer where the birth of Christ is mentioned as it is in the prayer after communion. The alternative wording of the prayer contains the more eschatological note of joy and hope at the return of the Lord at the end of time.

Either of the Advent prefaces may be used on this Sunday, where the first is the more eschatological and the second speaks of the ministry of John the Baptizer and emphasizes our preparing to celebrate the birth of Christ. The second and third of the memorial acclamations would be appropriate selections throughout Advent as would the fourth invitation to pray the Lord's Prayer.

The solemn blessing for Advent is presented as the conclusion to the liturgy in the texts of the Sunday. Of the prayers over the people, the first and the fifth prayers are appropriate since the first speaks of the kingdom to come, and the fifth speaks of remaining faithful to the Lord and rejoicing in his mercy.

Since the invitation before the opening prayer of this liturgy notes that the season of Advent is now drawing to a close and the prayer over the gifts states that Christmas is now drawing near, we see that the design of the editors of the reformed calendar, in making this Sunday incarnational in emphasis, has been fulfilled in the mass formula. While the role of Mary is stressed in all three cycles of the Lectionary on this fourth Sunday, in no other year is it as explicit as it is on this Sunday. In the "A" cycle the coming of Emmanuel is announced in Joseph's dream (Matthew 1:18–24), and in the "C" cycle the visitation of Mary to her kinswoman Elizabeth is described (Luke 1:39–45). Yet, the most explicit text about Mary's role in the incarnation of the Word of God is recounted in the gospel for this Sunday, the annunciation to Mary (Luke 1:26–38).

Such annunciation stories are common in the Scriptures, and even a first reading of this text reveals that there is more here than historical detail. Here we are on the level of significance and meaning, rather than on the level of recounting the bare facts of history. The theology underscored here is important for an understanding of the role of Mary and of the longed-for Messiah. His coming is not a work of human agency, but is the result of the work of the Holy Spirit and of the Most High. This Jesus is called the Son of the Most High, and the inheritor of the throne of David as the summit of all the hopes of Israel. Yet, the other details of the story underscore the message of the epistle reading from Romans, that there is a mystery of Jesus Christ, and that the gospel is the revelation of this mystery that the Savior would be born of human stock and share our human life. The Old Testament reading from second Samuel also leads us from the historical to the theological level, for the contemporary circumstance which the author describes is later elaborated and given another meaning, since it became a Messianic text where the throne of David is now reserved for Jesus alone.

The role of Mary in all of this is not to be forgotten, however, as her response at the end of the gospel is certainly a key to understanding her place in the work of salvation. "I am the servant of the Lord" is certainly a model of obedience for all believers.

What has to come to pass would be realized through the power of the Spirit. How it came to pass was because a maiden responded in full faith to the incredible; she said yes to what was apparently impossible; she trusted in a word that certainly seemed preposterous. And all this because she believed and trusted in the Lord. Mary can truly be called a model of fidelity to be imitated by all Christians.

For this, the last Sunday of Advent, the planning committee may appropriately choose the same penitential rite it has used through the season. The most appropriate for Advent is the third form with the second or third set of invocations. On this Sunday the third is especially apt because of the reference to "Son of God and Son of Mary." And yet, for the eschatological themes of the season, the second set of invocations is still appropriate.

The shorter opening prayer is incarnation-redemption oriented, whereas the alternative prayer speaks more specifically about the Virgin Mary who placed her life at the service of God's plan. The prayer over the gifts speaks of the role of the Spirit who sanctified Mary at the annunciation and who now sanctifies the gifts brought to the altar for sacrifice.

The second Advent preface is most suitable for use on this Sunday and is quite specific in speaking of Mary who bore Jesus in her womb with love beyond all telling. During the eucharistic prayer, the use of the second or third memorial acclamations would be appropriate to underscore the eschatological references of the Advent season. Similarly, the fourth invitation to pray the Lord's Prayer would be an appropriate choice.

The solemn blessing for Advent is appropriate for this Sunday as a fitting conclusion to the unity established through the four Advent Sundays. Of the prayers over the people, number 3 is presented in the Mass formula and speaks of cherishing the gifts received at the eucharist. Other appropriate selections are number 12 and number 22, which speak of serving the Lord and doing his will.

SUNDAYS OF ADVENT "C" CYCLE

FIRST SUNDAY OF ADVENT

An exegetical principle that is of prime importance in understanding a given scriptural passage is that the writers of the scriptures often adopted and adapted previously existing units of material and traditional sayings to the religious experience of the community in which they lived. Hence to uncover the original purpose of a writing and the original setting in which the Word was first proclaimed is helpful, not only to uncover its original meaning, but also to understand how to apply that text in the present. Authentic passing on of the tradition involves the interpretation of a past statement in the present, not merely the repetition of a text.

It is important to keep this principle in mind when dealing with the scriptural texts for this Sunday since all deal with the coming of the promised One, and yet the differing circumstances of the different communities help enrich the understanding of what Israel, the early Church, and a later Church community understood by this coming.

The reading from Jeremiah this Sunday is most likely the work of a later hand than that of Jeremiah the prophet, and is the application of a saying of Jeremiah to a later situation. The application of the prophet's message for the later community was that they not grow slack in their anticipation of the promised One who was to come from David's lineage.

The reading from first Thessalonians reflects the imminent parousia which Paul anticipated early on in his preaching. The message here is clear—that the second coming was to be soon and that before this coming of the Lord Jesus the community should live as closely as they could to the moral standards set by Christ.

The gospel from Luke reveals a constant theme of the evangelist, that the community called the Church was by no means an afterthought in the Christian dispensation. Rather, it is the means by which all believers in every age can come near to the salvation worked by God through Christ until his second coming. The Church is a prime factor in the continuance and vitality of the Christian life which community members are to live. While Luke uses much of the apocalyptic imagery of the evangelist Mark, his own editorial additions are most significant. His main concern is not only to indicate the apocalyptic nature of Christ's coming, but to instruct the present Church to be on their guard, that the great day of the Lord's coming will suddenly close in, that they should pray constantly for the strength to escape whatever is in prospect, and that they should stand secure before the Son of Man.

The themes expressed in these readings are typical of those of the first Sunday of Advent in all three cycles of the Lectionary, that of the second coming of the Lord and the kind of hope and watchfulness that can be truly called eschatological. Yet, of all the readings, the Lukan gospel would seem to describe most adequately the situation of the Church today, for the second coming seems far distant in the categories of thought and time. The situation of the Church in the "middle of time" between the past coming and the future coming of Christ could be a most appropriate focal point for consideration this Sunday. As Luke urges his community to be on guard and be aware that they are indeed living between the times, so the present Church may be served well with this same kind of admonition.

This Sunday's liturgy contains important Advent themes: the urgency now about our preparation for that final day, the constant need to be watchful for the signs of the Lord's coming, the necessary call to ever faithful conduct in accord with the gospel, and the hope for a full realization of what is still to be completed in the advent of Christ.

For the introductory rite of the liturgy the rite of blessing and sprinkling with holy water would be suitable when used with the first form of prayers which refer to our present share in life eternal. Should the planning committee choose the third form of the penitential rite, they could use the second set of invocations which speak of the Lord's coming in the past to gather the nations, his coming in the present in word and sacrament, and his coming in the future with salvation for his people.

An appropriate response to these invocations would be the ancient chant *Kyrie, eleison*, with the emphasis on Christ the Lord who is ever merciful.

The first form of the opening prayer refers more directly to the kind of ethical orientation Paul speaks about in the second reading, whereas the alternative form of the prayer has more of the expectation and hope-filled motif proper to the general theology of the Advent season, especially with the invitation to prayer that in Advent we may pray with longing and waiting for the coming of the Lord.

The first Advent preface is prescribed for use this Sunday and speaks clearly of the past coming of the Lord as a man and his future coming when the promised salvation will be ours.

The second or third memorial acclamations containing the direct invocation that Christ come in glory would be appropriate for this season, as would the fourth invitation to pray at the Lord's Prayer, which speaks of the coming of the kingdom.

The prayer after communion reflects the theology of the season by mentioning our present love for the things of heaven and asking for the Lord's guidance on earth.

The solemn blessing for Advent is provided as part of the Mass formula and is a most fitting choice for all the Advent Sundays. Of the prayers over the people, number 1 about being led to life everlasting, and number 5 about remaining faithful to the Lord are appropriate alternatives.

To underscore the continuity of the Sundays of Advent it would be helpful to select some of these same options for use on all four Sundays.

SECOND SUNDAY OF ADVENT

While the liturgy of Advent was reformed so as to place a strong eschatological emphasis in the first part of the season and to make the second part more clearly oriented to Jesus' birth (December 17 to 24), the liturgy of this Sunday contains both Advent themes, and demonstrates that they cannot be artificially separated. Beginning with this Sunday and continuing next week the important figure of John the Baptizer is given a prominent place in the gospel texts and in the liturgy of the day; hence, the obvious emphasis on Advent as a season prior to the commemoration of the Lord's birth. Yet on the other hand, the very clear emphasis in the liturgy of the first Sunday of Advent on the Lord's second coming is amply treated this Sunday as well, with the obvious exaltation and joyful expectation proclaimed in the first two readings. It would be important for the planning committee to determine which of these themes to stress in the celebration.

The first reading from Baruch is fitting because it refers to and reflects well the gospel reading, and because at the same time it speaks about traditional Advent images such as salvation coming from the East, waiting in an almost exalted expectation for the coming Holy One, and the joy that fills the hearts of those who prepare for his coming.

The responsorial psalm reiterates the joy and hope of the waiting community, with the response acclaiming the Lord who has done great things for us, and thus has filled our hearts with joy.

The second reading continues some of this emphasis and also gives an ethical exhortation fully consonant with the nature of the season. In the reading Paul prays that the Lord will complete the good work he began in the community and exhorts his followers to learn and discern the things that really matter.

The gospel proclamation about John the Baptizer begins with a listing of historical people and seemingly unnecessary details about time and place, but all this is important for the evangelist, for he understands John to be the last in the line of Old Testament prophets and the herald by word and deed of the coming Jesus. Therefore he uses a device typical of the beginning of the prophetic books, to situate the words of the prophet in a specific time and place. Also, John's concern is that the people repent and prepare for the coming Lord, who will inaugurate a new baptism in water and the Holy Spirit. It is important to note here that baptism by John was a response to and a sign of accepting his preaching; hence the obvious theme that Advent is a time for hearing and probing the word of evangelists and prophets.

The last part of the gospel returns to some more general and typical Advent themes in reflecting the imagery of the first reading and in using Isaiah 40 as a basis of development. The eschatological note is struck even here in a gospel whose main character is John who was the last of those who heralded the first coming of the Lord.

The rite of blessing and sprinkling with holy water would be an appropriate introduction to the liturgy this Sunday since John's baptism in water is mentioned. Keeping in mind the difference between John's baptism and Christian initiation, the rite could be introduced by noting the importance of interior purification and a change of heart that must always accompany any ritual gesture or sacrifice.

Should the planning committee choose the third form of the penitential rite, the second set of invocations about the comings of the Lord—past, present, and future—would be a helpful reiteration of Advent theology. In addition, the third sample set of invocations using titles of Christ would also be suitable.

Both versions of the opening prayer speak in terms of waiting and watching for the Lord's coming in glory, but the second choice would appear to be more ethical in orientation and would reflect the exhortation of the second reading.

The first Advent preface is suggested for use this week and contains many eschatological images appropriate for the Advent season. The second or third of the memorial acclamations would be an appropriate choice for this liturgy with the stress in each on the second coming of the Lord. Another way to underscore this aspect of Advent would be in using the fourth invitation to pray the Lord's Prayer.

While the first of the prayers over the people is presented for the final blessing in the Sacramentary, and is an appropriate Advent selection, the use of the solemn blessing for Advent would be a preferable option, especially if it has been used throughout the season. Other prayers over the people that would coincide with the day's liturgy would be number 5 about remaining faithful to the Lord, and number 16 about consolation in this life and in the life to come.

THIRD SUNDAY OF ADVENT

A central theme which runs through the Scripture readings for this Sunday is that of true Christian joy and hope which comes from a knowledge of the nearness of the Lord. In the former liturgical calendar this third Sunday was known as "Gaudete" Sunday, the one joyful day in what was otherwise understood as a penitential season. In the present reform the entire season is defined in terms of a joyful expectation.

The note of quiet joy, the gift of the peace of Christ, the hope that comes from trust in him alone, and the consolation which this offers in present times of trial, are all noted in this day's liturgy and form the major focus of attention.

The reading from Zephaniah begins with "Shout for joy," and promises a renewal of God's love. The psalm clearly speaks of the joy and gladness of the season due to the presence of the great and holy one among his people.

The second reading from Philippians speaks most clearly about rejoicing at this time of anticipation, and in fact is the source of the entrance antiphon for this day which is retained from the former liturgy: "Rejoice in the Lord always."

Another and equally appropriate theme of the readings concerns the communal dimension of preparation for the Lord's coming. In the second reading Paul reminds this community to dismiss all anxiety and to present their needs to the Lord in prayer.

The gospel continues the theme of anticipation by stating that the people were filled with longing and questioning whether or not the Messiah had come in the person of John. The gospel also gives three specific examples of the social dimension of this season—that one should live in charity, be fair with all people, and not denounce others but treat all respectfully. The gospel also mentions the judgment to come with the Lord, another clear and constant Advent theme, by using the images of fire and the winnowing fan.

For planning this celebration the committee could choose the theme of the joy of the season or the communal nature of our preparation for the Lord's coming, or it could continue to emphasize John's mission of preaching and baptizing as brought out in last week's liturgy. The continuity of the season is obvious should any of these themes be selected for emphasis and proclamation, but an overriding concern should always be that of the incompleteness of the Christian life that will not be fulfilled until the Lord comes again.

The rite of blessing and sprinkling with holy water would be an appropriate introduction to the day's liturgy especially because of the references to Jesus' baptism in the Holy Spirit, a baptism which Christians have received and which they renew at the eucharist each Sunday.

Should the committee prefer to use the third penitential rite, the second set of sample invocations about the comings of the Lord would be a most fitting choice. The third sample set of invocations would also be helpful as the titles of Christ are utilized in it.

Both invitations to pray at the opening prayer speak of the joy of the Advent season and hence support the scriptural themes of the day. The shorter opening prayer is more incarnational in emphasis (as is the prayer after communion), while the alternative form is more eschatological, about looking forward to the Lord's return at the end of time.

Either Advent prefaces 1 or 2 may be used this Sunday, and the selection should be determined by whether the liturgy centers on eschatological themes (preface 1) or more incarnational themes (preface 2). The use of the second or third of the memorial acclamations would reiterate the eschatological theology of Advent, as would the use of the fourth invitation to pray the Lord's Prayer.

The solemn blessing for Advent, in the Sacramentary, is a most fitting conclusion to the liturgy. Of the prayers over the people, number 4 about the Lord as the fulfillment of our longing and number 15 about serving the Lord with joy are both fitting choices to coincide with the theology of this season.

FOURTH SUNDAY OF ADVENT

It was the intention of the editors of the Lectionary to make this fourth Sunday in Advent focus on the incarnation of Christ and to emphasize the role of the Virgin Mary in the coming of Christ. The tradition of the Ambrosian liturgy on this Sunday is to emphasize Mary's role in the incarnation and this custom is reflected in all three cycles of the reformed Roman Lectionary. In the "A" and "B" cycles the scene of the annunciation is recounted, and here in the "C" cycle the gospel scene is that of the visitation of Mary to her cousin Elizabeth. The parallel circumstances of the two women and the importance of the birth of their sons in the history of salvation is obvious and indeed could well be a theme to emphasize this Sunday. Certainly, the figure of Mary is central on this day and the gospel reading about her blessedness being due to her trust in and reliance on the Lord's words to her is a most important model for the Church to imitate.

The alternative form of the opening prayer mentions the time when the Virgin Mary placed her life at the service of God's plan, and the prayer over the gifts speaks of the power of the Holy Spirit which sanctified Mary in her vocation as servant of the Lord.

The second Advent preface, which may be used this Sunday, mentions John the Baptizer and Mary specifically, and notes that the virgin mother bore Christ in her womb with unbounded love. The major theme of this Sunday is the example and qualities of Mary the Mother of the Lord.

A second appropriate theme in the day's readings and prayers concerns the relationship of the Incarnation to the redemption won in Christ. The second reading from the letter to the Hebrews speaks of the sacrifice of Christ and how it was the will of the Father that he sanctify those to come after him as his followers by the free offering of his body as the perfect sacrifice.

The free gift of his body was the chief aim and direct result of the incarnation, and this is reflected in the first form of the opening prayer which speaks of the suffering, death, and resurrection of Christ which leads the Church to salvation. The revelation of the birth of Jesus is a prelude to his act of redeeming sinful humanity.

Should the celebration of this Sunday liturgy be centered around the person of Mary, the rite of blessing and sprinkling with holy water could be introduced by reference to the Holy Spirit, whose power strengthened Mary in her doing the will of the Father, and who is the source of all grace and strength.

Should the committee choose the third penitential rite the invocations of the third model prayer would be the most appropriate to use since these refer to the Son of God and Son of Mary, as well as to the Word made flesh and the splendor of the Father. The second model invocations would also be suitable since they reiterate the themes of the whole season about the comings of Christ.

The alternative form of the opening prayer speaks directly of Mary's role in the incarnation as does the prayer over the gifts. The second or third of the memorial acclamations could be chosen for the liturgy because they emphasize the final coming of the Lord in glory. Using the fourth invitation to prayer at the Lord's Prayer would also reiterate this emphasis on the coming of the kingdom.

The solemn blessing for the Advent season would be a preferable conclusion to the liturgy in order to emphasize the unity of the themes of the Advent season. Of the prayers over the people number 5 about the Lord strengthening his people and number 24 about the Father's blessing on those who put their trust in him (as did Mary) are appropriate.

Chapter Two

Christmas Season—"The Beginning Of Our Redemption"

CHRISTMAS AND EPIPHANY IN HISTORY
AND THE CONTEMPORARY REFORM

The General Norms for the Liturgical Year and the Calendar state that the Christmas season is second only to the celebration of Easter in its importance, and that Christmas is the only celebration other than Easter to have an octave in the revised calendar. Unlike Easter, however, Christmas always had a fixed date of December 25, which date was always associated with the feast of the Nativity. The first notation of the feast of Christmas is in a calendar of the fourth century, but the feast has deep pre-Christian origins which helped determine its importance and date of celebration. In pagan Rome the second half of December was the Saturnalia, a festival of the turning of the year. The pagan cult of the sun also came to be part of the festival in the third century. Hence, in the fourth century there emerges the Christian feast on December 25 to counteract this pagan feasting, where the clear intent was to replace the cult of the sun with a feast of the coming of the true light through Christ. However, it should be noted that the prior sun-worshiping did not die a quick death, for in the fifth century Leo the Great was disturbed that worshipers arriving for the morning eucharist on Christmas would first bow to the sun before taking their places in the Christian assembly.

Christmas developed further as a result of the Christological controversies of the fourth, fifth, and sixth centuries which concerned the meaning of the incarnation and the person of Jesus. The emphasis on Christmas led to a lessening in importance of the originally more prominent feast of the Epiphany.

From its origins in the East, Epiphany spread in Gaul first and then to Rome. Originally it was closely connected with the baptism of Jesus and the initiation of new Christians into the faith. Later, in the fourth century, it became connected with the Nativity in theme. While Epiphany was closely connected with the initiation of new Christians in Gaul it never had this association in Rome. While there were other themes associated with Epiphany, recovering exact origins and sources of such themes is difficult. However, it can at least be said that Epiphany was observed throughout the Church from the latter half of the fourth century and reflected the birth of Jesus, the baptism of Jesus, the miracle of Cana, the turning of the year, a festival of lights, and even in one place it is cited as a festival with elements of the transfiguration as its theme. We can also say that by the end of the fifth century in the East, December 25 commemorated the birth of Christ and January 6 commemorated essentially the baptism of Jesus. At Rome at this same time December 25 commemorated the birth of Christ, and January 6 commemorated the visit of the Magi. As a result of Gallican influence the celebration came to be outlined as follows: December 25—Nativity, January 6—visit of the Magi, Sunday after Epiphany—baptism of Jesus, and on the Sunday following—the miracle at the wedding feast at Cana.

What is clear is that the celebration of Epiphany was, from the very beginning, very rich in theology. As is stated in the antiphon at evening prayer on Epiphany: "We celebrate a holy day adorned by three miracles: this day, a star led the Magi to the manger; this day, water was changed into wine at the marriage-feast; this day, Christ, for our salvation, vouchsafed to be baptized by John in the Jordan."

In the light of this early history it is not surprising to find that in the revised calendar the Christmas-Epiphany season includes the following themes: December 25—Nativity, Sunday following—Holy Family, January 1—solemnity of Mary, January 6 (or on Sunday as in U.S.)—Epiphany, Sunday following the Epiphany—Baptism of the Lord. What is also interesting to note in the revised Lectionary is that on the second Sunday of the year (the first Sunday of the year is the Baptism of the Lord) the gospels for all three cycles are taken from the gospel of John. In year "A" the text is John 1:29–34 about the confession of John the Baptizer; in year "B" the text is John 1:35–42, which repeats John's confession of

Jesus as the Lamb of God and also contains the disciples' recognition of the Messiah; and in year "C" the text is John 2:1–12, the miracle of the wedding feast at Cana. Once again, there is evidence here that the seasons flow into each other and are not so strictly separated as they might appear.

The season of Christmas begins with evening prayer 1 of Christmas and extends to the Sunday after Epiphany, the Baptism of the Lord. Prior to the reform of the rite, the feast of the Purification of Mary had been understood to end the Christmas season and was celebrated on February 2. One of the reasons why this feast took on such importance was the fact that one element of the Christmas-Epiphany symbolism is that of light. The prayers speak again and again of Christ coming into the darkness of this world and the readings speak of Christ's coming as the life and light of all.

Although the feast was called the Purification of Mary, the current reform returns to the primary meaning of the feast as the Presentation, for what is central in the Temple event concerns Jesus. The custom of blessing candles on this day and of walking in procession is retained in the Sacramentary, noting that this is forty days after the feast of the Nativity. Christ is acclaimed as the light of all nations and the glory of all peoples. Yet, it should be noted that this feast now occurs in "ordinary time" and that there is no mention in the Sacramentary that this celebration "ends" the Christmas season, although it had been the custom to so regard this feast. The norms for the Liturgical Year cite the Sunday after the Epiphany as the end of the Christmas season.

The season of Advent, Christmas, and Epiphany are to be considered together in the revised calendar. The overview is to see the mystery of the coming Lord, from the first Sunday of Advent through the Baptism, as a unified cycle, separated from the season of our redemption in Lent and Easter, and the season of the year which ends with the solemnity of Christ the King, which celebration itself already leads to the theology of the first Advent Sunday.

THEOLOGY AND SPIRITUALITY OF CHRISTMAS

The elements which influenced the development of this liturgical season are first, the emphasis on the theology of Christ under his different aspects and titles, and second, the account of what occurred in the early years of Jesus' life on earth. While both of these elements are still found in the revised celebrations of the season, the historical details are subsumed under the far more important theme of the theology of the incarnation. What we do when we celebrate liturgy is not to repeat each year what are, in fact, unrepeatable historical events. Rather, we celebrate them and renew ourselves through our immersion now in the mystery of the life, death, and resurrection of Jesus. The key to understanding Christmas is that it is the celebration of the interchange whereby the Son of God is born a son of a virgin mother, and humanity is raised to share in divinity because divinity is now shared in humanity. The alternative opening prayer for the Mass of the Vigil of Christmas states: "With gratitude we recall his humanity. . . . May the power of his divinity help us answer his call to forgiveness and life." The prayer over the gifts at Midnight Mass states: "By our communion with God made man, may we become more like him who joins our lives to yours." The third Christmas preface states: "Your eternal Word has taken upon himself human weakness, giving our mortal nature immortal value."

The joining of the historical with the more theological aspects of Christmas is exemplified very clearly in the development and theme of the three Masses of Christmas—at midnight, at dawn, and during the day. The first to develop was that on the day itself, and the present Lectionary retains the custom, derived from the fifth century, of reading the letter to the Hebrews 1:1–6 and the gospel of John 1:1–18 at this Mass. These readings do not relate the expected Christmas story (indeed there is no such recounting in either John's or Mark's gospel), but they concentrate on Christ as the Incarnate Word, who brings light to shatter the darkness of this world, who took on human flesh, but who at the same time gives us a vision of the Father's glory.

This theology is clearly reflected in the opening prayer for the Mass during Christmas day: "Lord God, we praise you for creating man and still more for restoring him in Christ. Your Son shared our weakness: may we come to share his glory."

The second Mass to evolve was that at dawn, and the last was the celebration at midnight. Both of these Masses originally recounted the Christmas story, and the revised Lectionary retains these readings. Yet, what is interesting is that the first readings of both Masses are taken from the book of Isaiah. In the Mass at dawn the Isaian text presages the coming of the Savior and calls the people to experience redemption. At midnight the reading speaks of the coming of the Wonder-Counselor, God-Hero, Father-Forever, and Prince of Peace, whose coming will allow the people who walked in darkness to see the great light. Hence, in all the liturgical celebrations for Christmas the readings point to the implications of the incarnation as well as to the recounting of the events surrounding the birth of the Savior.

And yet, such a theology does not end with the celebration of Christmas day itself because these same themes recur throughout the whole of the season. In the preface for the Epiphany we pray: "Now that his glory has shone among us you have renewed humanity in his immortal image." And the opening prayer for the feast of the Baptism of the Lord states: "May we who share his humanity come to share his divinity."

The season and the celebration of Christmas is not primarily a commemoration of Jesus' birth. Rather it has the deeper meaning that Jesus has inaugurated the reign of God in our midst. The birthday of Jesus as a King is not primary. What is central to the feast and season is an appreciation that this same Christ guides us still, that the dawn of God's rule came in Jesus, and his kingdom was firmly established by his birth. Christmas is not only a day but it is rather a hope in a state of life given to us now and shared among those who believe. It is a time of manifestation, of special remembering, that in Jesus the birth of a child also means that the King of all nations is forever with us. It means that his manifestation to earthly kings in the Epiphany is the showing forth of this Savior to all the world. It means that his baptism by John the Baptizer is the beginning of his public ministry which was the reason for his coming among us. The reign of God is now among us and the bond of God with all people cannot be broken. Jesus the Child is the Anointed One of God. His incarnation leads to his life-giving death and resurrection. As the prayer over the gifts states at the Vigil Mass of Christmas: "may we celebrate this eucharist with greater joy than ever since it marks the beginning of our redemption."

The assurance and promise of this season is not only that Jesus was born like us in humanity, but that he is forever with us as our mediator, the Lord of all. He was born once in history, but he is still with us and works through us, so that the reign begun at his birth may spread and continue to expand through us in our own day. The reign of God came to us as a gift to be shared, and this fragile world is the place where it is to grow because of our faith and love. Christmas is not about the innocence and infancy of Jesus' birth. It is about the incarnation and irrevocable bond between God and all people promised to us once and established forever.

PASTORAL PLANNING FOR CHRISTMAS

Proper liturgical planning is based on the above-mentioned liturgical and theological presuppositions and it should reflect them. If we make too much of the birthday of a King we may lose the real significance of what it means to be sharers in Christ's divine life now. If we emphasize too much the trappings surrounding the first Christmas night we may obscure what that event means. If we place too much stress on the historical details of the scripture readings we may paradoxically lose the significance of that event for our present lives.

And yet what makes the liturgical celebration of these most sacred mysteries different from private reflection about them is the fact that the liturgy is filled with sacred moments and is the setting where ordinary categories of time and space have no meaning and are no longer operative. In a sense, liturgical time happens when ordinary time and the community enter into God's timeless and unbounded love for his people. The grace-filled event of God's taking on human form is renewed annually so that we may be graced by the peace and love of Christ in a most special way—in community. The liturgy makes sense since it is here that the people gathered in the name of the Lord stand apart from ordinary life to be filled with God's uncommon grace. The sacred liturgy is the setting in which we meet the sacred in God who became one like us, so that this sacred event might continually lift up and raise our mortal lives to bring God's love to others. Liturgical time and liturgical space mean something not only because the community lives more fully according to God's Word, but also because that community has taken steps to reach beyond the now to what is everlasting, so that their lives are made ever new in Christ.

With regard to church decor for the Christmas season it would be appropriate to utilize the same furnishings through the whole season, thus underscoring in externals what is established in the theology of this season. The liturgical color prescribed for the season is white for festivity. An altar frontal could be made of white material to emphasize the mood and expression of the season as one of joy and rejoicing that the Lord is in our midst. Liturgical hangings for the season are also appropriate and might even use the same symbols (not words) as those used in Advent.

The colors should be white with some contrasts, but the retention of the symbols of Advent in the banners will show the relationship of Advent to the rest of the Christmas season. Here the motif of prophecy-fulfillment would be obvious. And yet, the fulfillment in Jesus still needs the perfection and completion of the second coming of the Lord, when "God will be all in all." Hence, the use of the same symbols will convey fulfillment, but not completion.

A word should be said about the use of the light theme in the Christmas season. In many of the readings the reference to darkness-light is clear, as evidenced in the first reading for the Midnight Mass at Christmas: "the people who walked in darkness have seen a great light" (Isaiah 9:1). Hence, the use of candles and light for decor is an obvious choice. However, the season for light to proclaim "Christ, our light" is Easter, with the lighting of the Paschal candle at the Easter Vigil as the primary Easter symbol. Hence, the use of light must not become the main focus of attention at Christmas in order that it might be all the more emphasized as an important symbol at Easter. A restrained use of light would not be inappropriate.

Throughout the Christmas-Epiphany cycle the scripture readings are the same selections for all three cycles of the Lectionary. The only exceptions occur on the Feast of the Holy Family (Sunday after Christmas) and the Feast of the Baptism of the Lord (Sunday after Epiphany) when the gospel reading changes each year. Yet, even on these days the first two readings are the same for all three cycles.

The beginning of the gospel of Matthew is the gospel text for this celebration, and it combines Matthew's treatment of the genealogy of Jesus with the events surrounding Jesus' birth. The first part, Matthew 1:1–17, is constructed to show that this Jesus is the Messiah (as stated in vs. 16), that he is the term of salvation history that began with the promises to Abraham. There is a symbolism in the number of generations cited, in all forty-two, and for the author this number symbolism is significant since he eliminates, in fact, some names which should have appeared if he had wanted to construct an accurate historical account. Hence, even here we find the significance of the reading on the level of the evangelist's theology, and not merely in the fact that he recounts the events of Jesus' birth. In verses 18–25 the titles "Jesus" and "Emmanuel" are mentioned; the former means "Yahweh is salvation" and the latter means "God is with us." The use of "Jesus" indicates that this child is the hoped-for savior. The use of "Emmanuel" in this first chapter of Matthew parallels its usage in the last chapter (Matthew 28:20) which indicates the Lord's presence with his people from the event of his birth "until the end of the world."

What unifies this gospel passage is its Christology, for the author here presents graphic evidence that the eternal Son of the Father is also the God-man who shares our human nature, "a man like us in all things but sin." The point of the gospel pericope is not to reintroduce the Savior who is again with his people at Christmas, but to underscore that we who are his followers bear in our humanity the message and very presence of Christ in the world in which we live.

In the first reading from Isaiah 62 the utterance of the prophet follows upon a divine silence of some duration, but now there is another word from God's messenger. For the Christian community, however, this word and promise has now become the very presence of the person so longed for. The word has now come to be and is fulfilled; the name has been spoken and has already appeared. Again, Christological implications can be drawn from this reading where the names "my delight" and "espoused" may be used to understand and explain the mission of the Messiah.

The reading from the Acts of the Apostles is part of Paul's speech at Antioch Pisidia. The whole force and context of this speech is to summarize salvation history: the history of the Jews, the preaching of the Baptizer, the recognition of Jesus, the crucifixion, and resurrection. In this reading the titles attributed to Christ are "Jesus," "descendant of David," and "Savior."

The clear emphasis on both the humanity of Christ as well as a survey of the various titles used to describe him provide the basic themes of this evening's liturgy. The third penitential rite would be well chosen for this celebration, with the third set of suggested invocations, since the titles of Christ, "mighty God and prince of Peace, "Son of God and Son of Mary," and "Word made flesh, splendor of the Father" are used.

The opening prayer speaks of Christ as the redeemer. It also has certain Advent overtones in speaking about welcoming the Lord and his role as judge, thus making it a fitting conjunction between Advent and Christmas. The alternative prayer is more poetic and is more expressive of both the humanity and divinity of Christ. The theological understanding of the incarnation leading to the act of redemption is seen in the prayer over the gifts for in it we pray: "Lord, as we keep tonight the vigil of Christmas, may we celebrate this eucharist with greater joy than ever since it marks the beginning of our redemption." The liturgy here is clear in that it moves from reviewing the events surrounding the birth of Jesus to its ultimate goal—the paschal mystery.

There are three prefaces for Christmas in the Sacramentary, the first of which speaks of light and the vision of God's glory; the second speaks of Christ, Son before all ages and now born in time; and the third speaks of Jesus as Word and a new light. The second would seem to be the most appropriate for use at this vigil Mass. The Roman Canon is recommended for use because of the proper commemoration of Christmas.

The first introduction to the Our Father would be suitable since it speaks of praying in the words "our Savior" gave us.

The solemn blessing for Christmas could be used to conclude this celebration since it speaks of the Son of God, the Savior, and the Word. Of the prayers over the people, number 14 about the mystery of redemption would also be an appropriate selection.

The readings of the Mass at midnight indicate clearly the paradox of the celebration of Christmas. In the first reading the prophecy of the Book of Isaiah reveals, in a messianic interpretation, the depth of the seeming contradiction that God should take on human nature, and that we who are human by nature can now become like God in and through him. The darkness of this world has been shattered, for a light has come among us. Yet, the King of Kings is born in poverty; the Lord of Lords' only majesty was a mere manger bed; the Wonder-Counselor himself had to grow in wisdom, age and grace; the Mighty God assumed the form of the humblest of slaves; the Son of the Everlasting Father was born the son of a virgin mother; and the Prince of Peace came to live in a world divided by violence and sin. In the reading from Titus the paradox is continued, for the incarnation does not mean that all is completed in this event and so the author juxtaposes the grace of God appearing among us in the nativity with the final and still to come appearance of Christ at his return in glory. The gospel indicates that the heavenly messengers entrusted their divine message to the lowliest of all people, even considered at times a despised lot—the shepherds in Bethlehem. This is a night of wonder, paradox, and reflection on the mystery of God's love revealed in the birth of his Son.

In planning this liturgy it would be important to stress the paradoxical nature of the event of the incarnation and thus to go "beyond the retelling of the story" of that first Christmas night. The liturgy is a solemn commemoration of the love of God for us and for all people. We have been irrevocably graced in the event of the incarnation. The liturgy is a commemoration of our rebirth in Christ and a call to share his love with others.

The introductory rite could suitably be the third form of the penitential rite with the third set of invocations which speak of the person of Christ under titles used in the liturgy of the Christmas season. The opening prayer of the liturgy, with its stress on the night being made holy by the radiance of Jesus Christ, is a sort of preview of the first reading. The alternative prayer speaks of the same darkness-light theme, yet it joins it with the message of the letter of Titus about the one who is "still to come" by using such words and phrases as "foretaste" and awaiting the "fullness of his glory." The prayer over the gifts speaks of the communion of all humanity with God and the desire of the Christian people to "become more like him."

The preface for the Mass may be chosen from any of the three for Christmas. The first links particularly well with the light and glory theme of the reading from Isaiah and the opening prayer of the Mass. The second preface poetically expresses the paradox of the readings in coupling the unseen and the seen, the eternal God and Christ's appearance in time. The third preface joins both themes of the light shining in the darkness and the divinity and humanity of Christ our Savior.

The most suitable eucharistic prayer is the Roman Canon with the proper commemoration of Christmas.

The solemn blessing prescribed is that for the Christmas season and is a most fitting conclusion to the liturgy. Two simpler alternatives would be the first solemn blessing for Ordinary Time, which contains the text of the blessing of Aaron (Numbers 6), or the second solemn blessing for Ordinary Time which is from Philippians 4:7.

CHRISTMAS—MASS AT DAWN

As already noted, this dawn liturgy was the second of the three Christmas Masses to evolve with its readings that recount the events of the birth of Jesus. The gospel text from Luke is a continuation of the gospel read at midnight, and recounts that the shepherds went to see the child after the angels had announced what had come to pass in the cave at Bethlehem. An understanding of Luke's stylistic traits can help us uncover some of the theological implications in this narrative. Stylistically the passage has been influenced by certain motifs such as the angels appearing, the fulfillment of the prophecies of Micah, and the glory surrounding the praise proclamation to the shepherds. Furthermore, Luke states in two places in these five verses that the shepherds saw the child and then understood what had been told them by the angels. They rejoiced "for all they had heard and seen, in accord with what had been told them." The message of the angels in explaining what had taken place helped them to appreciate the sight of the child. The mystery made clear by this miraculous birth is that this child invites us to live with each other as children of one Father. It is by grace and adoption that we are made his people. In the letter to Titus these facts are emphasized as the author speaks of our regeneration as children of the Father. The responsorial psalm also indicates the meaning of the incarnation by stating that the Lord is born for us. It was not by any deeds that we had done, but it was by the grace and goodness of God that we have been given his grace and peace on earth (gospel acclamation).

The first reading from Isaiah 62 speaks of the community to whom this mystery would come, and calls them the holy people, the redeemed of the Lord. The theme expressed in this liturgy is our relationship to God and to each other in Christ. The Son of God was born in human form so that we could become like him and share his life and love with one another. It is on the basis of this new relationship with God through his Son that the author of the letter to Titus in chapter two speaks of ethical conduct consonant with our union with God.

An appropriate introduction to the liturgy would be the use of the third penitential rite with the third set of invocations containing titles of Christ. The light motif returns in the prayers of the Sacramentary for this mass, since light is mentioned in the entrance antiphon, is in the invitation to pray at the opening prayer, and is part of the text of both versions of that prayer. Both of these prayers speak of the revelation of the Word for all. The shorter version is ethical in its orientation since it prays that the light of faith will shine in our words and actions. The alternative version is more in keeping with the text of the reading from Titus, which expresses the theology of the revelation of the Word to all.

In the prayer over the gifts we pray that we may follow the example of Jesus and that we, the children of the Father, may again receive the gift of divine life in this eucharist.

Of the three Christmas prefaces the third would be the most appropriate to coincide with the theme of relationship in Christ since it states that in the incarnation God has become one with humanity and that humanity has become one with God. The second preface speaks of the birth of the Savior in time as a means of restoring unity to all creation and leading all people from exile to freedom. The use of the Roman Canon, with the proper commemoration for Christmas, would be appropriate at this liturgy.

The solemn blessing for Christmas would be the most

appropriate conclusion to this liturgy. Other solemn blessings that would be suitable choices are the first and second for Ordinary Time. Numbers 2 and 4 of the prayers over the people about perfect love for one another and finding in Christ the fulfillment of our longing would also be appropriate selections to conclude the liturgy.

CHRISTMAS—MASS DURING THE DAY

The readings for the Mass on Christmas day speak about the reign of God among us, rather than about the birth of Jesus. As noted above, the texts from Hebrews and John are the classic and most primitive readings chosen for proclamation at Christmas. It is in the light of these central texts that the liturgical commemoration of the incarnation should be seen.

The acclamation "your God is king" from the book of Isaiah is the community's acclamation of faith this day since in the incarnation of the Son of God, the kingdom of God, his reign and rule are inaugurated in our midst. The incarnation is the beginning of Jesus' mission; the birth of Jesus among us is the initiation of his ministry.

The reading from Hebrews speaks of the ministry of Christ, the creator and redeemer, who now is seated at God's right hand in glory. The pattern of Christ's life is to be imitated in our own lives, ministering to the needs of others in this life and sharing the glory of God forever at the Father's right hand.

The gospel reading is the familiar Johannine prologue in which the author states definitively that Christ became man by taking upon himself our human condition. Through this sharing in our humanity we come to see his glory as our Savior and Lord. In the incarnation Jesus definitively and irrevocably took on our humanity; the destiny of the believer on earth is even now to share in his divinity.

For the introduction to the liturgy the third penitential rite with the third sample set of invocations would be most appropriate. These titles of Christ join the vision of Isaiah ("mighty God and prince of peace") with the credal affirmations ("Son of God and Son of Mary") and the Johannine language of today's gospel ("Word made flesh and splendor of the Father").

The opening prayer of the Mass speaks of the weakness yet

glory of Jesus and should be used if the committee wishes to explore the implications of the gospel of John in this liturgy. The alternative opening prayer speaks of the light of Christ dawning in the darkness of the world, and should be used if the planning committee takes the references to "light" in the gospel reading as the main theme of the liturgy. (Yet, it should be noted that this theme is not so strong as it is in the Lectionary readings for the Mass at midnight.)

The preface for the Mass may be chosen from among the three Christmas prefaces. The first of these speaks of the light of salvation coming in the incarnation of Jesus. Yet, the second Christmas preface is the best choice in that it speaks of the unseen God, who existed before all the ages and became incarnate in human history in our time, appearing in our midst as one like us. This is the point of John 1:14, the center of the day's gospel. The third preface might also be considered because it can be seen as underscoring the humanity of Christ, speaking as it does of "human weakness" which was mentioned in the opening prayer of the liturgy.

The solemn blessing for Christmas is presented in the Mass formula for this liturgy and is most appropriate because the third part speaks of the Word of God becoming man, again a Johannine theme from the prologue used as the gospel text on this day.

FEAST OF THE HOLY FAMILY—SUNDAY AFTER CHRISTMAS

The placing of the feast of the Holy Family on the Sunday within the octave of Christmas establishes and gives sanction to some of the popular piety which was a part of the Epiphany time, specifically the Sunday within the octave of that feast. In the reformed calendar, however, the Sundays after Epiphany have been eliminated, save for the feast of the Baptism of the Lord, while the feast honoring the Holy Family has been transferred to the Sunday after Christmas. The celebration, however, must be carefully understood so that nostalgic reminiscences of the boyhood of Jesus do not become the focal point of the celebration. The feast celebrates the incarnation of the Son of God, and the fact that the Christian family of today must imitate the life of the Holy Family.

In planning this celebration the committee should not overemphasize the traditional family unit to the exclusion of members of the single-parent family, or to the exclusion of the divorced or separated. What is at stake in this celebration is the concretization of the love and peace of the incarnation.

The book of Sirach presents couplets in rhythmic style which speak of a son's devotion to his parents. This text and the theme of the liturgy speak of the quality of the family relationship, with patience as its chief characteristic.

The second reading is taken from what may be considered the "household code" section of the letter to the Colossians. This text may well be given the center of attention in planning the liturgy on this day.

Both in Colossians and Ephesians the structure of the letters is important, for in both the doctrinal section precedes the exhortation section. The key to both letters is found in understanding and appreciating that ethical conduct and moral exhortation only follow upon the revelation of the mystery of Christ as the meaning and goal of all creation. It is then that the author draws out the implications for moral-spiritual living. In this reading both the life of the Christian community at large (vss. 12–17) and that of the Christian home (vss. 18–21) are considered. Because Christians are "in the Lord" and because they are baptized into Christ Jesus, the moral life does not start from anything they can offer to God by way of virtuous conduct but rather from what God has done for them. Our faith in God, which is his gift to us, both demands and enables us to obey his will, which means to live his way. Thus, the power to act morally comes from God himself. According to this letter, moral conduct is based on love and forgiveness. We are exhorted to forgive as the Lord has forgiven us, and over all virtues to put on love. The love of God for us is always to be responded to in our love for one another.

Another important aspect of our moral-spiritual life is that we dedicate ourselves to prayer, for the author stresses dedicating ourselves to thankfulness, to singing hymns and songs to the Lord, and to doing all things in the name of the Lord Jesus. Therefore, the eucharist we celebrate on this feast is most important as the source of strength and encouragement we need as Christians to live in our homes, in the wider family of the Christian community, and in company of all our brothers and sisters in the family of humankind.

In every eucharist we pray to be forgiven "as we forgive those who trespass against us"; we proclaim that the eucharist is "for the forgiveness of sins"; and we are invited to offer each other the sign of the peace of Christ. These aspects of the eucharist are sharpened for our consideration as we join in recalling the exhortations of the readings this day during this common prayer of thanksgiving. Just as Christian moral action is derived from Christ's prior love for us, so the reality of the eucharist we celebrate is reflected in the way we live when the eucharist is ended and we are sent forth "in peace, to love and serve the Lord."

The gospel for the "A" cycle on this day is from Matthew and it provides more of a setting for the feast than it does historical details of what happened on the way home from Jerusalem. This feast of the Holy Family means that the Father's love was and is incarnate in Jesus, and that what is at the basis of our desire to grow in love and patience is first and primarily the love and patience which God shows toward us. It is God's gift to us, through his son Jesus, that we are able to respond lovingly to him as he reaches out to us in our daily lives. Such is the theology of the season as applied to this feast.

In the "B" cycle the gospel provides at least three possibilities for developing the meaning of this liturgy and for choosing options from the Sacramentary. The first element to be developed could be the recognition by Simeon and Anna of the child who is presented in the Temple, for to them was revealed the mystery of the incarnation. The second possibility concerns the humanity of Jesus and the fact that he went through the same stages of growth as any other human being does. The third possibility from the gospel concerning Jesus' family life in Nazareth, recounted in the last part of the reading, would also be a logical choice since this is one of only two places in the scriptures which describes the family life of Jesus.

The gospel reading in the "C" cycle for this Sunday contains the familiar story of the Holy Family's journey to Jerusalem for the celebration of the Passover. While the ending of the reading contains explicit reference to Mary who "kept all these things in memory," the fact that the solemnity of Mary, the Mother of God, is on January 1 would militate against using this as a major focus of attention this Sunday. The far more appropriate theme to emphasize is that of the family in which Jesus grew physically, mentally, and spiritually. Once again, this theme need not be restricted to natural family units since the text from Colossians as well as the two forms of the opening prayer both give the notion of family a wider scope.

The rite of blessing and sprinkling with holy water would be a helpful introduction to the liturgy since it sets the celebration of the eucharist within the context of baptism by which all become sharers in the Christian community.

Should the the planning committee prefer to use the third form of the penitential rite, the third set of the sample invocations would appropriately underscore the congruity of this feast with the whole Christmas season.

The natural family unit as a place for growth is noted in the invitation to pray and in the text of the opening prayer. It asks for peace in our families, with the Holy Family as a model. The invitation to pray and the alternative opening prayer speak of the family of God which shares his life, and the text of the prayer ends with a petition that we live in peace with all people.

The prayer over the gifts asks that this celebration may keep our families united in peace and love.

The preface to be used on this feast may be selected from the three provided for Christmas, any one of which expresses the unity of this feast with the whole Christmas celebration. Should the Roman Canon be chosen for proclamation, the use of the proper commemoration for Christmas would be another way to unite this feast with that of Christmas.

The solemn blessing for Christmas would be a most appropriate conclusion to this Sunday's liturgy. Of the prayers over the people, number 6 is suitable for this celebration. Other appropriate choices would be number 2, about having perfect love for one another; number 7, about the Lord's family continuing to enjoy his favor and devoting themselves to doing good; and number 23, asking the Lord to come and live with his people to help them remain close to him in prayer and close to each other in true love.

SOLEMNITY OF MARY, MOTHER OF GOD

This octave day of Christmas has had a number of themes for its celebration as a Christian feast. Originally, in the city of Rome this day took on great significance, especially after the Julian reform, and was a day of great festivity and rejoicing. The Christian celebration of the circumcision of Jesus came about as an attempt to set a liturgical time-frame into which the biological events of Jesus' birth and circumcision could be fitted. This feast, however, was first and foremost a Marian feast at Rome, and commemorated Our Lady as the Mother of God. It was the primary and only Marian festival native to Rome. Hence, the feast of the Circumcision, the octave day of Christmas, and a feast of Mary are all subsumed in the reformed calendar under the title of the solemnity of Mary, Mother of God.

The readings for the feast are comparatively brief and begin with the Old Testament book of Numbers containing the pronouncement of the Aaronic blessing. The reference to the "name" in the last verse requires emphasis and explanation since, for the Hebrew mentality, to invoke another's name was to indicate a relationship with that person. Furthermore, to "bless" means to praise, glorify, and extol someone; secondarily it means that a thing or a person is consecrated. Therefore, we bless God during the eucharistic prayer by proclaiming the redemption he has granted us through the name of his Son, Jesus. It is with this as background that we can understand more fully the reason why many prayers in the Sacramentary end by stating "in the name of Jesus the Lord."

The second reading from the letter to the Galatians speaks of the birth of Jesus, the Son of God, and speaks equally clearly about our status through Christ as adopted children of God. It is through and in the incarnation that people in every age may find access to the Father through his Son.

The gospel reading from Luke used on this feast speaks of the name "Jesus" given to the child and of the observance of the Jewish law of circumcision. This notion is found also in the second reading which speaks of being "born under the law."

Two major themes emerge for meditation on this feast. The first is salvation in the name of Jesus, as in the first and the gospel readings, and what it means to invoke the name of God at our worship. The second theme is that of the title of the feast, for the readings from Galatians and the gospel both speak of Mary's motherhood and her faith and trust in God's plan.

By way of introduction to the liturgy, the committee could well choose the third form of the penitential rite with the third sample set of invocations in order to underscore the unity of this celebration with that of Christmas. The choice of the theme for the liturgy will determine the choice of the opening prayer, for the short form is introduced with an invocation of Mary, the mother of the Lord, and the alternative prayer speaks of the name of Jesus.

The prayer over the gifts refers to the Mother of God and the first preface refers to the Blessed Virgin Mary. If the Roman Canon is chosen for proclamation on this feast, the proper commemoration of Christmas is used.

The final blessing for this feast may be chosen from the prayers over the people and is a blessing in the name of the Lord Jesus. An appropriate alternative would be to choose from among the solemn blessings for Christmas, the blessing on feasts of the Blessed Virgin Mary (no. 15), the solemn blessing for the beginning of a new year (no. 13), or the first solemn blessing for Sundays in Ordinary Time (no. 10), which is the Aaronic blessing proclaimed as the first reading on this feast.

SOLEMNITY OF THE EPIPHANY

Trying to discover the origin of the feast of the Epiphany is a difficult historical and liturgical problem. This day has a strong pagan background. In ancient Egypt, for example, the time of the winter solstice was celebrated as the turning of the year and a time of new beginnings. In the Eastern tradition, Epiphany was the commemoration of the Lord's baptism and manifestation as the Son of God. It was an important festival for the celebration of baptisms everywhere except Rome, for the Western tradition celebrated this day as the feast of the visit of the Magi. The themes for the feast, according to the tradition, include the nativity of Jesus, the baptism of Christ, the commemoration of the Cana miracle, and even the transfiguration. To say the least there is a certain ambiguity about the dominant theme of this feast. And yet, there is a richness in the theology and liturgy of this day as seen through history.

The readings of the reformed Lectionary indicate that the theme of the manifestation of Christ to all the nations is the primary emphasis of the feast. The reading from chapter 60 of the book of

Isaiah speaks about those who come to Jerusalem from afar, who bring the wealth of the nations in homage, and who experience the power of God. In its original context this reading referred to the return of the exiles to Jerusalem as a kind of reverse Exodus. The Christian interpretation emphasizes the Christ event as the manifestation of God's power and love which transcends the events of the Exodus and of the exile as well. The first line of the reading about "light" is another, quite dominant theme, as expressed in the prayers and blessing in the Sacramentary.

The reading from Ephesians tells of God's plan of salvation in which all nations become co-heirs, abolishing barriers between Jew and Gentile: God's love for all people.

The Matthean gospel text is the account of the adoration of the Magi as a proper and fitting response to the mystery of the incarnation. Wonder, awe, and mystery are responses of mortals as they come face to face with God through Christ. As with the other liturgical celebrations of the Christmas cycle, the important element of this feast is the birth of Christ.

The breaking down of barriers that divide is a lesson to be learned from the celebration of this feast. As the solemn blessing for Epiphany indicates, in our celebration we "experience his [Christ's] kindness and blessings." We are challenged to "be strong in faith, in hope, and in love," and to be "a light to all our sisters and brothers."

In order to show the essential unity of this feast with Christmas the use of the third form of the penitential rite with the third sample set of invocations would be a very appropriate way of introducing this liturgy. The use of the second set of invocations would also be a possibility because the first of them speaks of gathering "the nations into the peace of God's kingdom."

The opening and alternative prayers of the liturgy both speak of the revelation of the Son of God to the nations and of the incarnation of Jesus as a light for all peoples. In the prescribed preface for Epiphany, Christ, as the light of all peoples, is pictured as the glory of God among us to restore our fallen humanity.

The Roman Canon is an appropriate text to proclaim on this feast because it includes a special commemoration for Epiphany, which speaks of Jesus who "showed himself in a human body."

The theme of the light of Christ as the light for our guidance as his followers is part of the prayer after communion.

The solemn blessing for Epiphany may be chosen as the conclusion of the Mass since it refers to the light of the world and the guidance of a star. For a simpler conclusion to the liturgy the committee could appropriately select number 7 of the prayers over the people, which also speaks of the light of God's grace coming upon us.

THE BAPTISM OF THE LORD

The commemoration of the baptism of the Lord marks the end of the Christmas season since the time "of the year" begins on the following day. Theologically this is a most fitting conclusion to the season for, like the whole liturgical commemoration of Christmas-Epiphany, the reading and prayers this day help to focus our attention on the implications of the event of Christ's birth and life among us. The feast is a fitting climax to the season of expectation and hope in the comings of the Lord in Advent and his manifestation to all the nations in Epiphany. The feast of the Lord's baptism commemorates the inauguration of his earthly ministry and his status as servant of his Father. The first reading from Deutero-Isaiah is the first of the celebrated "servant songs" in this Old Testament book. The selection of this text is hardly arbitrary for these songs greatly influenced the formation of the gospel narratives about Jesus' mission, especially the initial statements about his establishing the reign of his Father. Exactly who the original "servant" was at the time of the composition of the song is a matter of scholarly debate. What is clear is the identification of Jesus with the servant in this liturgy, for the work of both proclamation and action, as envisioned by Isaiah, are part of Jesus' mission in the world.

The selection from the Acts of the Apostles is interesting since it is the only New Testament writing, except for the gospels themselves, which speaks of the baptism of Jesus. It is a proper introduction to an understanding of Jesus' ministry since it indicates that he is anointed with the Holy Spirit, that he brings the good news of salvation to the poor, and that he heals those who are in the grip of the devil's power.

In the "A" cycle the gospel text is from Matthew and recounts the baptism of Jesus by John. Some scholars maintain that placing emphasis on the baptism of Jesus at the beginning of the gospel of Matthew has deep theological significance, for the picture of Jesus in this gospel is that of the new Moses, the giver of the law. As such, his legacy is a compendium of five sections, like the first five books of the Old Testament, the Torah. As in the opening verses of the book of Genesis, where the "mighty wind" swept over the waters, the Spirit hovers over the scene of Jesus' baptism to empower him to do the Father's work, no longer of creation but of redemption.

The gospel reading for the "B" cycle is from Mark 1:7–11. The imagery in this particular text is that of apocalyptic and revelation. The apocalyptic image of the heavens being torn apart is a revelation that Jesus is God's Son. The image occurs again in the scenes of the transfiguration (Mark 9:7) and the death of Jesus (Mark 15:39). The present reading is about God's Son, whose ministry is to be understood as a journey from his baptism, through his transfiguration, to his enthronement at his crucifixion. At each stage he is acclaimed as Lord. In the first two of these the manifestation is by a heavenly word accompanied by cosmic images. Hence, this text is to be seen both as the conclusion of the season of expectation and waiting, and the inauguration of a period of reflection on Jesus' ministry.

The gospel for the "C" cycle reminds us of the third Sunday of Advent in this same cycle since it speaks of the self-effacement of John the Baptizer before the coming Messiah and refers to him as the "mightier" one still to come. The first section of this reading (Luke 3:15–16) is part of the text of the gospel for the third Sunday of Advent, while the second section (Luke 3:21–22) speaks of the baptism of Jesus in the Jordan as the beginning of his ministry. The descent of the Spirit in the form of a dove, and the announcement "You are my beloved Son; on you my favor rests," is an important reference to the mission of Jesus, the Servant, who here fulfills the hopes described in Isaiah 63.

It should be recalled that in this "C" cycle of the Lectionary the recounting of the miracle at Cana is the gospel selection to be read on the second Sunday of the year, which is the Sunday after this feast. We again note that the liturgical cycles are connected rather than completely separated at this conclusion of this Christmas season, just as the first Sunday of Advent is connected with the preceding Sundays of the year, most especially the Sunday immediately preceding, the solemnity of Christ the King.

At this celebration of the baptism of the Lord the rite of blessing and sprinkling with holy water would be a suitable introductory rite since the keynote of the feast is the baptism of Jesus and the inauguration of his mission. This could be preceded by a comment connecting the event of Jesus' baptism with Christian baptism and the inauguration of the Christian life in witness and service.

Should the planning committee prefer the third form of the penitential rite, the third set of invocations about Christ could be used to unite this feast with the liturgical celebrations of the entire Christmas season.

The Sacramentary uncharacteristically offers two forms for the opening prayer, along with the alternative opening prayer. The first speaks of the descent of the Spirit on Jesus, the revelation of Jesus as the Son of the Father, and the plea that those reborn in baptism may be faithful to their calling. The second prayer reflects the nature of the Christmas-Epiphany season as it speaks solely of the humanity-divinity of Jesus. The alternative opening prayer is more poetic in structure and stresses our loving service toward others.

The preface proper to the feast of the Baptism of the Lord includes the scene at the Jordan, the voice from heaven, and the descent of the dove as parts of the imagery of the scene. It concludes by describing Jesus' ministry as bringing good news to the poor, thus recalling the gospel and the first reading. (It should be pointed out that despite the fact that the fourth eucharistic prayer contains much of the same imagery about the mission of Jesus, it should not be used on this particular Sunday because it is always to be used with its own preface. Since this feast has a preface of its own, one of the other eucharistic prayers should be used with it.)

The prayer after communion parallels the development of the opening prayer since it views the Christian life in terms of deeds rather than words. This is a fitting prayer after communion since it is at the eucharist that we renew our commitment to the Christian life and receive the grace and strength of God to fulfill that commitment. In addition, the eucharist is the weekly renewal of our union with Christ in baptism as seen in the option on Sundays of using the rite of blessing and sprinkling with holy water to begin the liturgy.

For the final blessing the planning committee may choose either the one for Christmas or for the Epiphany and thus indicate the continuity of this feast with the whole liturgical season. Appropriate choices from among the prayers over the people would be number 7, as presented in the Mass formula for the feast, and number 9 about enjoying Christ's love and spreading it among others.

Chapter Three

Season of Lent and Holy Week—"The Commemoration of Our Redemption"

LENT AND HOLY WEEK IN HISTORY AND
THE CONTEMPORARY REFORM

The General Norms for the Liturgical Year (no. 27) clearly define Lent as a preparation for the celebration of Easter, a time of renewal when members of the community recall their baptism, and a time of reconciliation with each other before the feast of Easter. The central theme of the season is conversion—a radical redirection of one's whole life according to the gospel of Jesus, who surrendered his life as the price which he paid for our salvation. Baptism is the initial moment of our conversion and is the sacrament of regeneration. Yet, conversion is a process which is not completed once and for all by the celebration of the sacrament. Rather, the continual challenge for the Christian is to redefine his or her life according to the gospel and so become a more deeply committed member of the Body of Christ, the Church. The season of Lent is a preparation for a second baptism in the sacrament of penance for the already initiated, as much as it is a preparation of the uninitiated for baptism itself.

One of the aims of this book is to insure the unity and integrity of worship during a given season or cycle of the Church's year. Thus the season of Advent was viewed as a season of preparation for the second coming of Christ at the end of time as well as for the commemoration of the incarnation of the Son of God, as celebrated in liturgies from Christmas to the Baptism of the Lord, the Sunday after Epiphany.

The same principle of continuity of the Church year and the unity of all the celebrations of a given cycle is even more apparent and important in the cycle from Ash Wednesday to the solemnity of Pentecost. The celebrations of Holy Thursday, Good Friday, and the Easter Vigil (the "Easter triduum") are the most important celebrations of the entire church year (General Norms, no. 59, 1) and these are supported on either side by the season of Lent as preparation and the season of Easter as a fifty-day period called the "great Sunday." This liturgical cycle can best be described as a triangle where all the liturgies through the season are seen as parts of the whole and yet where the "high holy days" of the Easter triduum retain their central significance. Such a diagram may be conceived as follows:

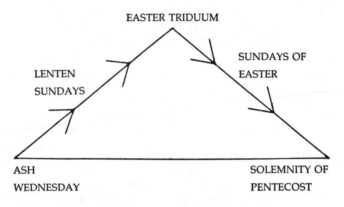

EASTER TRIDUUM

SUNDAYS OF
EASTER

LENTEN
SUNDAYS

ASH
WEDNESDAY

SOLEMNITY OF
PENTECOST

From the earliest days of the Church's life, Sunday was the day for liturgy, especially for the celebration of eucharist. While the Jewish observance of the sabbath remained on the seventh day, Christians saw Sunday as the "eighth day," the eschatological day, the day on which Christians would commemorate the Lord's rising from the dead and the dawn of the new age of risen life through, with, and in him. It was only later that the idea of a special commemoration of Christ's death and resurrection developed into an annual "great Sunday" celebration called Easter. The night before and the day itself were the original core of the liturgical observance of this important yearly festival during the first three centuries. At this same period the obvious link between these two days and Friday was made and the Easter celebration became known as the triduum, the "three days" from Friday to Sunday.

Part of the inspiration for an even greater expansion of the liturgies of these days, and the addition of special liturgies on Thursday, came in the fourth century. Residents in Jerusalem and pilgrims to the holy places celebrated liturgy in the places where the events of Jesus's passion and death occurred. Hence the liturgy of these days came to match historical events and places. This tendency toward historicization expanded the primitive unity of the paschal celebration and divided it into individual parts. Yet, these parts always referred to the unity of this annual solemn commemoration. What is involved here is important for our understanding of liturgy generally, and for an appreciation of the liturgy of the three days, the paschal triduum. Liturgy is a commemoration of the death and resurrection of the Lord, and all liturgy is a participation in the enduring salvation won once for all in Christ. Hence, the most appropriate appreciation of the days of Holy Week as they emerged in the city of Jerusalem is to see each in relation to the others.

The historicization of the celebration which took place during the fourth century was an entirely appropriate evolution in worship, for the unity of Christ's death and resurrection was maintained, despite different liturgies in different places through the week. The commemoration on Good Friday was not just of Christ's death, but it was also of the risen life shared as a result of the resurrection. Similarly, the commemoration of Easter and new life in Christ was always linked to the death Jesus freely endured.

What occurred in the subsequent evolution of Holy Week, however, did not always reflect this unity. Certain medieval developments may be called "dramatizations" whereby these holy days came to be seen in isolation, and it was not long before their unity was not understood. People's spirituality centered on a tableau of unfolding scenes of Jesus's passion and death, with passion-oriented piety receiving principal emphasis. Dramatization, allegory, and the suffering Jesus came to dominate the liturgies of these days, despite the fact that the texts of the liturgy often retained their original precision and balance.

The recent revisions in the Holy Week liturgy and the Lectionary reflect a return to the more traditional understanding of Easter whereby each celebration in the triduum refers to the entire Easter mystery. Hence, suffering and death are not seen in isolation, and resurrection is intrinsically connected with the commemoration of Jesus' death. The reading of the Passion is now confined to two days in Holy Week, Passion (Palm) Sunday and Good Friday. Its presence in the Passion Sunday liturgy highlights the theme of the entire week, the Paschal Mystery. Hence, this Sunday, with the blessing of palm and processions is intrinsically connected to the whole of Holy Week; it is not just a representation of Jesus' entry into Jerusalem.

The reading of the Passion according to John on Good Friday is significant because in John's theological perspective the cross is a symbol of hope, and not just the place for the suffering and ignominious death of Jesus. For John, the cross is a throne of glory, the place where the manifestation of the glory of the God-Man, the King and Ruler of all, takes place once for all in splendor and glory.

The crucifixion is not merely the scene of the death of Jesus; it necessarily points beyond itself to the term of the Paschal Mystery—the resurrection and glorification of Jesus. The cross is no longer merely the place of death; it is the place where death came to an end and life began for all ages. The human skull often pictured at the foot of the cross in Christian art reminds us that Adam's sin, which brought the reign of sin to the world, has come to an end in the sacrifice of the new Adam, Christ. The death we have inherited from Adam, visualized by a human skull, is transformed by the life we receive from the cross of Christ: "The tree of man's defeat became his tree of victory; where life was lost, there life has been restored through Christ our Lord" (preface of the Triumph of the Cross). "The power of the cross reveals your [God's] judgment on this world and the kingship of Christ crucified" (preface of the Passion of the Lord 1).

A proper appreciation of the revised liturgy for Holy Week understands Passion Sunday as the overture to the commemoration of the paschal mystery celebrated in Holy Week, and it sees the days of the triduum as emphasizing in various ways the death and resurrection of Jesus with each celebration intrinsically connected with the others. The season of Lent prepares the Church for these solemn liturgical celebrations by providing appropriate liturgical themes encouraging ascetical practices. The Easter feast is also extended for the following fifty days, culminating in the solemnity of Pentecost.

LENT: A SEASON FOR COMMUNAL
CONVERSION AND RECONVERSION

The conventional understanding and interpretation of the season of Lent often tended to be individualistic in outlook and perspective, but today it is seen rather as a time for communal conversion and communal reflection on the demands of the gospel. The recently revised sacramental rituals of penance and of the Christian initiation of adults (as well as the rite of baptism for children) stress the need for communal conversion as a preparation for celebrating the sacraments.

Initiation

One of the basic principles of the new rite for the initiation of adults is that the preparation of the candidates requires them to progress toward conversion in the midst of the Church (Christian Initiation of Adults, no. 4), and that what is involved here is also a communal reconversion. There are four stages envisioned in initiation: evangelization and precatechesis, the catechumenate, the period of purification and enlightenment in Lent (nos. 7, 52) culminating in the celebration of initiation at the Easter vigil, and the period of postbaptismal instruction.

The outline of this process is classic in its format, and yet it is very challenging for the contemporary Church since it requires much soul-searching on the part of the already baptized as well as on the part of the candidates as to what it means to be initiated into membership in the Body of Christ. The recent revisions in the initiation of adults and children stress the fact that baptism is not just the concern of parents and godparents, or those closest to the candidates, but it is a community concern. All members of the local church are to see themselves as helping in the formation of new members. Lent is a time for the conversion of those to be initiated at Easter and for the reconversion of those already reborn by water and the Spirit.

This period of purification in Lent is concretized in the Sunday liturgies for the third, fourth, and fifth Sundays (sometimes called the "scrutinies"). These liturgies are centered around the gospel texts assigned to these days in the "A" cycle of the Lectionary:

Third Sunday—John 4:5–42, the meeting of Jesus with the
  Samaritan woman: theme of WATER.

Fourth Sunday—John 9:1–41, the cure of the man born blind:
  theme of LIGHT.

Fifth Sunday—John 11:1–45, the raising of Lazarus: theme of LIFE.

These texts are so significant for an appropriate understanding of Lent that they may be used even during the "B" and "C" cycles of Lenten Sundays. They are especially appropriate when the parish community is involved in the rite of Christian initiation of adults. The careful planning of the liturgy of these Sundays in Lent helps to make the Easter Vigil, for which these Sundays prepare, a most significant celebration. By highlighting the images of water, light, and life, the initiation of new members to the faith and the renewal of faith of those already baptized can be made more effective.

The parish community also is expected to share the conversion process of their brothers and sisters through acts of penance and prayer (no. 21). Hence, the reorientation of initiation in the revised rituals sees the whole process as taking place among those already baptized together with whom the newly initiated will share corporate life in the local parish community.

Penance

The ecclesial dimension of initiation is the substructure for the revised rite of penance, leading to reconciliation in the Church community. The introduction to the rite states that the Church has never failed to call men and women from sin to conversion (no. 2), that in penance members are reconciled with the Church, where this penance is expressed through confession made to the Church (nos. 4, 5, 6). The celebration of the sacrament is always an act in which the Church proclaims its faith (no. 7). Also, the act of penance itself may take the form of prayer, or self-denial, particularly in the service of neighbor in works of charity. These elements underline the fact that sin and forgiveness have a social aspect (no. 18). It is this social aspect and the ecclesial focus of the new rite of the sacrament that calls for liturgies of the sacrament of penance during the season of Lent (no. 13). The homilies for these celebrations are to stress the social aspect of grace and sin, which realities affect the whole body of the Church (no. 25).

The liturgies of the third, fourth, and fifth Sundays of Lent in the "C" cycle of the Lectionary are most appropriate for emphasizing the theme of penance and conversion. By carefully planning the liturgies of these Sundays the community can celebrate this sacrament effectively at common penance services. The following helpful themes emerge on these Sundays.

Third Sunday—Luke 13:1–9, the necessity of repentance and the parable of the fig tree: theme of REPENTANCE.

Fourth Sunday—Luke 15:1–3, 11–32, the parable of the prodigal son and the celebration of the son's return: theme of RECONCILIATION.

Fifth Sunday—John 8:1–11, the woman taken in adultery and Christ's forgiveness: theme of FORGIVENESS.

Ash Wednesday: An Example

The structure of the liturgy of Ash Wednesday indicates the communal dimension of Lent whether the community emphasizes initiation or penance in liturgy planning and communal efforts at renewal.

On this first day of Lent the first reading from the prophet Joel speaks about the communal need for repentance since it is an invitation to "call an assembly," to "gather a people," and to "notify the congregation." Indeed, repentance is the keynote of this season. The second reading, taken from second Corinthians, envisions reconciliation in terms of an act involving God and his people. The direct result of repentance and conversion is the reconciliation of the community with God and each other.

The traditional practices associated with the season of Lent were essentially communal in origin and import—fasting, almsgiving, and prayer. The first reading of the Friday after Ash Wednesday brings this out clearly since the words from Isaiah 58:1–9 speak about the kind of fast that the Lord requires. It is a fast of "releasing those bound unjustly," "setting free the oppressed," "sharing your bread with the hungry, sheltering the oppressed and the homeless, clothing the naked when you see them, and not turning your back on your own." Indeed, the kind of fasting envisioned here is for the good of the entire community and is part of a whole process of directing one's life to the service of the larger group.

The traditional understanding of the season of Lent as a communal exercise is most helpful in interpreting the theology and practice of the period of forty days. Often enough conventional catechesis tended to individualize these practices; the present reform makes this season a valuable time of spiritual reform and renewal for the whole community.

THE LENTEN SUNDAYS: AN OVERVIEW

With the reform of the Roman calendar many of the traditional liturgical aspects of the season of Lent have also undergone change. The former distinction between the first four weeks as Lenten time and the last two weeks as Passiontide is now eliminated. The season is now understood as a unit from Ash Wednesday through the six weeks of Lent. The fourth Sunday no longer has the semifestive quality of the former "Laetare" Sunday. While the word "laetare" is still the beginning of the entrance antiphon and rose-colored vestments may still be worn, the mood of the day is the same as the rest of Lent: prayerful, reflective, in preparation for the coming feast of rejoicing and triumph at Easter. Therefore the fourth Sunday is no longer a joyful hiatus in the "penitential" liturgies of the Sundays of Lent. Instead, each Sunday liturgy builds on the other to present a positive reorientation of the believer toward baptism in Christ and its attendant responsibilities. Furthermore, the fifth Sunday of Lent is no longer called "Passion Sunday": this term is now more appropriately used to describe the former "Palm" Sunday since this is the only day in Holy Week, other than Good Friday, when the Passion narrative is proclaimed.

Sundays "A" Cycle

The Sundays of Lent themselves, especially in the "A" cycle of readings, present fundamental aspects of the Christian life in relation to baptism, the sacrament of regeneration (see diagram, "Sundays of Lent"). The first Sunday contains the Matthean account of the temptation of Jesus. In all three cycles of the

Lectionary the temptation of Jesus is proclaimed as the overture to what Lent is all about: our identification with Christ in weakness and paschal triumph. In the words of the preface for this Sunday: "His fast of forty days makes this a holy season of self-denial. By rejecting the devil's temptations he has taught us to rid ourselves of the hidden corruption of evil, and so to share his paschal meal in purity of heart, until we come to its fulfillment in the promised land of heaven."

SUNDAYS OF LENT

"A" CYCLE	"B" CYCLE	"C" CYCLE
1. Temptation of Jesus	Temptation of Jesus	Temptation of Jesus
Mt. 4:1–11	Mk. 1:12–15	Lk. 4:1–13
2. Transfiguration	Transfiguration	Transfiguration
Mt. 17:1–9	Mk. 9:2–10	Lk. 9:28–36
Initiation: Sundays 3-5		*Penance: Sundays 3-5*
3. Samaritan Woman	Jesus death and resurrection	Fig tree parable
Jn. 4:5–42	Jn. 2:13–25	Lk. 13:1–9
4. Man born blind	Lifting up of Son of Man	Prodigal Son
Jn. 9:1–41	Jn. 3:14–21	Lk. 15:1–3, 11–3
5. Lazarus raised	Grain of wheat	Woman in adultery
Jn. 11:1–45	Jn. 12:20–33	Jn. 8:1–11
6. Passion Account	Passion Account	Passion Account
Mt. 26:14–27:66	Mk. 14:1–15:47	Lk. 22:14–23:56
Triumphal Entry	Triumphal Entry	Triumphal Entry
Mt. 2:1–11	Mk. 11:1–10	Jn. 12:12–16

The second Sunday presents the Matthean account of the transfiguration of Jesus which itself places the passion, death, and resurrection of Jesus in the perspective of his transfigured glory.

In the preface we pray: "On your holy mountain he revealed himself in glory in the presence of the disciples. He had already prepared them for his approaching death. He wanted to teach them through the Law and the Prophets that the promised Christ had first to suffer and so come to the glory of his resurrection." As noted above, the gospel texts for the third, fourth, and fifth Sundays of Lent in the "A" cycle are from the evangelist John. They are taken from the great Johannine discourses on new life in Christ: the Samaritan woman, the man born blind, the raising of Lazarus. The prefaces for these Sundays reflect these texts by stating: "When he asked the woman of Samaria for water to drink,

Christ had already prepared for her the gift of faith. In his thirst to receive her faith he awakened in her heart the fire of your love." The season of Lent is here reaffirmed as a time for spiritual reawakening to the richness as well as to the demands of Christian faith. The preface for the fourth Sunday links the gospel text with the underlying Lenten theme about Adam's sin and Christ's conquering sin and death: "He came among us as a man, to lead mankind from darkness into the light of faith. Through Adam's fall we were born as slaves of sin, but now through baptism in Christ we are reborn as your adopted children."

The preface for the fifth Sunday reflects the raising of Lazarus and the Church's participation in sacraments which offer a share in Christ's life now for the believer. "As a man like us, Jesus wept for Lazarus his friend. As the eternal God, he raised Lazarus from the dead. In his love for us all, Christ gives us the sacraments to lift us up to everlasting life."

The selection of these texts restores an ancient tradition in which they were used primarily for liturgy and the catechesis of those coming into the faith at Easter.

The sixth Sunday of Lent is Passion Sunday and both the account of Jesus' entry into Jerusalem at the beginning of the liturgy and the account of the passion are taken from the evangelist Matthew. This day's celebration is the pivotal one, for the Sundays of the Lenten season culminate on this day and the liturgy points to and sets up the solemn liturgical commemoration of the "three days" from Holy Thursday evening to Easter.

Sundays "B" Cycle

The first two Sundays of Lent in the "B" cycle contain the same references to the temptation of Jesus and the transfiguration, but this year the gospel texts are from Mark's account (see diagram, "Sundays of Lent").

On the third, fourth, and fifth Sundays of the "B" cycle, the gospel selections are taken from the gospel of John, although they are not the same as those assigned for the "A" cycle. On the third Sunday the reading is from John 2:13–25 about the cleansing of the Temple area by Jesus and the reference to the destruction of his body and its being raised up in three days. This is a fitting text for proclamation in the middle of Lent for it stresses the significance of the forty days as a time of renewal and commitment in faith to the Lord whose death and resurrection are the source of all real life. The gospel for the fourth Sunday is from John 3:14–21, the Nicodemus dialogue, wherein key statements concern the lifting up of the Son of Man, the requirement of belief on the part of the followers of Jesus, and living in his truth. The gospel for the fifth Sunday of Lent is from John 12:20–33 concerning the grain of wheat falling to the earth and dying so that it can produce fruit. The parallel message and its application to the contemporary congregations is that those who "hate [their] life in this world" will have eternal life in Christ.

On Passion Sunday the gospel texts, the triumphal entry into Jerusalem and the Passion narrative, are from Mark.

Sundays "C" Cycle

The gospel of the evangelist Luke is used in this cycle of the Lectionary (with the exception of the fifth and Passion Sunday, see diagram, "Sundays of Lent"). The readings of the first two Sundays are about the temptation and transfiguration of Jesus. The gospel of the third Sunday (Luke 13:1–9) is about the necessity of repentance, as shown in the parable of the fig tree. The gospel of the fourth Sunday (Luke 15:1–3, 11–32) recounts the parable of the prodigal son and the Father's forgiveness in the face of evil or sin. The gospel of the fifth Sunday is about the woman taken in adultery and Christ's forgiveness and admonition to sin no more. On the sixth Lenten Sunday, Passion Sunday, the gospel readings from Luke recount Jesus' entrance into Jerusalem in triumph and the account of his passion and death.

PASTORAL PLANNING FOR LENT

In the Sacramentary there are two forms of the introductory rite of the Eucharist. The first, and one that would be preferable to use through the whole Lent and Easter season, is that of blessing and sprinkling with water. The other form (the penitential rite) is recited (or sung) with no accompanying gesture. The gesture of kneeling in this rite could be an effective way of directing attention to the reflective mood of the liturgy in the Lenten season.

The Sacramentary provides new prefaces for those Sundays of Lent when the gospel texts are other than the Johannine texts about the Samaritan women, the man born blind, and the raising of Lazarus. In addition, the two eucharistic prayers for reconciliation are suitable for use throughout the season. There is a solemn blessing for the "Passion of the Lord" which is appropriate for use throughout the season. In addition there are some twenty-four prayers over the people to choose from when the celebration does not require such an elaborate conclusion. As has been the custom of the Western rite for some time, the Alleluia is not sung in Lent, nor is the Glory to God.

The prescribed vesture for the season is violet. An altar frontal similar to the one described for use in Advent may also be used for Lent. The use of hangings or banners which have the same colors as those in the altar frontal will also create an atmosphere attuned to the meaning of the conversion called for in Lent. The use of the same hangings as those used in Advent would be inappropriate since each season is very different in theme and theology.

The use of various forms of crosses is most appropriate for Lent, whereas symbols such as the root of Jesse and the peaceable kingdom are appropriate for Advent.

The conventional practice of covering statues and images during "Passiontide" (now eliminated as a separate part of Lent) is left to the discretion of the national episcopal conference. The decision of the bishops of the United States is to leave them uncovered. In countries where the custom still prevails, they are covered only until the beginning of the Paschal Vigil. This practice avoids the dramatization that used to occur when the statues were uncovered at the singing of the Gloria on Holy Saturday: the Sacramentary provides that, if possible, crosses are removed from the church at the time of the stripping of the altar after the liturgy of Holy Thursday evening. To be emphasized is the starkness of the sanctuary area during Holy Week, not the addition of color for its own sake and distraction. The mood of the season is simplicity and starkness, reflecting the urgency of conversion to the gospel.

An important part of most parish calendars for the spring is the celebration of first communion and confirmation. The season for eucharist is Easter, not Lent, and for confirmation it is Eastertime. The major themes of the lenten season include initiation and conversion; hence communal penance services, including the celebration of "first penance," are entirely appropriate.

It was during the season of Easter (fifty days) that the regular practices of daily celebration of eucharist evolved. Thus to interrupt Lent with the celebration of parish first communions destroys the nature of the Lenten cycle.

One of the almost forgotten reforms of the liturgy since the Second Vatican Council is the Liturgy of the Hours. One purpose of reform is to restore this prayer to the people and not to have it remain a clerical preserve. One season which would call for such nonsacramental Word celebrations is Lent.

Daily prayer services based on the Liturgy of the Hours are a preparation for the community's Easter eucharist.

A very effective way of particularizing the season of Lent for a given community is to plan the season around a particular theme, such as initiation, reconciliation, and so on. Then the planning could cover the liturgies from Ash Wednesday through to Holy Week with special reference to specific elements of the community's prayer and practice. At the beginning of the liturgies of Passion Sunday and the Easter Vigil, the presider is free to adapt the introductions to reflect the journey undertaken by local communities in Lent. It is important not to allow the liturgy of Lent and Holy Week to "carry themselves." It is true that there is a richness in this season, but the richness needs focus and direction from the group planning the service of the whole community. What occurs in the annual commemoration of our redemption should not be the repetition of "last year's" liturgy. Rather there should be an ever new and deepened appropriation of these same central mysteries. This is done through skillful planning, with an eye toward applying the same paschal mystery to the circumstances of Christians removed some twenty centuries from those foundational events. The needs and attitudes of communities change frequently and the liturgy planning should reflect those needs and changes. The One who is the same yesterday, today, and forever is the Lord Jesus.

SUNDAYS OF LENT "A" CYCLE

FIRST SUNDAY OF LENT

The gospel of the temptation of Jesus, read on this Sunday in all three cycles of the Lectionary, is the traditional reading for this day.

Although the season of Lent begins on Ash Wednesday, this is the first Sunday liturgy in Lent which allows for deeper reflection on the meaning of the season. For this reason it should be treated as a beginning, and emphasis should be placed on the nature and purpose of Lent as a time of preparation for the paschal feast. In fact, the rite of election for the initiation of adults is to take place on this Sunday, if possible (Rite of Christian Initiation of Adults, no. 140), and in the text of the prayer for the elect it states: "Today we begin Lent and look forward to our celebration of the life-giving mysteries of our Lord's suffering, death and resurrection" (no. 148). Hence, this is indeed a day of beginnings for the elect and of renewal for those already living as members of the Body of Christ.

The first reading from the book of Genesis expresses in mythical imagery the fall of our first parents and our consequent need for redemption. A myth, it should be remembered, is not necessarily a story that is untrue, despite the conventional association of myths with false tales. In a religious context a myth is rather the recounting of a profound religious truth and insight. Today's reading reveals our need for a savior. The completion of this Genesis mythology comes at the Easter Vigil with the proclamation of the Exsultet which speaks lyrically of Adam's "necessary" sin, and of Christ's redemption conquering the evil that has resulted from this sin. Hence the story of the fall cannot merely be assigned to what happened once upon a time to Adam and Eve, for the import of the text is that the creation and fall are continual happenings, that each of us is made in the image and likeness of God as were our parents, and that the story of their fall is the story of our own as well. Adam's story is that of Everyman. A me-centered universe results in sin; a God-centered universe results in virtue. The reading from Genesis prepares the way to the reading from Romans which states that sin entered the world through one man and that grace and redemption entered the world through the God-man. Through the first Adam, sin, death, and condemnation became the heritage of humanity; through Christ, the second Adam, forgiveness, life, and redemption are the heritage of the believer.

The gospel of the temptation of Jesus continues the theme of evil, sin, and death and our need to choose and align ourselves with the goodness, virtue, and life which are ours through Christ.

The theme of the choice between the two is a fitting introduction to the Lenten season for it is a time for cooperating with the grace and life brought to us in the second Adam, Christ.

The opening prayer of the liturgy speaks appropriately about Lent as a preparation for Easter, but the alternative prayer deals more extensively with the imagery of the Genesis reading and of the tension between the profession of faith by believers and the faithless age in which we live. The prayer over the gifts asks that the reception of the eucharist may change our lives, a theme that is continued in the prescribed preface of the first Sunday in Lent which reiterates the necessity of avoiding evil and clinging to the good, with Christ's temptation serving as a model for us. The solemn blessing of the Passion of the Lord is presented in the Mass formula and speaks clearly of how Jesus' suffering, death, and resurrection give us new life in this season. Yet this solemn blessing may be replaced by the simpler form taken from the prayers over the people, of which number 4 concerns avoiding evil, number 6 speaks about cleansing our hearts, and number 15 speaks of avoiding what is displeasing to God.

The rite of blessing and sprinkling with holy water may be a fitting introduction to this Sunday liturgy (and all the Sunday liturgies of Lent) because of the close association of this season with initiation. Should the third form of the penitential rite be used, the fourth set of invocations about reconciliation with each other and Christ's healing the wounds of division and sin would be appropriate, as would the fifth set about Christ granting pardon and peace to the sinner (the reconciliation motif of Lent) and bringing light to those in darkness (initiation).

SECOND SUNDAY OF LENT

Christians gather at the eucharist each week to renew and deepen their common faith in God. Conventional descriptions of faith often treat it as a gift from God, while the term "the faith" has been used to describe the Christian communion to which one belongs as opposed to other churches. Today's first reading gives us a more "existential" model of faith which emphasizes the believer's trust and dependence on God.

Contemporary reflections on "blind faith" and Kierkegaard's "leap in the dark" find a valid example and expression in the life of Abraham, called by God to leave his homeland and to follow God's word and will alone. While faith has a logic and there are reasons to prompt a response of faith, there is also an illogic in what causes us to trust in the God we cannot see. Abraham as the father of all believers is given to us as an example of obedience and faith as a response to God's call. Similarly, our response to the word of the Lord at liturgy requires obedience and deeper trust in him.

The reading from second Timothy takes the call of the first reading and deepens its meaning to include growth in holiness as a gift from God through Jesus, for it is through him that we have life and immortality. Both holiness and faith need constant deepening and growth, and it is for this reason that Christians gather at the table of God's word and supper.

The gospel of the second Sunday of Lent in all three cycles is the transfiguration of Jesus. In accordance with the readings of the "A" cycle this year's account is from Matthew. Paradoxically, it is the transfiguration which leads Jesus to his passion, death, and glorious resurrection. His "exodus" from glory to glory, from transfiguration through humiliation and death to resurrection forms a constant theme in Christian theology. The setting for the passion of Jesus begins with the revelation of his glory to Peter, James, and John. The response of these men to the manifestation of God's glory on the mountainside should be our response to the power and the glory of the Lord revealed at the eucharist. Our experience of God at the eucharist is inviting, yet distant, familiar yet filled with mystery and awe, intimate, yet marked by our need for complete re-creation at his hands.

The opening prayer of the liturgy asks the Lord for his grace to open the hearts of believers to hear his word at this celebration. The alternative prayer refers more clearly to the readings and to the glory of the transfiguration, for in Christ's light we find the fullness of life and truth. Our response to this revelation can only be that of dependence on his word and wonder at the vision of his glory.

The prayer over the gifts asks that the already believing Christians may be made holy by the sacrifice of Christ's body and blood; the basis of this prayer is the exhortation of second Timothy. The prescribed preface of this second Sunday of Lent speaks of the transfiguration and links it explicitly with Christ's suffering and humiliation prior to entering his glory at the resurrection. The prayer after communion describes the holy mysteries as being celebrated so that those on earth may share even now in the life to come in God's kingdom.

As noted for the first Sunday, the rite of blessing and sprinkling with holy water or the third form of the penitential rite with the fourth or fifth set of invocations would be appropriate ways to introduce the liturgy. The solemn blessing of the Passion of Our Lord or a selection from the prayers over the people would be a fitting conclusion to the eucharist. From the prayers over the people, number 5 about being blessed and remaining faithful to God's love, number 7 about the Father's gift of light, or number 9 about belief and the gift of God's love would be appropriate choices.

THIRD SUNDAY OF LENT

In the revised rite for the Christian initiation of adults, the third, fourth and fifth Sundays of Lent are given prominence in the process of initiation. Historically those enrolled in the catechumenate at the beginning of Lent came before the bishop on these three Sundays for scrutinies, exorcisms, and instructions. In the Sacramentary the title of this third Sunday indicates that the first scrutiny of the catechumens before the community is held on this day. The readings of the Lectionary were chosen to give prominence to this day for they speak of the primary intention of the Lenten season—to prepare catechumens for their initiation into the Church and to lead the baptized to a deeper appreciation of their baptism in Christ.

The first reading from the book of Exodus has been chosen to reflect the theme of the gospel of the day. There is a reference to the crossing of the Red Sea and the doubts of the Israelites about God's promises to them. At God's command Moses strikes the rock and water gushes forth, thus allaying for the time being the people's anxiety. The responsorial psalm is a commentary on the event for it draws attention to the danger of hardening our hearts to the voice of the Lord. The place where the Israelites quarreled among themselves and doubted God, "though they had seen [his] works," is called Massah and Meribah—temptations.

In the second reading justification is described as the gift of

God's love and the in-dwelling of the Holy Spirit. While we were still sinners Christ made us righteous, and while we were unworthy he made us worthy of adoption by the Father.

The gospel reading is taken from the gospel according to John. This evangelist uses many images to describe the Son of God: Jesus is seen as the living water; as the bread of life, as the only true vine, as the only shepherd we can call "good." The reading this Sunday speaks of faith, regeneration, allegiance to the word of God, and worship in spirit and truth. The issue for believers is to examine how faithful they are in allegiance to the Lord, and how deeply committed they are to the word of God when the world offers so many other immediate but superficial joys.

The opening prayer of the liturgy recalls that fasting, prayer, and works of mercy are essential parts of the Lenten season. The prayer over the gifts speaks of our forgiving others as the proper and required response to God's love for us. In the prescribed preface for this Sunday, the gift of faith given to the woman at the well is shared by all the baptized at the eucharist so that their hearts may be filled with the fire of divine love. The prayer after communion reflects the theme of the prayer over the gifts in speaking of the forgiveness granted us in Christ. Should the rite of blessing and sprinkling with holy water be used to introduce the liturgy this day, reference should be made to those to be initiated in water and the Holy Spirit at Easter and those who are the faithful people of God because of their already accomplished initiation. Of the sample sets of invocations for the third form of the penitential rite, the fifth about raising the dead to life and bringing light to those in darkness reflects well the initiation orientation of this Sunday. Similarly, the sixth set about raising us to new life, the forgiveness of sins, and being fed with the Lord's body and blood reflect the sacraments whereby we are renewed in faith; hence it is also a possible choice.

The solemn blessing for the Passion of the Lord may be used to conclude the liturgy, especially if the scrutiny of the catechumens takes place this Sunday.

Other choices from the prayers over the people include number 6 about a complete change of heart, number 10 about the people who hope for God's mercy, and number 15 about avoiding what is displeasing to the Father.

This Sunday was formerly called "Laetare Sunday" since its mood and theme was one of hope and rejoicing that Easter was near. In the reformed calendar this Sunday is not different from the other Sundays of Lent even though the entrance antiphon still begins with the Latin word *laetare*. This Sunday has significance in the tradition of Lenten observance because it is the day for the second scrutiny. The first reading from first Samuel speaks of the Lord's choice of David as the anointed one. Initiation involves our response to God's initiative in calling us to salvation and to full life in him.

The reading from Ephesians is particularly significant because throughout the season of Lent the community has been urged to cast aside deeds of darkness and to walk in the brilliance of the light of Christ. In this reading the darkness-light theme, which is so apparent at the Easter Vigil and in baptism, is found for the first time in Lent. The believer must leave aside the deeds of darkness and live according to the justice and truth of God through Christ, the light. This reading emphasizes that the preparation of a person coming to faith is one of moral formation as well as instruction in the teachings of the Christian faith. The preparation of adults to be baptized has as much to do with the moral choices and deeds of asceticism as it does with instruction and teaching.

The gospel reading dominates the liturgy by its length and significance. The miracle story of Christ's healing the man born blind is amplified in typical Johannine style by references to and explanations about light, water, and Jesus' origins. The reference to Christ as the light of the world and to the symbolism of water as new birth is clear, for in his death and resurrection the sightless see eternal truths and the "seeing" become blind because their sight has been limited to seeing only worldly things.

The discussion about Jesus' origins is a typical Johannine approach: we know his natural parents, so why does he seem to come from another place and lineage? The point is that if we ask this question we do not know his true origins at all for he is from above, and to follow him where he goes requires a new birth for the believer.

The theme of light pervades the liturgy of the word, a light that is not a possession to be contained but a gift to be shared, a gift which clarifies and illuminates the things of the world so that we do not rely on human powers for our salvation, but rather acknowledge the divine origins of our Savior.

The opening prayer of the liturgy presents the community as waiting eagerly for the feast of Easter, hence placing this season in the frame of preparation for Easter. The alternative opening prayer, however, is a paraphrase of John's gospel: Jesus is the Word who comes into the sinful world to lead all peoples to his light. This Johannine terminology continues in the prayer over the gifts as the Word is pictured in conflict with the world. The prescribed preface of the Sunday, with its oblique reference to the man born blind, describes Jesus as the Lord who came to be a light for the darkness of this world. The preface also speaks of the fall of Adam and the need for salvation in Christ, thus harking back to the theme of the first Sunday of Lent. The prayer after communion speaks about enlightenment for all who come into the world, who are given direction, and who are shown the "way" by the light of the gospel.

The rite of blessing and sprinkling with holy water would be a fitting introduction to this liturgy, especially if it had been used last week at the first scrutiny. Should the third form of the penitential rite be used, the fifth set of sample invocations about Christ bringing light to those in darkness is a good reflection of the light theme of the gospel. The solemn blessing of the Passion of the Lord would be an appropriate choice for the conclusion to the liturgy as would number 7 of the prayers over the people, which speaks about the coming of the light of Christ upon the Church. The prayer over the people presented in the Mass formula for this Sunday is less suitable than these other options because it refers in general terms to the suffering and agony of Jesus, rather than to the specific scripture texts of this liturgy or to Lent leading to initiation.

FIFTH SUNDAY OF LENT

This Sunday marks the third Sunday for the scrutinies of those to be initiated at Easter, and the final Lenten Sunday before the beginning of Holy Week. The liturgy of the word for this Sunday speaks of re-creation, resurrection, and new life.

The selection from the Old Testament prophet Ezekiel is taken from the chapter about pouring forth the Spirit upon the "dry bones" in the valley of his vision. The prophet speaks of restoration by an act of God through the Spirit; it was through him that the people first were saved from oppression in Egypt. It is by his power that they will be saved again and restored as the people of God. One meaning of the reading can be applied to the resurrection to new life, a theme clearly reiterated in succeeding apocalyptic literature and finally present in the death and resurrection of Jesus.

The reading from Romans states that through Christ the whole person of the believer is saved, raised up, and redeemed. The realm of the flesh is the realm to be left behind, and the realm of the Spirit is where true life is to be found. But there is no hellenistic dichotomy here between flesh and spirit (or body and soul) since the believer lives with the Spirit of God enfleshed in his body so that his whole person will live in conformity with that Spirit. The gospel reading brings to a climax the Johannine discourses for Lent. The story of the raising of Lazarus is climaxed by the statement of Jesus, "I am the resurrection and the life." What is required of those who wish to be saved is belief in him and his life. The scandal of the cross is that he who is the resurrection and the life first had to suffer and die. Only by dying could he enter into his glory. In baptism the believer dies to former ways of life and renounces them in order to rise fully in the new life of Christ.

The opening prayer of the liturgy speaks of the salvation Christ offers us and uses typical Johannine imagery. The alternate opening prayer speaks specifically of the necessity of Jesus' suffering and dying to bring new life to believers who then must work in this world to transform and restore it.

The prayer over the gifts speaks of the forgiveness of sins as part of the cleansing offered at the eucharist so that those who are enlightened by the Christian faith may be governed by the light of Christ. The prescribed preface for this fifth Sunday of Lent describes Jesus the man, who wept for his friend, and Jesus the mediator of God's grace, who raised Lazarus from death and restored him to life. The sacraments are means whereby the community of believers receives the same gift from Christ. The prayer after communion describes the body and blood of Christ shared at the eucharist as the bond of unity between the Church and her Lord. The rite of blessing and sprinkling with holy water would be a suitable introduction to the celebration, especially when the third scrutiny of catechumens takes place during the liturgy. For the invocations for the third form (c) of the penitential rite, sample number 5 would be appropriate because of the reference to Jesus' raising the dead to life and giving light to those in darkness. The solemn blessing of the Passion of the Lord is a fitting conclusion to the liturgy, as would be number 17 of the prayers over the people about the necessity of suffering leading to glory. Once again, the prayer over the people presented in the day's Mass formula is less satisfactory since it is more general than other possibilities offered in the Sacramentary.

SUNDAYS OF LENT "B" CYCLE

FIRST SUNDAY OF LENT

To grasp the meaning of the readings assigned for this Sunday, one must take into account that the narration of events by the sacred writers was colored by their own experiences. To recall the story of the figure of Noah and the flood almost immediately conjures up images of destruction, while the passage from Genesis 9 is not really about destruction, but about God's will to preserve life, a will that is universal in scope, mediated through the covenant with Noah, where the initiative for this salvation comes from God himself. Stated concisely, these readings give us a very positive overture to the themes of Lent, where the covenant with Noah initiated by God is carried through in Christian baptism, the subject of the second reading. This is demonstrated on this first Sunday of Lent when the rite of election of the catechumens takes place. This step in the initiation process is significant, for candidates are now in the last stages of preparation and will be initiated in this same local community at the Easter Vigil. Hence, the celebration of Lent graphically demonstrates the notion of covenant from this first Sunday through to the Vigil of Easter.

All of the scripture readings this Sunday are to be seen within the context of the victory of Christ, as he triumphs over the Spirit of evil in the gospel of Mark. In this gospel Jesus is pictured as the one empowered by the Spirit of God to overcome the evil powers that tempt him. The scene is important for the plan of his gospel, which often pictures Jesus' life and that of his followers as a conflict between the forces of good and evil. His triumph is as much a model for the later Church as it is an account of Jesus' personal victory.

The texts from Genesis and first Peter may be seen together as an example of biblical "typology," whether the author of the epistle has used the event of Noah and the flood for his own purpose in treating Christian baptism. The ark is pictured here as a symbol of baptism, just as in the later history of the Church the ark would appear as the "type" of the Church offering salvation, and where the water of the flood would be associated with the water of baptism.

All three readings form a fitting inauguration for Lent as they can easily be applied to the experience of the Church where the salvation offered by God and ratified in baptism must be responded to in the subsequent lives of the initiated. This baptismal orientation is an appropriate focus for liturgy planning on this first Sunday, for this theme reemerges through the whole season. Communal preparation in Lent leads to communal initiation at Easter. Communal penances and reform lead to communal rejoicing and deeper conversion at Easter.

For the introductory rite this Sunday, the rite of blessing and sprinkling with holy water can be used with an introductory comment about those to be initiated at Easter and those who have already been initiated whose Lent is for recommitment. Should the third form of the penitential rite be used instead, then the fourth or fifth set of sample invocations would be appropriate to reflect the positive themes of Lent in acclaiming the deeds of Christ. The opening prayer seems the more fitting this Sunday since it speaks of this time of preparation for Easter and the death and resurrection of Jesus, whereas the alternative opening prayer would appear to be more suited to the first reading in the "A" cycle since it contains a poetic reference to the creation of man. For the composition of the general intercessions, the petitions in the Sacramentary Appendix I for Lent, with numbers 5 and 6, are appropriate for use throughout the season. As to the preface, it should be noted that in all there are nine prefaces for the season, five of which are suggested for use on the five Sundays, while the other four are for weekdays or for the third, fourth, and fifth Sundays in the "B" and "C" cycles. For this Sunday the Sacramentary suggests using the preface for the first Sunday of

Lent about the temptation of Jesus, or Lenten preface 1 or 2. The first of these would appear to be the most suitable. For the blessing at the end of the liturgy the solemn form for the Passion of the Lord is suggested, and would be a most suitable choice for all the Sundays of Lent. Of the prayers over the people, number 6 about a change of heart and number 17 about the redemptive love of Christ are suitable choices in the light of the day's readings.

SECOND SUNDAY OF LENT

The story of Abraham's willingness to sacrifice his son Isaac in accord with God's command was interpreted in many different ways by generations of Jewish commentators. In early Judaism, the recounting of the original story was important, whereas in later Judaism the emphasis on Isaac's voluntary surrender took on atoning significance and became associated with the sacrifice of the paschal lamb. It is no wonder that this story became a type of the sacrifice of Jesus who was obedient to his Father's will. This emphasis is found in the eucharistic prayer of Hippolytus now adapted as the second eucharistic prayer in the Roman Catholic liturgy: ". . . before he was given up to death, a death he freely accepted."

The story of Isaac is reflected in the responsorial psalm which mentions the death of the Lord's faithful ones as "precious"; the psalm also states that we offer our sacrifice of thanksgiving to the Lord.

The New Testament reading contains a passage (Romans 8:32) that applies the Old Testament text to Christ, by affirming that God did not spare his own Son, Jesus, but willingly gave him over for the sake of all.

While at first sight the gospel speaks of the other side of the paradox of suffering by recounting the scene of the transfiguration of Jesus, it too is set in the context of Paul's statement, and that is the prediction by Jesus that he will have to suffer before entering into his glory. This earthly revealer of the will of the Father freely accepted death for the salvation of all people. Hence, just as the resurrection can only be interpreted properly within the context of the passion and death of Jesus, so this text of the transfiguration can only be appreciated adequately when set within the context of the passion. This is an important point for Mark, since his community most likely was under some form of persecution and it was the intention of the author to stress the suffering of the Savior as a model for his followers. The suffering Church must take up its own cross in imitation of its Lord. Furthermore, it is no coincidence that the scene of the transfiguration is on a mountain, the place of special revelations from the time God spoke to Moses on Mount Sinai to Jesus' death on Calvary. In addition, the voice from the heavens is important as the divine confirmation of the passion prediction and the revelation of the Son of God in the transfiguration. This same voice was heard at Jesus' baptism, and the affirmation of the soldier on Calvary that the dying Jesus was the Son of God is all part of Mark's plan to emphasize Christ's divinity robed in flesh, and the glory of Jesus achieved only because of suffering.

The theme which underlies the texts on this second Sunday of Lent is that of the paradox of Easter and Good Friday, of glory-sharing and cross-bearing by Jesus and for later communities of faith. The rite of blessing and sprinkling with holy water would be a fitting introduction to the liturgy this Sunday because by being initiated into the community of Christ, we are initiated into a share in his suffering and his glory. This theme recurs in the funeral liturgy where the body of the deceased is blessed with water and the following is said: "By baptism into his [Christ's] death we were buried together with him . . . if we have been united with him by likeness to his death, so shall we be united with him by likeness to his resurrection." Should the third form of the penitential rite be used, the fifth set of invocations would fit in well with the readings for they speak of being raised from death to life and of our receiving light from Christ. Both opening prayers refer to the day's liturgy where the shorter prayer speaks in terms of the gospel imagery of hearing the word, and finding the way to glory (cf. Mark 8:27), and the alternative prayer refers to the transfiguration in terms of light, darkness and the voice from heaven. This second text would seem to be more appropriate should there be present at the liturgy members of the community who are preparing for initiation. The prayer over the gifts speaks of forgiveness of sin at the eucharist, a familiar and traditional pattern often found in this prayer.

The preface for the second Sunday of Lent is most fitting for this day since it speaks about the transfiguration and also refers to Christ's first having to suffer and so come into the glory of his resurrection. Alternatives to this text are numbers 1 and 2 of the seasonal Lenten prefaces. During the eucharistic prayer, the fourth acclamation, about the cross and resurrection of Jesus, would be a fitting community response.

For the conclusion of the eucharist, the solemn blessing for the Passion of the Lord would be most suitable, while number 8 of the prayers over the people or number 14 about the mystery of redemption would also be appropriate.

THIRD SUNDAY OF LENT

Beginning with this Sunday and continuing on the fourth and fifth Sundays of Lent, the scripture readings from the "A" cycle may be substituted for those assigned for this Sunday in either the "B" or the "C" cycles.

This substitution would be entirely appropriate and it is decidedly preferable when these Sundays are used as part of the rite of Christian initiation of adults. In this case, the ritual masses in the Sacramentary as well as the special proper commemoration in the Roman Canon may be used at the liturgy. A commentary on these readings from the "A" cycle appears above.

The first reading for this Sunday in the "B" cycle is the Exodus account of the ten commandments. It is likely that Moses took already existing codes of conduct and gave them a new interpretation based on the revelation of God to his people. The important thing about the revelation of Sinai is that it marks the beginning of God's covenant with his people, and that this relationship with him is the basis of moral responsibility. What is presented in this text is not an ethical code derived from nature, but a revelation from God on morality which has perennial validity for the Christian when read in conjunction with New Testament morality, especially that of the Sermon on the Mount (Matthew 5).

The responsorial psalm continues the theme of this reading by praising God for his revelation in creation and for the revelation of his law. In the second reading from first Corinthians, Paul counters the Jewish and Greek search after signs and wisdom by stating clearly that for the Christian the sign and wisdom is the cross of

Christ. What appears as folly in the cross is in fact wiser than human wisdom and God's "weakness" is more powerful than human strength. The reading from the gospel of John tells of the cleansing of the temple area. In contrast with the synoptics, the setting for this event in the fourth gospel is the beginning of Jesus' ministry. Here Christ shows that in him the former dispensation has come to an end, and that temple worship is now only to be carried out through the temple of his body. The temple precincts are now replaced by the body of Christ, in his glorified humanity. In any event, worship and authentic piety are through, with, and in Christ. Furthermore, the reference to the approaching Passover, as well as the reference to "three days," are unmistakable references to Christ's passover which transcends that of Israel.

Of the many Lenten and profoundly theological themes in the readings for this Sunday, two would appear to be suitable as coinciding with the liturgical and pastoral themes and emphases of Lent. On the one hand, the cross and risen body of Christ are signs of the new dispensation of Christian worship, and these two form the core of the Christian faith. The Church is now preparing for the celebration of the passover of the Lord, whose passion, death, and resurrection sounds the death knell to mere external piety, for now our hearts are to be scrutinized and the only security can be from faith and trust in the Lord alone.

The cleansing of the temple has not yet been completed, for our worship assemblies are always open to the demand of Jesus in today's gospel—that we make our religious practices sincere and honest expressions of faith.

The second theme which emerges in today's celebration comes from the first reading where the religious person's dealings with God are paralleled with dealings with other people as well. While there is often the temptation to see our spiritual lives and our service to others as two separate entities, they are, in fact, united, according to the Exodus reading. Love of God and of neighbor stimulate us to follow the Lenten practices of fasting in order to share with others and giving alms that others may also enjoy goods of this earth, so that all may glorify God. Reference can also be made to specific parish Lenten programs where support for those to be initiated is a community concern, where penance services remind us of the social damage caused by sin, and where collections of food and clothes are an important ascetical practice of this season.

The rite of blessing and sprinkling with holy water would be a suitable introduction to this liturgy, with an introduction so phrased as to encourage the congregation to authentic worship. Or, the third form of the penitential rite may be used with invocations taken from the fifth and sixth set of models in the Sacramentary, where the Johannine theme of light and our need for the food of the body and blood of Christ would be appropriate selections. The opening prayer speaks about the season of Lent, of penance and good works, whereas the alternative prayer is about preparing for Easter by sharing with others now. The prayer over the gifts speaks of God's forgiveness as a result of the eucharist, and of our need to forgive others. Hence it is a prayer that coincides with the theme of our relations with both God and neighbor.

In accordance with the instructions in the Sacramentary, the preface for the third Sunday in Lent is appropriately used with the readings from the "A" cycle. In line with the themes of the "B" cycle texts for today, the first preface of the Lenten season about preparing for the celebration of the paschal mystery and our service of neighbor is a suitable choice. The fourth memorial acclamation about the cross and resurrection setting us free would be an appropriate response of the community during the eucharistic prayer. The solemn blessing of the Passion of the Lord would be a suitable conclusion to the liturgy. Of the prayers over the people, number 2 about love for one another, number 9 about sharing the love of God, and number 23 about true charity for one another are appropriate selections from which to choose.

FOURTH SUNDAY OF LENT

The dominant reading in this liturgy is the gospel text containing the important dialogue between Jesus and Nicodemus. This discourse has stylistic traits which recur throughout the fourth gospel wherein the author uses an incident from the life of Jesus as the basis of an extended revelation about who this savior is and what he demands of his followers. Significant words such as "belief," "light," "truth," and the "world," all used here, recur again and again in the other discourses of John's gospel. The use of the term "world" is most important for this evangelist; it does not mean a place that can be determined by geographical boundaries, but rather means those who do not follow the Lord, who do not follow his way or truth. The difficulty in believing is that despite professing faith in God, one must still live in the world, and yet not be overcome by it. Believers cannot withdraw from the world, but they must realize that true values and security come from ever-deepening acts of trust in this Lord and in his Word.

The demand of faith, alluded to in the second reading from Ephesians, is a prerequisite for the author's discussion of the implications of Christian baptism. For this author, one who is baptized already shares in the death and resurrection of Jesus and is justified by faith, not by any personal merit or good works. And yet what is equally striking in the reading is the insistence at the end of this text (and in the rest of the letter) on moral actions and deeds of sanctification. Justification is by faith alone; yet one's response to it and its consequence are deeds of sanctification.

The first reading from second Chronicles about Israel's exile and return may help set a framework for these themes as some commentators see here a "type" of Christ's death and resurrection, and a "type" of the Christian observance of Lent. These themes could also be applicable to the Church that shares the characteristics of suffering in exile with the people of Israel.

Appropriate reflections on these texts would be on the two themes of baptism and penance, as well as on the meaning of our moral and spiritual lives in the world of our day. In addition, the theme of cross as our salvation, based on the gospel reference to the lifting up of the Son of Man, should not be overlooked as a possible theme for the liturgy this Sunday. The rite of blessing and sprinkling with holy water is again a most appropriate way to introduce this liturgy because the readings refer to baptism and the kind of moral life which should be its result. Should the third form of the penitential rite be used instead, the sixth sample set of invocations is appropriate because it speaks of being raised to new life and the forgiveness of sins.

The opening prayer speaks of the continuity of Lent with the celebration of Easter and of being reconciled with Christ, whereas the alternative prayer speaks of our growing in love and following the example of Christ's love in accepting suffering and death. The prayer over the gifts and the prayer after communion both speak of the "world," an important theme as seen from the Johannine perspective. For the composition of the general intercessions, the second set of Lenten prayers in the appendix to the Sacramentary is helpful, for it speaks of those who are baptized and those preparing for baptism. Since the preface for the second Sunday of Lent coincides with the gospel text from the "A" cycle, the use of the second preface of the Lenten season, about a time for renewal in spirit and setting our sights not on the world that is passing but on the world that will never end, would be a suitable selection. Or the committee might choose one of the eucharistic prayers for reconciliation. The solemn blessing for the Passion of the Lord is most appropriate for use this Sunday. Or, number 9 of the prayers over the people about those who believe in Christ and who share Christ's love, or number 18 about this life and the life to come, are appropriate conclusions to the liturgy.

FIFTH SUNDAY OF LENT

The gospel of this Sunday is the dominant reading, and it has Johannine characteristics of the gospels of the third and fourth Sundays of Lent in this cycle. The position of Philip is reminiscent of Nicodemus' position in John 3, since the main import of the reading does not stress the person of the inquirer but rather Jesus' discourse in the light of Johannine theology. Furthermore, the setting of the reading for this Sunday is the Passover festival, as it was for the reading on the third Sunday of Lent. This text is very important for an appreciation of the Johannine understanding of the passion and death of Jesus. Here the discussion concerns a grain having to die in order to bear fruit; the application is then made to Jesus who must suffer and die in order to draw all people to himself. But what makes this text so interesting is that whereas the other evangelists treat the agony in the garden, John's only indication of Jesus's hesitating to be crucified is implied in the question, "What should I say—Father save me from this hour? But it was for this that I came to this hour." Hence, the Johannine portrait has Jesus resolute in his acceptance of the cross, not merely as an instrument of suffering, but more importantly as the place where his glory will be manifested for the final and most important time. The glory spoken of in the prologue (John 1:14) will now come to full term in the event of the crucifixion. For John, the cross is not an instrument of suffering—it is the throne of the King of all, who ascends this throne in purple robes to signify his office and exalted position. The supreme revelation of who Jesus is will come at the crucifixion. In John's perspective Jesus does not shrink from it—he willingly accepts it.

This text is important as a preparation for the rest of Lent and for Holy Week. At times popular piety has tended to isolate the crucified Jesus from his resurrection because a positive understanding of the crucifixion was lacking. A true understanding of the Johannine passion narrative read on Good Friday reveals the depth and richness of the evangelist's theological insight into the passion of Jesus.

The first and second readings amplify the theological significance of the gospel reading for they are equally rich in the theology they express. The Old Testament reading from Jeremiah 31 is the prophecy of the new covenant to come, understood by those who hear it this Sunday as having been fulfilled in Jesus. Unlike the old covenant, this covenant in Jesus has a law written in the hearts of those who believe, and it extends beyond the original bounds of Israel to all people. The text of the fourth eucharistic prayer "again and again you offered a covenant" not only summarizes the Old Testament revelation of God to his people, but it also summarizes our relationship with the Father through Jesus. In the epistle to the Hebrews, part of which is read this Sunday, Jesus is our intercessor and high priest, as exemplified in his continual offer of love and mercy. Indeed, the Sunday eucharist is our weekly covenant renewal, by which we not only renew our baptism, but by which God's salvation is offered to us "again and again." The two themes which appear most clearly in these readings are that of the Johannine understanding of the cross and the new covenant we now share through our great high priest who himself suffered for our salvation.

The rite of blessing and sprinkling with holy water would be the most suitable introduction to the liturgy this Sunday, especially since the first reading speaks of the new covenant which is mediated in the Church through baptism. Should the third form of the penitential rite be used, invocations which acclaim Christ as the one who freely accepted death, who was raised for our justification, and who intercedes at the right hand of the Father would fit in well with the readings. The opening prayer speaks in Johannine terminology of Jesus' love for those in the world, whereas the alternative prayer speaks about this Sunday as part of our preparation for Easter. The prayer over the gifts continues the emphasis on preparation for Easter and mentions the forgiveness of sins, a petition often found in this prayer.

Since the fifth Sunday preface for Lent is geared to the "A" cycle when the gospel of the raising of Lazarus is read, the use of the first of the seasonal prefaces in Lent (Lent 1) would be an appropriate choice for this Sunday, for it speaks about the "great events" of Christ's passion, death, and resurrection as indicated in the day's readings. In accordance with this emphasis, the use of the fourth memorial acclamation, about the cross and resurrection, would be a suitable response of the community during the eucharistic prayer. The use of either of the eucharistic prayers for reconciliation would also be appropriate. The solemn blessing of the Passion of our Lord would be the most appropriate form of dismissal. Of the prayers over the people, number 12 which speaks of avoiding evil and leading lives of service, would be a good choice. Other appropriate selections include number 6 about the Lord's care for his people even when they stray (covenant theme), or number 22 about being strengthened by the eucharist.

SUNDAYS OF LENT "C" CYCLE

FIRST SUNDAY OF LENT

In all three cycles of the Lectionary, the gospel for this first Sunday of Lent is the synoptic presentation of the temptation of Jesus. This is the traditional text for the opening of the Lenten season. In the "C" cycle some of the dominant motifs of the Matthean text (formerly read each year on this day and now read only on the first Sunday of Lent in the "A" cycle) are reproduced by the Lukan author with little variation. These presentations of the temptation are in stark contrast to that of Mark where the more positive aspects of this event are stressed. The scene of the temptation of Christ at the beginning of Lent is at once an overture to the season to come and a paradigm of the whole of a believer's

rt of the season since it speaks of this time as a season
ation and of keeping watch with Christ.

face for the next Sunday of Lent should be chosen this
cause of its obvious reference to the devil's tempting of
he introduction to the Lord's Prayer, the presider could
use the third of the sample introductions, which speaks
for God's forgiveness and pledging to forgive others,
 major theme of Lent. The introduction to the sign of
ld be fittingly emphasized and expanded to include this
ne of reconciliation. Not only is this an important
theme but it is also an important aspect of the rites in
on for the reception of the eucharist. The prayer after
on reflects most clearly the gospel text of the day since it
t we live according to the words of the Lord and always
ist, "our bread of life." The solemn blessing of the Passion
rd is provided as the conclusion to this eucharist and is a
ing conclusion to the Sunday liturgies of the whole season.
rayers over the people, number 6, about having a complete
f heart and following the Lord with greater fidelity, is an
iate choice, should the committee determine that a briefer
on would be preferable.

D SUNDAY OF LENT

reading of the story of the transfiguration was the traditional
for this second Sunday of Lent, and this custom is renewed
 of the three cycles of the revised Lectionary, with the
t of Luke read this year. There are some obvious Lukan
ses in this version of the story, the most significant being
 Jesus' resolute acceptance of his journey to Jerusalem
 he would undergo his "passage" from suffering and death to
fully in the glory of the Father. The city of Jerusalem is
cant for Lukan theology as the place toward which Jesus
ys for the most significant acts of his life, in giving that life
hers so that they might come to share life eternal. And it is
the city of Jerusalem that the missionary efforts of the early
ch proceed in the Acts of the Apostles.
at the transfiguration is a most significant revelation is evident
its setting on a mountain (a common site for such important
ations in the scriptures, such as the mount of the beatitudes,

life. Even those who are already r
baptism are constantly tempted to
gods, and to enjoy passing pleasur
as the time of Jesus' sojourn in the
to the sojourn of the people of Isra
factor in the Church's keeping the

The issue presented in the readin
required of a believer during this Le
for kingdoms and power, and how c
whether Jesus "is running with us."
love: "Your ways, O Lord, make kno
a heightened sensitivity about the ten
whatever forms. For us the significanc
Christ's triumph alone, but in our nee
off evil powers and temptations that d

The first incident, about the devil te
power to turn stones into bread for foo
"Not on bread alone shall man live," cl
congregations to decide what in this life
what leads to perdition. The second tem
the kingdoms of the world and the Lord
makes us think of the situation of the be
beliefs and goes a-whoring after other lo
while that there is one God alone to be a
temptation makes us think about how oft
the test by pitting our wills against his.

For planning this Sunday's liturgy the c
the use of the rite of blessing and sprinklin
introductory rite. Should the presider use tl
penitential rite, he may profitably use the f
invocations about reconciliation in Christ an
our sin and division as aspects of the Lenter

The opening prayer would be an appropri
since it speaks of the general orientation of tl
alternative prayer is better not used in the "C
and wording reflect more clearly the imagery
Genesis, which is the first reading on this Sun

The first of the sample formulas for the gen
Lent is a helpful model for the composition of

this first pa
of reconcil
The pre
Sunday b
Jesus. As
profitably
of asking
certainly
peace cou
same the
seasonal
preparati
commun
prays th
seek Ch
of the L
most fitt
Of the
change
appropr
conclus

SECON
The
gospel
in eacl
accou
empha
that o
where
share
signifi
journ
for o
from
Chu
Th
from
reve

and the mount of Calvary). It is also significant that Jesus' clothes become dazzingly white, and at the end a voice from the heavens comes from the cloud overshadowing the disciples into which Moses, Elijah, and Jesus enter. But the revelation of the transfigured glory of Christ means much more than that he is one among three important figures in salvation history; indeed the voice from heaven confirms him as the only one to be called God's Son. This is the servant of the Father's will whose death and resurrection is the culminating act of God in history until Christ's return in glory. The soon to be accomplished events of Jesus's suffering, death, and resurrection are the events of salvation which replace the former Exodus event in the Old Testament.

The significance of this story is not that we glimpse what the resurrected Christ will be like after his death, as if the resurrection were merely a happy ending to an otherwise brutal series of events. In reality the resurrection is the prism through which we view the suffering and death of Christ and the suffering and death we experience in our own lives. Each and every Christian receives a vision of the glory of Christ in the transfiguration—a vision which sustains us through the suffering and deep disappointments of this life. Suffering as well as glory, death as well as resurrection, are the lot of the believer as first they were the vocation of the God-man.

The Lukan emphasis on Jerusalem becomes significant not so much as the historical setting of the passion, death, and resurrection of Christ, but as a means of allowing "Jerusalem" to stand as a symbol of this present congregation's own very real and crucial passage from death to life. In imitation of Jesus each of us can be as resolute as he was in accepting his journey to Jerusalem and its consequences. The rite of blessing and sprinkling with holy water is a most fitting introduction to the liturgy for this Sunday as it is throughout the Lenten season. Should the third form of the penitential rites be used, the fifth set of sample invocations about Christ's raising the dead to life, bringing pardon and peace to the sinner, and light to those in darkness would be an appropriate reflection of the readings for this Sunday.

Both versions of the opening prayer emphasize responding to the Word of God. In the opening prayer, hearing the Word is a way of sharing in the glory of Christ, and in the alternative prayer the voice of the Word of God is that which "restore[s] our sight that we may look upon your Son." For the prayer of the faithful this Sunday, the first set of intercessions in the Sacramentary appendix is a helpful model for the structuring and composition of this prayer. The preface for the second Sunday of Lent reiterates the theme of the gospel by speaking directly of the transfiguration where Christ revealed himself in glory, and tells that "the promised Christ had first to suffer and come to the glory of the resurrection." The prayer after communion also reinforces the theme of the scripture readings as well as indicates the place of the eucharist in the life of the believer, for it states that it is through these holy mysteries that we on earth come to share in the life to come. The solemn blessing of the Passion of the Lord would be a fitting conclusion to this liturgy, as it would be for all the Sundays of Lent, especially since the prayer over the people (no. 8) which the Sacramentary suggests for use today bears so little resemblance to the rest of the liturgy. Should the committee decide on a simpler dismissal taken from the prayers over the people, number 1 about being led to everlasting glory would be an appropriate choice.

THIRD SUNDAY OF LENT

Beginning with this Sunday and continuing through the fourth and fifth Sundays of Lent, the scripture readings from the "A" cycle may be substituted for those assigned for this Sunday in either the "B" or the "C" cycles.

This substitution is decidedly preferable when these Sundays are used as part of the rite of Christian initiation of adults. In this case, the ritual masses in the Sacramentary as well as the special proper commemoration in the Roman Canon may be used at the liturgy. A commentary on the readings from the "A" cycle appears above.

The selection from the gospel of Luke read this Sunday presents two rather bizarre examples of destruction which at first might put one off. Yet, their value lies in their depicting the judgment that has come upon the people of Israel as a warning to them to change their ways. The example of the fig tree that bears no fruit expresses this graphically, and yet the danger of immediate destruction is softened by the period of a year's grace before final destruction.

The application of this passage to the present Church involves self-scrutiny on the part of the baptized to determine to what extent they live lives in accord with their profession of faith. The temptation to grow slack and to become insipidly neutral is a constant one for the believer; hence this gospel about repentance and the constant need for renewal of that faith commitment is significant.

The obvious relation of this gospel to the season of Lent is made clearer in the texts of the opening prayer, both of which speak of the Lenten triad of prayer, fasting, and giving of alms as the means whereby Christians in this season signify their return to God and their concern for fellow Christians.

One characteristic of this kind of continual repentance is forgiveness and, while the gospel does not speak of this directly, the references to forgiveness in the prayer over the gifts, in the prayer after communion, and in the Lord's Prayer are obvious reflections of the gospel reading. In addition, the sacrament of penance may be referred to as an example of the forgiveness continually offered by God to those who turn to him in repentance. Penance and reconciliation are attitudes by which the Christian should be known and the Lenten season is a most appropriate time to emphasize the Lord's grace of reconciliation. That grace and favor, however, are not for the individual alone; they are gifts to be shared in the community of the local church.

The rite of blessing and sprinkling with holy water is the most appropriate introduction to the liturgy this Sunday because of the setting of the present celebration of the eucharist within the context of a profession of faith first pledged in the waters of baptism and now continually renewed in the eucharist.

Should the presider use the third form of the penitential rite, the fourth set of sample invocations about Christ's reconciling his followers with one another and with the Father, his healing us from the wounds of sin, and his ever-present intercession before the Father would be appropriate.

Both versions of the opening prayer speak of prayer, fasting and giving alms as important means whereby the believer turns to the Lord, but while the opening prayer speaks of being comforted in our efforts by the Father's love, the alternative prayer reflects the theology of the season by mentioning Lent as preparation for the joy of Easter.

While there is a preface in the Sacramentary for the third Sunday of Lent, it refers to the gospel of the "A" cycle and therefore should not be used at this celebration. Rather, of the four more general Lenten prefaces, the second about the Lenten season as a time for renewal in spirit, purifying hearts, and serving the Lord in true freedom, would seem to be the most appropriate choice. The committee might want to choose one of the eucharistic prayers for reconciliation for use today and for the next two Sundays. This would be a subtle reiteration of the reconciliation motif of the readings. The theme of forgiveness noted in the prayers of the Sacramentary is found in the third invitation to Lord's Prayer and could be complemented further by an alternative wording to introduce the sign of peace this Sunday. The solemn blessing for Lent is provided in the Mass formula for this Sunday and is a most appropriate conclusion to the liturgy. An alternative blessing from the prayers over the people can be chosen from number 4, asking the Lord to make the community holy, or number 6 about his granting us a complete change of heart.

FOURTH SUNDAY OF LENT

The gospel for this Sunday, a traditional one for the Lenten season, was formerly assigned to Saturday of the second week of Lent. Its place here in the Sunday liturgy of the "C" cycle is a welcome adjustment. The themes which make this gospel most appropriate for Lent are the images of the father who is most lavish in his care for the repentant son and almost over-generous in his concern for him. The prodigal son who turns from a life of sin to the father's good graces sets an example for the Christian to follow in the season of Lent, while the other son's attitude is an object lesson in what not to do and how not to act when our heavenly Father's love is expressed to another. The "good" son's attitude of strict "justice" and wanting nothing but his due, while natural enough and found so often even in our own experience, is shown to be harmful since it places limits on the father's love and mercy. When separated from mercy and love, justice can become a most un-Christian attitude, and no virtue at all.

The gospel proclaimed this Sunday is from chapter 15 of Luke's gospel which also includes the parables of the lost coin and the lost sheep. Luke's intention in those parables is to show that it is only the faithful and constant love of the Father that leads Jesus to seek out and search for a seemingly insignificant sinner even though he could count on his other righteous followers. The beginning of this Sunday's gospel, which is the opening of chapter 15, about welcoming tax collectors and eating with sinners, is a most appropriate image for the Church's celebration of the eucharist. This fellowship meal is by no means a "nice" gathering of the pure, saved, totally honest, and fully repentant. Rather, the eucharist is a meal of reconciliation, repentance, and forgiveness for the sinful Christian. It is by hearing the preached Word of God and by celebrating his redeeming presence in this sacrament that the Christian comes to be cleansed, purified, forgiven, and aided in the Christian life. By no means is the eucharist a reward for doing good; it is a means of sin-forgiveness and a most important sign of mercy for those who call on the Father for his grace and favor.

The liturgy of the word also points to the rite of penance where the image of the prodigal son is alluded to again and again. A proper understanding of God's love and mercy can help people to approach this sacrament more often. Where the former practice of the sacrament tended to relegate the aspects of healing and conversion to a secondary place, the present ritual directs attention to the Father's healing love and his concern for sinners who, in the light of today's reading, might be considered as sons or daughters who want to go on their own way with no direction or support from the Father.

The rite of blessing and sprinkling with holy water would be the most appropriate introduction to the liturgy this Sunday because it not only expresses the unity of the Sundays of Lent, but also because it refers to the cleansing waters of baptism and to the renewal of this "living spring of your life within us" as we come to the celebration of the eucharist. Should the presider use the third form of the penitential rite, the fourth set of sample invocations, about the Lord reconciling us with one another and with the Father, and his love which heals the wounds of sin and division, would be most appropriate. While the opening prayer mentions the act of reconciliation in Christ, the alternative prayer contains a more complete statement in rather poetic imagery of the peace of Christ in a sinful world, the gift of reconciliation for all peoples, and asks that the present community express real love and concern for one another in imitation of the Father's love (and so not act like the more logical and "justice"-bound son).

For the general intercessions the planning committee might wish to use the second of the model forms for the Lenten season from the appendix to the Sacramentary since it speaks of the closeness of the celebration of Easter and mentions specifically those to be initiated at Easter. One might also add a petition asking that those already baptized may renew their commitment to Christ in this community.

The preface for this Sunday should be selected from either of the first two general prefaces for Lent, since the preface for the fourth Sunday of Lent is designed to reflect the gospel of the "A" cycle. The first general preface for Lent refers to the coming celebration of the paschal mystery and recalls that these events give vitality to the Christian life; the second text speaks of this season of renewal and our need for penance and self-control. Or the committee might want to use one of the eucharistic prayers for reconciliation.

For the introduction to the Lord's Prayer the presider could fittingly use the second of the invitations to prayer since it speaks of calling God our Father, hence a reference to the image of the father in the gospel. The solemn blessing of the Passion of the Lord is an appropriate conclusion to the liturgy. Of the prayers over the people appropriate selections include the one provided in the Mass formula (no. 17) which speaks of the love which is shown in Christ's death, and number 6 about the Lord's care for his people even when they stray, and his granting them a complete change of heart.

FIFTH SUNDAY OF LENT

This Sunday's gospel reading is taken from the gospel of John, and yet most exegetes agree that this pericope is most un-Johannine in style and vocabulary. In fact, while this reading from John is obviously different from the Lukan gospels in the "C" cycle, some interpreters hold that today's reading is more Lukan than Johannine. Yet, the authenticity and origin of this text is not the point on this Lenten Sunday; it is more important to discover what this text has to say about forgiveness, not only for the woman caught in adultery, but for the members of the present Church.

The issue here appears to be a contrast of attitudes—that of

Christ and that of the condemning crowd. The crowd tries to trick this new rabbi, Jesus, by stating that according to the prescribed Mosaic legislation, this woman should be stoned. Yet, this new teacher declares the newness of his teaching by challenging the sincerity of the woman's accusers rather than condemning the woman herself.

Jesus offers his mercy, love, and forgiveness but in such a way that at the same time he encourages the woman to stop sinning. The cutting edge of this gospel for the present community is that it learn to forgive as the Father forgives; it is here that the two-edged sword of the scriptures really probes and penetrates, for this is precisely where we are often weakest. Most of us enjoy the image of the good shepherd when we feel like the lost sheep, and it is indeed a comfort to know that we are being sought out to be saved. Most of us enjoy the image of the prodigal's father ready to forgive his son and always prepared to kill the fatted calf in celebration. But the problem often arises even as we are being forgiven, for our smallness makes us less willing to extend that same mercy and love to others. Even after being forgiven, we are often not imitators either of the good shepherd or the father of the prodigal son. The heart of the gospel is that we become like Christ and have his attitude, and not have the attitude of the condemning crowd.

The very structure of the eucharist, the sacrament and sacrifice of the Lord's favor and grace to us, places the Our Father before the reception of communion, that those who are gathered in the name of the Lord might pray and actively show that same forgiveness to each other that they receive in the eucharist. The present reform of the Roman rite places the sign of peace soon after the Our Father as a gesture of what was prayed in the Lord's Prayer. With the main theme of the gospel about forgiveness, and these examples from the liturgy of the eucharist, the gospel for this Sunday leads almost naturally to reflection on the quality of our penance and the integrity of our celebrations of the eucharist. Jesus continually condemned empty rituals and lifeless gestures. The challenge of the gospel is to make these gestures and prayers living realities and life-filled attitudes for the Christian. The rite of blessing and sprinkling with holy water is the most appropriate introduction for the Sundays of Lent and would be most appropriate this Sunday. Should the presider use the third form of the penitential rite, he may wish to underscore the themes of the gospel by using the fourth or fifth set of sample invocations. The opening prayer speaks of the love of Christ inspiring the Church to follow his example, while the alternative opening prayer speaks of turning selfishness to self-giving and living in imitation of Christ. Hence, both prayers at least mention that the Christian's present life should be modeled after Jesus in his ministry.

The prayer of the faithful could follow the plan of the second sample form of intercessions for Lent, especially because of the reference to the nearness of the Easter celebration and the petition for those to be baptized at Easter. The preface for this Sunday may be chosen from either the first or second general prefaces for the season of Lent, since that assigned for the fifth Sunday of Lent reflects the gospel of the "A" cycle about the raising of Lazarus. The use of either eucharistic prayer for reconciliation would also be appropriate today. The third of the sample invitations to pray the Lord's Prayer, about forgiving others as we ask forgiveness, reflects the teaching of the gospel very well, and an expanded introduction to the sign of peace would be a graphic example of the kind of life-style and attitude envisioned in the gospel. The solemn blessing for the Lenten season would be the most appropriate conclusion to the day's liturgy. However, should the prayer over the people be used instead, number 12 about being freed from every evil and serving the Lord would be suitable. Other prayers that can be used would be number 2 about showing perfect love for each other, and number 9 about sharing God's gift of love with others.

HOLY WEEK: LITURGY AND SPIRITUALITY

While the six Sundays of Lent form an introduction and preparation for the Easter Vigil, the last of these Sundays, now called Passion Sunday (formerly "Palm") prepares more directly for the celebration of the rest of Holy Week. In the introduction before the blessing of palms at the beginning of this day's celebration, the presider may refer to the Lenten programs which the parish has undertaken to prepare for Easter. This can also be an appropriate time to stress the importance of this week as the week of the Christian Church. The note struck in the Passion Sunday liturgy between triumph and passion can also be underscored here since it is the theme of the entire week, where each celebration relates to the others and forms a liturgical and theological unity.

An axiom of liturgical study is that the more ancient ceremonies of the Church are found preserved in the most important days of the Church year. As applied to Holy Week, it would seem apparent that this refers not only to the outline of the ceremonies themselves, but also to the parts of the ceremony which are in the form of symbolic words and actions. No other week of the year has so much rich symbolism in it, and no other time of the Church year has such a depth of liturgical gesture to accompany the ceremonies. With regard to the most ancient practices of the Church year being retained on the most important days of the year, the example of the guidelines for Holy Thursday serve as an example. Under the heading of the Evening Liturgy the instructions state that the tabernacle is to be empty for this liturgy, and that a sufficient amount of bread should be consecrated for communion on Thursday and Friday. Furthermore, with regard to the distribution of the eucharist on both Thursday and the Easter Vigil, the instructions specifically recommend the distribution under both forms of bread and wine. Hence, the more ancient and more liturgically sound elements of the tradition are conserved in these instructions. As an example of the symbolic practice during Holy Week, we may note that palms are prescribed for Passion Sunday; the washing of feet on Holy Thursday; the bread and wine for eucharist on that special night; on Good Friday the cross is venerated and given special prominence. At the Easter Vigil, light in the form of the new fire and the lighted Easter candle in the midst of the darkened church is a most powerful symbol, as is water used for initiation and the renewal of baptismal vows at the Vigil and on Easter Sunday. During this holy week the elements noted in the readings used throughout Lent are now exemplified in ritual form:

HOLY THURSDAY	GOOD FRIDAY	EASTER VIGIL
Foot Washing	Word	Light
Eucharist	Cross	Water
Service	Communion	Life
	Passion	Baptism
	Triumph	Eucharist

For example, the water referred to in the dialogue with the Samaritan woman and the reference to Jesus as living water are brought to full term in the Vigil ceremony; the healing of the man born blind and the proclamation of Jesus as the light of the world is again brought to graphic expression in the powerful symbol of darkness and light at the Easter Vigil.

And yet, it is important to realize that while images and symbols have been used in the gospels of Lent and the liturgy of Holy Week, they possess a depth of meaning and significance that cannot be explained simply by reference to these gospel texts. For example, the very fact that the Vigil takes place in springtime, and that the major symbols include water and light opens up the whole range of natural symbolism that is latent in the liturgy of these celebrations. Historians of religion and anthropologists have noted that water ceremonies and light festivals have been a part of the religious orientation of peoples in cultures that have never heard the gospel message. Furthermore, even the ritual use of the symbols mentioned in the Lenten gospels does not do justice to the biblical imagery, where both the water and light are inherently ambiguous elements. Water can be destructive as well as productive; it can mean thirst or fertility and the goodness of the earth. Also, light can mean Christ as the light, the light which led the Israelites through the desert, the light that was a sign to astrologers to investigate the birth of Jesus, or it can mean the fire that will come to destroy the earth at the end of time. Therefore, while the symbolism of Holy Week should be emphasized as much as possible, no attempt should be made to exhaust the meaning of each symbol by giving some sort of scholastic dissertation about it.

Gestures are also an important part of the planning and execution of the liturgies in Holy Week. A primary, and primitive, gesture of the week is the procession, for besides its value for the presentation of the gifts, and for the reception of the eucharist at Mass, it has a special significance when it takes place on Passion Sunday when the palms are carried, on Holy Thursday when the transfer of the Blessed Sacrament is made, on Good Friday at the veneration of the cross, and on the Easter Vigil as the community follows the Easter candle into the darkened church for the beginning of the night watch of the resurrection.

The gesture of the presider bending down and kneeling to wash the feet of twelve parishoners is a powerful action and a sign of the love of Christ poured out on his disciples. The prostration on Good Friday is also a powerful sign of recollection, homage, awe, and reverence at the mystery to be commemorated that day. The procession with the cross (whether veiled or unveiled) is important for it heightens our awareness of an image that is always in our churches. It also parallels the procession to come at the Vigil when the cross is replaced by the light of the risen Christ.

The kissing or venerating of the cross is one way for the assembled community to speak their faith and to acknowledge personally that it is from the wood of the cross that our redemption has come.

We are sprinkled with water at the Vigil to renew the vows of our baptism and to symbolize our act of faith this night when Christ was raised from the dead.

PASSION SUNDAY

It should be recalled that the celebration of the events of Holy Week form a closely knit unity and no one aspect of the paschal mystery should be understood apart from the others. It is true that the Easter triduum includes Holy Thursday, Good Friday, and Holy Saturday in the reformed calendar, but each celebration, while retaining its own focus and emphasis, is in no way isolated from the other liturgical celebrations.

There is one central mystery of our faith; this is the week for its most solemn commemoration, but the commemoration is of the mystery in its entirety. Hence, to emphasize the crucifixion on Good Friday without regard for the resurrection on Easter, or to celebrate resurrection joy on Easter day itself without regard for the suffering and death of Christ, is to misuse the liturgy. There is no step-by-step "imitation of Christ" this week. There is rather a continued celebration of the one event of redemption won for us by the passion, death, and resurrection together.

The liturgy of Passion Sunday is a perfect example of this since the triumphal entry of Jesus into Jerusalem is only a subsidiary theme in the celebration, and the reading of the passion of the Lord is the major focus of the liturgy. The obvious drama and acclamation of Jesus as King must not be allowed to be the major emphasis of the day, for as soon as the procession enters the church the mood of the liturgy changes from acclamation to solemn and sober reflection on the passion and death of Jesus.

Liturgically, the celebration of Passion Sunday is like the other Lenten Sundays in that it prepares for the celebration of the Easter Vigil, but it also looks to the celebration of Holy Thursday and Good Friday as well. In many ways it is the overture to the week since it contains all the themes to be emphasized from this to the following Sunday.

The liturgy of Passion Sunday begins with the gathering of the community in a place outside the church (so they can then in procession move to the place of the eucharist); they already hold palms in their hands. After the greeting, the presider introduces the liturgy with the model text found in the Sacramentary or, preferably, with an introduction that is composed by the planning committee, since it should reflect as closely as possible the preparation of this particular community for Holy Week and Easter. It may stress penitential practices, the baptism of adults at the Easter Vigil, or the acts of charity in which the community was engaged this Lent. This introduction should also mention that all of this was in preparation for the celebration of the suffering, death, and resurrection of Jesus. Indeed, the introduction should highlight that it is this week that makes all the difference, not merely this Sunday.

The priest then blesses the branches with holy water and may choose one of two prayers, the first of which emphasizes the branches, and the second of which emphasizes the people's disposition for this expression of their faith and prayer. Both prayers stress our imitation of Christ and our faithful following of him. The gospel account of the triumphal entry into Jerusalem follows.

The readings are specified according to the cycles of the Lectionary with a choice offered in the "B" cycle between Mark's or John's accounts. The presider may choose to preach a homily after the gospel proclamation in order to develop the rich themes of this liturgy and to help the community focus attention on the passion narrative to come. During this liturgy as well as during the other celebrations of Holy Week our communal reflection should be on the cross of Christ, the means of our salvation. It is the cross which Christ endured in order to share his risen life with the Church.

The first reading of the eucharist is from the third servant song of Deutero-Isaiah and shows that the servant of Yahweh is obedient and totally submissive to the Father's will. The only recourse for him in his humiliation and trial is to cry out to the Lord, his only hope.

The second reading of the day is from the Christ hymn of Philippians, chapter 2, and again Jesus' voluntary surrender of his status as the eternal Son of the Father is emphasized.

The passion account from one of the synoptic writers now follows and dominates the liturgy of the word this Sunday.

The prayers of the Sacramentary reflect very well the nature and theme of the day, for the opening prayer is the keynote of the whole of Holy Week. It declares that Jesus is a model of humility and our imitation of him as Savior and Lord must necessarily include imitation of his humiliation and suffering. The alternative opening prayer, with overtones of the reading from Philippians, also includes the theme of the letter to the Romans, to the effect that one man justifies all by his one sacrifice. The alternative form is not as clear on the motif of suffering as is the opening prayer, but may be selected if the presider emphasizes in his homily the obedience of Jesus in doing the Father's will.

The prayer over the gifts speaks of Christ's sacrifice in the eucharist as winning for us the Father's mercy and love.

The prescribed preface for Passion Sunday presents in fine poetic style the theme of Holy Week—the sinless one who gave himself for sinners, the innocent one who redeemed the guilty, and the dying and rising of Jesus which enables us to share in his eternal life here on earth. Because of the almost word-for-word similarity between the preface and the second memorial acclamation, this acclamation should be used during the eucharistic prayer after the narrative of the Lord's Supper.

The prayer after communion reinforces the theme of the other prayers of the liturgy because it speaks directly of the death and resurrection of Jesus.

The solemn blessing (no. 5) provided in the Mass formula should be used on such a solemn day, for it speaks of the humility of Jesus in his willing service of others, his death on the cross, and the resurrection to which we are all called. The theme of the entire week is presented as a unity of events and as a single sacrifice of Christ.

Planning

The celebration of the Lord's entry into Jerusalem with the distribution and blessing of palm branches is prescribed for every celebration of the liturgy on Passion Sunday. Some form of the procession is required, even if the rites for the solemn or simple entrance are used. The procession should begin in some place other than the church itself. It may begin in a church hall, school auditorium, or in an open place sufficiently removed from the church to allow for a procession into the church.

The assistance of ushers to direct people from the church to the place of meeting is very important, since it will help the community assemble in such a way that all can see and hear the prayers, blessing, and homily.

The use of a microphone system in this place of gathering is a necessity for, depending on the nature of the place and size of the congregation, the sound can often be lost, especially if the gathering is held outdoors.

The choir should not be gathered in a single spot for this introduction since the singing will then be isolated in one place. They should mingle with the rest of the congregation, both here and in processing.

The distribution of palms takes place as the people assemble and the blessing takes place while they hold the palms in their hands.

The directions in the Sacramentary state that a minister carrying a suitably decorated cross is to head the procession into the church. The carrying of a processional banner at the head of the procession as well as the carrying of other hangings and decorations for the church for Holy Week may be a suitable adaptation in the liturgy. Carrying banners with the symbols of Holy Week helps to create an atmosphere of meditation on the entire paschal mystery rather than allowing the triumphal entry of Jesus into Jerusalem to be isolated as a separate event.

The color of the vestment of the day is red for royalty, instead of violet for penance, and the presider changes from the red cope to the chasuble as he enters the sanctuary for the liturgy of the word.

There is no penitential rite after the procession, since the prior ceremony takes its place; the presider invites the community to prayerful reflection on the readings of the day by immediately praying the opening prayer.

Since the Passion account is the main text proclaimed this Sunday, attention should be paid to the gestures and signs which accompany it. The use of two smaller lecterns along with the main pulpit would be a way to draw attention to this reading. Furniture is best moved during a liturgy and only the furniture needed at a given celebration should be present in the sanctuary area. Keeping this in mind through all of Holy Week can help to emphasize the signs, symbols, and gestures for each liturgy. Eliminating all but the necessary elements for a given liturgy can avoid the sanctuary "clutter," and confusion of signs.

HOLY THURSDAY—EVENING MASS OF THE LORD'S SUPPER

Historically, the term triduum sacrum refers to Good Friday, Holy Saturday, and Easter Sunday. Holy Thursday was in a different position because it was a day for the solemn reconciliation of penitents, the blessing of oils to be used for sacraments at the Easter Vigil, and an evening of vigils in preparation for the celebration of Good Friday with its emphasis on the cross of Christ.

As early as the fourth century, communities gathered for all-night vigils of common prayer and reflection on the significance of the passion of Jesus. The reconciliation of penitents was held in place of the liturgy of the word. Since baptism was regarded as the initiation into the eucharistic assembly, the reconciliation of penitents as a second baptism was done on Holy Thursday and the community could partake of the paschal communion.

In the reformed rites of Holy Week, the evening Mass of the Lord's Supper on Holy Thursday is the beginning of the triduum sacrum, and the restoration of the Chrism Mass on Holy Thursday morning in the cathedral church of the bishop of the diocese is considered still part of the season of Lent. According to the directions in the Sacramentary, no Masses without a congregation are permitted on Holy Thursday, and the only celebration of the day in a parish is the single celebration in the evening.

Another mass may be permitted, but in no way is it encouraged in the directives. All should try to attend the evening celebration, which is entitled "Evening Mass of the Lord's Supper." The readings and prayers of this eucharist celebration also stress the theme of service to others. The liturgy commemorates the last supper Jesus celebrated with his disciples, and his act of washing their feet. It was during this meal that Jesus instituted the eucharist by inviting his disciples to "Do this in remembrance of me." At that Last Supper Jesus also gave the command to serve the needs of one another as he humbled himself to wash the feet of his disciples. This evening's commemoration of the washing of the feet of the disciples is to remind us of the connection between the eucharist celebration and the service we offer our brothers and sisters as we go forth "to love and serve the Lord." We gather at the eucharist as a community of fellowship in the name of the Lord Jesus, and as members of that community we are to wash the feet of others symbolically by answering and serving their needs. We do not live in isolation, nor do we celebrate the eucharist in isolation. For in the words of one of the Fathers of the early Church, "If we live alone, whose feet will we wash?"

The liturgy of the word this evening begins with the commemoration of the Passover meal as a foretaste of the eucharistic meal we now commemorate. The second reading is the Pauline account of the institution of the Lord's Supper, and the gospel reading from St. John describes the washing of the feet and the service which Christians are to offer each other.

The new Sacramentary prescribes that the homily this evening should explore the principal mysteries commemorated in the Mass: the institution of the eucharist, the institution of the priesthood, and the Christ's command of love and concern for each other.

The opening prayer of the liturgy describes this eucharist as memorial of the institution of the eucharist; the prayer over the gifts speaks of the eucharist as a continual memorial of our redemption; the preface for the celebration is that of the holy eucharist; and the Roman Canon is proclaimed with the proper *communicantes* for Holy Thursday.

After the prayer after communion, there is a procession to the repository. The community is encouraged to remain after the service for adoration of the sacrament at the repository until midnight. According to the directives of the Missal, all-night adoration and adoration on Good Friday morning are eliminated.

The days of Good Friday and Holy Saturday are days without public reservation and adoration of the Sacrament. The purpose of this reform is to emphasize the celebration of the eucharistic liturgy, rather than simply to be concerned with adoration, as was often the case in the past. After midnight the eucharist should fittingly be removed to another place until the Good Friday service.

Planning

It should be borne in mind that this evening liturgy is part of the triduum and not an anticipation of Easter. The tone of the liturgy is grateful and yet incomplete; not as joyous and complete as is the Easter Vigil.

The ritual gesture of the washing of the feet of twelve parishioners is central in this celebration. The themes of the institution of the eucharist and priesthood are part of the heritage of Holy Thursday, but they must be seen in the context of what the gospel proclaims and what these gestures symbolize. The choice of the twelve parishioners should be given some attention. Some parishes choose leaders of various parish or civic groups. Others prefer to invite people who are less visible in the community, yet whose service and witness are strong and truly Christian. The action of taking a basin, water, and towels should not be disguised or made a mere token. This action is important symbolically and, therefore, the presider should be deliberate in his movements. Depending upon how the church is designed, the twelve can be seated together for this ceremony near the altar, in the sanctuary area, or even interspersed through the assembled community. The point is not to make these people feel "honored"; rather, the intention is to demonstrate our unity in the community, Christ's love for us, and ours for each other.

In the Chrism Mass for Holy Thursday (often celebrated earlier in the week at the diocesan cathedral) the bishop and priests are given an opportunity to renew their commitment to priestly service. While this practice is part of the Chrism Mass today, it has no traditional foundation. Some planning groups have tried to adapt this ceremony for use at the parish evening liturgy, but it is needless to do so because the gesture and sign of commitment to serve is done ritually at the foot washing. To do otherwise would tend to clericalize a liturgy which is essentially communitarian in tone, emphasis, and import. Authenticity here is what matters: the sign must be true and backed up with continued service. The celebration of eucharist this day must show that service to others, on the part of both clerics and laity, is what Christ calls for. The new directives for Holy Week also state that the distribution of the eucharist under both forms is an important option this evening. The stripping of the altars takes place after the liturgy has ended and without the presence of the congregation. From now on the church awaits the liturgy of Good Friday.

GOOD FRIDAY—CELEBRATION OF THE LORD'S PASSION

Historically, the rites surrounding this day varied from place to place. As time went on, a service of the word, the adoration of the cross, the distribution of communion, and an afternoon Vesper service emerge as elements which form the background of the contemporary revision of the liturgy of this day.

The earliest chronicles of this celebration give prominence to two things: the proclamation of the Passion according to St. John, and the solemn intercessory prayers in the primitive Roman form. These prayers include an invocation and statement of the purpose of the prayer, a pause for silence, and the concluding formula. The only day on which this form of intercession is prescribed is Good Friday, although it may be used at other celebrations as well.

The adoration of the cross and the distribution of communion were originally a separate service in the afternoon about the time when, it was supposed, the crucifixion took place. The evening Vesper service also emerged as a prominent focal point for popular piety. These rites all contributed to the recent revision of the liturgy of Good Friday which envisions the service as being held in the afternoon. It is composed of an opening prayer, readings, including the Passion according to St. John, the solemn intercessions, the adoration of the cross, and the reception of communion.

Theologically, this day also has a certain ambiguity and paradox in its theme and orientation. The theme of the day would obviously be one of somber reflections and tragedy if it were to be merely a historical reminiscence of the death of Jesus. However, the liturgy is not such a reminiscence or reenactment. While the liturgy is stark in its simplicity and somewhat sober in the reflection it evokes, it is nonetheless a celebration of the paschal mystery—not merely death in isolation. The passion narrative read on Good Friday is from St. John, whose clear and constant theology is that the cross is not simply an instrument of suffering and death, but rather a sign of hope and victory. The cross is the throne of this king's glory, the place where the manifestation of the glory of the God-Man takes place in such a way that the death of Jesus points beyond itself to the term of the paschal mystery—the resurrection and glorification of Jesus as Christ. It is no longer a place of death; it is the place where death came to an end and life came to all.

In the reformed liturgy of Good Friday the altar is not covered— the only day in the Church year when this is prescribed. Furthermore, the vesture worn by the presider is red, a symbol of royalty here, not violet to symbolize penance, or black to symbolize death. The first part of the celebration is the liturgy of the word, introduced by a silent procession of ministers to the sanctuary, a pause for silence and prostration, and the offering of the opening prayer.

The beginning of the liturgy with the opening prayer and no other ceremonies can be traced as far back as the time of St. Augustine. Also, the use of the Roman form of the intercessions is a more primitive form than the Byzantine litany-type prayers. The first form of the opening prayer is apt because of its reference to the paschal mystery, while the optional form speaks more clearly of the imagery of the sin of Adam, and the likeness of God and man joined in the life of Jesus.

The first reading from the Fourth Servant Song of Isaiah, which is interpolated again and again into the New Testament, refers to Jesus and is so interpreted by its place and proclamation in the liturgy of Good Friday. He is the perfect servant, who surrendered himself to death that the will of the Father should be accomplished through him.

The reading from the letter to the Hebrews speaks of the priesthood of Christ and states that through his obedience to the Father's will, he is now able to save all who follow him in obeying the Father. Because of his paschal sacrifice he is now the source of eternal life for all who believe.

The Passion according to St. John is the perfect complement to these readings and the perfect selection for Good Friday since it proclaims Christ as king who resolutely goes to his death for others. There can be no agony in the garden in St. John's gospel because this is Jesus' finest hour. Jesus is well aware of what is to happen and does not shirk his responsibility; rather he is eager to do the will of him who sent him. In the first chapter of this gospel, John the Baptist bears witness that Jesus is the Lamb of God who takes away our sins. St. John's gospel presents the death of the Lamb of God at precisely the time when the passover lambs were slaughtered for Temple sacrifice. The implication of this theology is clear—Jesus is the perfect Lamb of God who obediently goes to the slaughter.

The proclamation of this gospel in the liturgy indicates clearly that we are not to shun the sacrifice of Jesus at Calvary, but should rather rejoice, for they are blessed who find salvation in it and wash their robes in the blood of the Lamb.

After the proclamation of the Passion (preferably by three readers), the presider may preach a brief homily. His comments should underscore the aspect of the cross as the tree of eternal life and the source of salvation. We do not mourn the death of Jesus on Good Friday; instead we acknowledge the cross as our salvation in gratitude and respect. The general intercessions conclude the liturgy of the word, and the planners are free to choose from among the ten those which they understand to be most appropriate for the community.

These intercessions are introduced by the "invitatory," which itself may be rewritten in the light of local needs or concerns. The more particularized these prayers become, the more effective they will be as prayers of the local congregation. Yet, like all general intercessions, they should reflect universal as well as local needs.

The veneration of the cross is the second part of the liturgy of Good Friday. The ministers take either the veiled or uncovered cross and carry it in procession to the sanctuary, stopping three times to proclaim, "This is the wood of the cross . . ." and inviting the veneration by the congregation.

The veneration of the cross can be an effective rite or it can degenerate into mass confusion and boredom. The directives speak of the use of a single cross for the veneration of the congregation. Other crosses may be used if each person is to come forward for the veneration. Another option would be to use the single cross, the one carried in procession, and take it to different parts of the church and ask one group of people at a time to kneel in silence before it. Individual veneration of the cross could take place after the liturgy if the people so wish. This part of the liturgy invites much pastoral adaptation and planning for it to be as effective and complete a sign of reverence for the cross as possible.

The third and final part of the liturgy is the distribution of holy communion. The altar is covered for this part of the ceremony with the altar cloth, upon which are placed the corporal and the Sacramentary. The transferral of the Blessed Sacrament from the place of reposition to the altar is accomplished with no ceremony. The distribution of the host follows the Our Father, the embolism, and the invitation to partake of the Lamb of God. Both of the prayers after communion are suitable conclusions to the ceremony since they both speak of the resurrection as well as the passion. The prayer is followed by a silent procession of the ministers to the sacristy.

The Easter triduum lasts until the celebration of the Easter Vigil Mass, and the directions of the Sacramentary indicate the kind of activity that is desirable during this time. At the introduction to the celebration of Good Friday, the Sacramentary has the direction that the sacraments are not celebrated on Friday or Saturday, and this includes funerals, weddings, and even the sacrament of penance. Pastorally it may be difficult to eliminate the hearing of confessions on these two days, but a positive step in the redirection of pastoral practice regarding penance would be giving the emphasis to a communal celebration of the sacrament of penance on Tuesday or Wednesday of Holy Week, thus imitating the practice of the early Church of reconciling penitents before the eucharist on Holy Thursday. Furthermore, the scheduling of weddings should prove no difficulty provided those making the arrangements are aware that weddings are not allowed on these days, for the Sacramentary describes these as days of meditation of the events of the passion and death, and anticipation of the resurrection. On Holy Saturday, Holy Communion may only be given as viaticum.

EASTER VIGIL—NIGHT WATCH OF THE RESURRECTION

The night vigil of Easter begins the feast of Christians. In the words of the Exsultet: "This is our passover feast, when Christ the true lamb is slain, whose blood consecrates the homes of all believers. This is the night when Christians everywhere, washed clean of sin and freed from all defilement, are restored to grace and grow together in holiness."

It is the night of nights, the highest holy day of the Christian Church, for we are renewed, made whole again, and reborn in the redemption of Jesus who is raised triumphant from the grave.

According to the new Sacramentary, this is a night vigil and should be so scheduled that the theme of darkness and light becomes obvious; according to the directions, it should not be celebrated before nightfall. It is a night of light, illumination, and rebirth in water and the Spirit. It is a night for initiation, and reinitiation; it is a night of renunciation and allegiance; it is a night of commitment and speaking faith; it is a night of proclamation and exaltation; it is a night of transformation and regeneration.

In the revised rites, the Easter Vigil is composed of four parts, each of which has its own symbolism and richness, yet each of which needs the other parts for completion and fulfillment.

Service of Light

This is the first part of the Vigil celebration and should begin with the community, or at least a part of the community, gathered outside the church for the blessing of the new fire. The presider greets the assembly and inducts them into the celebration of the night watch. The suggested text describes the passing of Jesus from death to life and our identification with him in passing from sin and evil to new life in Christ at this Vigil. The introduction to the text may be rewritten to fit the needs and concerns of the local community, and should reflect the initiation to be celebrated which has been prepared for during the season of Lent.

The presider then blesses the fire and lights the Easter candle from the fire. The candle itself is the symbol of Christ; the decorations which customarily adorn the candle are now optional.

The use of incense and red nails was a conscious attempt to decorate the candle, the symbol of the risen Christ, with the spices and instruments of the passion and burial of Jesus. Depending on local circumstances they may or may not be used. If they are chosen they should be added to the candles before the ceremony so that after blessing of the new fire, the candle is lighted and the procession begins. The deacon, or other minister, takes the candle and begins the procession into the church toward the sanctuary followed by the community. The deacon sings or proclaims: "Christ our light" three times, and after the third proclamation the candles of all those in the congregation are lighted from the Easter candle. (The Sacramentary prescribes the use of candles by the congregation.) The deacon then places the Easter candle in the stand, incenses the candle and book, and begins the Exsultet, the Easter proclamation. The directions in the Sacramentary indicate that the lights of the church are put on as the candle is placed in the stand. A pastoral adjustment could be made here and the lights left off until after the singing of the Easter proclamation. This gives obvious emphasis to the light of the candles, a major symbol of the Vigil ceremony. After singing the proclamation, the people's candles are extinguished and not used again until the liturgy of baptism.

Liturgy of the Word

The second part of the service is the proclamation of the word of God. Nine readings are assigned for this night, seven from the Old Testament and two from the New Testament. The two New Testament readings are prescribed, and some or all of the Old Testament readings may be selected provided the reading about the passage through the Red Sea is among them.

The decision on the number of readings is one that depends on local circumstances. One way to vary the wordiness that can sometimes be created by reading many of the selections is to vary the response to the readings. After one there can be a sung responsorial psalm; after another a recited psalm. Each of the lessons is followed by a collect type of prayer. The first reading (from the book of Genesis) about the creation should be proclaimed since this is the feast of commemorating origins and redemption. We were made in the image and likeness of God and renewed in that image through the death and resurrection of God's Son. The imagery of water makes it an especially appropriate reading for the Easter Vigil. The reading from the book of Exodus 14:15 to 15:1 is prescribed since it relates the passage of the Israelites through the Red Sea; they walked through water to freedom because of an act of God. The reading of the selection from the prophecy of Ezekiel is also appropriate since it speaks of the pouring forth of clear water to cleanse the people who had gone astray. The Lord will come and sprinkle clean water on them, give them a clean heart, and pour forth his Spirit on them and renew them to live according to his statutes. The reading from Romans 6 is the classic text of the Easter Vigil because of the explanation of Christian baptism and the dying and rising of the believer who is plunged into the death and resurrection of Jesus at baptism. The gospel is taken from the synoptic accounts of Easter morning.

While in the former practice, the Gloria received great emphasis, as did the Easter alleluia, a more restrained proclamation should mark the glory of God during the liturgy of the word. The Gloria is incarnational in emphasis, whereas the progression of the scripture readings leads to the proclamation of the gospel as the Easter text. The Easter alleluia is appropriately emphasized before the gospel and may well be repeated after the gospel. Pastoral planning is important for this night of nights, especially in the liturgy of the word, to show the progression from creation to the redemption of Israel, to our redemption in baptism and this feast commemorating the resurrection of Christ.

Liturgy of Baptism

The third part of the Easter Vigil is that for which Lent has prepared—the initiation of adults and children into the Church and the profession of faith on the part of those who were members of other Christian churches. Catechumens and sponsoring families and godparents should be seated in the assembly in such a way that they receive due attention. The presider introduces this part of the liturgy in a way that shows how what is about to happen to the newly initiated is also related to those already initiated. The celebration of confirmation for adult catechumens takes place as part of the ceremony, and this is done by the presider as part of the liturgy. The renewal of baptismal promises by the whole community should take place in such a way that all those assembled experience a personal renewal in faith and recommitment to the faith into which the catechumens are baptized. In some dioceses the Easter Vigil is now emphasized as one very significant occasion for a communal initiation of infants. This is certainly to be encouraged. And yet the Rite of Christian Initiation of Adults should receive as much emphasis in planning so that this night can be focused on the font of baptism where all are equal in Christ.

The conclusion of this part of the liturgy involves the sprinkling of the entire community with holy water. This should be carried out so as to allow the symbol of water to be experienced, not just looked at, by all. The use of a glass baptismal font or basin for water can also help in directing attention to this fundamental element of Easter liturgy, and could also be used throughout the whole season to continue its symbolic emphasis.

Liturgy of the Eucharist

Because of the length of the Vigil or a legitimate preoccupation with initiation at baptism and confirmation, the liturgy of the eucharist can sometimes be eclipsed. Yet, such should not be the case since it is initiation into the eucharistic community that this vigil service has been all about. The weekly renewal of the covenant of baptism takes place at the table of the Lord's word and eucharist. Hence, emphasis should be placed on this eucharistic liturgy as the new heaven, the new means for sustaining members by the food and drink of eternal life. The presentation of the gifts by the newly-initiated and the distribution of communion under both forms express the richness of this symbolism. The use of the Roman Canon with the proper commemorations for Easter is appropriate, as is the solemn blessing of Easter at the conclusion to the liturgy.

EASTER SUNDAY

Like the celebration of the Easter Vigil, the celebration of the eucharist on Easter Sunday is a celebration of light and rebirth by water and the Holy Spirit. Easter is indeed *the* celebration of the entire Church year; it is the fulfillment of the Lenten preparation of the community, and is the central mystery of our faith. While strictly speaking the most important celebration of the liturgy is the

Easter Vigil, there is an unavoidable problem inherent here—for most of the community the Vigil is, in fact, not their celebration of Easter. Rather Easter Sunday itself is the most popular day of the Church year, and the eucharists celebrated on Easter day need, therefore, as much care, attention, and planning as that of the Vigil itself. In the revised Sacramentary some of the elements which characterize the Vigil are also taken over to the celebration of the eucharist on this morning, and these should be used in such a way that the community which was not present the night before can still participate in an Easter eucharist that has the solemnity, grandeur, and splendor that it deserves.

The most important adjustment in the Sacramentary is that the profession of faith is replaced at all Masses on Easter with the renewal of baptismal promises. The introduction to this ceremony, which follows the homily, may be reworded, and this can be done to heighten the connection between this day and the preparation for it during Lent, as well as to note this day as the climax of some specific parish Lenten programs. For the renunciation of Satan, two forms are provided, the first of which declares what it means to renounce evil and is more expressive of the purpose of Lent, to struggle with evil in our lives and to live as God's children. The second is shorter and more conventional.

The second element of the Easter liturgy that should be duly emphasized is the alleluia before the proclamation of the gospel. Just as at the Vigil the night before, the proclamation of this gospel almost demands a grand introduction since it proclaims the most important element of our faith. While the guidelines for the Easter Vigil state that the alleluia is to be solemnly intoned by the presider, it may be preceded by a suitable musical selection which would serve to heighten the awareness that this is the most important Easter reading.

Another way of emphasizing the eucharist on Easter day would be to utilize the option provided regarding the gospel to be proclaimed. For all three cycles of the Lectionary the gospel of Easter day is the same, John 20. It is also permitted to use one of the gospels of the Vigil, which provides a reading for each cycle: Matthew 28:1–10, Mark 16:1–8, and Luke 24:1–12. In addition, the Lectionary notes that for afternoon liturgies on Easter, the text about the disciples on the road to Emmaus may be proclaimed, Luke 24:13–39 (found in the Lectionary, no. 47).

At the introductory rite of the Mass, the presider could acclaim Christ as present as the Risen Lord of this congregation and in this way introduce the sung Glory to God. The first reading for the liturgy of the word is one of the speeches from the Acts of the Apostles, which presents in summary fashion the key to the Christian faith, "Christ has died, Christ is risen, Christ will come again." No other profession or doctrine of the faith comes close to being so central as the Easter mystery. The sacred author of Acts is at pains to emphasize who Jesus is, not just what he did on the first Easter morning, for he is the judge of the living and the dead, he is the Lord who grants forgiveness of sins, he is the Paschal Lamb who is still active in the work of redemption.

The call of Peter in the Acts pericope is a call to imitate the apostles in becoming witnesses of the resurrection, not merely by words but by deeds. This is also the theme of both Pauline readings assigned for this day, for in both, statements are made about Christ and the believer, followed by the demand that Christ's witnesses live their faith. Baptism in the name of Jesus initiates a person into a life lived according to his teaching, a life of witnessing to his truth. We are to clean out the old leaven and replace it with a totally new principle and source of life. The gospel reading from John shows how Peter himself was transformed from a doubting, hesitant follower to an active proclaimer of the risen Lord because he saw and believed. He made the decision of faith and did not remain in doubt and uncertainty.

Seeing, however, is not believing; Peter decided to become a believer rather than wait for proof. His decision to believe meant that he was determined to do God's will. This witnessing is also evident in the speech in Acts.

The alternate gospel that may be chosen for an afternoon liturgy on Easter is that of the disciples on the road to Emmaus. This moving post-resurrection appearance of Jesus concerns the love of these followers for their Lord and the greatness of his love and generosity for them. They speak to each other about Jesus' passion and crucifixion, and the risen Lord appears to them. On one level, this moving account could lead to a homily on the paschal mystery where the suffering necessary to precede the joy and glory of Easter should not be forgotten. Our sufferings and hardships in imitation of Jesus should always be seen as part of the mystery of the resurrection. The recounting of the breaking of the bread would also be an appropriate basis for emphasizing the eucharistic character of this season, where the community is reminded that just as the disciples "saw" but only later came to have their eyes opened to recognize their Lord at the moment of bread-breaking, so our sight of these sacred mysteries should always lead to an ever deeper perception of his presence with us.

The opening prayer of the liturgy directs our reflection not only to the event of Jesus' resurrection, but to reflection on what resurrection means, for by it we are all saved and raised to new life in him; his power is now at work in us. The alternative opening prayer takes up the ending of the gospel reading of John and refers to the Lukan account of the suffering and death which necessarily preceded the Lord's resurrection, humiliation which must also precede our own exaltation.

The rite for the renewal of baptism vows follows the homily and should be introduced by pointing out the reason for the Lenten preparation and the reason why Christians gather weekly at the eucharist.

The first preface of Easter mentions the suffering and death of Jesus along with the resurrection to new life.

The prayer after communion describes the resurrection as the fulfillment of God's plan of re-creating us and restoring us to eternal salvation.

The solemn blessing of Easter Sunday should be used today and throughout the season because of the solemnity of Easter.

Chapter Four

Season of Easter—"The Fifty Days"

According to the Introduction to the Sacramentary, Easter is a
festival of fifty days wherein all the days from Easter Sunday to the
solemnity of Pentecost comprise the "great Sunday," the one feast
of the Lord's resurrection (General Norms for the Liturgical Year,
no. 22). In the revision of the calendar, Easter retains its octave, as
does Christmas, but Pentecost does not. Instead, the norms (nos.
24, 26) emphasize the days from the solemnity of the Ascension to
Pentecost as a time of preparation for the coming of the Holy
Spirit, the last stage in the glorification of Jesus. Ascension is no
longer to be understood as the close of the Easter season, but rather
marks an intensive preparation for the Spirit's coming. Pentecost is
revived as the day which ends the Paschal time, for on the next
day the cycle of "ordinary time" resumes.

Pentecost may be understood as the feast of the outpouring of
the Spirit on the community which waits in anticipation for the
second coming of the Lord. In a manner of speaking, Advent looks
forward to the second coming, yet prepares for the commemoration
of the incarnation of the Son of God and his manifestation to all
the nations of the earth. Lent prepares the community by special
prayer, fasting, and almsgiving for the celebration of the sacred
triduum of Holy Thursday, Good Friday, and the Easter Vigil, and
then Easter itself looks to Pentecost when the coming of the Spirit
sustains the community until the second coming, commemorated in
the last Sundays of the Year and in Advent. The central
celebrations of the Church year are Easter and Christmas, framed
by the season of Advent and the solemnity of Pentecost.

The celebration of Pentecost has its roots in Judaism, in the Feast
of Weeks mentioned in Deuteronomy 16:9–12, a joyful agrarian
festival of thanksgiving for the first harvest of the year. Originally a

grain festival, in later Judaism it became a festival in commemoration of covenant-renewal and the Law given at Sinai. The term *pentecost* also stems from the number symbolism of seven days times seven weeks, making forty-nine, and then adding one to make the total fifty, a number symbolizing perfection or completion. Hence, the completion of the Exodus-Passover festival was held fifty days later at Pentecost in Judaism, and in the Christian calendar the completion of Easter is celebrated fifty days later as well.

That Pentecost was central to the primitive Easter celebration is shown by the fact that at one point in the development of the Church year, the term "Pentecost" referred to the whole season from Easter to Pentecost day itself. This period was one of joyful celebration of Christ's resurrection, hence fasting and other penitential practices were suppressed, as was kneeling during the liturgy; standing was associated with Christ's rising from the tomb. Furthermore, Pentecost was originally the feast of both the Ascension and the coming of the Holy Spirit, but by the end of the fourth century we have evidence that Ascension came to be celebrated separately forty days after Easter. The number symbolism of forty is important as reflecting the same number of days of fasting during Lent, in imitation of Jesus' fasting for forty days in the desert before his ministry, the forty days of the flood in Genesis 7:17, and the forty years of the Exodus (Exodus 12). The current revision of the calendar, by closely associating Ascension with Pentecost, and emphasizing the total Easter season of fifty days, is a return to a more traditional form of Church usage.

Liturgically, the season of Easter was *the* time for the eucharist, the paschal communion. After the celebration of the Easter Vigil, the new converts were invited back to the church during the following week (the octave of Easter) to receive instructions about what had happened to them at the Vigil, as well as to help them understand the implications of Christian initiation. During this week, the newly-baptized wore white robes given to them at the ceremony on Easter, and put them aside on the Sunday following the post-baptismal instruction, which Sunday was called *dominica in albis*. In the new order of initiation of adults, this post-baptismal instruction period is revived in accord with the practice of the early Church.

For the Sundays of Easter, the customary first lesson from the Old Testament is eliminated in favor of a reading from the Acts of the Apostles. The gospel readings are taken from the Gospel of St. John, except on the third Sunday of Easter, where the appearance of the risen Christ to the apostles on the road to Emmaus is recounted from the Gospel of St. Luke. The reason for this change from the customary readings from the Old Testament and the Synoptics is that the earliest Lectionary lists available show that the community reflected on the beginnings and expansion of the Church in the Acts, and on the readings from the Johannine "spiritual Gospel."

In the "A" cycle, the second reading on Sundays is taken from the first letter of Peter, in the "B" cycle it is from the first letter of John, and in the "C" cycle it is from the book of Revelation.

For the liturgical planning of this season, penitential elements of the eucharistic celebration should be downplayed, and the emphasis should be on the joy of the resurrection symbolized in art, gestures, and hymnody; of alleluia, praise, and unrestrained joy. It is the most natural time for the planning of first communion in parishes, as well as planning for the sacrament of confirmation.

PASTORAL PLANNING FOR THE SEASON—
EUCHARIST AND ANOINTING

Since the Easter season is the time of great emphasis on the eucharist, two pastoral practices which may be introduced, reemphasized, or developed more completely in parishes are the use of special ministers of the eucharist at parish celebrations and for the communion of the sick in their homes. More lay involvement in the ministry to the sick and elderly should be encouraged. While the use of special ministers at the eucharist is a common practice, using these same people in the parish ministry to the sick is a practice that has much historical background, and could quite fittingly be explored as a parish project, especially during this season.

Historically, there is evidence that lay people once brought the eucharist home on Sundays for anyone who was sick, so the absent member of the community could participate in the Sunday celebration. Intercessions for the sick of the community, a common practice now with the revived prayer of the faithful, has its origins in early liturgical practices. Hence, ministry to the sick was understood to be a concern of the community, clerical as well as lay. This notion is revived in the Introduction to the revised Rite of Anointing and Pastoral Care of the Sick, where it states that it is fitting that all baptized Christians share in caring for the sick in mutual charity (no. 33). Like the other sacraments, anointing has its communal aspect and this is to be brought out as much as possible in the rite (no. 33). The family and friends of the sick person have a special share in this ministry of comforting the ill, yet all Christians are to share in this ministry by visiting and comforting the sick (nos. 34, 42). The document also urges that sick people should be given every opportunity to receive the eucharist, "even daily, if possible, especially during the Easter Season" (no. 46). In accordance with the nature of the Easter season, the following suggestions may help the community to participate in this ministry.

The first suggestion is to have a communal anointing liturgy for the elderly and sick. Such a celebration would require special attention to many details like transportation to and from the church, provision for some nursing care to be available if needed in church, assisting those going to the altar for the anointing and the reception of the eucharist, and after the liturgy, perhaps a parish reception for all those who have been anointed.

If there are any nursing homes in the parish, it might be possible to schedule a regular eucharistic celebration in the home. Members of the parish could form a committee to prepare the patients for the liturgy, to bring them to the room for the Mass, to sit with them during the liturgy, and to assist them in returning to their room at its conclusion. Such a committee, depending on the number of patients involved, could be designed on a one-to-one basis where these parishioners would not only help on the day of the liturgy, but also take on the responsibility of visiting the patients more often, perhaps weekly, as a sign of personal concern. Also, for the liturgy itself, a music group from the parish could help with the singing of hymns, especially since much of the liturgy is "new" or strange to the elderly. The patients can join in the responses and can also recite or sing the Our Father. Extending the sign of peace to all the elderly would also be an important gesture for the celebrant since he can show by this sign his real concern for those with whom he celebrates this liturgy. Special ministers of the eucharist who administer the sacrament to the sick and elderly in their own homes could read a passage or two from scripture, pray with the patient, and in general, make the visit one of comfort and understanding. Many parishes have St. Vincent de Paul societies as well as Christian service or community action committees of parish councils whose members might be the first to participate in such programs. Also, the young people of the parish could be involved as a part of their religious education programs so that theory and practice are both understood to be a part of the faith. The young people might even take on the responsibility of the music for the liturgies in nursing homes, assisting the priest at Mass, and setting the alter for the celebration.

SUNDAY EUCHARIST

The Easter candle, lit for the first time from the new fire of the Easter Vigil, is placed in a prominent place in the sanctuary between Easter and Pentecost and should be lit for all liturgical services in this season, and should be incensed whenever incense is used during the fifty days. Since Pentecost marks the end of the season, the Easter candle is no longer extinguished on the solemnity of the Ascension, and, therefore, the candle should burn prominently until then. After Pentecost it can be placed in the baptistery for use at baptisms and funerals.

The color of the vesture for the season is white, and the cloth or frontal for the altar should be white as well. Liturgical hangings or banners should be made of white and contrasting colors and should reflect the season of new life, fulfillment, rejoicing and joy at the season. Using the symbols of the Lenten season—for example, a series of crosses—but changing the colors from penitential violet to the white of Easter is appropriate.

The other sign of the Easter season that should be used to the fullest is water. The rite for blessing and sprinkling with water should be a part of every Sunday eucharist. The introductions to the blessing should be reworded weekly, and the prayer for the actual blessing should be taken from that of the Easter season, the third of the options in the Sacramentary.

All penitential elements in the eucharist should be eliminated in this season of sung Alleluias, water, candles, and lights. If at all possible, the congregation should be invited to sing the Glory to

God since it falls flat and does not convey its power, significance, and exaltation if merely recited, especially during the Easter season.

The season of Easter is *the* season for the sacrament of the eucharist. While recent emphasis on daily reception of the eucharist during Lent has proven to have pastoral benefits, the nature and character of the Easter season almost demands the same emphasis and publicity. Many parishes have inaugurated the practice of preaching at the weekday eucharist only on the weekdays of Advent and Lent. One way to emphasize the Easter season would be to preach daily during this season as well.

For the season of Easter (after the first week), the first reading of the weekday Lectionary is a continuous reading from the Acts of the Apostles; the gospel is from St. John. These sacred books were thought to provide ample instruction and formation during the Easter season for those candidates baptized at the Easter Vigil, and should also provide the same formation for those who annually renew their baptismal promises at Easter.

The celebration of a parish First Communion can be introduced and prepared for by a series of para-liturgies, or even by a series of special eucharistic celebrations at a regularly scheduled Sunday liturgy. The whole parish can thus take part in preparing both the first communicants and their parents for the sacrament of the eucharist.

The use of incense as well as the use of water and light at the Sunday liturgies of the Easter season, at least at the main parish eucharist, emphasize the importance of this season by a direct appeal to the physical senses. Many churches today scarcely ever use incense, yet it can lend a degree of solemnity to a celebration.

SUNDAYS OF EASTER "A" CYCLE

SECOND SUNDAY OF EASTER

As a result of the Second Vatican Council, the Church of our day has seen major changes in her prayer, organization, and outlook toward the world in which we live. Again and again members of the Church ask for clarification of what has changed and why changes were necessary. Questions such as: "Where is it all going?" and "What is it all about?" are asked with greater frequency and intensity. The readings of today's liturgy present a perspective from which we can and should ask such questions.

The first reading from the Acts of the Apostles gives four "marks of the Church" which should be obvious to all. Granted that the text presents an idealized picture of the primitive Church, the major theme of the reading is fidelity—remaining faithful to an ever-faithful God who invites us to make sure we live according to the profession of faith we made at our baptism. Life in the Christian community is the second aspect of fidelity, and as it was more than an abstract ideal in the early Church, it should also be a characteristic of the present Church. Concern for others in love is the expression of our love of God, and Christians should give to the world an example of love and concern for all people.

Two other essential aspects of Church life are the breaking of the bread and prayers. Scholars will debate the specific meaning of these phrases, but what is certain is that table fellowship in the early Church was a sign of the messianic banquet to come in the kingdom. The dedication of the first Christians to personal prayer was equally important in helping them to keep their balance between the pressures of the world around them and their commitment to the faith.

The second reading of the liturgy from first Peter (read on all Sundays in the "A" cycle) is in the nature of instructions to the newly baptized, about the new birth they received and how they should hold to that faith despite trials and suffering, for sufferings help faith mature.

The gospel reading is the account of the revelation of the risen Jesus to Thomas, and the confession of Thomas that the Lord is indeed risen. The gospel passage shows that faith does not come because one has seen, but rather because one has heard the word of the Lord and trusts in that revelation. Thomas is an example of those who believed in Jesus before the resurrection, but who awoke to a new and more mature faith in the resurrected Lord. We ourselves need to make our acts of faith repeatedly because faith is dynamic, not static. The profession of faith is not easily made, especially when we are faced with suffering and difficulty. (This gospel text is read on this Sunday in the "B" and "C" cycles as well.)

For the introduction to the liturgy, the rite of blessing with holy water would be appropriate because of obvious Easter associations. Of the sample sets of invocations, number 6 containing much Johannine language would be suitable.

The opening prayer of the liturgy refers to the baptismal setting of first Peter where sin is washed away and we receive new birth in the Spirit. The alternative opening prayer speaks more specifically of the risen life we share in Christ, and tells us that we should look for his presence among the living, not the dead.

The prayer over the gifts speaks of baptism as a new creation. The prayer after communion refers to the "Easter sacraments," that is, to baptism and the eucharist, the means by which we communicate with the risen Christ. The preface of the day is the first of the Easter season, and the solemn blessing for the Easter season would be an appropriate conclusion to the liturgy.

THIRD SUNDAY OF EASTER

Since the approval and promulgation of the Constitution on the Sacred Liturgy, there has been a major shift in liturgical piety. The new orientation is away from emphasizing the validity of a sacrament and rubrical perfection in the "performance" of a sacrament, to one that is concerned with an experience of the risen Lord through the community's celebration of thanksgiving and praise of the Father. The gospel story related on this third Sunday of Easter presents a moving portrayal of how two of Jesus' disciples experienced the risen Lord on the road to Emmaus. This pericope is so important for the development of the Easter season that it is now read at the Sunday eucharist, whereas formerly it was used on the Monday after Easter Sunday. While a basic theme of the readings of Easter is water and baptism, the theme of this gospel is the eucharist as the sacrament which continues and deepens what was pledged at the font of baptism. The very style of the gospel story shows that it is a special resurrection appearance story, for the references to their hearts burning when the Lord explained the word and their recognizing him at the breaking of the bread indicate that the author refers here to the experience of Christ as the eucharist. Christ's interpretation of the scriptures led the apostles not so much to intellectual assent; rather it caused their hearts to burn with hope and enthusiasm. The risen Christ was revealed to these two men in the breaking of the bread; today as we listen to the scripture readings and the homily, our hearts are opened to Christ, who will accept our gifts of bread and wine and make them into his body and blood for our nourishment.

Today's first reading consists of Peter's speech about the meaning of Christ's suffering, death, and resurrection. The second reading is a continuation of the first letter of Peter; the believer who has been delivered from sin at baptism is required to live in a totally new way. The image of the blood of the Lamb provides an important link between baptism and the eucharist. The readings speak of the coming of the full reign of Christ in which believers will continually share because they have already shared in the blood of the Lamb of God at the eucharist.

The prayers of the liturgy in the Sacramentary have clear eucharistic associations. But they speak not merely of remembering the past sacrifice of Jesus; they speak as well of the coming of the full reign of God at the end of time. The alternative opening prayer is the better option because it speaks of the word of God and asks that we who witness to the resurrection of Jesus may rise from the realm of death with him in a like resurrection.

The prayer over the gifts notes the eschatological nature of the eucharist by speaking of the perfect joy to be shared in heaven.

Any of the Easter prefaces may be used, but the third is most appropriate because it speaks of the Lamb of God, and of Christ as victim, priest, and advocate interceding on our behalf.

The blessing provided in the Sacramentary is one of the prayers over the people, yet it could be replaced by the solemn blessing of the Easter season.

FOURTH SUNDAY OF EASTER

"Good Shepherd Sunday" was formerly celebrated on the second Sunday after Easter (the Sunday following Low Sunday). In the revised Lectionary and Sacramentary, this image of Jesus is the basis for reflection on this fourth Sunday of Easter instead. In all three Sunday cycles of readings, parts of the Johannine discourse are read: year "A," John 10:1–10; year "B," John 10:11–18; year "C," John 10:27–30. The meaning of images such as Jesus as the sower and the shepherd are often difficult to explain to a society as modernized, sophisticated, and institutionalized as ours. Despite these difficulties, the Good Shepherd is among the most appealing of New Testament images for it presents Christ as actively searching out the lost, not to bring them to trial and cross-examination, but to return them to the fold.

The responsorial psalm introduces the shepherd theme with Psalm 23, and the second reading from first Peter ends with a reference to the shepherd as the guardian of the community. The first ten verses of the "good shepherd" chapter of John's gospel speak about Christ as the gate of the sheepfold, and as the keeper of the sheep. Salvation is offered only for those who call upon his name, for he is the only perfect sacrifice acceptable to the Father. As members of his flock, we gain salvation through him.

The prayers in the Sacramentary are replete with references to the readings of this Sunday since the shepherd theme is carried through all three cycles.

The opening prayer invokes Christ as the shepherd who leads us to the Father, and the phrasing is that of the gospel of John. The alternative opening prayer uses the language of the responsorial psalm. The selection of which prayer to use depends on the central focus of the liturgy.

The preface may be chosen from any of the Easter prefaces, but the second, with a reference to the "gates of heaven," or the third, with reference to Christ as the Lamb, priest, advocate, and victim, seem most appropriate.

The prayer after communion speaks of the eternal shepherd who feeds the flock of Christ with the eucharist as a foretaste of the bounty of the promised land in the kingdom.

The solemn blessing of the Easter season as printed in the text of this Sunday should be used. Number 6 of the prayers over the people would be a suitable alternative because it refers to the Lord's care for his people even when they stray.

FIFTH SUNDAY OF EASTER

The Second Vatican Council emphasized that sacraments are community celebrations, not just private enterprises between the minister and the person "on whom" a sacrament is conferred. The very structure of the initiation of adults into the Church envisions the active involvement of the community at the scrutinies on the

Sundays of Lent and their support at the ceremony of baptism. The celebration of the eucharist has been so revised that lectors, cantors, servers, ushers, artists, and musicians all have a proper and significant role to play in what was once regarded as the priest's preserve. The faith of the community and their calling as a priestly people requires their full participation in the liturgy.

One of the texts which presents this notion of the faithful's priesthood is the end of today's second reading. The part of the text, "chosen race, royal priesthood, holy nation, God's own people" needs careful examination because it is often overused. The connotation is that a chosen race is also a race of mutual service; a royal priesthood is also a community of humble servants; and God's own people set apart for the things of the Lord are at the same time a people who must live and work among people of all persuasions. It is precisely amid such diversity that Christians must show forth their faith. But the real key to all of these titles for the people of God is the concept of holiness. Being initiated into the community, the priesthood of the faithful, means that there must always be a constant and continual growth in holiness. God has acted out of his boundless love in making us part of his family, so we are to grow in holiness to share that love with others. This growth in holiness is not a clerical or "religious" preserve as the pericope from first Peter shows, for the sacred author is speaking to all the baptized.

The reading from the Acts of the Apostles is a difficult text for New Testament scholars because the exact "institution" of the diaconate and the real exercise of that ministry in the early Church is disputed. Whether or not seven men were set aside for the temporal affairs is hard to substantiate. It is clear, however, that charitable concerns are not foreign to the sacred community of believers and that there must be an obvious connection between the affairs of God and the affairs of men. This service theme is carried through in first Peter, where baptism means joining a community where the concerns of others become as real as one's own.

The gospel shows how we should check on our progress in sanctity. To what extent is a pious exercise or act of charity helping one grow in the way, truth, and life of the Lord? In one sense, we are all deacons, dedicated to works of charity, and yet we are all contemplatives, dedicated to growth in holiness and personal prayer.

Both texts of the opening prayer of the liturgy present a general theme for prayer rather than a specific reference to the readings of the day. The prayer over the gifts speaks of the exchange of gifts, a sort of transaction between the community and God whereby the bread and wine become the body and blood of Christ. The prayer also uses the Johannine terminology of the gospel to speak of the Lord's truth. The Sacramentary recommends that Easter preface 5 be used this Sunday. However, the first preface for Sundays in Ordinary Time could be used because it refers to the royal priesthood of the faithful. The prayer after communion is related to the prayer over the gifts and to the gospel, for it speaks of new life in Christ because of the reception of the eucharist.

The suggested blessing of the day is taken from the prayers over the people; it could fittingly be replaced by the solemn blessing of the Easter season (no. 7).

SIXTH SUNDAY OF EASTER

The time between the solemnity of the Ascension and the Vigil of Pentecost is a time of preparation and expectation for the coming of the Holy Spirit (General Instruction of the Roman Missal, no. 26). The coming of the Paraclete is emphasized in today's first reading and gospel which speak of the "Holy Spirit," "another Paraclete," and the "Spirit of truth."

In the first reading, from the Acts of the Apostles, Peter and John are sent from Jerusalem to Samaria to be ministers of the coming of the Spirit to the new converts in that town. These people had already been baptized in the name of the Lord Jesus, and the imposition of the apostles' hands completes the initiation of these converts. It would be an anachronism, however, to equate the coming of the Spirit and the laying on of hands in this instance with the present sacrament of confirmation. St. Luke's concern is to emphasize the work of the Spirit in convert-making and in personal conversion rather than to distinguish moments and times of what have come to be two sacraments of initiation in the later Church. According to Luke, the Spirit is the source of vitality for the believing Church after the resurrection of Jesus, and the work of the Spirit is the cause of the missionary expansion of Christianity; the time of the Church is the age of the Spirit.

The reading from first Peter indicates that the destiny of all believers is to live in the realm of the Spirit. In the gospel of John, the Paraclete is the promised Counselor and Advocate whose power enlivens the community of believers. Jesus leaves the Church, but a new appearance and manifestation of the power of God will take place. The link between the three readings is that the Paraclete is soon to come to strengthen us in our profession of the faith.

The prayers from the Sacramentary do not reflect the specific theme of the readings but are of a general nature and have an Easter theme. The eucharist is an Easter sacrament according to the prayer after communion, and is the means of our being forgiven and worthy of the "sacrament of love" (prayer over the gifts).

The alternative opening prayer speaks of our resurrection through the power of Jesus, a theme which also occurs in the second preface for the Easter season, which may be chosen for proclamation. The solemn blessing of the Easter season is suggested in the Sacramentary. An alternative would be number 23 of the prayers over the people, which speaks of remaining in the Lord's love and close to him in prayer.

SEVENTH SUNDAY OF EASTER

Since the octave of Pentecost is no longer observed, and the calendar no longer refers to "Sundays after Pentecost," this Sunday should appropriately emphasize the coming of the Spirit, and the watchfulness and prayer which marked the days prior to the first Pentecost.

The first reading from the Acts of the Apostles describes our own situation as well as the situation of the early community. This group first gathered in the upper room for the Last Supper with Jesus and they now gather together again to await the gift of his Holy Spirit. The same is true of the present Church, for we gather at the eucharist to proclaim the death of the Lord and we celebrate this Sunday in particular to await the coming of the Paraclete. In the view of the author of the Lukan gospel and Acts, the city of Jerusalem, the site of the upper room, has a theological significance that transcends its importance as the cultural center of Judaism. In the Gospel, Jesus is portrayed as making his way to this city to suffer and die, and in the Acts it is from this city that the apostles are sent forth to bring the gospel to the ends of the earth. Most particularly, the community spends time in prayer while awaiting the coming of the Spirit.

The reading from first Peter reiterates that suffering for the faith is part of the life of a believer. Just as Holy Week cannot be fully understood without constant attention to the event of Easter, so the glory and joy of the Easter season cannot be appreciated fully without adverting to the fact that the follower of Jesus must walk in trial and suffering as well.

The unity of suffering and glorification is a major theme of the gospel of John from which today's gospel reading is taken. This part of the gospel has been aptly described as the "last will and testament" of Jesus (E. Käsemann). The "hour" of Jesus had finally come—the hour of triumph, glory, and the exaltation of Jesus. It is in this light that the Johannine gospel views the death of Jesus. At Cana, Jesus protested that his hour had not yet come; now it is upon him, that through the cross he may call all people to his Father. Jesus prays for those whom the Father has given him, that while still in the world, they may not become part of the world. The trial for the believer is to remain faithful to the word of God while still living among nonbelievers. The unifying theme of all the readings is a prayerful expectancy of the coming of the Spirit who will keep believers faithful to the word of God, despite suffering and trial.

The prayers of the Sacramentary coincide with the gospel theme of glory. In the opening prayer the eucharist is the setting of a present sharing in the glory of Christ; in the prayer over the gifts the eucharist is a foretaste of the eternal glory of the kingdom; and in the prayer after communion the glory of the risen Christ is given to the Church to share at the sacrament of the Lord's body and blood.

The second preface for the Ascension could be used since it locates the celebration between the ascension of Christ and the coming of the Spirit; or the solemn blessing for Ascension (no. 8) could be used in place of a prayer over the people. (If this solemn blessing is used, the words of the first invocation "this day when . . ." might be adjusted to "this time of the Ascension.")

SUNDAYS OF EASTER "B" CYCLE

SECOND SUNDAY OF EASTER

During the "B" cycle, the Sunday readings are as follows: the first reading is from the Acts of the Apostles, and the gospel pericopes are from John (except on the third Sunday of Easter when the gospel is from Luke 24, and the second reading is from the first epistle of John.

The first reading of this Sunday is one of the familiar summaries of the activity and life of the early Christian community. This text from Acts emphasizes the sharing of goods among the members of this ideal Christian Church. The purpose of the author is not to present a blueprint for the activity of the Church in succeeding generations; it is to focus our attention upon the community's constant concern for the poor, a major characteristic of the early Church.

The second reading from first John speaks of the belief and love of those who were begotten by God to become his children. One of the obligations of members of the community is to continue to grow in their affirmation of faith, especially as they face an unbelieving world. The message of this epistle is clear—faith is the only power that conquered or will conquer the "world" and its evil.

The gospel of John, about the evening of the first day of the week and the appearance of Jesus to the disciples and to Thomas, is read on this Sunday in all three cycles of the Lectionary. The reading points out the need to believe in the risen Lord. It was not sufficient that the disciples should have known the earthly Jesus and respected him as their teacher. What was at stake was their acceptance of him as their risen and exalted Lord.

The incident of doubting Thomas still challenges the Church as a community of faithful Christian believers living in an unbelieving world. It is up to Christians to make their faith in the unseen Lord become visible in their love and service to others. The risen Jesus appeared to the disciples; he comes to the community gathered at the eucharist this Sunday through his Word and through the sharing of the eucharistic meal. With the disciples we may ask ourselves: How shall we receive him? How will we allow our lives to be affected by communion with him?

The issue that faced the infant Church is the same that faces us today, to profess and speak our faith amid a world that seeks wisdom other than God's, a world that propagates falsehood while the Christian seeks for Truth Incarnate, that prefers darkness rather than the light of Christ, that tries to remain aloof from the suffering of the poor and oppressed.

The rite of blessing and sprinkling with holy water would be the most appropriate introductory rite to use throughout the Easter season because of the emphasis on baptism and eucharist as Easter sacraments. The third of the prayers of blessing may be used during this season because it emphasizes the rich heritage of the symbolism surrounding water: the Red Sea as an event of salvation, Jesus' baptism by John in the waters of the Jordan, and our sharing now in holiness by use of water. (It is interesting to note that while the above rites understand the symbol of water in a positive way, the alternative opening prayer offers another aspect of water, its destructiveness. Here water is symbolic of death—the death we undergo with Christ, and from which he raises us by his power.) The opening prayer is oriented toward baptism and uses the imagery of the Spirit, water, and blood of the second reading from first John, while the alternative form speaks of our sharing now in the new life of God's people.

The model for the general intercessions during the Easter season may help in the composition of today's prayer as it speaks of Christ's rising from the dead, our belief in him, and our sharing in the joy of the resurrection. The prayer over the gifts speaks of the theme of the Easter faith and baptism, and of the offerings at the altar for the eucharist.

The first preface of Easter is to be used on this Sunday, and if the presider proclaims the Roman Canon, he should use the proper commemoration and invocation of the Easter season.

The prayer after communion is particularly appropriate for this season as it speaks about our sharing in the Easter sacraments.

The solemn blessing for the Easter season may well be used this Sunday, for it is a most appropriate conclusion to the eucharist. Other appropriate selections would be number 5 of the prayers over the people, about strengthening the community to remain faithful to the Lord, and number 24, about the children who put their trust in the Father (in accord with the important theme of God's children in the first letter of John).

On this Sunday the gospel reading is Luke 24:35–48, about the appearance of the risen Jesus in Jerusalem. It is the one exception to the use of the gospel of John for the Easter season. The first reading this Sunday is from the Acts of the Apostles and is part of Peter's speech in the temple, in which he summarizes the kerygma of the glorification of the servant Jesus, the death of the author of life (or better, the one who leads to all life), and the necessary suffering of the Messiah. It is important to realize that the speech is a device used by the Lukan author of Acts to convey his own ideas, and it is not necessarily a verbatim report of a discourse of Peter himself. (A case in point would be Paul's speech on the Areopagus in Acts 17:23–31 and his opening remarks in his letter to the Romans, 1:18–23. In the former, Paul speaks of man as capable of a knowledge of God through the use of his reason; yet in the latter, natural reason leads not to a knowledge of God but to an awareness of man's inability to be saved except through the revelation of God. Hence, the theology of the author of Acts is placed in the mouth of Paul in the Areopagus, whereas the authentic Pauline teaching is enshrined in Romans.)

The Lukan Christology implied in the passage from Acts is amplified in the second reading from the first letter of John containing references to Christ as an offering for our sins. The meaning of the paschal mystery can be illuminated by the homilist's making a positive statement about Jesus' enduring the cross and being raised for our salvation. Such an approach would be helpful for a community whose piety may have overly stressed Christ's passion at the expense of emphasis on the resurrection.

A liturgy in line with the eucharistic aspects of this season can stress the second reading and the gospel, where the intercession of Jesus on our behalf forms the basis for the forgiveness of sins at the eucharist. The gospel pericope about Jesus' eating of fish has unmistakable eucharistic overtones. Because "B" cycle for the season of Lent has emphasized the Christ's passion, it is likely that the community would be better served by emphasizing the eucharistic import of today's readings.

The rite of blessing and sprinkling with holy water is an appropriate introductory rite this Sunday because of the eucharistic theme of the Easter season and because baptism is seen as our incorporation into the eucharistic community. Should the presider prefer to use the third penitential rite (c), number 6 of the sample invocations of Christ, speaking of him as the one who raises us to new life, who forgives sins, and who feeds the Church with his body and blood, would be most appropriate this Sunday.

Both opening prayers speak of sharing in the glory of the resurrection. The planning committee may wish to begin including in the general intercessions those who will be confirmed or have received the eucharist for the first time during this Easter season. On this Sunday with its eucharistic theme, a petition could also be added for the sick or elderly who are not present for the eucharist this Sunday, but who will receive the eucharist during the coming week.

The preface for this Sunday may be chosen from among those of the Easter season: the second, about Christ's death as our ransom from death, and his resurrection as our rising to life; the third, about Christ's intercession as the Lamb once slain who lives forever; and the fifth, about Christ as the priest, the altar, and the lamb of sacrifice, are all appropriate to the eucharistic emphasis of the day.

Should the presider proclaim the Roman Canon, he should be aware that the Sacramentary allows the proper commemoration of Easter to be used only on the second Sunday of Easter.

The sign of peace this Sunday could reflect the communion among the members of the community as well as with the Lord in the eucharist.

The prayer after communion is most appropriate as it speaks of sharing in the Easter mysteries at the eucharist.

The solemn blessing of the Easter season is a good conclusion to the liturgy for all the Sundays of Easter, yet of the prayers over the people, number 3, about having received heavenly gifts, and number 18, about people desiring to relive the mystery of the eucharist would also be appropriate selections.

FOURTH SUNDAY OF EASTER

In all three cycles of the revised Lectionary, the gospel text on this Sunday is taken from parts of chapter 10 of the gospel of John concerning Christ as the Good Shepherd. The text read on this

Sunday in cycle "B" was formerly used on the second Sunday after Easter, along with an epistle reading from the first letter of Peter also referring to the shepherd. With the new Lectionary readings and prayers of the Sacramentary, this fourth Sunday of Easter may now be considered "Good Shepherd Sunday." The Johannine author of this Sunday's gospel speaks of Jesus as the shepherd who "knows" his flock and who gives them "life." Jesus calls himself "good," which also means that he is the true and perfect shepherd. He shows the depth of his love for his flock by laying down his life so that through him they may come to "know" the Father and share in Jesus' Sonship.

The first reading from the Acts of the Apostles concerns a miracle worked in the name of Jesus who, as the rejected stone, is the cornerstone who heals those who call upon him. The second reading from first John continues the relationship theme of the gospel by speaking of the Father's love bestowed on his children through the Son. The key to the theology of these readings is the image of the Shepherd. This image relationship is reflected in the first letter of John, where the flock of the shepherd mentioned in the gospel is seen as the children of God. It would be far better to stress the idea of "children" rather than that of "sheep," for the former image implies the possibility for growth in knowledge and wisdom on the part of the community—hardly a conspicuous characteristic of sheep.

The image of the Good Shepherd in today's liturgy is the dynamic latent in the first reading from Acts, where a man was cured by the power of the name of Jesus. The idea of healing and strengthening the community through the celebrations of the sacraments in the name of Jesus has received much emphasis in recent years. Obvious examples include penance as healing those broken in spirit and weighed down by their sin; the eucharist as a sacrament of healing and strengthening; the anointing of the sick as healing and protection of the ill, elderly, and infirm. It is of the nature of liturgy that we gather "in the name" of the Trinity at the eucharist; we call upon the name of Jesus at the conclusion of many of the prayers of the liturgy; at baptism we give the child a name which will signify his Christian identity as well as family heritage. All of this could be treated in terms of the Good

Shepherd and his people, his flock, and the Father and his children.

The rite of blessing and sprinkling with holy water is the most appropriate introductory rite in the Easter season, and a reworded introduction about our worship in the name of the Lord could be a helpful introduction to the readings of the day. Should the presider wish to use the third penitential rite as the introduction, he could use the seventh set of invocations suggested in the Sacramentary, written in typical Johannine style, about Christ as our way to the Father, as giving us the consolation of truth, and as the Good Shepherd who leads men to everlasting life. Both prayers contain specific reference to the shepherd theme of the day; the opening prayer states that Christ is our Shepherd; the alternative opening prayer uses the imagery of Psalm 23 as well as that of today's gospel, about people hearing the shepherd's call even though they walk in the valley of darkness.

The general intercessions suggested for the Easter season could be appropriately adapted, especially since the first petition mentions the Good Shepherd.

The prayer over the gifts speaks of the Easter mysteries celebrated at the eucharist, and the prayer after communion speaks of the Lord watching over the flock of the redeemed and leading them to the promised land.

Of the Easter prefaces the second, about "life" and "light," and the fifth, about the Advocate always pleading our cause, are both written with Johannine terminology in mind and are appropriate selections for this Sunday.

The solemn blessing for the Easter season is the most suitable conclusion to the eucharist, yet of the prayers over the people, number 6, about caring for the community even when they stray, and number 24, about the Father protecting his children, are appropriate selections as well.

FIFTH SUNDAY OF EASTER

Beginning today, the Sunday liturgies rise to a climax on the feast of Pentecost. For example, the readings for this Sunday speak of the Church throughout Judea, Galilee, and Samaria being at peace and enjoying the increased consolation of the Holy Spirit.

This is the same Spirit mentioned at the conclusion of the second reading, who incorporates the community into the Father as the branches are incorporated into the vine, a symbolism which is stressed in the gospel for this day. On the sixth Sunday of Easter, we will recall that the Spirit is poured out on the Gentiles as well as on the circumcised; on the solemnity of the Ascension, the promise of the Spirit to the infant Church is proclaimed in the first reading. On the seventh Sunday of Easter, the reading from first John and the gospel text, where Jesus promises to send the Paraclete, declare that the Spirit is the means of remaining in God. Whether the parish has undertaken a special preparation for Pentecost or not, at least these Sundays could be used to emphasize the role of the Spirit in the life of the Church, especially since there is no special time after the feast itself to dwell on the Spirit in any systematic way. This would also be an appropriate time to use the readings of the Pentecost Vigil to emphasize the various aspects of the ever-mysterious Spirit for study groups, parish meetings, or for the parents whose children are preparing for the sacrament of confirmation. With the development of the charismatic movement in the Catholic Church, these texts would seem to generate more than passing interest in most parishes.

Two themes having to do with the Spirit's role in our lives could be developed on this Sunday. The first theme concerns the dependence of Paul as well as the early Church upon the apostles for the word they preach. Paul enjoys fellowship with the other apostles and is dependent on them for many elements of the tradition which are to be handed on in his ministry. The whole problem of what it means to be a member of a traditional community like the Church, bound by the scriptural tradition about Jesus and bound by the historical development and adaptation of that tradition throughout its history, is an important one for the Church to face in our day. Hence, emphasizing the Acts reading about tradition and carrying on the heritage of the apostles would be a helpful selection.

The other theme, from the second reading and gospel, is that of God's in-dwelling in the community and the challenge which the community faces if it is to share that new life. Today's gospel reading (John 15:1–8) will be continued next Sunday (15:9–17); the present portion is more of an evaluation and encouragement to self-questioning than the pericope which will follow. Today's gospel is closely allied to the theme of the second reading about keeping in perspective both elements of the Christian—our acts of love for others and the love that God has for us. The gift of the in-dwelling of God in his people and their total dependence on this gift requires that the community reflect on its obligation prior to celebrating the Spirit's coming. These themes are profoundly ecclesiological; the first concerns the implications of tradition for the Church today, and the other concerns the solidarity of God with his people, and his people with each other as a result of the gift of his Spirit.

The rite of blessing and sprinkling with holy water would be an appropriate introduction to the liturgy, especially if the committee undertakes to rewrite the introduction to the rite in terms of these coming weeks as a preparation for the solemnity of Pentecost. The presider may use the third penitential rite, however, because the invocations in example number 6—about our being raised to new life, our sins being forgiven, and being fed with the body and blood of Christ at the eucharist—are in accord with the themes of the day.

The opening prayer asks that the Lord look with love on his people, reflecting the theme of in-dwelling, and the alternative opening prayer speaks of the God of all nations and all ages, coincident with the theme from the Acts of the Apostles.

Preface 2 of the Easter season contains the Johannine imagery of "children of light" and "life" and so coincides with the gospel and the second reading (1 John 3:18–24); the third preface refers more directly to the paschal sacrifice of Christ and speaks of the Advocate who pleads our cause before the Father.

The rite of peace could be stressed by rewording its introduction in the light of our sharing with each other because we share in the in-dwelling of the same love of God, through Christ the vine, in the power of the Holy Spirit.

The solemn blessing for the Easter season would be the most appropriate conclusion to the liturgy, and yet of the prayers over the people, number 5, about the community remaining faithful to their Lord, and number 7, about his shedding light on the community so they may continue doing good, would also be appropriate alternate forms of blessing.

SIXTH SUNDAY OF EASTER

Those who have been accustomed to think of baptism as the sacrament of initiation, with eucharist and confirmation as completely separate from it, may be confused by today's first reading. In this account of the baptism of the members of Cornelius' household, it was while Peter was speaking, and before water baptism took place, that the Spirit came upon the people. What the author of Acts is stressing here is the fact of the activity of the Spirit in conversion and the necessity of water baptism through the Church, for to him water baptism and the Spirit are inseparable. It is not necessary to go further into the matter.

The second reading presents an alternative theme to that of the activity of the Spirit in Acts, by speaking of the love we should have for one another based on the firm foundation that God has loved us, and continues to love us first. We come to know his love through his Son, who was an offering for our sins. Hence, the fact that God is love is evident from the actions of the Son and the redemption won for us by his death and resurrection.

Jesus' love is made explicit in the gospel text, which declares that there is no greater love than that of laying down one's life for one's friends. Our service to others is based on Jesus' ultimate act of self-giving on the cross. We have been called through him to share new life, joy, and friendship with the Father.

Both themes of this day's liturgy could be understood as remedial education to counteract some contemporary misunderstandings. For the first, the presence of the Spirit even before baptism can help correct the assumption that confirmation is *the* sacrament of the Spirit. Also, the various ways the Spirit acts within the "institutional" Church in the book of Acts helps us to realize the freedom with which the third person of the Trinity still acts in today's Church.

The rite of blessing and sprinkling with holy water is the most appropriate introductory rite because it recalls the sacrament of baptism as the first coming of the Spirit to us, and as our initiation into the community of those loved by God. The eucharist can then be seen as both a continuance and renewal of that love as God's gift to us. Should the presider choose the third penitential rite, invocations about Jesus, his life and love incarnate, and his death for our salvation would be suitable.

The opening prayer speaks of the joy of the resurrection of the Lord and of our lives of love in response to this joy, while the alternative opening prayer seems less preferable since its theme is the suffering Jesus endured so that we might share in his joy in eternity.

The prayer over the gifts continues the theme of the gospel and second reading by speaking about the sacraments of the love of God.

Each of the Easter prefaces speaks of our joy because of the Easter season, yet number 2, about the children of light sharing everlasting life, would be most appropriate to coincide with the Johannine imagery of the gospel and second reading.

The sign of peace could also be emphasized this Sunday because of the acts of love we are to show for others.

The prayer after communion speaks of the eucharist as an Easter sacrament, a fitting conclusion to the celebration of the renewal of our baptism into the death and risen life of the Lord.

The solemn blessing of the Easter season would be a most appropriate choice for the conclusion of Mass, as would number 2 of the prayers over the people, about perfect love for each other; number 8, with the prayer that the Lord keep us in his love; and number 15, about avoiding what is displeasing to the Lord and serving him with joy.

SEVENTH SUNDAY OF EASTER

Since this Sunday is between the solemnity of the Ascension and Pentecost, its planning and celebration should reflect the intention of the reformers of the liturgical calendar that this day, along with the weekdays between these two feasts, be a time of reflection, prayer, and expectation for the sending of the Spirit on Pentecost.

The later chapters of the book of Acts are read on the weekdays during this time as are the sixteenth and seventeenth chapters of the gospel of John containing the discourse of Jesus at the Last Supper, his farewell, and high priestly prayer. These chapters especially could be utilized in a series of daily homilies or special services since they recall the themes of Christian mission in the world and the prayer of Jesus for his followers, who are to continue to carry his message to the world.

The first reading from Acts is from the beginning of the book, and while it interrupts the progression of the continuous reading, the incident recounted, according to the chronology of John, took place between the Ascension and Pentecost. What is far more important than chronology, however, is the theological import of the text. The selection of Matthias as one of the Twelve shows that membership in the Twelve required association with the Lord from his baptism to his ascension. For the author, to be an apostle was to be more concerned with missionary activity, while to be one of the Twelve meant to be a bearer of the authentic tradition of the Church, having first learned it from the Lord. The author's concern here is not only the community for whom he wrote originally. He is also speaking to the members of the Church in succeeding generations: they, like the first community, would have to be faithful to their Lord and to the authenticated tradition about him handed down from the earliest eyewitnesses. The first theme of today's liturgy then, can be the fidelity of the Church in our day to the traditions it has received from the Lord, all the while recognizing that revisions in Church practice are necessary at times because of changing circumstances and the promptings of the Spirit of God. This familiar theme of the book of Acts could be the basis for reflection on how to discern the Spirit's presence in various movements in the Church.

A second theme of the liturgy could be drawn from the second reading and the gospel, in both of which recur the Johannine theme of how we show God's love by the way we love one another. The gospel speaks of mission as well as of witnessing in our lives to the presence of God. This means that a person involved in mission work in the world must also draw ever nearer to the Word through prayer and personal holiness.

Today's gospel recounts that Jesus spoke of consecrating himself "for their sakes . . ."; he is to be understood as saying that he is the new and true sacrificial victim who takes the place of the victim which was offered in the Old Law as a sign of the community's contact with the sacred. Through union with the "consecration" of Jesus in his sacrifice, Christians come into such intimate contact with the sacred that all actually share in God's own life. This is what sanctification means.

The rite of blessing and sprinkling with holy water would be a most fitting introduction to the liturgy of this day, especially so if the introduction were reworded to pray for the invocation of the Spirit on the water and on the community.

The invocations of the third penitential rite could be adapted to express the terminology of the Johannine gospel by referring to Jesus as our way to the Father, as the one who gives us the consolation of the truth, and who intercedes for us at the right hand of the Father. The opening prayer speaks of remaining faithful to the Lord until the end of time, whereas the alternative opening prayer speaks very poetically of God's plan of salvation, the center of which is the consecration of Jesus in the gospel reading.

The general intercessions should refer to the community's preparation for the coming celebration of Pentecost and to those preparing for initiation or confirmation on Pentecost.

Both the prayer over the gifts and the prayer after communion use the Johannine terminology of the glory of God now shared in his Body, the Church.

The preface for this day may be chosen from the two provided for the Ascension; the first places the liturgy of this Sunday in the ambience of the ascension, and the second links the resurrection with the event of the ascension.

The solemn blessing for Ascension would be the most appropriate conclusion to the liturgy, but the words of the first invocation should be adjusted to refer to "this time of ascension" rather than to the day itself.

SUNDAYS OF EASTER "C" CYCLE

SECOND SUNDAY OF EASTER

The gospel proclaimed on this Sunday is the same for all three cycles of the Lectionary and recounts the appearances of Jesus to the disciples on the evening of the resurrection and during the following week. The text contains stylistic traits most characteristic of the Johannine writer, such as Christ's greeting of "Peace," the note of the unity of the Father and the Son, and the assurance of sharing in the power of the Holy Spirit. Yet, the central character in the story is certainly Thomas and his profession of faith in the Christ. The words of Jesus indicate that indeed "seeing" does not guarantee "believing," and in fact, many who have never "seen" now "believe." Taking this a step further in the light of Johannine theology, we must understand that the "signs" which Jesus worked and the miracles which he performed do not automatically force anyone to accept Christ as savior. What happened in the earthly ministry of Jesus, his working of signs and wonders, is but a help toward or prelude to faith, which after all, is a gift from God in the light of which we share the new life of the risen Jesus.

The season of Easter is a time for probing more concretely into what "Easter faith" means. While the former apologetic stressed what was reasonable and demonstrable about faith, more recent approaches stress faith, not as a personal possession, but rather as an orientation to the Lord, made possible through incorporation into the Christian community.

The reading from the Acts of the Apostles about the characteristics of the primitive Christian community is an important supplement to the gospel of John, for the individualism often drawn from John is balanced and complemented here by reference to the communal dimension of faith and life in Christ. While Luke's descriptions of the Church are often overlaid with editorial complimentary statements, the point of such texts is to recall to the present Church its need to grow as a community in the peace of Christ.

The text from Revelation (read on all the Sundays of the "C" cycle) contains many significant elements characteristic of this scriptural book, but it particularly emphasizes that Christ, the one who is first and last and who now lives with his people, is the source and center of the present Church. The vision of the risen Christ is the vision which characterizes the Christian Church and therefore, the individual believer. That vision is meant to be sustained and nourished by our present experience of eucharist, *the* sacrament of the Easter season. Indeed, blessed are they who have not seen, but believe (gospel acclamation), and more blessed are they who once came to belief (gospel acclamation) and who now seek to grow in that belief in this season of the Lord's resurrection.

The rite of blessing and sprinkling with holy water is the

appropriate introduction to the liturgy on this and all the Sundays of Easter because of the baptismal nature of Easter. Should the presider opt for the third form of the penitential rite, the sixth set of sample invocations, about the Lord raising us to new life in him, our being forgiven our sins, and Christ feeding his people with his body and blood, is most appropriate to reflect the Easter season.

While both forms of the opening prayer speak of baptism as our means of sharing in the new life of Christ, the alternative opening prayer has a more complete and specific reference to growth in faith in the community, and is preferable should the presider wish to emphasize the communal nature and experience of faith.

The model for the general intercessions for the Easter season in the Sacramentary Appendix may help the planning committee in composing their own prayer by referring to pastors who serve the flock of the Church; and to the present community's need for faith and the strength necessary to witness to the resurrection.

The prayer over the gifts cites the Church as the people who share now in a new creation in Christ; the prayer after communion asks that the Easter sacraments live forever in the community (to continue its common vision of the risen Lord).

The first preface of Easter is prescribed for proclamation on this Sunday since this day ends the octave of Easter, and since the prayer speaks directly of the paschal mystery of Christ. Should the Roman Canon be selected as the anaphora this Sunday, the presider should include the proper commemoration of Easter.

For the memorial acclamation, form "B" would be an appropriate choice as it coincides with the text of the preface.

The introduction to the sign of peace this Sunday could be reworded to reiterate the greeting of Christ in the gospel of the day.

The solemn blessing for the Easter season is provided in the Mass formula as the conclusion to the liturgy, and is an appropriate selection for the whole Easter season.

Should the presider wish to substitute one of the prayers over the people for solemn blessing he may find the following helpful: number 2, about always remaining faithful to the Lord; number 9, about the community of faith, that they may enjoy the gift of the Lord's love and share it with others; and number 17, about the

Lord looking on his people now with the same love he showed by suffering the agony of the cross.

THIRD SUNDAY OF EASTER

Unlike the gospel readings for the third Sunday of Easter in the "A" and "B" cycles, from parts of Luke 24, today's readings in the "C" cycle is from John 21:1–19 or 21:1–14.

This reading concerns another appearance of the risen Christ to the disciples, noted in the text as the third since the resurrection, and has many eucharistic overtones. The appearance of Jesus to the disciples while they were fishing, their acknowledgment that "It is the Lord," the use of bread and fish to feed them, and the invitation to eat the meal he prepared for them on the lake shore are significant elements in the story. Yet, the specific mention that Jesus "took" bread and "gave" it to the disciples is the most direct reference to the feeding of the community with his bread, now understood in the Church as his sacramental bread and cup at the eucharist.

The shorter pericope offers the planning committee ample material to draw from should they wish to elaborate on the eucharist as the Church's share in the life of the risen Christ, indeed a most appropriate theme for the Easter season.

The longer reading includes the section on the profession of love by Simon Peter and his deputation to a position of leadership in the early Church, with a warning that he would have to endure many trials as a result. The text from Acts concerns bearing witness to the "name" of Jesus, and the implications which this witnessing necessarily brings with it. Peter and the apostles answered their inquisitors by stating firmly their faith in Christ, and the lesson ends somewhat romantically with references to their joy at having been found worthy to endure trials for the name of Christ. The homilist has an opportunity to join the reading from Acts with the longer gospel reading and speak of the eucharist as the sacrament of growth in Christ, which gives the believer strength to continue in the Christian life.

The second reading from the book of Revelation contains rich imagery and significant themes about the person of the Lamb that was slain.

The eucharist is more than a present share in the risen life of Christ in a general way; it is seen as the strength and grace which the present Church, as the Church in every age, needs to endure persecution "for the name." While today's sufferings for the faith may be less than those which the early Christians experienced, there are subtle temptations all around us to make us conform to the standards of the world rather than to the demands of the gospel. To live a truly moral life, the Christian needs the strength that comes from faith in Christ and from sharing in the bread of his life and the cup of his eternal salvation.

The rite of blessing and sprinkling with holy water is the most appropriate introduction to the liturgy this Sunday as a reminder of the covenant of baptism in the life of the believer.

Should the presider wish to use the third form of the penitential rite, the sixth set of invocations provides the most suitable reflection of the themes of the liturgy of the word because it speaks of being raised to new life in Christ, of being forgiven our sins by the death and resurrection of Christ, and of our being strengthened at the eucharist with his body and blood.

It is preferable to use the alternative opening prayer if the theme of the day's liturgy concerns bearing witness to the Lord, since it speaks of the eucharist as our help and strength in that task. The prayer also expresses confidence in our Easter hope, and asks the Lord for strength to answer his call.

The general intercessions for the Easter season again provide a good model for the prayer of the faithful, especially because of the reference to the theology of this season and the inclusion of the petition about asking the Lord for faith and strength to bear witness to the resurrection.

The preface to be proclaimed this Sunday may be one from the second to the fifth options provided for the Easter season. The third speaks specifically about the paschal Lamb who was once slain and who now lives forever, and the fifth speaks of Christ as the priest, altar, and sacrifice of our salvation.

The solemn blessing for the Easter season is most appropriate for the conclusion to the liturgy, as is the modified form of number 11 of the prayers over the people provided in the Mass formula of the day. Other appropriate concluding blessings are number 18 of the prayers over the people, about the present community seeking to relive the mystery of the eucharist and lead a new life in Christ; and number 22, about receiving the Lord's strength to do his will.

FOURTH SUNDAY OF EASTER

Today's reading, John 10:27–30, with its image of Christ the Good Shepherd, is a welcome text to ponder. This chapter is used in all three cycles of the Lectionary on this Sunday and the gospel acclamation (Alleluia) for the three cycles captures the teaching of this text by speaking of the shepherd: "I know my sheep and mine know me." Jesus' knowledge of his sheep means his care for his people; he allows no one to snatch them out of his hand.

The gospel proclamation on this and the following Sunday, where Jesus is pictured as the Good Shepherd and the Son of Man, raises the question of Jesus' identity. As shepherd he explains his love for his sheep and his knowledge of who they are. As Son of Man who died and rose for their salvation, he now invites them to share his love with each other. Taking both these Sundays together, the liturgy might well emphasize these important images of the Risen Lord and also show how unity and love among the members of the Church is a response to the Lord's first loving them. Both readings speak of the implications of Christ's passover from death to life and how the present Church is to live the resurrected life he shares with it.

Today's reading from the book of Revelation coincides well with the theme of the shepherd, since those who are depicted as having survived a great trial and who have washed their robes white in the blood of the Lamb are also those who have the assurance of the Lord's love for them. Never more shall they hunger or thirst, for their shepherd will feed them and lead them to springs of living water; never again shall they mourn as those who have no hope, for he will wipe away every tear from their eyes.

It is especially in the light of this significant reading from Revelation that both this text and the gospel proclamation provide ample foundation for a liturgy whose theme explores the identity of the risen Lord.

The first reading from the Acts of the Apostles, if taken together with that of the following Sunday, gives an insight into the preaching of the early Church in the persons of Paul and Barnabas. The mission directed primarily to the Jews is now to be a mission to the Gentiles—a theme which the reading for next Sunday also explores. The preachers also warn that those who follow the Lord will necessarily have to endure trial and sufferings.

The rite of blessing and sprinkling with holy water would be the most appropriate introduction to the liturgy this Sunday, especially when the introduction is so worded as to include the fact that we who gather this Sunday share a common and comforting vision of the Lord in Christ the Good Shepherd.

Should the third form of the penitential rite be used, the seventh set of sample invocations contain typical Johannine terminology and imagery about Christ who shows the way to the Father, who gives us the consolation of the truth, and who is the Good Shepherd who leads his people to everlasting life.

The invitatories to both forms of the opening prayer speak of the Lord who leads his people through distress, and while the first form of the prayer is more succinct in style and form, the alternative opening prayer is more poetic and expanded with some parts taken from the imagery of Psalm 23.

The sample general intercessions of the Easter season underscore the theology of the season while mentioning specifically the Good Shepherd as the model for Christian pastors in their service of their people.

The preface to be used this Sunday may be chosen from the second to the fifth prefaces of the Easter season, and it would seem that the third, about Christ still being our advocate and pleading our cause before the Father, is most consonant with the Lectionary readings of the day.

The sign of peace could be suitably emphasized this Sunday because of the gospel implication that the unity of the Father and Son ought to be reflected in the life of the community as it is symbolized in the sacrament of the eucharist.

The prayer after communion continues the shepherd theme of the day in speaking of the eternal shepherd who redeemed the flock with his blood.

The solemn blessing of the Easter season is the most appropriate conclusion for the Sunday liturgies of this season, yet should the presider prefer to use one of the prayers over the people instead, number 1, about the Lord leading his people to everlasting life, and number 6, about the Father's care for his people even when they stray, are both appropriate choices.

FIFTH SUNDAY OF EASTER

The principle of the unity of a liturgical season has been a major principle of our interpretation of the Sundays of each cycle of readings. The gospel proclaimed on this Sunday in the season of Easter illustrates this principle since it speaks of the Son of Man being glorified, a glorification that was only possible because he accepted death on a cross so that men could draw their share in his risen life from that same cross of salvation. The seasons of Lent and Easter are more than logically juxtaposed; they are to be interpreted as mutually intertwined in theology and liturgical practice. Just as the gospel of the second Sunday of Lent was about the transfiguration as an earthly foretaste of the glory of the risen life of Christ, so this fifth Sunday of Easter, with the theme of the suffering and death of Christ, is intimately related to his resurrection. The Lenten Sunday saw the coming passion of Jesus in the light of his glory; today's reading does just the reverse. So, those who share now in his glory must follow his example in extending his love to all as required by his new commandment. The parallel between Christ and his followers is stated explicitly, for just as Christ loves his disciples, so they, in turn, are to show their love for one another.

The book of Revelation provides a different theme for the liturgy of this Sunday, and follows closely upon the vision described in last week's second reading. Here the vision is of the new and heavenly Jerusalem, the new place of God's dwelling among his people, and the assurance that everything is indeed new in Christ. Now a believer will no longer weep alone, as the Lord will wipe away every tear; there will be no more death, no more crying out or pain—all things are new in him and are found to be ever-new by those who share their life of faith in him. The text from Revelation is indeed a most comforting revelation of who this Christ is and of his eternal love for mankind.

The reading from the Acts of the Apostles continues the description of the preaching and missionary activity of Paul and Barnabas. For those who follow the reign of God as inaugurated in

Christ, these apostles can promise nothing for sure but trials and hardships. And yet, the paradox of suffering in the midst of joy in the Holy Spirit is here expressed as it was at the end of last week's reading from Acts.

This Sunday, the planning group could capitalize on the missionary dimension of Christianity by specifically stressing that missionary preaching and activity is a task to be shared by the community.

The theme of the liturgy, based on the gospel about the death and the risen life of Christ, could be shown as relevant to the second reading, about the newness of the life of grace shared in Christ, or with the first reading, about the missionary expansion of the early Church and the missionary demands that are placed on every Christian.

The rite of blessing and sprinkling with holy water would be the most appropriate introduction to this liturgy, especially if the introduction refers to our share in the death of Christ at our baptism and our continual share in his sacrifice in our daily lives.

Should the third form of the penitential rite be used, the fifth set of sample invocations, about raising the dead to life in the Spirit and bringing light to those in darkness, or the sixth set, about being raised to new life in Christ, being forgiven our sins, and being fed with Christ's body and blood at the eucharist, are appropriate selections.

The opening prayer, about our common vocation as children of God and serving him in true freedom, reiterates the invitation of the gospel to serve the Lord by serving each other in love.

The formula for the general intercessions during the Easter season is a helpful guide for the composition of this prayer this Sunday, especially because it speaks of Christ's rising from the dead and mentions prayer for those in sorrow—an element of the second reading from Revelation.

The preface to be proclaimed this Sunday may be taken from the second to the fifth of the prefaces for the Easter season; the fifth would seem to be most appropriate since it speaks of Christ's offering himself on the cross, by which act he gave himself for our salvation.

The solemn blessing for the season of Easter would be the most appropriate conclusion to this liturgy as it is throughout this season.

Number 17 of the prayers over the people asks the Lord to look with love upon his people, the same love which Christ showed as he delivered himself to death on a cross; this same love is the new commandment to be lived by the community of the Church as stated in the gospel of the day.

SIXTH SUNDAY OF EASTER

As has already been noted, we are now at a time in the Church's life when emphasis on the theology of the Holy Spirit has been revived in the Western tradition, and popular piety has come to reflect this emphasis as well. The calendar reform in the Roman rite eliminated the octave of Pentecost, however, the time when Church communities could capitalize on such popular devotion and emphasize the Spirit's role in our lives.

While the appropriateness of this action has been debated by many, the clear directions of the General Norms for the Liturgical Calendar about the preparation for the solemnity of Pentecost have often gone unnoticed. This document states that the weekdays from the solemnity of the Ascension to the Saturday before Pentecost are a preparation for the coming of the Holy Spirit (no. 26). While formerly emphasis was placed on the Pentecost octave after the feast, emphasis is now placed on preparing for the coming of the Spirit. It might be well for the planning committee to utilize the themes of the liturgies on this and the following Sunday as well as the solemnity of the Ascension, to encourage adequate preparation for and reflection on the commemoration of the sending of the Spirit to the Church at Pentecost.

While there are a number of themes that can be drawn from the liturgy on this sixth Sunday of Easter, that of the importance of the Spirit is certainly a major one among them. The gospel text from Jesus' farewell discourse to the disciples speaks of loving the Lord, keeping his word, and relying on the Paraclete still to come who will instruct and remind the Church of what Jesus taught. For John it is absolutely essential that Jesus leave them so that the Spirit, the Paraclete, the Advocate, might come and preserve them in the truth which Jesus came to teach. A major task of the Spirit is to preserve the Church in unity of faith, but the kind of unity that is based on fidelity to the word of God, and not necessarily a unity that requires rigorism in liturgical practice.

The reading from the Acts of the Apostles describes what has come to be called the "council of Jerusalem." The controversy at issue in the early Church concerned the observance of Mosaic Law by those Gentiles subject to the Law before their conversion. The resolution of the controversy is stated in terms of conscious reliance on the Spirit, as the beginning of this section of the text attests: "It is the decision of the Holy Spirit, and ours too, not to lay on you any burden beyond that which is strictly necessary. . . ." Hence, an obvious theme connected with these readings and which reflects as well the present experience of the Church is our common dependence on the Spirit in times when diversity of thought, perspective, and expression are the order of the day. A simplistic solution would be to demand absolute uniformity; the more evangelical solution is to persevere in the unity of the Spirit and in conformity to the Word spoken in Christ, again assured by the gift of the same Spirit.

An alternative theme of the liturgy would be to consider the new temple of the Lord as described in the second reading from the book of Revelation. Indeed, there is no longer any one holy city or holy place when compared to the holiness of the Lord and the holiness of his people. The new Jerusalem is not built by hands, nor on natural foundations of stone; the new people of God are founded on the Lord and the solid foundation of his love for man.

The rite of blessing and sprinkling with holy water would be an especially appropriate introduction to this Sunday's liturgy, with its theme of the coming of the Spirit. It is that same Spirit who brought us to the Lord for the first time at baptism, and it is that Spirit who keeps us in the unity and love of the Father.

Should the presider prefer to use the third form of the penitential rite, he may wish to substitute these or similar invocations: "Lord Jesus, you raise us to new life, you heal our divisions by the gift of your encompassing love, you keep us faithful to you by the gift of your Spirit."

Both opening prayers speak in a general way of the death and resurrection of Christ and provide a fitting context for the celebration of this Sunday in the Easter season.

The model of the general intercessions for the Easter season is helpful for these prayers throughout the season. On this Sunday, additional petitions about true Christian unity and about this time of the Church year as a preparation for the coming of the Spirit are most appropriate.

Of the Easter prefaces to be proclaimed this Sunday, the third, about Christ as our intercessor on whom we can always rely, would seem to be a most appropriate selection.

To emphasize the sign of peace this week would be in accord with the farewell of Christ to his followers, and its introduction could be so worded as to underscore the importance of the Spirit in ensuring our unity in Christ.

The solemn blessing for the Easter season is provided in the Mass formula for the conclusion of the liturgy; of the prayers over the people, numbers 2 and 23 both speak of our love for each other as a result of sharing in the eucharist.

SEVENTH SUNDAY OF EASTER

The words of the first preface for the season of Ascension declare that "the joy of the resurrection and ascension renews the whole world," and the placing of this Sunday just before Pentecost makes the obvious association of these events with the coming of the Spirit—a major theme for the liturgy this Sunday.

The gospel text is from the farewell discourse of Jesus to his disciples, in which he speaks of his unity with the Father and prays that this unity may be fulfilled in the community of his people. The reading also uses a significant word in Johannine theology—the "world." The unity of the Christian Church functions in the service of the "world" by its witnessing to the unity of Christ and the Father. Furthermore, the glory to be shared by the Church is a glory not only for the members of the community themselves, but for the sake of the "world."

Christ also speaks of his life living on in them, but again this life is not a quality to be kept as a special possession; it is a presence that is for the service of the wider "world" and always more extensive than personal salvation.

The first reading speaks of the Spirit specifically and shows that as Stephen witnesses to Christ, the Spirit is with him for courage and strength. Stephen here becomes a model for us; we are drawn to witness to the power of Christ's resurrection, and we rely, as the present Church must, on the Spirit. Whereas the Eastern Church has always emphasized the power and presence of the Spirit, it is only recently that the Western Church has put this notion thus prominently in the foreground. In some Eastern theology, the Spirit was so identified with the community of believers that the doxology of liturgical formulas often spoke of giving glory to the Father, in the Son, through the Spirit who lived with the Church.

One way the homilist could explore the Spirit theme of the liturgy as well as the theology of the whole season would be to emphasize that Pentecost is the end of a liturgical cycle and also the beginning of another. For just as the newly baptized must continue to grow in the fullness of Christ, so the already initiated need this annual season of Easter to ponder more deeply and profoundly the meaning of their baptism into Christ. Furthermore, the celebration of the Easter mysteries through these fifty days must not give the impression that Christians can so rely on the merits of Christ's death and resurrection that they need not renew and redouble their efforts of witnessing him in the world.

It is by the power of the Holy Spirit that the present Church prays, lives, and witnesses to the resurrection and ascension of Christ. And between his ascension and second coming, it is this same Spirit who keeps us in Christ as his witnesses in the world. This transitoriness of the present and a need to look to the future is most fully amplified and expanded in the second reading from the book of Revelation, the last part of which was often used in liturgical gatherings as the memorial of all that has been accomplished in Christ and all that is yet to be when he returns at the end of time.

The rite of blessing and sprinkling with holy water would be the most appropriate introduction to the liturgy this Sunday as the final celebration of the Easter season.

Should the presider prefer to use the third form of the penitential rite, invocations such as the following may be helpful: "Lord Jesus, you raise the dead to new life in the Spirit; Lord Jesus, you feed us with your body and blood until you come in glory."

Both forms of the opening prayer contain clear eschatological motifs; the opening prayer itself emphasizes more specifically the text from Revelation in the second reading, and the alternative opening prayer stresses the presence of the risen Christ who leads us to the vision of the Father's unlimited love.

The general intercessions this Sunday should help link the

liturgy of the Easter season with that of the solemnity of Pentecost, and should contain prayers about the fidelity of those initiated at Easter, the continued faithfulness of the whole Christian Church, and the presence of the Spirit to keep us united in the Father's love.

The proclamation or first preface for the Ascension would seem to be the more appropriate this Sunday because it speaks of the destiny of Christ as the destiny of the Christian Church, and unites the mysteries of the resurrection and ascension of Christ.

Should the presider use the Roman Canon this Sunday, the proper commemoration of the time of Ascension should be included.

The solemn blessing for Ascension would be the most appropriate conclusion to the liturgy this Sunday, with the proper adjustment made in the first part of the blessing about the time of the Ascension, not just the day of the feast itself.

Of the prayers over the people, number 1, about being led to everlasting life; number 2, about our love for each other and remaining faithful; as well as number 23, about remaining close to each other in prayer and true charity, are all appropriate choices as the conclusion to the liturgy.

SOLEMNITY OF ASCENSION

By the late fourth century, the Church came to celebrate a commemoration of the Lord's exaltation and commissioning of his followers to preach his gospel forty days after the feast of the resurrection. While some New Testament writers join the original event of the ascension with the resurrection itself, others, primarily the Lukan author, place it forty days after the event of Easter. It is this latter tradition which is reflected in today's readings. The first two readings are the same for all three years in the Lectionary. At the heart of the reading from Acts is the affirmation that when the Spirit comes on the disciples they will become Christ's witnesses to the end of the earth. In the reading from Ephesians, the author adverts to Christ's present exaltation at the right hand of the Father, and the mystery that both Jew and Greek share in the revelation of Christ. Here, the resurrection and ascension are understood to be one continuous act of the Father's love now shared by the Church, the Body of Christ.

In the "A" cycle, the gospel text is the conclusion of St. Matthew's Gospel and contains many important Matthean stylistic traits. The place from which the apostles are sent forth is a mountain, an important place of revelation throughout the Scriptures, from the giving of the Torah to Moses on Mt. Sinai, to the preaching of the beatitudes by Jesus at the sermon on the mount, to the missionary discourse in this reading. The apostles fall down in homage as a profession of faith in the risen Lord, but Matthew adds the note that some of these men also "doubted." This is not the first time the evangelist does this, for in the miracle of the stilling of the storm in Matthew 8:23–27 the apostles, the ones who should have had a firm faith and confidence in Jesus, are precisely the ones who lacked it. The lesson here is that the presence of doubts and fears will beset believers in every age just as they beset the apostles. Faith in any age has its insecurities and problems, but this fact should not paralyze the believer. The main point of the story is the commission and sending forth of the apostles. They are sent to make other disciples by their preaching and example. The spread of Christianity from a ghettoized Judaism is the theme of today's reading from the Acts. The command is to teach all that Jesus taught, and to baptize all people in his name. The support and strength the apostles will need for this task in the early Church is still needed for today's missionaries. This need is the presence of Emmanuel, "I am with you always," a promise made in the early chapters of Matthew, which declare that the Messiah will reign with us forever.

The gospel for the "B" cycle is taken from the ending of Mark's gospel, where Jesus commands the disciples to go into the whole world proclaiming the good news. They will do so empowered by the Lord Jesus who is now seated at God's right hand. The readings of this feast emphasize the sending forth of witnesses to continue the work of proclaiming Jesus' good news, and the exaltation and present intercession of the Lord at the Father's side. The celebration of the eucharist on this day is important, since it is in the liturgy that we participate in the love of the Lord interceding for us before the Father. Besides, we are also commissioned each time the celebration has ended to go forth and be witnesses of the gospel in which we believe.

In the "C" cycle, the first part of the Lukan text about Christ's leaving his apostles presents the kernel of the faith that is to be proclaimed; the second part speaks of the apostles' return to Jerusalem, the place from which the missionary activity of the Church goes forth. The plan of the author of Luke-Acts is to specify that the Church in his day is living in an age in which the Spirit is most active in ensuring fidelity to the gospel of Christ and to the love of God poured out in Christ. The assurance of the spirit's presence is an unfailing source of the vitality and confidence of the community.

The rite of blessing and sprinkling with water would be a most suitable introduction to the celebration of today's Mass provided it could be so worded as to reflect the connection between the celebration of sacraments and Christian mission.

The prayers of the liturgy in the Sacramentary indicate that our ascension to the Father is our destiny, just as Jesus' ascension was his destiny. The prayer after communion speaks of the divine life we share in the eucharist as a foretaste of the eternal life we shall share in the kingdom.

The prayer of the faithful should reflect the nature of this solemnity in its association with the whole of the Easter season, and should contain as well petitions about the community's preparations for the coming solemnity of Pentecost.

The preface for the day may be either of those for Ascension, where the first speaks of Christ as head of the Church and reiterates that his ascension is our destiny as well. The second selection is briefer and a more concise statement of the connection between the resurrection and the ascension.

Should the presider use the Roman Canon, the proper commemoration for Ascension should be used.

The solemn blessing for Ascension is presented in the Sacramentary for use on this feast and is a fitting conclusion to the celebration since it speaks of Christ's exaltation at the Father's right hand.

While formerly the Easter candle was to be extinguished after the proclamation of the gospel on the solemnity of the Ascension, the directives now state that the Easter season continues to the solemnity of Pentecost. Hence, the paschal candle and all other sanctuary appointments that have been used since Easter should remain until Pentecost.

SOLEMNITY OF PENTECOST—VIGIL MASS

The celebration of the solemnity of Pentecost is not a reenactment of the first Pentecost day; rather it celebrates the completion of the paschal season, and the fullness of the risen Christ who dwells now with the Church in the power of the Holy Spirit. While this is true for both the vigil Mass and the texts of the day of Pentecost itself, it is easier to understand the theological implications of the feast from the texts of the vigil. Although none of the readings of the vigil refer to the first Pentecost, they nevertheless are invaluable as giving the scriptural basis for the theology of the celebration. This vigil Mass returns to the custom of having an Old Testament lesson precede the New Testament reading and the gospel; the one to be read this evening is to be taken from one of four suggested texts. At least three of these texts have been noted as forming part of the background of Acts 2 on the event of the first Pentecost; they provide valuable insights into the meaning of the Pentecost event for the early Church.

The first suggested text is from Genesis 11, the incident of Babel. Here the text of Acts 2 should be recalled to see what features have been emphasized in relation to the Spirit. With both Genesis and Acts in mind we may say that it is by the power of the Spirit that the confusion resulting from the incident at Babel has now become clarified; where the product of human invention ended in confusion, the result of God's gift of the Spirit is clarity. Because of the Spirit, the barriers of Babel are overcome and the divisions caused by language are ended with the preaching in tongues as a gift of the Spirit.

The second reading from Exodus 19 tells of Moses' experience of God and how Israel becomes God's special possession. The event is marked by cosmic occurrences such as thunder, lightning, clouds overhead, and trumpet blasts before the Lord coming with fire. Similar occurrences form the setting for the coming of the Spirit on the apostles. The third text is from Ezekiel, whose vision of dry bones becoming a mighty army is used as a type of the activity of the Spirit, who takes what is dry, arid, desolate, and even dead and makes it alive by imparting vigor and vitality through its life-giving and preserving power. The fourth selection is from Joel, which prophesies that the Spirit will come upon all, not just on one specially elected people, when men's divisions are ended. Then young men will see visions and old men will dream dreams.

The responsorial psalm for the Mass develops many of these themes. The Spirit's manifold works in all the creatures of the earth and his activity as ever-renewing the face of the earth are cited.

The New Testament reading is from Romans 8, about the Spirit as the beginning of the hoped-for end times, where the Spirit's gift is seen not as the total completion but as the first-fruits of the age to come. Expectation, hope, our groaning now in anticipation of final completion, are all elements in this text from Paul. Also noted are the important characteristics of the Spirit who enables us to pray as we ought.

The gospel is the pericope from John 7, about the Spirit coming as water on those who believe, and the glorification of Jesus as necessary before the coming of the Spirit. From all of these readings it is clear that this feast celebrates God's presence in an ever more powerful way with his community. Thus he enables it to see visions, achieve maturity because of the Spirit's vitality, pray because of the Spirit's prompting, and still live in hope because the first fruits of the end times are already present in the Spirit.

As part of the preparation for this celebration of the vigil and for the day's Masses, the planning committee could explore ways in which the sanctuary decor for this feast could be enhanced by images or symbols reflective of the readings. The powerful symbols of light, water, fire, wind, unity, life, and peace are all essential parts of the celebration of Pentecost.

The rite of blessing and sprinkling with holy water could provide a key to the community's awareness of the presence of the Spirit already with them because of baptism.

The opening prayer speaks of the function of the Spirit in uniting all nations of the earth. The alternative opening prayer concerns the fifty days of the paschal feast, the openness necessary for receiving the Spirit, and the power of the Spirit to overcome the divisions of the world and make of many people one voice in faith and praise. The third prayer speaks of the light and strength of the Spirit.

The theme of unity runs throughout these prayers as it does

through the prayer over the gifts, the preface of this day, and the solemn blessing of the Holy Spirit.

If the presider uses the Roman Canon, a special commemoration for Pentecost is provided.

SOLEMNITY OF PENTECOST—MASS DURING THE DAY

For more complete background to the feast and the scripture readings, see above for the Mass of the Vigil.

There is a tendency in the interpretation of the Christian liturgy to historicize feasts and seasons in order to dramatize or recreate again events as they once happened in sacred history. And yet, the liturgy itself resists quite strongly any theology which would support this kind of activity. The season of Advent is a time of preparation for Christ as he comes to us now, and as he will come to us, not as he came two thousand years ago. The celebrations of Holy Week are understood as a unit; no one event is isolated from the others. The celebration of Pentecost is not the historical reminiscence of the first Pentecost. The festival of Pentecost marks a completion, for the Spirit is given anew to those who believe in order that they might complete God's work on earth. The Spirit is a gift, but not a possession to be selfishly hoarded. The Spirit is manifested only in our giving.

The first reading for this Sunday recounts the event of the first Pentecost, a feast which had its Jewish roots and came to be celebrated as a renewal of the covenant between God and the people of Israel, with specific recollection of the giving of the Law to Moses at Sinai. Today's reading recounts the descent of the Spirit in style that is reminiscent of the Old Testament account of the Tower of Babel, where men and women became confused by their own stubborn wills. But now, the reading points out, the coming of the Spirit ends this confusion and barriers of language and nationality are no more.

The responsorial psalm summarizes the nature of the day as it prays that the Spirit come now to renew the face of the earth. Just as the Spirit hovered over the waters at the dawn of creation, as Jesus gave up his spirit at his death on the cross, and as the apostles received the Spirit at Pentecost, we pray this psalm that the world may be enlivened by that same re-creative Spirit. This power of God was active before time began, was active as well in historical time in the life of Jesus, and will be active for all future time among those who believe.

The reading from first Corinthians speaks of the Spirit as the bond that unites the different gifts and talents of the community. The differences between Jew and Greek, male and female, are transcended by the Spirit who is over all, not to stifle anyone but to bring all gifts together for the good of all.

The gospel proclamation ties in with the Genesis story of the creation of man, for as Yahweh breathed into the clay of the earth and made man, so Jesus the God-Man breathed on the apostles to commission them to go forth to proclaim his peace.

In the opening prayer, the Spirit is envisioned as preaching through the believing Church to show the present reality of the power of God. The alternative opening prayer, however, is much more appropriate, for it is filled with biblical and liturgical imagery. It proclaims God as the Father of light, a reference to the termination of the Easter season. The wind and flame refer to the first Pentecost of the first reading; the love which binds all together is reflected in the reading from St. Paul. It may be that the prayer has too many allusions and therefore is difficult to understand, but if proclaimed slowly and distinctly, it can be a very effective opening to the celebration.

The prescribed preface of Pentecost shows this day as the completion of the Easter season, for now it is the Spirit who continues to renew the face of the world.

The prayer after communion speaks of the vigor of the Spirit who initiates our mission; the gifts we possess are varied but are to be used in the work of evangelization.

The solemn blessing of Pentecost is prescribed for use and is filled with biblical imagery about the Spirit.

Chapter Five

Sundays in Ordinary Time

ORDINARY TIME, THE SEASON OF THE YEAR

Before the reforms which have taken place in the liturgy, the Sundays between the Epiphany and Lent were called Sundays after Epiphany, and the Sundays between Pentecost and the season of Advent were called Sundays after Pentecost.

In such an arrangement, the Sundays were seemingly allied in some way with the feast which they followed. Such, however, was not the case. The readings, and indeed, the whole spirit of the celebration of these Sundays had at best a slight relationship with the preceding feast or season.

In the reformed liturgy, these Sundays are given a new nomenclature. They are called Sundays "throughout the year" or Sundays "in ordinary time." The emphasis here is not on the relationship of a Sunday celebration to some previous feast or season, but to the scripture readings that give each Sunday a general theme that fits in with the overall cycle of readings for years "A," "B," and "C."

The Lectionary is thus a primary factor in the planning of these Sunday liturgies, and the task of the presider and worship committee is first to understand the scripture readings before selecting options from the Sacramentary. Once the committee has determined the main scriptural theme of a given Sunday or a series of Sundays, it can determine the penitential rite, opening prayer, preface, eucharistic prayer, and blessing texts to be used, as well as compose the introduction to the liturgy, the prayer of the faithful, and any other comments to be made during the celebration. The cooperation of presider and committee is crucial at this stage since selecting the theme of the Mass and the homily for a given Sunday is the fundamental task of liturgy preparation.

In the commentaries that follow, the gospel text and the Old Testament reading will determine the major theme of the Sunday, and the second reading from the New Testament will determine the alternative theme for the day.

For the Sundays of the "A" cycle, the gospel is from the evangelist Matthew in semicontinuous selections. The Old Testament lesson is chosen to correspond with the gospel. The second reading in the "A" cycle is taken from the letters of St. Paul: first Corinthians chapters 1 to 4 (second to eighth Sundays), Romans (ninth to twenty-fourth Sundays), Philippians (twenty-fifth to twenty-eighth Sundays), and first Thessalonians (twenty-ninth to thirty-third Sundays).

For the Sundays of the "B" cycle, the gospel is from Mark in semicontinuous selections, with the exception of the seventeenth to the twenty-first Sundays of the year when the gospel of John chapter 6 is used. The intention here is to develop the miracle of the multiplication of the loaves (Mark 6:30–34), the gospel for the sixteenth Sunday of the year in this cycle. The second readings in the "B" cycle are from the epistles: first Corinthians chapters 6 to 11 (second to sixth Sundays), second Corinthians (seventh to fourteenth Sundays), Ephesians (fifteenth to twenty-first Sundays), the letter of James (twenty-second to twenty-sixth Sundays), and the letter to the Hebrews chapters 2 to 10 (twenty-seventh to thirty-third Sundays).

For the Sundays of the "C" cycle, the gospel is from Luke in semicontinuous selections. The second readings in the "C" cycle are taken from the epistles: first Corinthians chapters 6 to 11 (second to eighth Sundays), Galatians (ninth to fourteenth Sundays), Colossians (fifteenth to eighteenth Sundays), Hebrews chapters 11 and 12 (nineteenth to twenty-second Sundays), Philemon (twenty-third Sunday), first Timothy (twenty-fourth to twenty-sixth Sundays), second Timothy (twenty-seventh to thirtieth Sundays), and second Thessalonians (thirty-first to thirty-third Sundays).

SUNDAYS OF THE YEAR "A" CYCLE

SECOND SUNDAY IN ORDINARY TIME

It may seem strange to begin the "season of the year" with the second Sunday, rather than the first. In reality, however, the first

Sunday of the year is the feast of the Baptism of the Lord, and this second Sunday continues that theme with a consideration of the incarnation of the servant, Jesus.

The reading from the Second Servant Song of Isaiah clearly reflects the theme of the Epiphany about salvation to the ends of the earth. The servant of Yahweh is the one who is a light to all the nations so that the saving power of God may reach to the ends of the earth. The gospel reading of the day is the single exception to the rule that all the Sunday readings of the "A" cycle come from Matthew's gospel. There is no explicit recounting in John's gospel of the baptism of Jesus, but this reading comes closest to it. The servant of the first reading is described in the gospel as the Lamb of God who takes away the sins of the world. The incarnation of the Savior is to be understood now in terms of the redemption he was sent to accomplish; the birth of the Messiah leads to the death and resurrection of this servant, that all might be saved through his one sacrifice. The responsorial psalm clearly links the two readings since the refrain is "Here am I, Lord; I come to do your will."

The readings tell us that Jesus was the perfect servant of the Father, and that we too become servants of the Father's will, strengthened by the blood of the Lamb of God. Jesus was the only servant of the Father ever to fulfill completely the prayer, "Your will be done," for he freely accepted and gave himself up to death that others might share life through his sacrifice.

The alternative theme of the liturgy is found in the beginning of first Corinthians, portions of which will be read for the next six Sundays. The community at Corinth may best be described as a feeble church of sinners. Nonetheless, Paul addressed them as "holy" because they call on the name of the Lord Jesus Christ. The introductory greeting of this epistle has been adapted as one of the greetings for the beginning of the eucharist and should be used this Sunday: "The grace and peace of God our Father and the Lord Jesus Christ be with you." Sending greetings of grace and peace are standard introductions to the epistles, and some consideration of what these mean might prove helpful to the congregation. The Corinthian church is called a part of the Church of God, but only a part of the whole. There is no such thing in Paul's terminology as a church in isolation, either from other churches or from the whole Church.

The opening prayers of the liturgy are both introduced by references to the peace of Christ. The first refers to the grace and peace mentioned in the second reading, but the alternative opening prayer is preferable if the theme of the liturgy is taken from the gospel reading. In it we pray that the Father will help us submit to his will as did the servant Jesus, the Lamb of God.

Number 3 of the prefaces of Sundays in Ordinary Time, about salvation from a man like us, the Lamb of God, or number 7, about all things being restored through the obedience of Christ, are those which coincide best with the day's readings.

The prayer over the people number 11, could be used as a fitting conclusion to the celebration focused on our obedience to the Father's will. The dismissal (form c), about the community going in peace (the first reading) to love and serve the Lord (the first and gospel readings), is a good option.

THIRD SUNDAY IN ORDINARY TIME

The gospel lesson today presents Jesus as more than an ordinary teacher, or a preacher of a system of thought. He was not a theoretical philosopher, nor did he propound a set of abstract propositions. His concern was with making people whole, not just improving their mental capacities or thought processes. Jesus is the preacher of the new kingdom, the herald of Good News of the Father, but he is equally the healer who binds up the wounds of those in need.

The alleluia verse of the liturgy sums up the gospel proclamation by stating that Jesus preached the gospel and healed the sick and infirm. The ministry of Jesus was one of words as well as deeds. In the gospel, Matthew presents Jesus as beginning his ministry, proclaiming: "Reform your lives, the kingdom of heaven is at hand." He gathered his followers to assist and carry on this ministry, and went about curing the people of every kind of illness and disease. Matthew makes a point that Jesus began this mission outside the established Jewish circles of his time, thus indicating that Jesus is the Messiah for all nations.

The Isaian reading coincides with the gospel for it also indicates that those in Galilee, here called the Gentiles, will also experience a light that will come into the darkness of their lives, and from this light all the world will come to believe.

Third Sunday in Ordinary Time A   **169**

The responsorial psalm, in which the Lord alone is proclaimed as our light and salvation, reflects the theme of the readings. From him alone comes healing as well as wisdom.

The second reading, from first Corinthians, provides the second theme of the liturgy. Paul appeals for unity since the church at Corinth was experiencing the deep wounds caused by dissension. This characteristic of the church at Corinth can easily characterize many contemporary local churches. How to change cliques into a genuine community, how to encourage dominant personalities to discover that the not-so-dominant also have a voice, and how to encourage the individualists to open themselves to the entire gospel is a constant task of ministry. Since this Sunday occurs near the week of prayer for Christian unity, today's gospel may provide an excellent occasion to preach on the still disunited Christian Church. Effective ecumenism comes not by decrees from the central offices of administration, but develops from the experience of local congregations who begin to work on common programs to meet local needs.

The prayer over the gifts and the prayer after communion, where we pray that the salvation offered us in the eucharist may bring us salvation and a share in the joy of the kingdom, reflect the eucharistic theme of today's celebration. The opening prayer about unity and peace is in the spirit of the second reading. The alternative opening prayer speaks of the light and vision of the glory of God which the community experiences at the eucharist.

Appropriate prefaces from among those for Sundays in Ordinary Time would be number 1, for the darkness/light theme is mentioned at its conclusion; or number 5, about the marvels of the power and wisdom of God, as exemplified in the words and deeds of Jesus.

The prayer over the people could be number 7, about the light that has come to the community from this eucharist.

FOURTH SUNDAY IN ORDINARY TIME

The statements of the Sermon on the Mount, recounted in today's gospel reading, require critical reflection on the part of the believer to discern where values lie and true principles rest.

St. Matthew has stylized the blessing statements of Jesus by casting them in the form of a discourse of the Master as he sits on the side of a mountain. In Jewish circles the giving of any teaching on a mountain would immediately conjure up significant recollections of the giving of the Torah to Moses on Sinai. These statements of Jesus, and the setting of the scene, indicate that Jesus is teaching a new way of life. Jesus, in these beatitudes, is turning the wisdom of the world upside down. He is telling his hearers how they will be brought into his kingdom by living according to God's rule here on earth. To live by this rule is to live according to the new law.

The nine groups of people exalted by Jesus are not those exalted by worldly society. The world does not bless the poor in spirit (as well as the poor in fact), those mourning, the meek, those who show mercy, those who are peacemakers. Finally, the world will persecute and insult those who profess their faith in Jesus.

The Old Testament lesson from Zephaniah was selected to correspond to the teaching of the sermon, especially with its concentration on the humble who are exalted. The same first beatitude is used as a response to the psalm, a sign of its priority over the other beatitudes.

The second reading, part of the continuous reading from first Corinthians, links up with the other two lessons since it contrasts God's love for the downtrodden with the way the world treats them. The Christian's only boast is to boast in the Lord; for the man of God, this is his only wisdom; for the man of the world, this is only foolishness. The readings concern the "haves" and the "have-nots," the "privileged" and the "underprivileged." More importantly, how does one decide the difference between the two, and whose wisdom is the measure?

The prayer over the gifts and the prayer after communion ask that this eucharist may help us attain salvation and continued growth in faith.

The opening prayer refers to the readings as it echoes their theme of loving others the way God loves them. The alternative opening prayer speaks of how God has formed us into a community in the image of his Son.

Preface number 2 of the Sundays in Ordinary Time, about Jesus humbling himself, and number 8, about God's gathering his people into a community to praise his wisdom, as opposed to the wisdom of the world, would seem most appropriate.

Since the time of the Reformation, the debate over "faith" and "works" as essential for salvation has continued to occupy the attention of believers. What has often happened, however, is a misguided emphasis on the one to the exclusion of the other. To emphasize in the letters of Paul to the Romans and Galatians that faith alone brings justification, or to isolate the saying in the letter of James about faith being dead without good works, is to do an injustice to the revelation of the whole New Testament. The readings of this Sunday provide a proper perspective for this debate by showing that believers have no choice but to be both "salt" and "light."

The first reading, which also occurs in a longer version on the Friday after Ash Wednesday, points out that fasting should lead to works of charity and regard for the poor, and is not to be used merely as a means of self-discipline. Fasting for show (cf. Matthew 6:1-6, 16-18) is to be replaced by fasting so that the goods of the earth may be shared by those in need. The reading emphasizes that those who care for the poor will themselves be healed of their sins, and God's light and protection will be theirs.

The responsorial psalm, by speaking of the just man as light, links the Old Testament with the gospel of the day, which refers to Jesus' followers who are "the light of the world." The gospel tells us that just as salt enhances the flavor of food, and is sometimes used to preserve it, so the followers of Christ are to help others realize their potential for good, but not dominate them. True believers do not stand aside and dwell on their gifts as possessions. To have the faith of justification means showing that faith in works of sanctification, showing that one believes in God by being a light for others. The alternate theme of the readings is found in the second lesson from Paul's first letter to the Corinthians. The true paradox of Christianity is that by the cross of suffering and death we have been freed from sin and share a new kind of life with God. The scandal of Christianity is the scandal of the cross.

The prayers of the Sacramentary speak in general terms of the eucharist and are applicable to the readings only in the case of the prayer after communion, which asks that the believers help bring salvation to the world, and in the alternative opening prayer, which uses the language of the Sermon on the Mount about beatitude for the poor in spirit.

The selection of preface number 1 for Sundays in Ordinary Time, about the characteristics of the community which has been called out of darkness into the light of Christ, can help expand the theme of the Old Testament and gospel readings; the use of Sunday preface 2 would help amplify the theme of the second reading about Jesus' birth from a virgin mother and how his suffering on a cross brought life to the world.

Number 7 of the prayers over the people reflects the main theme of the readings about salt and light; number 17 of these prayers speaks about the necessity of the cross of Christ for bringing salvation.

SIXTH SUNDAY IN ORDINARY TIME

The gospel reading today continues from the Sermon on the Mount and contains the clear statement of Jesus that he has not come to eliminate any part of the Law and the prophets. Jesus came to fulfill the Law, that is, to show by his life and teachings what the Law was really designed to accomplish—a new way of life based on the Father's love for all people. The Old Testament reading from Sirach tells how one is free to choose between fire and water; between life and death; that is, to abide by or not to abide by the commandments of God. The responsorial psalm reinforces this teaching by exalting the law of the Lord, the precepts which are to be kept diligently.

The long form of the gospel shows how Jesus gives a new thrust to the commandments of the Law. Adultery is not only taking another man's wife, it is the desire to possess unlawfully the pleasures of the flesh. The commandment forbidding murder is seen by Jesus as not merely refraining from taking a human life, but as condemning anger against others—a sort of murder kept in the heart.

No one of us can say that our motives are always the best, our reasons for doing things always single-hearted. Thus we must realize that we cannot answer Jesus' call to a "better righteousness" by ourselves alone. In the midst of our best efforts to do God's will, we must rely on his grace. We are not left to our own devices to withstand temptations; we are given the grace and peace of God our Father through the same Jesus who reveals the "new" Law.

The alternate theme of the readings is found in the continuation of first Corinthians, about the wisdom of God and the wisdom of man. Here Paul does admit wisdom on our part, and in order that this not be misunderstood as a contradiction to last week's reading, reference should be made to both readings in the preacher's homily.

The opening prayer points to the decisions called for in the gospel and Old Testament readings about doing what is right and just. The alternative opening prayer ties in with the wisdom theme of the epistle reading, as it too speaks of the wisdom of God taking flesh in the person of Jesus Christ.

The prayer over the gifts speaks of obedience to the word of God and can refer either to the morality mentioned in the gospel reading or to the wisdom of God spoken of in the second. The only oblique reference in a preface to reflect the alternate theme of the readings is number 8, about praise for the wisdom of God in all his works. The main theme of the readings finds adequate expression in preface number 7, where Christ is seen as a model for all believers, and in number 2 of the prayers over the people as well as in number 6, about greater fidelity to his commands.

SEVENTH SUNDAY IN ORDINARY TIME

The Old Testament reading from the holiness code of Leviticus (today's first reading) and the last portion of the Sermon on the Mount (today's pericope from the gospel of St. Matthew) indicate in no uncertain terms that no one can follow the teaching of Jesus about offering no resistance to injury, turning the other cheek, loving one's enemies, and even praying for one's persecutors, without faith and the help of grace. The end of the gospel reading admonishes us to be made perfect as the Father is perfect. But we are "made perfect" by sharing in the very holiness of God if we follow his commandments (first reading) by sharing the perfect love of Jesus for all people. Thus these apparently impossible demands of Christ—that we "turn the other cheek"—can be carried out by weak and vacillating human beings if they have faith in Jesus and cooperate with his grace.

At the celebration of the eucharist, the Christian Church comes face to face with the transcendence and sanctity of God so that we who are redeemed and sanctified by the eucharist can and must redeem and sanctify the situations in which we live. Sacraments are encounters with the all-holy, and a natural response is that of Peter: "Depart from me for I am a sinful man" (Luke 5:8). But the Lord does not depart or retreat; he remains to give the follower the possibility of renewing and living again according to Jesus' teaching. The need to transcend national barriers, political and personal philosophy, the bonds of race, and even religion in order to fulfill the extraordinary kind of love which Jesus came to teach is only possible because he first brought that extraordinary love to his followers. He who shared the very holiness of God from all eternity came to be one of us, that we who know sin might come to know redemption and holiness through him. For this reason communities gather weekly to renew and deepen their own experience of the holiness of God.

The alternate scriptural theme is taken from the conclusion of Paul's counterattack on the position of some of the Corinthians who claimed that they had better and wiser teachers and philosophers than those who preach the wisdom of Christ. The wisdom of this world is passing; the wisdom of God lasts forever.

The opening prayer speaks of the wisdom and love revealed in Jesus and of our desire to imitate him in word and deed. The alternative opening prayer has the same theme about faith in the word of God and how our every act may show our share in the life which Jesus offered us. Because both prayers speak of living the faith, they are particularly helpful to reflect the theme of the gospel, in which the reference to wisdom coincides with the second reading as well. The prayer over the gifts speaks of this offering in Spirit and truth which brings salvation. The prayer after communion corresponds well with the gospel theme in calling the community to live the example of Christ's love shared at the eucharist.

Preface number 8 of Sundays in Ordinary Time speaks of God's wisdom; preface number 6 speaks of the love of God and the gift of the Spirit dwelling in the community. This preface also links the celebration of the eucharist to the assembly who are members of the body of Christ. An appropriate prayer over the people to reflect the main scriptural theme is number 2, about the Lord's protection and grace, or number 6, about following the Lord with greater fidelity.

EIGHTH SUNDAY IN ORDINARY TIME

Because of the revival of interest in biblical studies and recent developments in the explanation and understanding of the sacraments, the word "covenant" has become important in our religious vocabulary. The covenants of the Old Testament between Yahweh and Noah, Abraham, and Moses, as well as the "new covenant" promised in Jeremiah 31:31–34 and inaugurated in the ministry of Jesus, form a major part of contemporary catechetical emphasis and teachings.

The personal covenant between the believer and God begins at the sacrament of baptism, for in it God takes the initiative and welcomes the person into the community of faith. In the sacrament of the eucharist, that covenant is renewed and developed through the preaching of the word of God and the reception of the sacrament of the Lord's body and blood. The sacrament of marriage is a covenant of mutual and lasting fidelity between husband and wife, a covenant through which they also commit themselves and their love to God's love for them.

But in none of the biblical covenants is there question of equal partnership between God and his people. There is no equality with God, only a realization that his love and fidelity will far outlast ours; his act of graciousness can never be outdone or even matched by us.

The covenant with the people of Israel is the basis for the first reading from Isaiah, and it indicates that despite the infidelity of even religious people, God will be ever faithful. The imagery of mother and child is used to show God's abiding love for his people.

The gospel reading from Matthew is filled with examples of the care which God the Father has and shows for his people, for in it the model of family unity and the care of a father for his children is analogous to the love of the heavenly Father for his children. By baptism we are made free; free from attachments and undue concern about the things of the world; free to serve God by responding to the love of God in love of neighbor. The application of these readings to the eucharist is obvious, for at this sacred banquet we are again brought close to the source of all good things, the source of all grace and blessing.

The alternate theme of the liturgy is found in the conclusion of Paul's discourse on factionalism in the Corinthian community. It is not the personality of the preacher that is important, but that he preach Christ crucified; it is not the person of the minister of God's Word who is important, but the Word which he ministers. The overriding challenge is for preachers to be faithful to the Word they serve and to be dedicated, so that they do not hinder effective proclamation of Christ.

The opening prayer of the liturgy speaks of the freedom which belongs to those who share in the covenant of God. The alternative opening prayer is about the peace of Christ and witnessing to the gospel. The prayer over the gifts and the prayer after communion both speak of the eucharist as a foretaste of the fulfillment of the covenant in the kingdom.

Preface number 1 and number 8 of Sundays in Ordinary Time are appropriate selections since they both speak of the covenanted people of God who are holy and are the very body of Christ. A most appropriate alternate for the preface and eucharistic prayer would be to use the fourth eucharistic prayer with its own preface because of the section on the covenant and God's fidelity, even when religious Israel disobeyed him and lost his friendship.

For the prayer over the people, number 6, about blessing the people even when they stray, and number 24, about blessing those who put their faith in God and who need his strength, are most appropriate conclusions to the liturgy.

NINTH SUNDAY IN ORDINARY TIME

One of the characteristics of the evangelist Matthew is the catechetical orientation of his gospel, in which he provides illustrations and examples for the lessons he teaches. The gospel reading for this Sunday contains the dominant Matthean theme of showing the need for deeds as well as words, for action as well as theory, in the life of a believer. The point at issue is the integrity of the believer and the extent to which actions reflect the demands of faith. It is not those who say "Lord, Lord" who will enter the kingdom, but those who live by the word of the Lord. The same theme is reflected in Matthew 19:16–22 about the rich young man who knew the commandments and kept them, but who could not make an active commitment to follow Jesus. In Matthew 21:28–31, the man who had two sons asked them to go out and work in his vineyard; the first refused, yet ultimately did what his father asked while the second readily agreed yet did not keep his word. The lesson here is that the first son was the faithful one because he ultimately performed what was asked of him. Actions speak louder than words. Today's Old Testament lesson from Deuteronomy coincides with this gospel since it speaks of choices in the life of a believer: to choose God's commandments and thereby receive a blessing, or to choose other gods and incur a curse.

The alternative theme of today's celebration is justification by faith rather than by the mere observance of the law, as mentioned in the second reading from Romans where the emphasis is on the sacrifice of Jesus and on the fact that our redemption is from that one perfect act of love.

The prayer over the gifts speaks in general terms about the eucharist, but the prayer after communion carries through the theme of the Old Testament and gospel readings by asking that this community may show their faith by the lives they lead, not only by the words they speak. Preface number 7 of Sundays in Ordinary Time, about the example of Christ doing the will of his Father, would be most appropriate. Of the prayers over the people, number 2, about our love for each other, and number 11, about doing God's will, reflect this same theme. For the theme from Romans about justification by faith, the alternative opening prayer, about an increase in faith, is appropriate.

Sunday preface number 6, about the paschal mystery, the heart of the faith, and number 9 and number 24 of the prayers over the people, about belief in God and putting one's trust in God, also carry through the theme of the epistle to the Romans.

TENTH SUNDAY IN ORDINARY TIME

In the first reading for this Sunday from the book of Hosea, the prophet is concerned about the priority of mercy over performance of ritual sacrifice. Hosea does not want rituals abandoned; he wants them purified and properly used, not mindlessly and perfunctorily abused. Crude ideas about sacrifice need reforming, but religious persons still need the ritual of sacrifice.

The last line of this first reading recurs in the conclusion of today's gospel and therefore serves as an introduction to the gospel, in which our need for the table-fellowship with the Lord is emphasized. For Matthew it is important that Jesus eats with sinners to heal and strengthen them; it is only in Matthew's Last Supper account that we find the reference to the cup of salvation for the forgiveness of sins. Believers stand in need of the sacrifice of the eucharist to forgive sins and strengthen them in the Christian life. Throughout Matthew's gospel, God is shown to be a Lord of mercy, forgiveness, and love who saves us despite our human weaknesses and failings. In fact he strengthens us precisely because of our weakness, cleanses us because of our failings, and raises our human life to touch all that is divine in him. Hosea the prophet and Matthew the evangelist do not ask to hide behind sacrifices and rituals; they want God's people to share in his love at their liturgical celebrations, until the day when "sacraments will cease" and the pilgrim Church becomes the assembly of the elect who share eternal table-fellowship with the heavenly Father. This theme finds expression in the language of many prayers over the gifts, for they often speak of the forgiveness of sins as one of the reasons for the celebration of the eucharist.

The alternate theme for this Sunday is taken from the reading from Romans with the example of Abraham as the man of faith. The trust of this man was extraordinary since the promise that he would become the father of many nations at his age of one hundred was beyond human expectation and the natural course of events. The quality of faith more often than not involves trust in seeming contradictions.

Today's alternative opening prayer speaks of the love of God for us through Jesus. That we all are to grow in that love is the prayer over the gifts, and that the eucharist is a sacrament of the healing love of God is reflected in the prayer after communion.

Sunday preface number 3, about salvation through Christ, or number 6, about the eucharist as a promise and foretaste of the paschal feast of heaven, are appropriate selections for the liturgy.

The third prayer over the people, about cherishing the gifts of the eucharist, fits in well with the readings.

For the theme of the faith of Abraham, Sunday preface number 6 proclaiming the paschal mystery as the core of the faith is suitable, and the first of the prayers over the people speaks clearly of God's initiative in calling us to faith.

ELEVENTH SUNDAY IN ORDINARY TIME

The refrain of the responsorial psalm, "We are his people; the sheep of his flock," reflects the theme of both the Old Testament and the gospel readings, for we are a people chosen to do his will—a will that impels us to missionary concerns, not self-satisfaction in being elected. The reading from Exodus is a preliminary to the Sinai covenant where Israel is dearer to Yahweh than any other nation; Israel is to become "a kingdom of priests, a holy nation." They needed to grow in holiness and to become a mission-oriented group rather than remain a self-contained body. Israel was specially chosen and enjoyed God's favor, but that election was not to mean isolation and self-satisfaction.

The gospel of the day contains the summons of Jesus to the apostles to proclaim the imminence of the reign of God. It is only here at their commissioning that Matthew gives the names of the Twelve, not at their "election." In this instance Matthew differs from the accounts of the other synoptics in that he stresses the sending forth of the apostles, thus showing that they were not to keep the news of the kingdom to themselves. The statement at the end of this pericope about preaching first to the lost sheep of the house of Israel should not be taken to mean preaching exclusively to the original elected people, for at the end of this gospel (Matthew 28:16–21), Jesus commands the apostles to make disciples of all nations. Furthermore, the command to preach the coming of the reign of God is not a clerical preserve; the entire people of God, "a chosen race, a royal priesthood, a holy nation, God's own people," is to proclaim his mighty works (from preface number 1 of Sundays in Ordinary Time). The biblical doctrine of election invites critical reflection on the extent to which we Christians have evangelized the world. Have we treated the gospel as the preserve of a band of the elite? The second reading presents the alternative theme of justification, mediation, and the end of our estrangement from God through Christ Jesus. We were redeemed while we were still sinners because of God's act of love in the death of Jesus on a cross. It is through the sinless one that we have access to the Father, whom we worship at the eucharist, "through Christ our Lord."

The alternative opening prayer asks that we avoid selfishness and thus indicates the major theme of the day's readings. Sunday preface numbers 1 and 8 both speak of the body of Christ and the vocation of this chosen people. Of the prayers over the people, number 9 and number 23 speak of the gift of God's love for this community and the task of the community to share that love with others. For the theme of the mediation of God's love through Christ, from the epistle to the Romans, Sunday preface 7, about the disobedience of man and redemption through the obedience of Christ, would be the best selection; number 5 of the prayers over the people, about being faithful to the Lord and rejoicing in God's mercy, is a fitting blessing.

TWELFTH SUNDAY IN ORDINARY TIME

The call to be a prophet of God's word, to transmit his message and teach the gospel, has an enduring appeal and a certain romantic flavor. Yet, the scripture readings of this Sunday indicate that such a commission is necessarily difficult and will involve suffering and humiliation for the one sent forth.

The reading from Jeremiah has the tone and force of a lamentation psalm where persecutors are all around the just man, and his only strength is the Lord himself.

The gospel also speaks of the persecution that the apostles will have to endure as they preach the good news of Jesus; their only security is the knowledge of the presence of God with them. That the Son of Man had to suffer and die to bring redemption to all people means that his followers too will have to endure persecution for the sake of the gospel. There is no smooth progression from the event of Easter to the eschaton, and in the meantime, the pilgrim Church will be persecuted for the sake of the preaching of the gospel.

The theme of the second reading is about an important question theologically and pastorally—the biblical doctrine of original sin and redemption. The typology of Adam/Christ is important for a proper understanding of this doctrine. Original sin is to be understood positively in the sense that estrangement from God has been overcome in Christ. The sin of Adam which we inherit is transcended by the redemption we inherit through Christ. Emphasizing this biblical background can help the contemporary faithful regain a proper perspective of original sin, which has all too often been understood in a very negative sense (taken from the banishment of Adam and Eve in Genesis).

The alternative opening prayer speaks indirectly of the persecution that believers will have to endure when they must choose between the inconstancy of this world and the Lord's faithful covenant.

Preface number 2 of Sundays in Ordinary Time about the humility and suffering of Jesus is an appropriate selection since it is a foretaste of the suffering and persecution which the Church will experience throughout its lifetime on earth.

Of the prayers over the people, number 5, about remaining faithful to the Lord, and number 7, about the suffering and agony of the cross, are equally suited to the message of the readings.

For the theme of the Adam/Christ typology, the prayer after communion assures the community of the redemption of Christ as it is experienced in the eucharist. Of the Sunday prefaces, number 3, about Christ's restoring sinners to God's friendship, or number 8, about our sin and Christ's redemption, are appropriate options.

Of the prayers over the people, number 14, about the mystery of redemption, reflects again this theme of lost innocence and redemption.

THIRTEENTH SUNDAY IN ORDINARY TIME

From the visits of the holy man Elisha to the house of the Shunemite woman (first reading), to the command of Jesus to receive prophets and holy men (gospel reading), to the custom of the early Christians to share all things in common (Acts 2:42–46), and the admonition of Paul to make hospitality our special concern (Romans 12:13), the practice of generosity and hospitality has been one of the marks of the believing Church. The Rule of St. Benedict instructs the monks in the most cloistered and remote settings to receive all guests as Christ. The sight of Christians loving each other begins in charity of the most practical sort, in opening one's house to others. The message of the gospel contains three instructions: to leave family and friends for the sake of preaching the gospel ("let goods and kindred go, this mortal life also" of "A Mighty Fortress"); to take up one's personal cross for the sake of preaching the cross of Christ; and to welcome strangers and preachers of God's word as though welcoming Christ himself. To welcome a prophet is to welcome the very presence of God, and to welcome the prophet's word is to welcome the word of God. The identification of the prophet with him who sent him forth, and the holy man with the holiness of God is a significant scriptural theme. The cutting edge of this gospel is not how well they welcome the word of God that preachers direct to them. Hospitality means a welcoming of the word of God into the homes and hearts of believers.

The alternate theme of this Sunday is the classic baptismal text of the Easter Vigil and the revised funeral liturgy—chapter 6 of the epistle to the Romans. The point at issue here is the quality of the lives of the believers who share God's life through the waters of baptism. The passage from death to life demands a continual passing over from one's former way of life to life lived according to the baptism we have received.

The alternative opening prayer speaks of God's truth and forming the lives of the community according to truth and love. The prayer over the gifts asks that those who share in the eucharist will also be faithful servants of the Lord. Preface number 8 of Sundays in Ordinary Time, about the characteristics of the Church as the body of Christ and the dwelling place of the Spirit, comes closest to the theme of the scriptures about the qualities of hospitality and generosity of the Church. Number 12 of the prayers over the people asks that those who receive the eucharist may serve the Lord always, one aspect of which is to welcome the presence of the Lord through the word of God mediated to us by his ministers.

The opening prayer is almost a perfect reflection of the reading from Romans 6 as it speaks of the situation of the believer before and after the regenerative bath of baptism.

Prefaces number 1 and number 7 of Sundays in Ordinary Time are both proper selections to correspond with this theme since the one speaks of sharing the glory of God through the cross and resurrection of his Son, and the other speaks of redemption through the obedience of Christ.

Of the prayers over the people, number 4, about avoiding evil, and number 7, about sharing Christ's light and devoting oneself to doing God's will, reflect the exhortation and instruction about baptism in the second reading.

FOURTEENTH SUNDAY IN ORDINARY TIME

The style and form of the first part of the gospel (Matthew 11:25f.) for this Sunday seem foreign to the design and plan of the synoptic accounts and appears more characteristically Johannine. The long discourses of John 14–17 begin as prayers to the Father in a fashion similar to that found in Matthew 11:25, "Father, to you I offer praise." The reference to "mere children" as recipients of God's revelation is a characteristic of the gospel of Matthew. For example, at the beginning of chapter 18 he alludes to the incident of Jesus and the little child where the Lord exalts the child's simplicity and declares that only those with a like simplicity could enter the kingdom.

In another context both in Mark and Luke, Jesus uses the example of a child and informs the disciples that those who seek greatness should rather seek the position of a child, the "least" in the eyes of this world. The association of Jesus with the lowly and his praise of simple wisdom are very much to the point of Matthew's gospel.

The selection of the reading from the prophet Zechariah as the Old Testament lesson indicates that the humility asked for by Jesus is the kind that he himself endured, for he came in meekness and without pageantry, yet his dominion could be to the ends of the earth. The example of the humble servant is the very person of Jesus himself, who invites us in the second part of the gospel to come to him for refreshment and rest. This gospel passage is also one of those used in Masses for the dead because of the comfort and hope it provides for those who mourn.

The alternate theme of the scripture readings is in Romans chapter 8, which contains one of the most important yet often misunderstood themes of St. Paul. The hellenistic dichotomy between the lower and higher nature is not found here, for flesh and spirit mean the whole person and the whole person stands in need of redemption by Christ. The Pauline teaching is not that only the spiritual element in our make-up is redeemed; rather our whole person is redeemed by the sacrifice of Christ. The vocation of the Christian, both "body" and "soul," is to live in conformity with the Spirit received at the rite of Christian initiation.

The opening prayer refers to the obedience of Jesus, the servant of the Father, and the example and model of our humility. The proclamation of the fourth eucharistic prayer with its own preface is a proper option for it clearly emphasizes the humility of the Messiah as envisioned in the first reading from Zechariah.

The prayer over the people could well be number 24 because of the reference to "children" who put their trust in God and the strength they receive from the eucharist, the sacrament of wisdom and refreshment. Both forms of the opening prayer refer to the saving power of God in redeeming the fallen world, while the alternative prayer refers to the redemption from sin.

Preface number 4 of Sundays in Ordinary Time, which speaks of our being reborn through the resurrection of Jesus, and number 6, about our identification with the Father through the Son and the Spirit, are appropriate choices to express the theme of today's second reading.

Of the prayers over the people, number 20, about filling the community with the love of God, his holiness, and the richness of his grace, reflects the generosity and love of God by which we are saved.

FIFTEENTH SUNDAY IN ORDINARY TIME

This Sunday the Lectionary begins a series of readings from Matthew's gospel in which Jesus speaks in parables. The parable is a story told in such a way as to shock the listener, to make him or her aware of the unusual that is so often overlooked in everyday life. The parable was a common form of discourse in early cultures and was used in the Jewish Wisdom writings and in rabbinic teaching.

Jesus used parables not just to make his hearers aware of the unexplored possibilities of life, but to direct their attention to him and to his way of life. Once this has been accomplished, the listener is faced with a choice: to live for Jesus or to live the selfish way of worldliness.

Like all parables, Jesus' parables tell a story. In today's gospel reading, the story is about the sower who sowed seed abroad in his field. Some of the seed bore fruit, and some did not. The story ends with the challenge to the hearers: "Let everyone heed what he hears."

The end of the gospel reading has Jesus telling his disciples what the parable means. He interprets it for them. The early Church also interpreted the parables narrated in the New Testament in order to make them relevant to the conditions and problems of the community.

In today's Church, the homilist has the task of applying the message and teaching of Jesus to conditions facing a culture and society far removed from the world to which the parables were originally addressed.

Today's first reading from Deutero-Isaiah gives us the clue to what Jesus' parables are designed to accomplish. They are to make us realize the power of God's word that not only causes the grain to grow and give a bountiful harvest, but that also works as a saving presence in our lives.

It is in this light, then, that we should try to understand today's reading from Matthew. Hearing God's word is not to be a passive experience of merely receiving information, but a means of re-creating us in God's image and likeness—a continual process of conversion.

The alternate theme of the scripture readings is the testimony of Paul in Romans 8 about present suffering and the glory of God. Suffering is inevitable in the Christian life and one who truly believes will have his or her share of hardships and trials. Yet, these are not ends in themselves, as there is hope that they will terminate with the full revelation of the glory of God. The theme and message of Paul is not to lose hope in the Lord, into whose risen life we have been initiated by baptism.

The opening prayer points to the truth of Christ, which comes from his word and guides us to follow his way. The proclamation of the word of God as part of the celebration of the eucharist is an invitation to growth in holiness, faith (prayer over the gifts), and love (prayer after communion). Of the Sunday prefaces, there is not one which reflects more adequately than the others the theme of the readings of the day. Number 20 of the prayers over the people speaks of the good news of salvation.

For the alternative theme from Romans, preface number 7 for Sundays in Ordinary Time, about the necessity of Christ's suffering leading to his sharing in the Father's glory, and preface 6, about the eucharist as a pledge of eternal glory with the Father, are equally appropriate selections. Of the prayers over the people, number 4, about the fulfillment of our longing, and number 16, about present consolation and a promise of the life to come, are proper selections for the final blessing.

SIXTEENTH SUNDAY IN ORDINARY TIME

The three parables which comprise the long form of the gospel for this Sunday may be termed parables of growth. The point at issue is the growth and expansion of the reign of God from insignificant origins to wide and significant expanse, from the size of the proverbially small mustard seed to the size of a remarkably large tree. The parable of the leaven in the mass of dough also indicates that the reign of God begins small but will grow to full stature. The parable of the weeds is also a parable of growth since both weeds and wheat remain until the harvest when they will be divided; the wheat will be gathered into the barn while the weeds will be burned. Yet, this is not the only message of the parable of the weeds; the discerning eye of the owner is interpreted allegorically to mean the judgment of the Son of Man as to the quality of the faith of the members of the Church. While the Church must grow and mature into the kingdom of the Father, there are also elements within the faith community which are not conducive to growth. Weeds as well as wheat, evil as well as good people, hypocrites as well as the sincere inhabit the Church. Church membership is no guarantee of salvation or an assurance of joining the elect in the kingdom of the Father. What really counts is integrity and fidelity in following the word of the Lord.

The judgment theme is emphasized in today's Old Testament lesson from the Book of Wisdom, where the author reminds us that true judgment depends not on the scales of the goddess justice, but instead on the mercy and love of God toward those who strive to live his life in response to his love.

The comparatively brief reading from Romans provides the second theme of the Scripture readings—the activity of the Spirit in helping us in our weakness to pray as we ought, for it is the Spirit who intercedes for us before God.

The alternative opening prayer is related to the theme of the parable of the wheat and weeds, for it asks that God's life may grow in us and also that we may be kept true to Christ's teaching as faithful members of his Church. Preface number 8 for Sundays in Ordinary Time, about the Church and the body of Christ, corresponds to the teaching that the Church is the community of those eager to conform themselves to Christ and become the dwelling place of the Spirit.

Of the prayers over the people, number 2, about remaining faithful to the Lord, number 5, about remaining faithful as well as rejoicing in God's mercy, and number 12, about serving the Lord with all our hearts, reflect the theme of the parables in the gospel.

The alternative opening prayer also reflects the second theme of the scripture readings, asking that the community be kept watchful in prayer, depending on the power of the Spirit for such fidelity. Sunday preface 6, about the Spirit as the foretaste and promise of the paschal feast of heaven, and preface 8, about the power and the dwelling place of the Spirit in the Church, is in line with the reading from Romans about the power of the Spirit helping us in our weakness.

SEVENTEENTH SUNDAY IN ORDINARY TIME

The recounting of the parables of the kingdom of God continues this Sunday with the ones about the treasure in the field, the pearl of great price, and the dragnet. Structurally the first two are similar to each other, while the third resembles the parable of the gospel of the sixteenth Sunday, the parable of the wheat and weeds. Yet, despite the difference between the two types of parables this Sunday, there is an important lesson in their juxtaposition. The person who finds the reign of God is so overjoyed and values this discovery so highly that he sells all that he owns to buy the field that contains the treasure, or he sells all his other possessions to purchase the really valuable pearl. The moment of the discovery of the kingdom is the moment of the act of conversion in the life of a believer.

The parable of the dragnet containing things which are valuable as well as worthless, where the things of value are kept and the useless things are discarded, is an image of judgment. The first two parables deal with the immanence and presence of the kingdom, whereas the third speaks of the end of the world when the faithful will be separated from the unfaithful. Like Solomon in the Old Testament reading, we must live according to the wisdom of God to be found among the elect. To prepare for the day of judgment, the faithful believers practice discernment in choosing things that will aid the life of faith and in avoiding those things that hinder that faith.

The theme of the second reading from the epistle to the Romans concerns the graciousness and mercy of God at work in calling people to himself, justifying them, and glorifying them as well. The reading points out that even before men and women existed, God loved them with an ineffable love. The biblical use of the term "predestined" does not refer to later theological opinions and systems. It refers to God's eternal plan of redemption for his people not as individuals, but as members of his body, the Church.

The discernment required of a believer who must await the complete establishment of the kingdom of God is reflected in the opening prayer of the liturgy, as it asks that we use wisely the blessings God has given to the world.

The prayer over the gifts contains a plea that we grow in holiness as we await fulfillment of the kingdom; the prayer after communion asks that we be brought closer to eternal salvation by the celebration of the eucharist. Preface number 8 of Sundays in Ordinary Time, about the Church as the body of Christ, reflects the imagery of the gospel parables, of those awaiting the fulfillment of the kingdom who celebrate in the meantime the saving presence of God in their midst at the eucharist.

Of the prayers over the people, number 2, about remaining faithful to the Lord; number 5, about remaining faithful and rejoicing in God's mercy; and number 12, about serving the Lord with all our hearts, all reflect the theme of the gospel of the day.

The alternative form of the opening prayer speaks of God's love at work in creation, and in the life he gives to us; the prayer over the gifts asks that we be made holy by these sacred rites and hence faithful in our lives to the love of God made manifest to us in Christ Jesus.

The infinite love of God is reflected in Sunday preface 3 as well as in preface 5, but in the latter the obligation to praise and glorify the Father prevents an overemphasis on God's love as sufficient for salvation.

Of the prayers over the people, number 20, about God's grace, would be the most appropriate to reflect the reading from the epistle to the Romans.

EIGHTEENTH SUNDAY IN ORDINARY TIME

In today's gospel, the setting of the miraculous distribution of food, the manner of the blessing of the bread, and the association of this reading with the first reading from Deutero-Isaiah are all as important stylistically as the event of the multiplication of the loaves and fish itself. In Matthew's narrative of the Sermon on the Mount, he presents Jesus as the new Moses who proclaims the will and law of his Father in much the same style and fashion as did Moses at Sinai. In today's gospel of the multiplication of the loaves and fishes, Jesus is again the new Moses because he feeds the crowds with bread as Moses fed the people with manna from heaven. He performs this act after crossing over to a deserted place by boat, a subtle reminder of Moses' crossing the Red Sea to fulfill God's plan to save the Chosen People.

Jesus takes the five loaves and two fishes, which are in themselves symbols of the eucharist. By blessing, breaking, and distributing the loaves he feeds not only the crowd, but also the disciples whom he would feed again at the Last Supper (Matthew 26:26) with the food of the eucharist by which he continues to nourish and sustain the Church.

The eschatological dimension of the miracle story is provided by the first reading from Deutero-Isaiah, where the banquet for the poor of his time is a promise and a foretaste of what will come in the completed messianic banquet in the kingdom. The table-fellowship of the Lord with sinners and those who need his healing power is renewed for the community of the Church as they gather weekly to break the bread of his word and sacrament until they will come to share the eternal table-fellowship with Christ in the kingdom of his Father.

The responsorial psalm, as it speaks of the Lord feeding his people, reminds us of the gospel reading with its eucharistic overtones.

The second theme of today's celebration is found in the concluding words of today's second reading: that nothing can separate us from the love of God which comes to us through Christ Jesus. The principalities and powers of which Paul speaks are forces which the people of his time conceived of as being harmful to men and women. There are many "powers" today which would harm Christians by weakening their faith in Christ.

Both the prayer over the gifts and the prayer after communion reflect the eucharist theme of the readings. Of the Sunday prefaces, number 6, which refers to the paschal feast of heaven, and number 8, about redemption through the blood of Christ, adequately reflect the scriptural theme of the gospel. The third eucharistic prayer fits in well this Sunday as it contains the line from the prayer over the gifts, "may he make us an everlasting gift to you." The prayers over the people which reflect the feeding of the multitude or the feeding of the Church with the sacrament of the eucharist are numbers 18, 19, and 23.

The opening prayer of the liturgy, about the everlasting goodness of the Father, is in tune with the theme of the reading from Romans about the everlasting love of God through Christ Jesus. Sunday preface 3 refers to the Father's loving plan of salvation through Christ; preface 6 speaks of the Father's love through Christ and through the Spirit (a major theme of Romans 8), and preface 7 speaks of the sending of God's Son as our redeemer to show forth the love the Father has for us.

Of the prayers over the people, number 8, about the continuance of God's love for us, and number 17, about the love which Jesus has shown us, are suitable choices.

NINETEENTH SUNDAY IN ORDINARY TIME

There are three important themes in the gospel for this Sunday: the power of Christ over wind and water, the significant position Peter enjoys in the early Church, and the calming of the apostles' fears at the return of Jesus.

The very setting and natural phenomena of the story recall the power of God at creation by separating the water (Genesis), the victory of God in saving the Chosen People from the waters of the Red Sea (Exodus), and the event recorded earlier in Matthew of Christ stilling the storm (Matthew 8:23–27).

The lordship which Jesus here shows over the elements, and which struck the apostles with wonder, has led some commentators, rightly it would seem, to see it as a sign of Jesus' bringing to fulfillment the work of creation begun by his Father. The gospel's emphasis on natural phenomena has a parallel in the reading from first Kings, when Elijah's experience of the presence of the Lord shows him that God cannot be identified with any natural phenomenon: because he transcends them all. Thus in the gospel, the apostles are led to acclaim Jesus as the Son of God because of his control over these forces of nature.

The prominence of Peter provides another theme for consideration as it is he who emerges to join the Lord and then, after a lapse of trust, returns with Jesus to the boat, an early symbol of the Church of Christ.

But it is the third theme, the experience of the apostles and their appreciation of the person of Jesus, that requires major emphasis. It is they who should have firm faith and confident hope in the presence of God with them. And yet previously, in Matthew 8:25, they cry out almost in despair for in the storm they fear death, just the way Peter cries out, "Lord, save me." In both instances these men, in their fear, call upon Jesus as "Lord," and still he can rebuke them: "How little faith you have." It is clear that Matthew's purpose in recounting these events is to convey to the Christians of his community, and to us today, that in the midst of doubts, Christians must rely on the presence of Christ in the community and renew over and over again their total commitment to Jesus.

The theme of the second reading from the epistle to the Romans concerns Israel's lack of faith in Christ as the Messiah. The anguish and pain Paul endures because they do not believe is the background against which he deals with the relationship between Jew and Christian in salvation history.

Only the opening prayer reflects the main theme of the gospel reading that we call upon the Father in faith at the eucharist.

Preface number 5 for Sundays in Ordinary Time, about the Father's rule over all his creation, reflects the theme of the Old Testament and gospel readings, about nature obeying his commands. Of the prayers over the people, number 5, about remaining faithful to the Lord, and number 24, about persevering in the faith, both correspond to the scriptural theme of proclaiming our faith and trust in the Lord to save us.

Sunday preface 1, about the characteristics of the chosen people of God, and preface 4, about the history of salvation, reflect the theme of the reading from Romans about our call to the community of faith. Number 6 of the prayers over the people asks that, as God cares for his people "even when they stray," so he may grant us a change of heart that we may follow him with greater integrity and fidelity.

TWENTIETH SUNDAY IN ORDINARY TIME

Today's gospel reading is about the Canaanite woman, a pagan, who asked Jesus to cure her daughter who was "troubled by a demon." Jesus answers that his mission is ". . . only to the lost sheep of the house of Israel." As she continues her plea, Jesus remarks that the food of children ought not be thrown to the dogs. The woman, not to be outdone in this sort of Eastern give-and-take, replies by stating that ". . . even the dogs eat the leavings that fall from their masters' tables." When we realize that the Jews of Jesus' day were accustomed to refer to pagans as "dogs," the woman's rather flippant reply shows that, although she was a pagan, she was nevertheless reaching out to the truth. Thus Jesus replies: "Woman, you have great faith," and cures her daughter.

This gospel reading is concerned not merely with the cure of the woman's daughter, but looks forward to the day when differences between Jew and pagan will be overcome in God's universal redemption that is open to all people without regard to ethnic or social differences.

Today's Old Testament reading and responsorial psalm point to the gospel message by placing emphasis on the universality of redemption. This pericope from third Isaiah is a return to the concept of the universal scope of redemption envisioned in the early chapters of the book ascribed to Isaiah. In first Isaiah, the Temple is not a place solely for Jews; it is the place where foreigners are welcomed, not merely tolerated. The holocausts and sacrifices are for all peoples. Such a universalist perspective is not the sole property of Jewish theology, for from the earliest Christian celebrations, the eucharist always had a "catholic" and "apostolic" orientation. In the *Didache*, the prayer (of the eucharist or grace over meals) asks that "as grain, once scattered on the hillsides, was in this broken bread made one, so from all lands thy church be gathered into thy kingdom by thy Son." The celebration of the eucharist is for the local community and "for all so that sins may be forgiven."

In the epistle to the Romans, Paul calls himself the apostle to the Gentiles (compare the statement of Jesus, about his mission "to the lost sheep of the house of Israel"), but still prays that the Israelite rejection of Jesus may one day be reversed. The lesson for the Church at Rome was to keep the community open to the Israelites.

Both scriptural themes converge on the need for universality in Christian congregations. This is reflected in the alternative opening prayer, which speaks of the love and care of the Father reaching beyond the boundaries of nation and race, because such boundaries should find no place in the hearts and experience of true Christians.

The proclamation of preface number 8 of Sundays in Ordinary Time, about the characteristics of the Church as the body of Christ and the dwelling place of the Spirit, coincides with both scriptural themes. An alternative selection would be the proclamation of the fourth eucharistic prayer with its own preface, since the prayer just before the Great Amen is for "all your people, and all who seek you with a sincere heart . . . and all the dead whose faith is known to you alone."

For the blessing at the conclusion of the eucharist, number 20 of the prayers over the people asks specifically that Christians may not be secure in isolation but may be filled with love for all.

TWENTY-FIRST SUNDAY IN ORDINARY TIME

Today's first reading from Isaiah, speaking as it does of the authority to open and shut, has a real connection with the gospel reading about Peter and the Lord's giving him "the keys of the kingdom."

Peter confesses his faith in Jesus as the Messiah. Jesus then declares that Peter is the "rock" on which he will build the Church, with the power of binding and loosing. Like Eliakim in the

Isaiah readings, Peter becomes "master of the palace" in God's Church. Peter becomes the cornerstone of the early community and exercises authority not on his own, but for the sake of the integrity of the faith and the unity of the Church. The authority of binding and loosing is to be exercised so that the community remains faithful to the revelation Jesus has taught them. Peter shares this authority with the other disciples, for Jesus uses these same words when he addresses them in Matthew 18:18 (the gospel of the twenty-third Sunday in Ordinary Time.)

One of the themes from the liturgy of the word is the conclusion of Romans 11 where Paul offers praise and thanks to God for including everyone in the salvation he offered, first to Jews, then to the Gentiles.

Both opening prayers speak about "oneness of heart" of the community, which is essential if proper authority is to be exercised in today's Church.

The prayer over the gifts asks that the people may receive the peace and unity of the kingdom even now as they share in the eucharist.

The theme of the confession of faith as that which binds the Church together is reflected in preface number 2 for Sundays in Ordinary Time.

Of the prayers over the people, number 5 asks that the people who celebrate the eucharist may remain faithful to the Lord, and number 20 asks that the God who has already granted us his mercy may continue to show his love for the Church and help us share that love for all people.

TWENTY-SECOND SUNDAY IN ORDINARY TIME

In the beginning of today's gospel, Jesus declares that he must suffer and be put to death before being raised up on the third day. He does not tell the precise way that he will suffer and die, for his purpose here is to present the pattern of his own life as the model for the believers who follow him. Jesus tells his disciples and all who will follow him throughout the ages that they will have to endure suffering and trials for their faith in him. They will imitate him by taking up their own crosses. The figure of Peter and his remonstrance of Jesus makes even the most ardent believers aware that it is easier to accept the messiahship of Jesus when it means glory and eternal life than when it involves denial, renunciation, and suffering.

The second theme of the liturgy of the word is taken from Romans 12:1–2, in which Paul asks the community to offer themselves as sacrifices by living according to God's will rather than abiding by what is the common life-style of this age.

The prayers of the liturgy do not reflect the main scriptural theme of the day, but the alternative opening prayer does reflect the second reading from Romans, as we pray that God's will may be done by the community and that what he values may become the values by which the Christian community will live.

Of the Sunday prefaces, number 2 speaks of the suffering and death of Jesus, number 4 refers to the suffering of Jesus, and number 8 refers to the blood of the sacrifice of the Lord; hence the theme of the first passion prediction in Matthew's gospel finds ample expression in these prayers. The best expression of this theme for the blessing is number 17 of the prayers over the people, which speaks of the love of God through the agony of Christ on the cross.

The theme of the exhortation in Romans 12 is only indirectly reflected in the reference to the characteristics of the pilgrim Church in preface number 1 of Sundays in Ordinary Time, where "we now proclaim the mighty words" of God. The exhortation that the community live according to the will of God is found in the prayers over the people number 4, about living a holy life, and number 9, about sharing the gift of God's love with each other.

TWENTY-THIRD SUNDAY IN ORDINARY TIME

The vocation of a prophet, as envisioned in terms of Ezekiel's oracles, is to judge the evil and the wicked and to dissuade them from their ways. The prophet has the responsibility of announcing the judgment of God (not his own judgment).

If the wicked do not heed the prophet's warning, they will die. But if the prophet does not warn the wicked, then the prophet will be held responsible for the death of the wicked. This reading, which leads us to reflect on our own responsibility for others, is further developed in the gospel reading, in which Matthew tells of Jesus' words about fraternal correction. The members of the community do not correct each other's behavior just to be critical or to show their own superiority over others, but to draw the erring brother or sister more fully into the heart of the loving community—the community of which Christ speaks: "Where two or three are gathered in my name, there am I in their midst."

The second theme for the liturgy of the word is from Romans 13 about love as the summary of the whole law of Christ. It may be regretted that this is the only part of the moral exhortation of Romans 12–13 which is proclaimed at the Sunday liturgy, yet this passage includes the whole of the law in a condensed form: "love is the fulfillment of the law."

The prayers of the liturgy do not directly reflect the main scriptural theme for this Sunday, but the alternative opening prayer does express the teaching of Paul in the second reading—in God alone are perfect justice, mercy, and love, and the follower of Jesus is to share these with the rest of the community. Sunday preface 8 is the most accurate description of the Church, which is called in the scriptures to fraternal correction and prayer. In this preface, the love of God and the sacrifice of Jesus are the basis of the love that is shared in the mystical body of Christ, the dwelling place of the Spirit.

Of the prayers over the people, number 2 about the love of believers for each other, and number 23, about remaining close to the Lord and to each other in prayer, carry out the main theme of the scripture readings.

Of the Sunday prefaces which praise God for his love for us, preface 2, about his humiliation, and preface 7, about the great love of Jesus as our redeemer, form the basis and model for the love for one another urged by Paul in the second reading.

Of the prayers over the people, number 2, about perfect love for one another, is the best expression in a blessing for the theme of the reading from Romans.

TWENTY-FOURTH SUNDAY IN ORDINARY TIME

Today's Old Testament reading from Sirach speaks of forgiving others so that "when you pray, your own sins will be forgiven." Here Sirach is urging forgiveness of one's transgressors rather than demanding the retribution that was allowed under Jewish law of the time. Thus Sirach's view advances beyond the law and reaches out in spirit to the teaching of Jesus as exemplified in the Our Father and in today's gospel reading. Forgiveness must come from the heart and be unselfish.

The responsorial psalm reflects the New Testament teaching about the Lord as kind and merciful, "slow to anger, rich in compassion." His kindness and mercy require that we show mercy to others.

In the beginning of the gospel, Jesus responds to Peter's question about how often one must forgive others by pointing out that the number of times forgiveness should be offered cannot be measured. We must respond to God's mercy by extending that mercy to others.

The second theme presented in the liturgy of the word comes from Romans 14, where Paul points out that we live and die responsible to God.

The opening prayer asks that we may experience the forgiveness of God in our lives, the way the official received mercy from his king and master. The prayer after communion asks that the experience of the eucharist will influence our actions so that others may receive the love of God from us which we receive at the sharing of the Lord's body and blood. Sunday preface 3 speaks of the infinite power of God's loving plan of salvation which may be understood as including his mercy and forgiveness. Of the prayers over the people, number 5 asks that the community always rejoice in the Lord's mercy, and number 23 asks that the community be strengthened by God's grace, and remain close to him in prayer and concern for one another.

The prayer over the gifts reiterates the second scriptural theme. Our responsibility to worship God leads us to pray and work for the salvation of all. Sunday preface 8 speaks of the unity of faith in the Trinity and then cites the Church as the Body of Christ, with expansive biblical imagery by which the Church in its many members and functions is still considered one. Of the prayers over the people, number 23 speaks of the unity of the Church based on fraternal love and prayer.

TWENTY-FIFTH SUNDAY IN ORDINARY TIME

Much of the imagery of the Bible is foreign to our everyday experience. The agrarian allusions affect fewer and fewer people, and talk of kings and kindgoms does not rest comfortably with those for whom democracy is a way of life. But these attitudes are symptoms of the much more basic problem involved with understanding the scriptures—our unwillingness to listen when the authors say what we would rather not hear, when the readings don't happen to agree with our already established life-style. And while all of this may be true in general terms, it is most especially true in the readings for this Sunday. The Old Testament reading from Isaiah states quite clearly that God's ways are not ours and his thoughts are not always our own. This fact becomes evident in today's gospel when, contrary to what we might expect in our selfishness, the Lord shows his mercy to those who do not seem to deserve it. The laborers who worked all day expected more than those who worked for just an hour. Even though they agreed on a wage, the fact that they worked more hours would, as we might think, require that they be given more. The strict economy of personnel management and the American way of life is slashed when this gospel is read, for strict calculation and reward are demolished in favor of a strong biblical lesson for all the members of the community; no one of us deserves the mercy of God, but when we receive it we should be more grateful. The problem arises when God shows it to "other" people. We become jealous when another receives God's favor, but are humbly grateful when we receive it ourselves.

The second scriptural theme for this Sunday is taken from the letter Paul wrote to the Philippians while he was in prison and in the throes of torment. Whether he will be killed or released, he maintains that his ministry will continue. If he is martyred, many will hear of his mission; if released, he will again be able to actively engage in preaching. The apostle uses this opportunity to teach his audience the meaning of death; for Paul, "life means Christ, hence dying is so much gain."

Both forms of the opening prayer speak of the justice of God at work through his mercy and love, and hence point to the lesson of the gospel about his generosity. Preface 2 of Sundays in Ordinary Time speaks of God's love for sinful man, and number 7 speaks of God's great love in sending us his Son as our redeemer. Of the prayers over the people, number 8 speaks about the Lord's generosity and love, and number 17 asks that the Lord look upon us with his love, the love which Jesus showed us by his passion and death.

The Sunday prefaces present the model of Christ's death as an example for the Christian, first in preface number 1 when his redeeming acts have made us his chosen people; in numbers 4, where suffering leads to rising to life everlasting; and in number 6, where the gifts of the Spirit who raised Jesus from the dead are a foreshadowing of our own Paschal feast in heaven.

TWENTY-SIXTH SUNDAY IN ORDINARY TIME

The selection of the Old Testament lesson from Ezekiel is an appropriate introduction to the gospel proclamation for this Sunday. The point at issue in the first reading is the determination of the individual believer to turn away from past sins and live according to what is right and just. The two choices presented for decision involve iniquity and wickedness on the one hand, and virtue and what is right and just on the other. The decision rests at the level of action, not mere verbal agreement. This sets up the gospel reading where the person of integrity performs acts of virtue and lives according to what is right.

The folksy parable of a father and his two sons, and the work to be done in their vineyard, soon leads to Jesus' statement that tax collectors and prostitutes gain entrance into the kingdom before those who say the right thing but do what is wrong.

A person's past does not necessarily determine his future life. What is important is the moment of conversion and true purpose of amendment. Repentance and conversion are continually necessary for the believer and should not be restricted to a special time or season like Lent.

The second theme of the scripture readings is from the second chapter of the letter to the Philippians. The short form of the reading indicates that the emphasis in preaching should be on the exhortation which precedes the Christ-hymn of the longer version. The key to the reading and the morality of this section of Philippians is that we are to model ourselves after Christ's act of self-emptying as he took on our human condition. We also must humble ourselves if we are to live in complete unanimity of love, without rivalry or conceit, never allowing ourselves to have a superior attitude toward others, for we are to look to their interests rather than to our own. Both scriptural themes require self-examination and conversion from a former way of life, and in both instances, we pray for the mercy of God to help us begin again with his help and guidance.

Both forms of the opening prayer speak of God's unbounded mercy and forgiveness and set the proper context for both themes of the liturgy of the word. Preface 7 of Sundays in Ordinary Time speaks of the great love of God who sent his Son as our redeemer, while number 3 more accurately reflects the theme of the Philippians exhortation since it describes the power of God to rescue and save us through the salvation wrought by the God-Man, Jesus.

Of the prayers over the people, number 6 tells of the Lord's concern for his people even when they stray; number 15 asks for God's mercy to help the faithful avoid what displeases the Father, and number 17 asks that the love of the Father which caused Christ to suffer for our salvation may continue to be with us in our need.

TWENTY-SEVENTH SUNDAY IN ORDINARY TIME

One of the principles of the exegesis and interpretation of the synoptic gospels is to compare the account found in one with its counterpart in the other gospels. This procedure is especially helpful in interpreting the parable in today's gospel, for traces of the original form of the parable as Jesus proposed it are found in Luke and in later writings, for example, the apocryphal gospel of Thomas.

Today's gospel reading from Matthew, about the tenants of the vineyard, is similar to the parable as found in Mark 12:1–12, and in Luke 20:9–19. In the Markan version, the reference to Isaiah 5:1–7, shows what the parable means: the vineyard is Israel, the owner of the vineyard is God, and the tenants are those charged with the religious leadership of Israel. The servants stand for the prophets, and the son sent to the servants is Jesus. In Matthew's version, which we have in today's reading, the allegory is expanded. The emphasis here is on Israel's rejection of the prophets and the Messiah. Hence, to facilitate the understanding of the Jewish-Christian community, Matthew lays special stress on the son of the owner of the field by relating Jesus to Psalm 118:22–23, about the rejected stone becoming the cornerstone. In allegorizing the parable, the primitive community relied on the song of Isaiah 5 to complete some of its details, and it is for this reason that his song is chosen for this Sunday's first reading. That the Lectionary editors want to emphasize the allegorical interpretation of the parable is obvious in the responsorial psalm, in which the vineyard of the Lord is identified with the house of Israel. The rejection of the Messiah can take on many forms and limiting it to the Jewish rejection of Jesus is only one. The Christian community, the new vineyard of the Lord, can also be tempted to reject Jesus.

The second theme of the liturgy of the word is taken from the letter to the Philippians, in which Paul speaks of the peace of Christ reigning in the heart of believers, and offering to the Lord every form of prayer as well as the quality of the lives we lead. The necessity of prayer for the full realization of the Christian vocation may be profitably explored especially at the Sunday eucharist.

The alternative opening payer is a fitting introduction to the Old Testament and gospel readings since it speaks about having the courage to stand before God's truth.

The reality of salvation despite people's rejection is the theme of preface 3 for Sundays in Ordinary Time; the disobedience and rejection are restored by the obedience of Jesus in preface 7. Either of these prefaces may be proclaimed to coincide with the liturgy of the word. Another choice would be to proclaim the fourth eucharistic prayer with its own preface, because of its emphasis on the rejection of God by humankind and the proclamation of the gospel to those who would accept it: the poor, the imprisoned, and those in sorrow.

Of the prayers over the people, number 2, about remaining faithful to the Lord, number 5, about fidelity and God's mercy, and number 6, about straying from belief and needing God's mercy for conversion, are all proper selections for this Sunday.

The opening prayer speaks of the peace of Christ and the way of his salvation and reflects the appeal of Paul in the second reading to dismiss our anxieties and let Christ's peace reign in our hearts.

Sunday preface 5 reflects the Philippian reading, for it speaks of the believer's vocation to return praise to the Father through the Son for the gift of the eucharist.

Of the prayers over the people, number 4, about being made holy and avoiding evil, reflects the moral instruction of the second reading; number 11 speaks of God's blessing which we receive at the eucharist to enable us to do his will.

TWENTY-EIGHTH SUNDAY IN ORDINARY TIME

Among the images of God in the Old Testament, few are as compelling as that of the provider of a banquet, the Lord who will extinguish death forever, the kind of God who is so concerned as to wipe away tears from those who mourn, who always remains with his people to shepherd them. This is the description of God found in today's Old Testament reading and the responsorial psalm. The early Church saw in the parable of the wedding banquet a likeness to the kingdom of God which will come in its fullness at the end of time. The first reading from Isaiah is also about the banquet that will come at the end of time, when God will manifest his power over all nations and peoples.

The gospel parable reminds us that, although we are invited to the banquet of the eucharist now and to the banquet of the end time, it is not enough just to "belong to the Church." We must be "properly dressed" for this banquet by living a life of good works, prayer, and sacrifice. That way we will be ready to greet the Day of the Lord when it comes at the end of life and at the end of time.

The second theme of the liturgy of the word is taken from an expression of gratitude on Paul's part for the charity of the Philippians, as he closes his letter to them. In thanking them, Paul also reminds them that whether hungry or well-fed, one must rely on the riches of God's grace to fill all our wants and desires.

Both the prayer over the gifts and the prayer after communion coincide with the theme of the banquet since they speak of the sharing in the eucharist of God's glory even here on earth. The Father's plan of salvation and the redemption through Christ form the core of preface 3 of Sundays in Ordinary Time. The love of God the Father in sending the Son and the Spirit is found in preface 6. Both are appropriate selections to carry through the theme of the image of God and the banquet of salvation.

Many of the prayers over the people speak of the love of the Father and the banquet of salvation, but number 18 is particularly appropriate because it emphasizes the reliving of the mystery of the eucharist and our constant need for rebirth by God's mercy.

Part of the alternative opening prayer also coincides with the second reading for it speaks of the loving kindness of the Father and of our reliance on his love and care for us. That the Lord supplies all our needs fully is part of the message of Paul to the Philippians, and is part of the prayer of praise we offer in Sunday prefaces 3 and 5.

Of the prayers over the people, number 19 reflects the theme of the second reading for it speaks of being enriched by God's mercy and love. Our response to that love is our prayer of praise, especially in the eucharist.

TWENTY-NINTH SUNDAY IN ORDINARY TIME

The task of the Church in her teaching role is to apply the perennially valid word of God to the changing circumstances of people's lives. The problem is determining just what a particular scriptural passage means almost 2,000 years after it was originally spoken or written down. And there is no more critical issue than that raised by today's gospel reading of the relationship between church and state. Recent Church statements do not endorse a complete separation between the secular and the ecclesial, the social and the religious. The very title of the Pastoral Constitution on the Church in the Modern World and the encyclicals of Pope John, *Pacem In Terris*, and of Pope Paul, *Populorum Progressio*, indicate that the Church must be involved in our everyday affairs, for we need clarification derived from the word of God. The biblical notion of the community of faith as leaven for the rest of society and of believers as a sign to the rest of the world of God's ways are very much in the forefront of recent Church teachings and emphasis. To be concerned with the things of God does not mean that the concerns of men are not important. However, the Christian's duty includes participation in promoting the common good of society.

The second scriptural theme for the day is from the opening of the first epistle to the Thessalonians. This is the earliest of Paul's writings and in it he compliments the community on the way they have proven their faith by being considerate in their love for each other, and by their constant hope in the Lord.

The introduction to the opening prayer and the text of the prayer itself clearly reflects the gospel of the day in praying for Christian service toward God and man, a theme which is also part of the prayer over the gifts.

Sunday preface 5, about man as the steward of creation, is the only one that reflects in any way the theme of the gospel. A far better choice would be to use the fourth eucharistic prayer and preface which emphasizes those who share the Christian faith but who must still live in and be a part of the world, that they may live no longer for themselves but for the Lord and the spread of his gospel.

Of the prayers over the people, number 11 about doing God's will in this world is an appropriate selection to reflect the main scriptural theme.

None of the prayers of the liturgy of the day reflect the theme of the reading from first Thessalonians, but Sunday preface 1, about the Church being called out of darkness by the power of God, and preface 8, about the community united to the Trinity, do coincide with the positive picture of the Church presented in this reading.

The example of the Thessalonian community in their love for one another can be the model of love for the assembly that is sanctified by the eucharist. This theme is found in numbers 2 and 9 of the prayers over the people.

THIRTIETH SUNDAY IN ORDINARY TIME

The context for the Gospel teaching about the greatest commandment of the Law is the question of the Pharisee about tribute to Caesar (as in last Sunday's gospel), the question of the Sadducees about the resurrection (Matthew 22:23–33), and finally the question of the Pharisee lawyer about priorities of the Law of God. Jesus responds to each of these difficult questions with surprising answers, such as the ones recounted in the gospel read today. Jesus took two parts of the Old Testament law about love of God and neighbor, and made these a new teaching by joining them together and calling them the basis for the whole law. These commandments of love as the basis for the Christian life is the thesis of the first letter of John. There he declares that to live in the light of Christ means unequivocally that we are to love our neighbor, and if we do not, we remain in darkness (John 2:7–11). Jesus gives no new commandment at all, but informs his questioners that these are the basis of his law.

The second scriptural theme continues the reading from first Thessalonians and in it Paul compliments this community on their adherence to faith in the one God as opposed to their former belief in idols. This reading could be applied currently to the questioning of present-day communities as to their many gods in this world and their allegiance to the one true God. To serve God means to serve him alone and not to be lost in the distraction of false gods.

The opening prayer of the liturgy asks that this community grow in love and do what the love of God requires in their lives, and so coincides with the theme of the gospel of the day. Also, the prayer over the gifts and the prayer after communion speak of rendering glory to the Father by our service to one another and of the hope that the sharing of the eucharist will have its effect in the lives of the community. Preface number 7 of Sundays in Ordinary Time speaks of God's love for us through Jesus, and of the eucharist as our continual sharing in that love. The expression of our love for God in love for others is the basis of numbers 2, 9, and 23 of the prayers over the people.

The alternative opening prayer corresponds with Paul's message to the Thessalonians in which he complimented their perseverance in faith in the one God. The prayer states that nothing good can come unless it comes from the covenant between God and man through Jesus' sacrifice.

One of the themes of the Thessalonian reading is the believer's imitation of the Lord, and this finds adequate expression in Sunday preface 3.

The blessing could well be taken from number 5 of the prayers over the people, about remaining faithful to the profession of faith, or number 24, about preserving those who believe from anything that endangers that profession.

THIRTY-FIRST SUNDAY IN ORDINARY TIME

Chapter 23 of the gospel of St. Matthew is a summary of the theologizing of Matthew about the situation of the community of his day. His approach seems quite harsh and very direct in its accusations and examples, but his concern for the Christian community has motivated the severity of this pronouncement.

There are two levels of interpretation of this Sunday's gospel—the level of the professionals in religion, and the level of the rest of the community. The problem with the professionals is essentially that they do not practice what they preach. The result is a heavy burden for the community. But the believers are not exonerated either, since all that is said about the professional purveyors of organized religion is said of the community in the same gospel. A religious practice that is socially acceptable and status-granting is not Christian. The level that the gospel reaches is the level of personal and communal conversion, which needs the constant goading of this and similar gospel proclamations.

The first reading states that God's people have wandered from the way of belief, a theme which Matthew asserts in many ways in chapters 6–7, but which he states explicitly in 7:13–14. "Enter through the narrow gate. The gate that leads to damnation is wide, the road is clear, and many choose to travel it. But how narrow is the gate that leads to life, how rough the road, and how few are there who find it."

The task of both preacher and the assembly gathered for worship is to open themselves to the gospel message: "The greatest among you will be the one who serves the rest."

The second theme of the readings is Paul's complimentary introduction to the letter to the Thessalonians where he thanks them for the reception they gave to the word that he preached to them. It is not a word that one preaches easily, but it is one that needs verbalization and application through the Church's minister. Paul is especially grateful, therefore, that the Thessalonians received the word as from God, not men. The preacher of the word of God is well aware of his responsibility in proclaiming and preaching that word, for he asks in the prayer before the gospel that the Lord will cleanse his heart and lips as he did Isaiah's. He is aware that it is God's word that is to be preached, not his own, or on his own terms.

Both of today's opening prayers speak in terms of the gospel, for they refer to living the faith and not merely listening to it. Preface 5 of Sundays in Ordinary Time speaks of the whole community offering their praise to the Father, not merely of the Church's minister. Sunday preface 1 speaks of the qualities of the Church which are needed to continue the praise of God's wisdom. Hence these two prefaces carry through the ideas of the second reading about remaining faithful to God's word.

Of the prayers over the people, numbers 2 and 5 speak of fidelity to the Lord and of being strengthened by the eucharist to live the faith.

A suitable blessing to reflect the theme of the preaching of the word is number 20 of the prayers over the people, which speaks of receiving the Good News.

THIRTY-SECOND SUNDAY IN ORDINARY TIME

The main point of today's gospel is the need for preparedness; in the case of the virgins in today's reading, it is preparedness for the coming of the bridegroom. This notion of preparedness has a special significance in today's liturgy because it looks forward to two weeks from today when we celebrate the feast of the coming of the true Bridegroom—Jesus Christ the King.

The virgins in today's gospel waited for the bridegroom with exaltation and joy, but the waiting became tedious and "they all began to nod, then to fall asleep."

How often we ourselves are like the virgins. Who among us has not found that preparing to meet Jesus the Lord in the weekly eucharistic celebration, to meet him in daily prayer and self-sacrifice, requires a level of perseverance that we tend to fall far short of? Like the virgins, we begin to nod and fall asleep.

But as today's reading says: "Keep your eyes open." With Jesus' help we will be able to do so as we prepare in today's liturgy to welcome Christ the Bridegroom whenever and in whatever way he will come to us; in the eucharist, in prayer, in joy, in sorrow, and finally, at the hour of our death.

The first reading from the book of Wisdom is about the need for watchfulness for those who seek the wisdom to know and serve the Lord. The responsorial psalm speaks of thirsting for the living God, even in, or more accurately, especially in the low points of our lives, so that we can reach from there to the heights of faith in God.

The second theme of the scripture reading this Sunday is from first Thessalonians where Paul addresses a practical and doctrinal problem faced by that community. Paul had preached to them and left them with the impression that the second coming of Christ was imminent. Some had died and the living were concerned about what had happened to them. Paul states firmly that the people should interpret these events in the light of faith and hope in the Lord. At the end of the reading he states that we shall all be "with the Lord unceasingly." Therefore, the hope which grounds the Christian faith is life eternal with God, and all will come to share this same existence no matter when they die.

There is much contemporary debate about death, dying, and theologies of suffering. This reading may provide such a theme for today's homily as a means of helping people to deal with these situations, leaving the subject of the last judgment as the homily topic for the feast of Christ the King.

All of the prayers for today's liturgy can be interpreted to reflect the readings of the day about living the faith with God's help, even in the unromantic and more difficult situations of life. Sunday preface 4, about the return of the Lord to heaven in glory as a pledge of our resurrection, and preface 6, about the foretaste of the paschal feast of heaven, reflect both scriptural themes of this Sunday: the watchfulness of the community until the Lord will come again, and the condition of those who sleep in death until the second coming of the Lord.

Of the prayers over the people, numbers 11 and 22 reflect the theme of the gospel reading as they ask that the community be aided by this celebration of the eucharist to do the will of the Father. Numbers 1 and 16 reflect the second reading, speaking of the life to come which we all shall share.

THIRTY-THIRD SUNDAY IN ORDINARY TIME

Last Sunday's gospel about the five wise and five foolish virgins, and this week's gospel about the three servants and the ways they took care of their master's money, are rising to the climax of next week, the gospel of the final judgment. Just as in the former Lectionary where the Sundays prior to Advent took on an eschatological orientation with judgment a prominent feature, these three Sundays provide different images of the theme, which tells us that we are to be ready at all times, for we know neither the day nor the hour when this judgment will take place.

Thirty-Third Sunday in Ordinary Time A 209

There are at least two levels of interpretation of this Sunday's parable from Matthew chapter 25; the teaching as it was enunciated by Jesus himself, and the interpretation of the primitive community with their consequent allegorizing of his teaching. The disposition of three sums of money always provides a certain intrigue and suspense, and the servants who are "industrious and reliable" are those who invest the money and make it earn more than its face value. Industry by itself does not necessarily deserve a reward, but the talents which the Lord gives to each in the community must be used industriously if they are to be developed for the benefit of all. To bury a talent, as the servant buried the silver coins, is to misunderstand the responsibility one assumes when receiving a gift: a reckoning of the way it is used will be exacted by the Lord. The allegorization of the parable is as follows: the "Lord" is Jesus, the servants are all of us, the reckoning is the final judgment, and the different results of the investment scheme are the different judgments we will receive. Matthew is clear that all will be judged and each one must grow and increase in faith on earth, not hide it or hinder its expansion.

The reading from the book of Wisdom speaks of the rewards "a worthy wife" will receive as a result of her labors, just as the loving, responsible followers of Jesus will receive their reward on the day of judgment. The homilist can choose the first reading and speak of the responsibilities of the married and family life and their rewards, or take the second reading along with the gospel (a happy coincidence that these should be read on this Sunday) and preach on the judgment that may be imminent, not merely to be relegated to the end times.

The alternative opening prayer this Sunday reflects the theme of the gospel since it speaks of the first coming of the Lord Jesus and how, until his second coming, the Christian community serves him in faith and love. The same Sunday prefaces recommended last Sunday are appropriate for this week: preface number 4 for Sundays in Ordinary Time, about the eventual return of the Lord in glory, and preface 6, about the Spirit as a foretaste of the paschal feast of heaven.

Both the second reading and the gospel speak of continuing to do the Lord's will until his second coming, and numbers 11 and 22 of the prayers over the people reflect this same theme and give it a eucharistic orientation.

SUNDAYS OF THE YEAR "B" CYCLE

SECOND SUNDAY IN ORDINARY TIME

There are several themes in today's gospel reading: the calling of the first disciples, their acceptance of Jesus as the Messiah, their readiness to follow him, and his giving of a new name to Simon.

Today, then, we may take as our main theme "What it means to follow Jesus." If we answer his call, we must, like the disciples, accept him as our Messiah and Savior. As Jesus changed Simon's name to Peter as a sign that he is now to live a new life of obedience to the Father, so Jesus gives us the power to live his new way of love and obedience to the Father.

The Old Testament reading about Samuel offers us a preview of obedience to God's will—an obedience that is reflected in Psalm 40 (today's responsorial psalm), and to which we respond: "Here I am, Lord; I come (to this assembly) to do your will."

The alternative theme of the day is taken from the first letter of Paul to the church at Corinth and concerns the perennially significant issue of sexual morality for the followers of Christ. Paul's followers had indulged in sexual excess and license because of their improper interpretation of his teaching. He now takes them to task and awakens in them a deep understanding of their status as people who bear God's Spirit in their very bodies. He tells them to respect their calling and vocation as God's chosen ones sealed at baptism by the power of the Holy Spirit. A Christian is one called to lead a life consonant with baptism in Christ, where the morality of the believer follows upon being transformed by Christ at baptism.

The treatment of sexual morality in this passage is continued for the next two Sundays. On the third Sunday of the year, the text concerns the imminent return of the Lord and Paul's advice for those who had wives to live as though they were not married. On the fourth Sunday, the text concerns the vocation of all believers as based on devotion to the Lord. The second reading for these three Sundays provides an excellent opportunity for a three-week series of homilies on personal sexual morality, as seen by St. Paul and determined by his theology and understanding of what it means to be a member of the Body of Christ.

The rite of blessing and sprinkling with holy water is the preferable choice for the introductory rite of Mass on every Sunday, as it sets the celebration of the eucharist in the context of the sacrament of baptism. The theme of today's celebration can well be that of the second reading about Pauline morality as based on the meaning of Christian baptism.

The alternative opening prayer is a particularly appropriate text to reflect the major theme of the day's liturgy since it mentions following the Father's call and embracing his will. Of the eight prefaces for use on the Sundays in Ordinary Time, preface 1 speaks of the community of the Church as the chosen race, a royal priesthood, a holy nation, and a people God claims as his own; hence it refers to those called to hear and proclaim the Word of the Father. For the alternative theme of the second reading, preface 6 speaks of the Spirit dwelling with the community and preface 8 speaks of sinners reconciled through Christ, both fitting reflections of the Church as the Body of Christ. Numbers 12 and 15 of the prayers over the people are suitable selections where the former mentions the Lord protecting his people from every evil, while the latter speaks of serving the Lord with joy. A suitable choice to reflect the alternative theme of the day would be number 2 about having perfect love for one another.

THIRD SUNDAY IN ORDINARY TIME

The readings for this Sunday might seem more suitable to the nature and theology of Advent or Lent than they are to a season called "Ordinary Time," for both themes reflect self-examination and living according to the word of the Lord. The gospel reading is from the beginning of Mark's gospel, about repentance and belief in the Good News, and the calling of the disciples Peter, Andrew, James, and John. In this text, the call to repentance is exemplified by the changes in life-style of the first four followers. For Peter and Andrew it was a matter of leaving behind their livelihood, and for James and John it was renunciation of familial ties, for now it would be the Lord's service that would bind them.

These first disciples are related to the contemporary Church in that they function for us not only as the first to hear the Good News and respond with faith, but also as models for our own conversion and repentance. Indeed, the fact that this text is not merely consigned to the Lectionary for Advent or Lent and is read on this Sunday is example enough that conversion and repentance should be a hallmark of the Christian's whole life, and not left just for special times and seasons.

The Old Testament lesson from the book of Jonah reflects the summons of the gospel, for the prophet was sent to preach repentance to the city of Nineveh which did indeed turn from evil to the ways of the Lord. The responsorial psalm also prayerfully joins the message of these readings by speaking of the Lord's ways, his paths, his truth, and his kindness.

Yet there is another aspect of these texts that might be worth exploring with the community this Sunday, especially since a clear lesson from the readings is that repentance is a life-time process. In the first reading, the prophet Jonah faces his task squarely and preaches repentance, yet earlier in the same book he hesitates and is reluctant to heed the Lord's call. The disciples in today's gospel reading respond immediately to the Lord's summons to follow him, but on other occasions they are pictured in the gospels as hesitant. A further consideration might well be that conversion as a life-long process is inaugurated by the sacraments of initiation, and sustained by the weekly eucharist.

The eucharist has always been considered a primary sacrament of reconciliation, and many parts of the celebration speak of conversion and the forgiveness of sin—the exchanging of the sign of peace, the petition for forgiveness in the Lord's Prayer, the words of the institution over the cup which speak of the blood of Christ for the forgiveness of sins. The words of the priest or the deacon after the gospel has been proclaimed ask that by this proclamation our sins may be blotted out. Indeed, a major theme of the Sunday eucharistic assembly is a recalling and renewing of our commitment to conversion and repentance, sustained by the Lord's word and sacrament.

The alternative theme for this Sunday also recalls the seasons of Advent and Lent, especially the former, since the text speaks of

acting in such a way that we realize the transitory nature of the things of this world, and the fact that we lead our lives between the times of Christ's resurrection and his second coming in glory. The specific example here is marriage, which for St. Paul (second reading) is still a most fitting vocation for the community of the baptized to continue in the Lord's work of re-creating the earth. Despite the fact that Paul's remark about "those with wives should live as though they had none," was based in part on the expectation of an imminent second coming, the validity of marriage is by no means negated. The vocation to virginity is also implied in this reading, and both marriage and the virgin state can be seen in the light of bearing witness to the kingdom of God which will be fully established at the second coming of the Lord.

The rite of blessing and sprinkling with holy water is a most suitable introduction to this Sunday's liturgy since the introduction to the rite could be reworded to reflect more specifically either of the themes of the liturgy, particularly about baptism and eucharist as special moments in our lives of repentance.

If the presider uses the third penitential rite (c), the second set of sample invocations about the kingdom of God, the strength for the Church now in the word and sacrament, and the return of the Lord in glory are most fitting to reflect the theme of the reading from first Corinthians. The alternative opening prayer refers to both the themes of the readings as it speaks of the Father directing our thoughts and efforts, and asks that our faults and weaknesses not obscure our vision of his glory.

The prayer over the gifts reflects the alternative opening prayer by referring to being made holy by the eucharist; the prayer after communion notes particularly well the eschatological note in the second reading by referring to the joy of the kingdom.

Preface 1 of Sundays in Ordinary Time reflects well the major theme of the readings in speaking of the vocation of the chosen race of the Church, and their being sharers now in his light while formerly they shared in the darkness of sin. For the alternative theme of the day, preface 6, about the Spirit giving us a foretaste of the paschal feast, and preface 8, about being far from the Lord's friendship and now being redeemed through his Son, are appropriate selections.

Solemn blessings in Ordinary Time number 3, about persevering

in good works and walking in charity and peace, or number 5, about walking in the ways of the Lord, would provide a fitting conclusion to a liturgy based on the major theme of the day.

Of the prayers over the people, number 6, about the Lord's care for his people even when they stray, and number 11, about the will of the Lord, are appropriate selections to reflect the major theme of the day, while number 1, with its reference to the life which the Lord has prepared for us, is a fitting reference to the eschatology of the second reading.

FOURTH SUNDAY IN ORDINARY TIME

Today's gospel about Jesus' cure of the man "with an unclean spirit" shows the power of Jesus over evil. In no sense is it to be understood in the light of today's sensational movies and stories about demonic possession.

The text primarily is meant to show Jesus' ministry in terms of power and authority: his authority to teach and his power to heal. This incident is one of many used in Mark's gospel to show that the devil's reign has come to an end with God's rule and power through Christ. The critical part of the text concerns the evil spirit saying "I know who you are," and Jesus replying, "Be quiet." This recognition by the evil spirit shows that a supernatural power is at work in Jesus, but if that be the only knowledge Jesus' followers have of him, then they misunderstand his real nature.

For Mark, the revelation of the glory of the Lord, and his healing and strengthening power through the gospel, is a way of initiating and enabling the community to understand and deal with the necessary suffering which each Christian must face. The recognition of Jesus' nature as the Holy One who still had to suffer is most important for Mark.

A secondary theme of this text is Jesus' healing and strengthening, which are to be main facets of the ministry of the later Church. Since the use of the term "evil spirits" possessing a man is to be understood as one way of describing sickness, the message for the later Church is to continue Christ's healing ministry in her sacramental practice and prayer life, for it is the Church with its Easter faith that sees the true meaning of Christ's ministry.

The Old Testament lesson balances the seeming overemphasis on

the deeds of Jesus in the gospel by presenting Moses as a prophet whose words are God's words, spoken in his name. The prophet often showed the power of God's words by performing wondrous deeds; so Jesus, the prophet, works miracles by his own power. Thus both the words and deeds of Jesus must be taken into account. The responsorial psalm speaks of hearing the Lord's voice (his words), recognizing his great works as creator and shepherd, and then opening our hearts to him in love.

The alternative theme from the second reading this Sunday is the third in the series of texts from first Corinthians about one's personal life and dedication to the Lord. The concrete example of this text concerns the unmarried. Here Paul teaches that marriage or continence is an appropriate way of life for the Christian provided that it serves the person's devotion to the service of the Lord. Which state to choose depends on the life of the person now, in the transitoriness of this present life, as the best way to prepare for the coming kingdom of God. One possible theme to be developed from this text would be the understanding of virginity and celibacy, practices by lay people as well as clergy, as suitable vocations in this life.

The introduction to the rite of blessing and sprinkling with holy water could be rewritten to mention the power of Jesus to heal and the power of the eucharist to strengthen us for our lives of faith. The rite would then serve well to introduce today's liturgy. Should the presider use penitential rite C, the eighth suggested set of invocations about Jesus who healed the sick, forgave sinners, and who now heals and gives strength to the present community is most suitable.

The opening prayer underscores the alternative theme of the day by speaking of the love of God for all people. The alternative opening prayer mentions Moses, who like Abraham, is one of the fathers in faith of the Christian community which finds its fulfillment in serving God and neighbor.

For the main theme of the day, preface number 1 for Sundays in Ordinary Time, about calling believers from darkness into light, and number 3, about the Lord's rescuing us by his power as God, are suitable choices. For the alternative theme, the notion of hope and expectation of the paschal feast of heaven is underscored in preface 6.

For the introduction to the Our Father, the third suggested text (c) about the forgiveness of sin reflects the healing power of Jesus now come to the present community in the eucharist. The fourth introductory text, about praying for the coming of the kingdom, suitably reflects the alternative theme of the day.

Of the solemn blessings for Sundays in Ordinary Time, number 3, about the Lord strengthening us in faith, and number 5, about the Lord keeping us from all harm, reflect the main theme of the day. Of the prayers over the people, number 18, about being reborn by the mystery of the eucharist to lead a new life, as well as number 24, about being strengthened against the attacks of the devil, are appropriate choices. For the alternative theme, number 4, about the Lord as the fulfillment of our longing, and number 16, about the life to come, are appropriate choices.

FIFTH SUNDAY IN ORDINARY TIME

This Sunday's gospel text from Mark, like last week's, concerns a healing miracle. In this text, Jesus is presented as much more than a miracle worker and faith healer. Mark's concern here is to underscore the words of Jesus, as well as the cure.

To the people of Jesus' day, a fever such as that of Peter's mother-in-law showed that evil was present. Jesus' cure of the woman was thus a sign of his power over evil. It should be noted that after her cure the woman "immediately began to wait on" Jesus and his disciples. This story thus gives us an example of a person who is saved from the power of evil and, as a result, is turned to a life of loving service of God and the neighbor.

The healing of Peter's mother-in-law—"raising her up"—is a reference to the raising up of Jesus in the resurrection. Also in this reading, Jesus refuses to accept the plaudits of the crowd— "Everybody is looking for you." For him to have done so would have made it seem that his gospel message was only for those who praised him, whereas it is for all people everywhere.

Jesus continually asks for faith on the part of his hearers, not only when a miracle has occurred or is about to happen; he also asks for understanding of his ways most especially when they do not correspond with our powers of reason or conventional ways of living.

That the miracle is not the only important point in the gospel can be learned from the Old Testament reading from Job and from the responsorial psalm. Job cries out in his misery that he will not see happiness again. The Lord is then pictured in the responsorial psalm as the Lord who heals the brokenhearted, who binds up their wounds, who sustains the lowly, and who casts the wicked to the ground. Despite the lamentation of Job, there is still a redeemer who heals and shows his love, and yet this love and care is not necessarily seen as immediately or as obviously as we might wish. This is consonant with the gospel, since to be a witness to the Lord means much more than seeing and seeking his cures; it means to place our trust in his ways and words, even if, and especially when, things do not evolve as we would wish. The issue in the major theme of this Sunday's readings is seeing beyond the miracles and alleviation of pain, to a firm trust built on the Lord in spite of our present sorrow and distress.

The alternative theme for this Sunday is from first Corinthians. It concerns Paul's ministry for the sake of the gospel, and the fact that he became "all things to all men" for this task. Paul's desire was to be with people to bring them to the revelation of the gospel entrusted to him. The text also more than hints at Paul's lack of success and unfulfilled expectations in some of the places he worked. Nonetheless, he unflaggingly pursued his vocation by carrying on his work because of the Lord's call. Paul's example should help us to realize that success in gospel preaching is almost always slow in being realized. Sowing the seeds of the word and ministering to the growth of the kingdom of God is always a task which has its trials and difficulties. The celebration of the eucharist based on this theme could be a celebration of hope amid apparent lack of success, and of faith in the abiding power of God's word.

The rite of blessing and sprinkling with holy water would suitably introduce the day's liturgy since its introduction could be rephrased in the light of the gospel reading to apply to the eucharist as our celebration of faith, prayer, and hearing the Good News of the Lord. Should the presider use the third penitential rite (c) for the introduction to the liturgy, the use of the eighth set of invocations would be appropriate, as would the sixth set speaking of Christ as raising us to new life in him, of the forgiveness of sins, and of the eucharist as strength and food for the community.

The alternative opening prayer speaks of the presence of the Lord and his constant support for us, his mercy and kindness, and his leading us to the kingdom of heaven, and therefore is a suitable reflection of the main theme of the day's liturgy.

The main theme of the day is also underscored in the third preface for Sundays in Ordinary Time, which speaks of the power of God at work in Jesus; the sixth is about the Father's love and hope of unending joy.

The alternative theme of preaching the gospel and of continuing the ministry of the Lord in the world is underscored in the prayer after communion, which speaks of the bringing of salvation and joy to all the world.

Of the solemn blessings of Ordinary Time as a conclusion to the liturgy, number 1, about the blessings of the Lord and his kindness, and number 5, about being kept from harm and living in lasting joy, reflect the main theme of the day. Number 2 of the prayers over the people, about restoring health of mind and body and keeping the community faithful to the Lord, is a fitting conclusion to the main theme of the liturgy. For the alternative theme, prayer number 9, about sharing God's love with others, and number 20, about the Good News of salvation, would be appropriate blessings in accord with Paul's missionary zeal, as well as Jesus' determination in the gospel to go to all who need his ministry.

SIXTH SUNDAY IN ORDINARY TIME

Today's gospel from the first chapter of Mark presents us with what is by now a familiar scenario. Jesus meets the leper, hears his request to be healed, takes pity on him, works the cure, tells the recipient to tell no one, and then retreats to "desert places." The leper is an outcast from society, for as described in this Sunday's first reading, the law required a leper to "keep his garments rent and his head bare," and "to dwell apart." The gospel notes the change in the leper's condition: from being "unclean" and outcast, he is now restored to society. The major theme of the liturgy this Sunday deals with the role of Jesus as healer.

But the healing work of Jesus was not limited to the miracles recounted in the gospels. His healing work continues to this day. In the sacrament of reconciliation, he heals us from whatever separates us from friendship with him, and restores us to an ever closer union with the Christian community. In the eucharist, he continues his healing work by infusing us with his own life so that we may turn from our selfish ways and imitate him by giving of ourselves to others.

The alternative theme of today's celebration is found in the reading from first Corinthians, in which Paul encourages his flock to imitate him as he imitates Christ so that "the many may be saved." Thus to imitate Paul, who imitates Christ, means to live in loving unity in the Christian community so that all may work together for the salvation of all.

The third penitential rite (c) has appropriate invocations to reflect the major theme of the day in sample formula 8, about the Lord healing the sick, forgiving sinners, and healing the present community. Sample formula 4 reflects the alternative theme of the liturgy as it speaks to Christ as reconciler, healer of wounds of division and sin, and intercessor on our behalf before the Father.

The prayer over the gifts speaks of the eucharist as our source of cleansing now and as that which will lead to life eternal.

The major theme of the day finds fitting expression in preface 5 of Sundays in Ordinary Time since it invites the community to join in wonder and praise of God for the wonders worked through Christ. For the alternative theme, preface 1 for Sundays in Ordinary Time speaks of the people of God, and preface 8 speaks of gathering all peoples into the Body of Christ.

For a blessing in Ordinary Time to reflect the main theme of the day, numbers 12 and 22 of the prayers over the people speak of protection from harm, and of strengthening the community to do the Lord's will. For the alternative theme, number 23, about true love for one another, and number 24, about the community seeking to love the Lord in all they do, are fitting selections.

SEVENTH SUNDAY IN ORDINARY TIME

The gospel readings of the past week have shown Jesus as the healer of bodily infirmities. Now Jesus will be shown as the one who also has power and authority to forgive sins.

Today's first reading from Isaiah, about God forgiving the sins of his people, and the responsorial psalm with its refrain asking the Lord to heal us from our sin, reflect the power which Jesus shares with his Father on our behalf.

The scene in the gospel also reflects the differences that were arising between the followers of the Jewish establishment and the growing Jesus movement. The concern here is how much authority this new teacher can claim for himself, as compared with the wisdom of the ages as discussed by the schools of Jewish rabbis. The most sensitive point is the problem of the forgiveness of sins. In the Old Testament, believers were invited to critically reflect on the state of their lives, to turn to God to ask for forgiveness, and to offer sacrifice to him as a sign of contrition and amendment. As might be expected, some felt that the offering of sacrifice was sufficient, and then went on and lived as they did before presenting the ritual offering. Rather than serve as a sign of dedication, the sacrifice all too often served as a business transaction to be gotten through and accomplished, with little or no sorrow or sincerity. Hence, it is all the more striking when Jesus shows his power to forgive sin. By doing so he puts the traditional concept of the forgiveness of sin in a new perspective, much to the dismay of the scribes. Integrity of intention, a contrite heart, purity of motive, and an awareness of dependence on God are what is important. Sacrifices and ritualization are only important in the light of these primary attitudes. The same is true for the sacramental practice in our own day, where rites should reflect proper dispositions.

The alternative theme of the liturgy of the word is taken from the second letter of Paul to the Corinthians, selections from which will be read from this Sunday to the fourteenth Sunday of the year. God's promise revealed and fulfilled in Jesus' "Yes" is the most important aspect of this text. God's fidelity is realized and fulfilled in Christ, while our worship of the Father and acknowledgment of the Father's will for us is to be through, with, and in him. Also, today's text ends with a reference to the Trinity in terms of the Father establishing the Church with Christ through the Spirit dwelling in our hearts.

The rite of blessing and sprinkling with holy water is an appropriate introduction to the liturgy for each of the themes of the Mass; the forgiveness of our weakness and the strength of Christ as our mediator with the Father are appropriate as introductions to the blessing itself.

Should the presider use the third penitential rite (c), the eighth set of invocations, about the Lord forgiving sins, healing the sick,

and now healing and strengthening the community is appropriate
to introduce the major theme of the day.

In both versions of the opening prayer, the alternative theme of
the day is stressed since the prayer speaks of the Son who reveals
the Father's wisdom and love. The prayer over the gifts fits in well
with this theme since it speaks of our worship in Spirit and truth.

Of the Sunday prefaces in Ordinary Time, preface 6, about the
gift of the Spirit raising Jesus from the dead, coincides with the
theme of the second reading. The major theme of the day is
emphasized by preface 1, about our being called from darkness into
the light; by preface 7, about the sinless one now redeeming us;
and by preface 8, about children wandering from the Father and
now reunited through the blood of the Son. This Sunday the
proclamation of either of the eucharistic prayers for reconciliation
with its own preface reflects the forgiveness offered to us despite
our past infidelity and sin.

The major theme of the day is also reflected in solemn blessing
5 in Ordinary Time, about the Father keeping us from all harm, but
is better reflected in the prayers over the people, where they speak
of our health of mind and body (no. 2); of the Father's care for his
people even when they stray (no. 6); and of protection from every
evil (no. 12). The alternative theme is underscored in number 5 of
these prayers, about remaining faithful to the Lord.

EIGHTH SUNDAY IN ORDINARY TIME

The text of the gospel on this Sunday combines the question of
why Jesus' followers do not fast as did those of John the Baptist
with the parables of new cloth and new wine to signify the
ministry of Jesus. The first part of the gospel, about there being no
need for fasting while the bridegroom is present, is prefigured in
the Old Testament lesson from Hosea, wherein the author
continually presents the relationship of God and his people Israel
as that of the marriage covenant. The second part of the gospel
reflects, if in a somewhat accommodated sense, today's New
Testament reading from second Corinthians on the New Covenant
in Christ.

The theme of the intimacy of marriage as a symbol of the
intimacy of the relationship of God with Israel is at the core of the
whole book of Hosea. The prophet writes from his lived experience

of a husband whose wife left him and whose account of such a broken relationship is bound to touch our hearts. The image of fidelity and infidelity is broadened to include Israel who, like an unfaithful marriage partner, spends her time chasing after other partners, that is, after other gods. Israel was a nation adrift, whose only security would come in returning to the One God who could grant it mercy, love and forgiveness. The prophet asks his hearers to repent and assures them of the Lord's kind response. The responsorial psalm affirms this by acclaiming the Lord who is kind and merciful, who deals with us not according to our sins but rather has compassion on us the way a father shows his compassion to his repentant children.

The first theme that can be developed on this Sunday concerns the need for fidelity while living in an unfaithful age.

The second theme is based on the parables of the new cloth and new wine as symbols of the messianic age. Mixing the new with the old is no answer, for what has come in the New Covenant of Jesus is totally new and all-encompassing. Jesus here is indeed a new rabbi, whose teaching transcends the limits of the old Law. The newness of this relationship with God through Christ is underscored in the latter part of the second reading where we learn that the written law kills, but that the Spirit gives life. Here the Christian's moral life is shown to be quite different from life under the Old Covenant because believers are essentially changed by baptism in Christ and because of the grace and love of Christ. This change causes a difference in responsibility because our ability to respond to the Lord's word is enhanced and strengthened through the grace of Christ now dwelling in us.

Depending on the selection of the theme of the liturgy this Sunday, the introduction to the rite of blessing and sprinkling with holy water could be adapted to include a statement that we come to the eucharist to renew our relationship with God, a God who, in the imagery of the prophet Hosea, calls us back to him in the intimacy of a sound and firmly founded marriage. Or this introduction could speak of the eucharist as the weekly renewal of the covenant of our baptism, with a deepening of our faith and an increased sense of our responsibility—essential parts of this celebration of renewal.

Should the presider use the third form of the penitential rite, invocations about Jesus teaching us the Father's will, drawing us to the Father's love, and offering grace to sinners would be suitable.

The opening prayer speaks of serving the Lord in freedom. The alternative opening prayer speaks of God's love amid the fragile peace and broken promises in this life.

The prayer over the gifts speaks of the bread and wine as signs of our renewed love and worship, and the prayer after communion speaks of the sacrament of the eucharist as offering the strength needed to bring us to eternal life.

Prefaces 1 and 8 for Sundays in Ordinary Time reflect the theme of the marriage relationship of God and believers. The first notes God's inviting us to be his people and calling us from darkness to light; in the eighth preface, his call is reiterated in terms of the Church being his people and the Body of Christ. The New Covenant through Christ is expressed well in preface 3, where the title to the preface notes that the salvation is accomplished through the God-Man's death and resurrection.

Preface 7 speaks of Christ as a new principle of life, love, and peace from God who acquits man's disobedience through the obedience of his Son.

Of the prayers over the people, number 2, about the community always being faithful to their Lord, and number 6, about greater fidelity, are appropriate selections to coincide with the theme of the marriage relationship of God and his people. The New Covenant brought through Christ is expressed well in prayer number 17, about Jesus' gift of his life and love for us, his followers.

NINTH SUNDAY IN ORDINARY TIME

The gospel this Sunday deals with the conflict between Jesus and the Pharisees about the requirements of the Mosaic Law. The incidents which bring this disagreement to the fore are the picking of grain by the disciples and Jesus' curing of a man's withered hand on the Sabbath. The setting of these incidents in the gospel of Mark is the end of the first section of the gospel concerning the authority of Jesus, and forms a fitting climax, as the Lord comes face to face with the Jewish establishment and their strict formulas of piety and prayer. The new teacher, Jesus, challenges by his actions some of the established ways of observing the Law, and his questioners become enraged at his seeming lack of respect and understanding of the traditions that went unquestioned before he began his teaching. Jesus' reply to his critics ends with the frank and unambiguous statement that the Sabbath is made for man, but also that he himself is the Lord even of the Sabbath rest. By the end of this episode, both the Herodians and Pharisees, members of different parties, and representatives of very different views about the Law and religion, conspire together to plot Jesus' downfall.

The gospel is well introduced by today's first reading from Deuteronomy about the commandments, particularly that about the Sabbath, where rest is enjoined on the Israelites. They are to refrain from work because they are to take the time to recall prayerfully their deliverance from their slavery in Egypt.

The responsorial psalm reiterates the message of the Deuteronomy reading by speaking about the solemn feast of the new moon which celebrates the power and might of the one God Yahweh who delivered the people from bondage. Reflecting on the first reading and the psalm, and giving special attention to the ending of the gospel with Jesus' statements of his lordship over all, could help us to consider how well and in what frame of mind we submit ourselves to Christ's law that we love our neighbor.

The second theme of the day is taken from Paul's second letter to the Corinthians, which contains a most moving account of the apostle's understanding of his ministry ("treasure") and the power which comes from God to perform his ministry effectively. The text is readily applied to all believers who, like Paul "are afflicted in every way possible." Also, like Paul, we may be struck down, but Jesus will never let us be destroyed. The all-embracing love of the Father through Christ makes all the difference in our struggle to live our faith.

The introduction to the blessing and sprinkling with holy water could be rewritten for this Sunday to include either theme of the readings of the day. The main theme could be emphasized by a statement about our gathering for worship as an authentic expression of our faith. The introduction to the second theme could center around the hope and encouragement that we receive when we celebrate the eucharist, and the power of God that we receive from the hearing and preaching of his word as well as from the table of the eucharist.

In the third penitential rite, the eighth set of invocations about the Lord's healing the sick, his forgiveness of sinners, and his strengthening of the community by his body and blood reflects both themes of the day.

Both versions of the opening prayer indirectly reflect the second theme of the day since they speak of the Lord hearing our call, providing for our needs, and increasing our faith at the liturgy.

The prayer over the gifts sounds a similar note by speaking of our being confident in the Father's love for us.

For the main theme of the liturgy, prefaces 1 and 7 of Sundays in Ordinary Time would be suitable choices.

The prefaces that most fittingly coincide with the alternative theme would be number 3, about our salvation through Christ, and number 6, about Christ as our hope of unending joy. Numbers 2 and 7 of the prayers over the people reflect our involvement in spreading the New Covenant we share in Christ.

The fourth and fifth of the solemn blessings in Ordinary Time, about the God of all consolation freeing us from all anxiety, giving us his gifts in this life, and keeping us from harm, as well as number 16 of the prayers over the people, about our sharing in the Lord's consolation in this life and in the life to come, also reflect the theme of the Pauline reading.

TENTH SUNDAY IN ORDINARY TIME

The gospel of this Sunday returns to a Markan theme noted before—the conflict between the forces of good and evil, and between good spirits and evil spirits. According to the prevailing Jewish tradition, the evil spirit, Satan, exerted powerful influence in the world; hence, when Jesus cast out devils, the Jews thought that he had to use a spirit of this world to perform this work. However, Jesus affirms that he drives out evil spirits not by Beelzebul, chief and leader of the spirits of this world, but rather by the spirit of the very holiness of God. What gives this text a character all its own, however, is that Jesus declares that the power of the Spirit is so important in his life and in the lives of those who follow him, that the ultimate sin is to disbelieve in the power of this Spirit or to be unaware of his rule now at work in Jesus and through him in the Church. Jesus' true family, then, is quite understandably defined as those who keep his word and who continue his reign, empowered by this same Spirit. True family and true relatives include those who adhere to and are supported by the Spirit of God. For application to contemporary congregations, the setting of the Old Testament lesson from the book of Genesis may prove helpful, for it is cast in the literary genre of myth and the language of symbol. The last verses of this selection have been discussed repeatedly, and have been thoroughly worked over for possible light which it sheds on the status of the Virgin Mary vis-à-vis the forces of Satan. What is proclaimed here, however, is the author's understanding of the sinful condition of mankind, and that although we are presently under the sway of evil forces and temptations, we are assured of ultimate victory and triumph empowered by God himself.

The symbol of the serpent and his hostility can be interpreted as the spirit of evil in the world, whose ultimate defeat is assured because of the Holy Spirit. The believing Church, between the resurrection and second coming of the Lord, and between Satan's initial defeat and his final destruction, finds itself supported by the Spirit in its daily struggle against the forces of death's realm, however subtle or overt. Our consolation now is the word of God, and we retain our status as members of the family of the Lord by our active and willing response to and cooperation with that word. Heard in the liturgical assembly, this word can be a purifying agent and a means of liberation from the forces of evil.

We are reminded in the responsorial psalm that as we call upon the Lord for help in our faith, he is ever-present as the Lord of forgiveness, kindness, and redemption.

The second reading for this Sunday continues the theme of last week's text about the hope and trust in God amid the difficulties often involved in living our faith. Today's reading reaches its climax with the affirmation that just as we know that our earthly dwelling will end in death, so we are equally certain that our everlasting dwelling awaits us in heaven. Hope in the face of death and the trials of the Christian life form the focal point again for the alternative theme of the readings this Sunday.

At the introduction to the rite of blessing and sprinkling with holy water, the presider may wish to speak of the strength of the power of the Spirit of God in the gospel, the same Spirit who came to us at our baptism, and who comes in the eucharist to renew in us God's image and likeness. The alternative theme of the eucharist as our source of hope and strength can also be a fitting introduction to this rite. Should the celebrant use the third of the penitential rites (c), the invocation of the fifth and sixth examples, about being raised to new life, our sins being forgiven, the eucharist as food, our life in the Spirit, and light being given to those in darkness, correspond well with the major theme of the day.

The opening prayer and the prayer after communion continue the major theme by speaking of the Spirit who teaches us the Father's truth and the healing we receive at the eucharist to lead us to salvation. The alternative theme of the day is noted in the alternative opening prayer which speaks of the community gathered at the eucharist as raised above the limitations of this world.

Prefaces 6 and 7 of those assigned for the Sundays in Ordinary Time reflect the major theme of the day in that the sixth speaks of the Spirit dwelling in us, and the seventh returns to the imagery of Genesis by noting that the gifts of God's grace were lost by disobedience and are now restored by the obedience of Christ. The note of Christian hope is struck in preface 6 as well, and this would be an appropriate selection for the alternative theme of the day, as would the selection of the fourth solemn blessing for Ordinary Time, which speaks of the God of all consolation and his freeing us from all anxiety. For the major theme of the day, number 12 of the prayers over the people, about the Lord freeing the community from every evil, would be an appropriate selection.

ELEVENTH SUNDAY IN ORDINARY TIME

The fourth chapter of the gospel of Mark, from which this Sunday's gospel is taken, is most important for it introduces the parable form of discourse so familiar in the gospels. In dealing with parables, it must be understood that generally there are three possible levels of interpretation: that of the words of Jesus, that of the primitive Church's interpretation of the passage, and that of the evangelist as he retells the story. The aim of today's parables is to show that just as seed takes time to grow and ripen, so the kingdom of God, which is already among us, will grow to its fulfillment in God's good time. The parables here are both agrarian. In the first one, the farmer sows the seed, but he cannot hasten its growth. Similarly, with the spread of the kingdom, we cooperate and work for it, but in actuality it is God himself who "builds the kingdom." The second example is that of the mustard seed which grows to become the largest of all trees. (What is important in parables is the point the author wishes to make, not the accuracy of the examples he uses. In fact, the mustard seed is not the smallest of all seeds, yet in its full flowering it is indeed great. Such botanical details need not detract from the meaning of the parable.) We are involved here with the language of myth, poetry, and symbol, and for the evangelist Mark, this is the way in which Jesus explains the reign of God.

Symbolic language also occurs in today's Old Testament lesson and responsorial psalm, both of which are concerned with the image of the tree, important in Old Testament revelation. From the beginning of the book of Genesis, through the account presented here from Ezekiel, to the just man flourishing like the palm tree and bearing fruit in old age in the psalms, to the tree that will sprout from the stump of Jesse and bring forth the Messiah in the book of Isaiah, the image of the tree has borne with it the revelation of God and his dealings with his people, Israel. The major theme of this Sunday, then, concerns the gradual yet guaranteed growth of the kingdom of God through God's own will and power.

The secondary theme of the day is from second Corinthians, which points out that the Christian's true dwelling place is with God and that while we live in the flesh in our mortal bodies, our task is to please God and be prepared for the final judgment. The theme of hope, and living as the Father would have us live in this life, is at the heart of this selection. There is no lasting city here on earth; our true destiny and home is in eternity.

For the introduction to the rite of blessing and sprinkling with holy water, the presider could introduce the major theme of the day by speaking about our need for the eucharist as a sacrament of our growth in Christ. Or he may introduce the theme of the reading from Corinthians by speaking of living our lives under the judgment of God, relying always on him as our hope. Number 7 of the third (c) penitential rite, about Jesus bringing the good news of the kingdom and showing us the way to the Father, would reflect the major theme of the day.

Both versions of the opening prayer reflect the alternative theme of the day: the opening prayer itself speaks of living according to the Father's will, while the alternative prayer speaks of living as one family in love.

Of the prefaces for Sundays in Ordinary Time, number 6, about our hope of unending joy, coincides with the alternative theme of the day; number 2, about God's plan of salvation, and number 4, about our entering the heavenly kingdom through Christ, reflect the major theme of the day.

The alternative theme is reiterated again in solemn blessing number 4 for Ordinary Time by speaking of hope, consolation, and freedom from all anxiety. The first of the prayers over the people is consonant with the major theme of the day in terms of leading to the life promised us by Christ, while number 15, about avoiding what is displeasing to the Lord, and number 16, about consolation here and in the life to come, are appropriate selections to reflect the theme of the text from second Corinthians.

TWELFTH SUNDAY IN ORDINARY TIME

The gospel text for this Sunday is the beginning of a section in Mark's gospel which deals with miracles and the power of God, through Jesus, over the works of nature. One way of interpreting the miracle of the stilling of the storm would be to see it as symbolic of God's power over the forces in the world that buffet the Church, here symbolized by the boat.

This nature miracle, with its symbolic overtones of saving people from the deep, reflects the beginning of the book of Genesis. God's power is revealed in his separating the waters and bringing forth dry land upon which mankind could safely dwell. The people of Israel passed safely through the waters of the Red Sea; the psalms declare the Lord's triumph over vast waters—all of which, like today's gospel, proclaim God's power over nature.

The image of the boat reminds us of the story of Noah and his being saved from the flood by means of the ark.

The example of the disciples being saved in the boat by their master is the familiar image of the Church as the bark of Peter, storm-tossed, but ever-dependent on the power of God triumphant through Christ to bring her to salvation and security. Obvious applications to the contemporary situation of the Church and the experience of many in insecurity of faith and in hesitancy of belief could be addressed, articulated, and dealt with in a liturgy centered on Jesus as the Church's true support and mainstay.

The Old Testament reading from Job refers to the creation stories and to the power which God exerts over storm and wave. The responsorial psalm also speaks of the Lord's power which hushed the storm to a gentle breeze and stilled the billows of the sea.

The gospel text exhibits particular Markan traits. The author emphasizes that it was late in the day, a natural time for bringing things to a safe completion, yet it is precisely then that the storm appears. The evangelist emphasizes the Lord's being asleep, especially at a time when the community needs his active direction. Further emphasis is placed on the disciples' fear. It is somewhat ironic that those who should be fearless because the Lord was present with them should be so frightened. These stylistic traits express Mark's continual affirmation that God was at work in the earthly ministry of Jesus, that faith is needed especially when the Lord seems to be far from us, or even "asleep."

The secondary theme of the day is from the second letter to the Corinthians, about living no longer for ourselves but for the Lord, a text that should be familiar to us since it is now part of the fourth eucharistic prayer. The reading stresses the newness of the creation we share through the death of Christ, and invites us to a new way of living in him. The new age of salvation that has dawned in him must continue to live within us as members of his Church, where mutual love and not mere human judgments are our hallmarks.

The rite of blessing and sprinkling with holy water could be introduced this Sunday by reference to the theme of the power of God at work in Jesus, a power which is now at work within the community at the eucharist. There could also be reference to the theme of the second reading about the new creation that believers share through their common baptism and lives of Christian service. Should the presider use the third penitential rite (c), the invocations from the fifth and sixth set of examples about the Lord's raising the dead to life in the Spirit, giving light to those in darkness, raising us to new life, and feeding the community with his body and blood, all apply to the theme of the day.

The opening prayers speak about the Lord's protection offered now to the Church; he is addressed as the God of the universe, who keeps his followers one in peace and love amid the uncertainty of this world.

The prayer over the gifts and the prayer after communion both reflect the theme of the second reading, about being eager to serve the Lord and the renewal of the new life in Christ shared in the eucharist. Preface 1 of Sundays in Ordinary Time, about recalling the mighty works of the Father, and number 5, about creation and the Lord's designs, refer at least indirectly to the major theme of the day.

Also reflective of the main theme of the day is solemn blessing 4 for Sundays in Ordinary Time, about the Lord's freeing us from anxiety and consoling us all the days of our lives. For the alternative theme, blessing 3, about the mercy of God enabling us to do good, is appropriate.

Of the prayers over the people, number 9, about the people who believe in God enjoying the gift of his love and sharing it with others, and number 11, about being ready to do God's will, reflect the alternate theme. Number 24, about the community putting their trust in the Lord and being kept from harm and free from the forces of evil, reflects the main theme of the day.

THIRTEENTH SUNDAY IN ORDINARY TIME

The gospel text for this Sunday contains two Markan miracle stories; the first, the raising of Jairus' daughter, and the other about the cure of the woman with a hemorrhage. Jesus not knowing who touched him and feeling power go out from him are means by which the author emphasizes the unlimited power of Christ. Yet, the conclusion of this miracle brings with it a theological point not stressed up to now in the gospel; that is, the faith of the woman heals, not just her touching Christ's garment. Jesus states that it was the woman's faith that healed her. This brings us to another level of appreciation of the miracles in the gospels. Faith in Christ was not only necessary for the healing of those in need during the earthly life of Jesus; it is also a necessity for the Church in any age. In fact, asking for healing from Christ, especially the healing of the eucharist, makes no sense unless it is within the context of one's faith in him. The axiom that miracles proved who Jesus was and is meets a severe challenge by the text presented here, since faith in him preceded any demonstration of his power.

Jesus' raising of the child should encourage us to consider this miracle in the light of Jesus' resurrection from death to new life, and the heritage of his followers who will also share in new life with the Father. These two miracles provide scriptural background for a consideration of how a Christian should face death in the light of the resurrection of Jesus. Another element in the story, the request of Jairus that Jesus come and lay his hands on the girl, may deserve the homilist's consideration. The laying-on of hands is a gesture found in the Old Testament, but it was not a sign of healing as it is in many cases in the New Testament. This healing gesture is part of the new rite of anointing, and is a suggested part of the rite of penance. Hence, this request for healing in the gospel can be linked with the gestures of healing in the sacramental life of the Church.

The Old Testament reading from the book of Wisdom presents the customary association in Judaism of sin with death, both of which have been overcome in the resurrection of Christ. Redemption by Christ is mediated most clearly in the healing and strengthening power of the sacraments of the Church. The responsorial psalm speaks of the Lord preserving those falling into destruction, and the assurance of the Lord's help for those in need.

Two main themes emerge from a consideration of the gospel and Old Testament texts this Sunday—faith in the power of Christ's resurrection and the sacraments as mediating his healing and strengthening. The alternative theme is from second Corinthians, where the apostle encourages the community to imitate the Lord and act generously toward those in need. Christ made himself poor, although he was rich, so that the community might be made rich by his poverty. The Christian community is enabled to be generous toward all, through charity in prayer as well as almsgiving. An examination of a parish's motivation for giving and whether it is overly self-directed, or truly an act of kindness toward those most in need, may prove an important theme for the day. The plenty spoken of in the latter part of the reading refers to sharing spiritual wealth as well as material goods.

The rite of blessing and sprinkling with holy water could be introduced by a comment about the need for faith on the part of those who celebrate the eucharist this day. Or, reflecting the day's alternate theme, the introduction could speak of generosity in prayer. Should the presider use the third penitential rite (c), the eighth set of sample invocations, about healing the sick, forgiving sinners, and strengthening the community, is an appropriate introduction in the light of the main theme of the gospel.

The opening prayer speaks of being called from darkness to light, and the prayer after communion mentions the eucharist as a share in the life of Christ, both expressing the theme of the gospel of the day. The prayer over the gifts, about serving the Lord faithfully, reflects the theme of the text from second Corinthians.

Of the prefaces for the Sundays in Ordinary Time, number 2, about the resurrection as the heart of the mystery of salvation, and number 4, about our sharing in life everlasting through the resurrection of Christ, express clearly the mystery of the eucharist and the pattern for the healing of the young girl in the gospel.

The sign of peace could be suitably emphasized this Sunday if the theme of today's liturgy is from the reading from second Corinthians. The main theme of the day is reflected in solemn blessing number 3 for Ordinary Time, about the God of all consolation freeing the community from all anxiety, as well as in number 5 of the prayers over the people, where the Lord is asked to strengthen his people. For the alternative theme, numbers 9 and 23 of the prayers over the people, concerning prayer for all believers, sharing and spreading that love, and remaining close to the Father in prayer and love for others, are fitting choices.

FOURTEENTH SUNDAY IN ORDINARY TIME

The major theme of this Sunday's liturgy concerns the gift of prophecy bestowed upon the prophets of the Old Testament, and the prophetic mission which was an essential aspect of Jesus' ministry. In the first reading from Ezekiel, the people to whom this prophet was sent are characterized as "hard of face and obstinate of heart . . . and a rebellious house." The people to whom Jesus speaks in the gospel story do him no honor, and he could work no miracle in that place because of their lack of faith.

The alternative theme of today's celebration comes from second Corinthians, where Paul describes his ministry in terms of his own weakness, a weakness that was strengthened by the power of Christ. Paul welcomed personal humiliation in imitation of Christ's humiliation in becoming man. While the main theme of the day concerns the difficulties encountered in preaching to the faithless, the second theme speaks of accepting our weaknesses in this life so that Christ may make us strong.

The rite of blessing and sprinkling with holy water could be introduced this Sunday with a comment about how the Church must preach the authentic word of God on all occasions. Or a comment could be made to the effect that in our human lives we experience weakness so that the Lord himself will be glorified. Should the presider use the third penitential rite (c), number 7, with its invocations about Christ showing us the way to the Father and bringing us the consolation of the truth, would be appropriate.

The opening prayer, and more precisely the alternative opening prayer, note the theme of imitating the weakness of Christ and his suffering to raise up a fallen world. This theme is carried through in preface number 2 for the Sundays of Ordinary Time, about the humiliation of Jesus' birth and death, and number 5 of the prayers over the people, about being strengthened by the Lord. The main theme of the day is at least noted in preface number 1 for these Sundays, which characterizes the Church as a holy nation, a people God chooses for his own, and hence one that bears his message and word. The use of the first eucharistic prayer for reconciliation with its own preface reflects the forgiveness offered to us despite our past infidelity and sin. Of the prayers over the people, number 11, about doing the Father's will, and number 22, about having the zeal to do his will, are appropriate.

FIFTEENTH SUNDAY IN ORDINARY TIME

Today's gospel reading from Mark concerns the missionary task of the Twelve to continue in their lives the ministry of Jesus and also to continue his role of proclaiming the repentance for sins as preparation for the establishment of the reign of God. The ministry of the Twelve, according to Mark, would mirror the work of Jesus in his authority over unclean spirits, in healing the sick, and in anointing them with oil. Yet they would not proclaim the reign of God, but rather would preach the necessity of repentance, and in this way, prepare for the preaching of Jesus himself. Since the reference to anointing with oil recalls the text of the letter of James, chapter 5, it might be appropriate to use this Sunday to emphasize the sacraments as extensions and instruments of the healing power of Jesus, especially to the physically ill.

The reading from the prophet Amos places this prophet firmly in the tradition of Old Testament prophecy as he proclaims that his vocation was not self-motivated and self-determined, but rather that it came from the call of the Lord himself. The setting of this text is particularly significant, as the conflict between Amos and Amaziah is the classic conflict between the prophet of God and the priestly class. The latter often resented the intrusion of the prophet, whose preaching would often result in severe rethinking of customary and accepted ways of religious expression. Such a critique is an ever-necessary function to guard against improper exercises of piety and the manipulation of religion.

The alternative theme of this Sunday is from the letter to the Ephesians, portions of which will be read from this Sunday to the twenty-first Sunday of the year. The epistle begins with the praise and thanksgiving offered to the Father through Christ, then continues with the doxology which runs through the first three chapters, followed by chapters devoted to the Christians' response to the revelation of God to them.

Many commentators have pointed to baptismal and eucharistic underpinnings of today's reading, and it may be interesting to note that the type of doxology (praise) which begins this reading is like the expressions of praise and thanksgiving and the recounting of the deeds of God's mercy and love for the community.

The letter to the Ephesians also stresses the mystery of God's love revealed through Christ. The headship of Christ and his universal rule would also provide a fitting theme for the homily this Sunday. It should be recalled that from the seventeenth Sunday to the twenty-first Sunday, the gospel reading is taken from John 6, as a way of extending the announcement of the miracle story of the multiplication of the loaves heard on the sixteenth Sunday. With most communities giving special emphasis to the gospel for these weeks, today and next Sunday might provide an opportune time to emphasize this second, alternative theme for Sunday liturgy.

For the rite of blessing and sprinkling with holy water, the introduction could emphasize either the healing and strengthening power of the eucharist or it could be an introduction to the eucharist as the act of praise and thanksgiving which the community offers to the Father through Christ. Should the presider use the third penitential rite (c), the eighth set of sample invocations about healing the sick, forgiving sinners, and the strength of the eucharist would be a most appropriate reflection of the main theme of the liturgy of the day.

The prayer over the gifts and the prayer after communion both speak of growth in holiness and faith through the eucharist, while the alternative opening prayer speaks of the love of God for us through Christ and the gospel.

Preface number 1 of Sundays in Ordinary Time, which characterizes the Church as a holy nation, and preface number 8, concerning those who are called to be God's people, reflect the main theme of the day. For the alternate theme, preface number 8, about the mystery of Christ, is an appropriate choice.

Of the prayers over the people, number 11, about doing the Father's will, and number 22, about having the zeal to do his will, also may be interpreted to refer to the mission of the Church today. For the alternative theme of the mystery of Christ and the Father's plan for the salvation of his Church, number 14, about the mystery of the redemption, and number 20, containing a doxology about all God's gifts and the riches of his graces, are appropriate choices for the blessing at the end of Mass.

SIXTEENTH SUNDAY IN ORDINARY TIME

In one sense, the subtitle for the main theme of the gospel reading for this Sunday as reflected in the Old Testament lesson and the responsorial psalm could be "the image and likeness of God" in the scriptures. While "natural theologies" and philosophical reasoning have helped and continue to help in giving some ideas about who God is and what we can know about him, the Christian religion is fundamentally a faith based on the revelation of the scriptures. Through reason, humankind can arrive at some conception of the "Other," but God's attributes as creator, redeemer, Lord of creation, and savior of his people, are known only through his revelation. The primitive images of gods of wind, fire, storm, and water give way in the Old Testament to a Lord of the people Israel, who continually cared for his chosen people. The intimacy of God with his people replaces the pagan images of God as distant and removed from his creatures. Such is the background for the references in today's gospel to a special revelation of Jesus as teacher of his people, and as one who feeds them with the instruction of his word, and who assumes the role of their shepherd. The Old Testament reading conveys the same images in terms of instruction for the leaders of Israel who had "scattered" the Lord's sheep instead of keeping them firm in faith and close to him. God is portrayed as a shepherd who will lead, not dominate his people, who will give them new leaders who will have their best interests at heart, and who promises a true king and Lord.

The responsorial psalm today is the twenty-third psalm, in which the Lord is likened to a shepherd who refreshes souls and guards his people on right paths through the dark valleys of this life, with its sorrows and trials. We are a people whose God is with us and who feeds and cares for us as a shepherd cares for his sheep. The reference to the table he spreads for his followers may be accommodated to refer to the eucharist where feasting and rejoicing mark his presence with his community.

Dwelling in the Lord's house (heaven) is our destiny; to dwell in this house in this world is to live by the grace offered to the Christian at the eucharist. The image and likeness of God which Jesus came to reveal to us is not a God of thunder, storms, fire, or distress; he is the gentle and loving shepherd who never leaves his flock untended and who seeks out and brings back those who are lost.

A homily on Christ the shepherd who feeds his flock by the food of his word and by his body and blood would reflect the revelation of today's gospel. The responsorial psalm could be used to amplify the theme of Christ, who feeds us with the sacrament of his body and blood.

The alternative theme of the day's liturgy is that provided in the second reading from Ephesians, wherein the author stresses Jesus' role as the bond of unity and peace between Jew and Gentile. Now the only thing that matters is faith in Christ, not physical descent. The tone of this section of the letter is one of doxology and thanksgiving, where the revelation of the mystery of Christ results in our becoming children of a common Father. Race, nationality, and origin are redirected now in the light of Christ's sacrifice for all people.

The rite of blessing and sprinkling with holy water could be introduced this Sunday with a comment about the love of Christ feeding us as his people with the food of his word and sacrament, reflecting the main theme of the day. A reference to the mystery of Christ's love as our newfound source of reconciliation could reflect the text from Ephesians. Should the presider use the third penitential rite (c), the seventh set of sample invocations about Jesus as the way to the Father, as giving us the consolation of the truth, and as the Good Shepherd, adumbrate the gospel theme of the day.

Both opening prayers—which speak of Christ showing mercy and continually drawing us from death to faith, hope, and love—reflect this gospel text as does the prayer over the gifts and the prayer after communion.

For the main theme of the day, preface number 6 of the Sundays of Ordinary Time, about the love of the Father, the Spirit as the source of our hope and joy, and our sharing now in the paschal feast of heaven, would be an appropriate selection. For the alternative theme, preface number 1, about Jesus' cross and resurrection as the source of all our life, and number 8, about Christ caring for his people even when they stray and hence being our source of reconciliation, reflect the text of the letter to the Ephesians. This alternative theme is expressed in solemn blessing number 2 of Ordinary Time, about the peace of Christ, and number 14 of the prayers over the people, about the mystery of Christ's redemption. For the main theme of the day, the blessing could be selected from numbers 6 or 16 of the prayers over the people, where number 6 speaks of the love of the Father even when his people stray, and number 16 asks for the Lord to care for his people.

SEVENTEENTH SUNDAY IN ORDINARY TIME

The gospel readings from this Sunday through the twenty-first Sunday of the year are taken from the sixth chapter of St. John's gospel. Because of the need which many parishes experience regarding eucharistic catechesis, these Sundays present opportunities to stress important liturgical and eucharistic aspects of worship. Since these readings may be used as the basis for a series of homilies on the eucharist, some exploration into their background and how they reflect the theological intention of John the evangelist would be in order. Any standard biblical commentary can provide much of this information and should be consulted before determining the topics for the homilies on these days.

The subject of the sacramentalism or sacramental teaching in John's gospel has been the source of much discussion among scripture scholars, and some observations that at least indicate three main methods of approach are in order here. Some exegetes interpret this chapter of John, as well as almost any other having indirect reference to the liturgy or sacramental life of the Church, as an illegitimate expansion of the Johannine author's intent. With regard to the gospel itself, R. Bultmann and E. Lohse are among those whose interpretation may be considered antisacramental. These authors maintain that the evangelist did not know of the later Church's doctrinal teaching about sacraments and that any reading into these passages of later Church teaching is quite unwarranted. For these interpreters, what is uppermost for John is not the sacraments as mediating salvation, but rather an individual's personal union with the Lord and personal faith in the Church. What is important, they say, is not the repetition of sacramental encounters, but a renewed emphasis on the quality of one's faith and the integrity of a person's trust in God. Bultmann cites a later ecclesiastical redactor as the editorial hand which is responsible for the sacramental tendencies in this gospel. For Lohse the specific passage of John 3 about baptism and 6:51ff. about the bread of life and what others cite as eucharistic overtones of this passage, are the work of a later hand. For these exegetes, then, the "sacramental" teaching to be found in the gospel is a work of later redaction.

A second line of argumentation concerning these texts is that represented by O. Cullmann, which is the opposite of the first approach. This author holds that references to sacraments, however direct or indirect, are to be taken quite seriously as providing the basis of much of the fabric of the fourth gospel. For Cullmann, the concerns of the second generation Christians and their sacramental practice is read into an earlier tradition in the gospels and emerges in the Johannine gospel as the way in which later Christians meet the Lord. For Cullmann, the washing of the feet of the Twelve at the Last Supper (John 13) refers to baptism and the eucharist, and the dialogue of Jesus and the Samaritan woman in chapter 4 of the gospel has definite reference to the practice of baptism in the Church.

What emerges from placing these two schools of exegesis side-by-side is an understanding of at least the extremes of the possibilities in interpreting the sacramental symbolism of this gospel. The antisacramentalism on the one hand, and the almost supersacramentalism on the other, are often distilled in the works of other exegetes where their interpretation of the same passages in the fourth gospel may be termed symbolic. Such writers respect Bultmann's interpretation about the evangelist's concerns in writing the gospel, but at the same time they understand that there is a level of interpretation of the gospel that can be considered apart from its literal and most primitive form. The symbolic interpretation prefers to speak of sacramental allusions and references in the gospel, rather than of the sacramental teaching per se of the gospel. Hence, whether texts such as John 6 can be used as substantiations of the institution of the sacraments is not at the heart of their concern. What is at stake, however, is that there are valuable references here to the present life of the Church, and that the symbolic level of interpreting baptism and the eucharist, as preached by many of the early Fathers of the Church, and as incorporated into the Lenten liturgy for the formation of candidates for baptism, is indeed legitimate.

From all of this, the planning committee should realize that there are varying ways in which respected exegetes have interpreted this chapter of John's gospel. The level of the symbolic can be explored in these weeks, but the evangelist's theological intent and his concern about faith in Jesus should be respected and incorporated as much as possible.

This Sunday's gospel is the account of the miracle of the feeding of the multitude and is the Johannine account of what the author has likely taken over from the synoptic tradition. Important here— even on the level of the presentation of the miracle without the next verses which form a commentary on it—are the unmistakable Johannine characteristics of style, language, and structure. The miracle is noted by the Johannine author as a sign, like that of the wedding at Cana and other miracles elsewhere in his text, which must be interpreted correctly in order to convey the true identity of Jesus and the demand he places on his followers in faith. Should the sign be misinterpreted, the result, as noted at the end of this reading, is the withdrawal of Jesus from the crowds, for they want to make him into something he is not. Furthermore, true to the style of John, the setting of the event is important. In this case, it takes place on a mountainside, familiar and most important for a Jew because it was on a mountain that the revelation of the Law was made to Moses. Also, the reference to the Passover symbolically links the multiplication of the loaves and fishes with the eucharist. Loaves and fish, early symbols of the eucharist for the Church, are used here to their full potential to indicate to the later reader and the later Church that this multiplication is not just another miracle, but a reference to the bread offered at the eucharist. The numbers used in the passage, five loaves and two fish adding up to the ever-important and highly symbolic number seven, and the twelve baskets with the food left over are themselves unmistakable points of interest and theological import for John. The note of abundance is also important and is reflected in the Old Testament reading from the second book of Kings, for here the community ate and had much left over. Furthermore, the eucharistic significance of the story is noted in the very words which the evangelist uses for the act of the multiplication: he took bread, gave thanks, and gave it to his followers. Any one of these stylistic traits can be the basis for the beginning of a series of homilies on the eucharistic import of this miracle and this chapter of John's gospel, and can also lead the community to appreciate the eucharist, which itself is symbolic and filled with many levels of meaning and significance.

The responsorial psalm unites the Old Testament and gospel passages by referring to the hand of the Lord that feeds us and answers our needs.

The alternative theme for this Sunday is taken from the letter to the Ephesians where the author, having finished his earlier dogmatic-doxological section (chapters 1–3), begins to explore the ethical import of his teaching. The author first treats the Spirit, whose activity in the community makes ethical conduct possible. The Spirit is primarily the source of unity for the community called the Church, and the Spirit is the source of the peace that binds it together. Thus, the Church is the one body of those who share faith in one Lord through the Spirit's power.

The unity of the eucharistic assembly is a major theme of every celebration of this sacrament, since the result of a worthy celebration is that we become "one body, one Spirit in Christ." The invocation of the Spirit during the eucharistic prayers asks that the gifts of bread and wine may become the body and blood of Christ, and that the community grow ever more closely united as the living presence of the Body of Christ on earth.

The rite of blessing and sprinkling with holy water would be a most significant introduction to the eucharist for these five Sundays, where the introduction could be reworded to speak of the eucharist as the means of the public renewal of the covenant of baptism by the community of the baptized. The eucharist is also the sign and source of our renewal in faith, which theme is important in the later sections of the sixth chapter of John.

For the alternative theme of the day, the eucharist as a source of unity and sign of our being united in Christ by the Spirit, the celebrant could use the third penitential rite (c), with the fourth set of suggested invocations about the unity of the eucharist. The sixth set, about Christ feeding the community with his body and blood, or the seventh set, which uses terminology appropriate to the gospel of John are also suitable.

Preface number 8, of the Sundays in Ordinary Time, about the power of the Holy Spirit and the Church as the dwelling place of the Spirit, coincides very well with the theme of the Ephesians reading. Preface number 1, about the community of the Church being called out of darkness into the light of Christ, and proclaiming the mighty works of the Father, would be an appropriate selection to coincide with the main theme of the gospel of the day.

For the blessing at the end of Mass, number 23 of the prayers over the people speaks rather poetically in line with the Ephesians reading of the unity we share in the Lord through our common prayer and the unity we experience through our true love for each other. For the main theme of the day, number 18 of the prayers over the people, about the mystery of the eucharist, seems most appropriate.

EIGHTEENTH SUNDAY IN ORDINARY TIME

The gospel for this Sunday is the beginning of what we might call the more specifically "eucharistic" section of the sixth chapter of John's gospel. The account of the miracle related last week is the basis for this week's reading wherein John relates the difficulty which Jesus encountered in trying to move his audience from being attentive to the miracle itself, to having them realize that this was a sign to be understood in faith, a sign to help them realize who the giver of the bread was. John's point is that the sign itself does not guarantee perception of the reality, and that to move from perception of Jesus as the giver of earthly bread to accepting Jesus as the giver of all life would take faith on the part of his followers. Jesus' real mission was not to be merely a worker of miracles, but to be the revealer of the Father, the same Father who fed the Israelites in the desert with manna and whose power was at work in the man Jesus in this miracle of multiplying and sharing the bread. The crowd asks what they had to do "to perform the works of God." Jesus replies that to have faith in him as the one the Father has sent is the mark of God. They were to look beyond the material bread they shared as a result of the work of the Lord, to the reality of the giver of all good things and the giver of all life. They were to understand that far more important was believing in Jesus as the bread of life, of real life, life eternal, and not just as the miracle worker dispensing food in an emergency. The most important element in this text is Jesus' statement: "I myself am the bread of life." Here the author wants to make clear that Jesus was declaring in definite terms that he is indeed the only source of life, true life from God; he is the mediator of the Father's love for all people. Just as Moses' followers had to look beyond the miraculous feeding with quail and manna in the desert to appreciate God's love for them, and consequently to respond to that love, so in the new dispensation through Christ, believers would have to see in

Christ the love of the Father—a love which would always help them to respond to his word in complete faith and confidence. Jesus is the bread of life, the living water, the true vine, and the good shepherd, leading his followers through him to the Father in heaven. The Father works through him, as he did through Moses, to enable others to come to believe in him.

The Old Testament reading and the responsorial psalm for this Sunday lead to a consideration of the Father's care for his people.

In both of these texts the references to bread have eucharistic connotations, and also point out the need for faith. The faith of the community is the basis for all the Church's sacramental celebrations; it is increased by the celebrations themselves. In this light, then, today's homily could explore the theme that the liturgy, the summit and source of the Church's worship, is predicated on faith in God through Jesus.

The second theme of the liturgy of the day is taken from the letter to the Ephesians where the strong baptismal background of the text is unmistakable. To "lay aside your former way of life," and to "put on that new man created in God's image," is what baptism means. Just as one had to put off the things of a former way of life and put on the Lord Jesus, so in the ceremony of the early Church the candidates put their old clothing aside to be vested later in a new white robe, a symbol of newness of life. The Fathers tell us that after immersion in water and being sealed with perfumed oil, the candidates wore white as a sign of their new orientation to God and to the way they would lead their lives. The fact that baptism is the source of new life, and that the Christian has to put off the old way of life to show allegiance to the Father, is an appropriate theme for this Sunday in accord with this text.

As an introduction to the rite of blessing and sprinkling with holy water, the theme of the sacraments as signs of faith which help us to grow in Christ would be an appropriate comment based on the gospel text. Mention of the eucharist as a source of strength for the community to live the new life that is theirs in Christ would be appropriate as well. Should the presider use the third penitential rite (c), the Johannine terminology of the seventh set of invocations would be appropriate to reflect the gospel of the day, while the fifth set of invocations, about being called from death to life in

Christ, to share in Christ's pardon and peace, is most suitable to reflect the secondary theme of the day from the reading from Ephesians.

Both versions of the opening prayer speak more clearly about the second theme of the day since they speak about being restored to life, being freed from sin, being close to the Lord, and receiving strength and support from him.

Preface number 1 of Sundays in Ordinary Time speaks about the community of the baptized being called from darkness to light, hence reflecting the theme of Ephesians, while preface number 7 speaks of Christ as our only redeemer and coincides with the main theme of the gospel of John.

For a blessing to coincide with the main theme of the day, solemn blessing number 3, about strengthening the community with proofs of love, number 18 of the prayers over the people, about the mystery of the eucharist, and number 20, about every good gift from on high, are suitable choices.

The selection of number 2 of the prayers over the people, about being faithful to the Lord in our love for each other, and number 4, about being holy and avoiding evil, suitably reflect the alternative theme from Ephesians.

NINETEENTH SUNDAY IN ORDINARY TIME

The main theme of this Sunday is taken from the gospel reading from John where the author speaks of the revelation of Jesus as the bread "that came down from heaven." According to St. John, there are two ways of living, one we know quite well, and one that is not so familiar. The one we know well concerns all that is around us, represented by the term "world"—the familiar, the known, the place where the customary occurs—and is filled with apparent security. The other is very different, for it is not bound by surroundings, or geography, or class in society; it is the realm bound by the word of God. The word which calls us and challenges us out of our security in this world invites us to live a new kind of life, where we no longer feel satisfied with the world, where the world's standards are seen as empty and false, and the world's security proves to be no security at all. For the celebration of the eucharist, the Church turns aside from the "world" to focus on the presence of the word of God whose instruction sharpens our vision and redirects our sights to realize all that the eucharist means—to achieve as best we can the delicate balance demanded by living in the world, but having a set of values often at variance with it; of being totally immersed in our humanity, but realizing all the time the constant call of the divinity in Christ. We are called to live our ordinary lives in such a way that others may see the extraordinary truth to which we are dedicated because of the revelation of Jesus Christ. As is evident in today's gospel, there was bound to be conflict and discussion about this Jesus who confounded the standards of the world, and even gave new and deeper meanings to sacred traditions of Israel. From now on the only good news would be his, the only inspiration and source of life would be from him, the only security would be found from trusting in him, the only way of life would be his way, the only definition of life would be the kind of life he came to give.

To live according to the life-style demanded by the gospel requires that we live Christ's life and rely on him in faith and trust. It is because we have been baptized and already share the life of God that we come to the eucharist to be strengthened on our way to life eternal. The food of the eucharist becomes for us, not a sort of accessory, but the very source of growth in the word of God. It is not just a religious ceremony for one hour a week, but it becomes a way of living our faith; it is our celebration of joy in the presence of the risen Lord and our hope and consolation to live life according to his word.

The Old Testament lesson and the responsorial psalm introduce the notion of the eucharist as food and the source of strength. Just as Elijah ate and drank and was sustained for forty days and forty nights, so the Christian in the eucharistic assembly is strengthened to live in this world as a believer, who continually heeds the summons of the word of God.

The alternative theme for this Sunday, from the second reading of the epistle to the Ephesians, continues the exhortation section of the letter with specific examples of the kind of conduct expected of one initiated into the Body of Christ. Not holding grudges, keeping one's temper, not raising our voices, keeping from name-calling, and avoiding spitefulness are possible for the believer because of the presence of the Spirit of God. The basis of Christian morality is the gift of the Spirit we have received at baptism. The strength to forgive others is from the Lord who has already forgiven us. To ask God's forgiveness requires that we also share his forgiveness with others.

The rite of blessing and sprinkling with holy water could be introduced by a comment about the nature of the Christian's life in the world or about the eucharist as the source and sign of reconciliation. Should the presider use the third penitential rite (c), the major theme of the day could be introduced with invocations from the sixth and seventh examples which speak of being fed with the Lord's body and blood, of Christ as our way to the Father, as the one who brings us the consolation of his truth, and as the Shepherd who continually leads his flock. For the alternative theme of the day, the fourth set of invocations, about Christ who reconciles us with each other and with the Father, who heals the wounds of sin and division, and who intercedes for us with the Father, is a suitable choice.

The alternative opening prayer, the prayer over the gifts, and the prayer after communion speak of the eucharist as the source of our growth in the life promised, and as the sacrament of our salvation. The opening prayer itself is more generally oriented to the reading from Ephesians, as it speaks in terms of the Spirit as the gift of God in the community.

This same theme of the Spirit dwelling with the community is mentioned in preface number 6 of Sundays in Ordinary Time. In preface number 8, the Spirit is seen as the source of Church unity with the Church as his dwelling place. The main theme of the day is reflected in preface number 2, about being destined for eternal life, and in number 4, about everlasting life from God, which in terms of Johannine theology comes from being reborn "from above."

To reiterate the theme of the letter to the Ephesians, the presider could suitably introduce the Our Father by using the third invitation of prayer, about forgiving others as we ask the Lord to forgive us. He might also expand the invitation to the sign of peace to signify the unity believers share in Christ through the Holy Spirit.

For the concluding blessing of the liturgy, the main theme of the day is noted in numbers 18 and 20 of the prayers over the people, and the alternative theme from Ephesians is noted in number 23 of

these prayers, about showing true love for others in the
community.

TWENTIETH SUNDAY IN ORDINARY TIME

It is the opinion of many exegetes that today's gospel pericope is
the most problematic of this sixth chapter of the gospel of John.
The question is: are these verses, which obviously have eucharistic
implications, the work of the evangelist himself or are they from
the hand of a later editor who was concerned to convey Johannine
theology in terms that would reflect the sacramental practice of the
early Church?

The reading begins with Jesus saying that he is the living bread
come down from heaven. Then he goes on to say in a striking way
that his flesh and blood is to be eaten and drunk. The flesh of the
Son of Man gives a share in true life with God.

In John's text, Jesus affirms most solemnly that the only way that
one can have life is through eating and drinking his very self, and
this communion insures life forever with the Father. In the light of
this gospel text, the result of ritual eating and drinking may be
interpreted as the major means by which believers can be united
with Christ, thus intensifying any preexisting relationship with him.

One way the worship committee can apply this gospel reading
would be to emphasize the eucharist as a communal meal in which
sharers come face to face with Christ. It could also be pointed out
that by sharing the sacramental meal of Christ's body and blood,
we receive through him the life of the Father.

The celebration of the eucharist could be the theme of the day,
especially since today's reading from Proverbs concerns feasting. To
share in the present meal of the eucharist is itself to anticipate the
fullness of divine riches and blessings in the eschatological feast of
heaven. This could also be a fitting theme for this Sunday since the
eucharist as an anticipation now of this feast of heaven is often
neglected in expositions on this sacrament.

The alternative theme of this Sunday comes from the reading
from Ephesians in which the author continues the moral
exhortation section of the letter by urging the faithful to be alert
and alive to the Lord's commands, and to be filled with God's spirit
instead of with intoxicants. The misuse of wine should be replaced
by reliance on the Lord's Spirit. The author points out how

Christians should behave, in contrast to the way "fools" act. The Christian life, if lived the way it should be lived, is itself a sign of opposition to the evil of this age.

For the introduction to the liturgy this Sunday, the rite of blessing and sprinkling with holy water could quite suitably be used with a reworded introduction about the banquet shared at the eucharist, and the Lord's invitation to share in his very life at this meal. The morality demanded of the Christian or emphasis on singing "praise to the Lord" reflect well the text of the letter to the Ephesians. The invocations in the sixth and seventh examples of the third penitential rite (c) could be combined to reflect the Johannine terminology of the gospel.

Both opening prayers speak clearly about the unity theme of the Ephesians reading. The prayer over the gifts and the prayer after communion both speak in Johannine terms of offering at the eucharist what the Father has given us so that we may receive the gift of communion with his Son, and so become one with Christ.

That we are called to offer praise to the Father for his many graces and blessings, as noted in the reading from Ephesians, is the theme of preface number 5 of Sundays in Ordinary Time, about praising the marvels of the Father's wisdom and power, and preface number 8, about praising the works of the Father. The main theme of the day is noted in preface number 1, about being called from darkness to light, and in number 2, about being destined for eternal life.

For the concluding blessing of the liturgy, the main theme of the day is noted in numbers 18 and 20 of the prayers over the people, and the alternative theme from Ephesians is found in number 23, about remaining close to the Lord in prayer and to each other in lives of service.

TWENTY-FIRST SUNDAY IN ORDINARY TIME

This Sunday's liturgy marks the end of the series of readings from both the letter to the Ephesians and the gospel of John; beginning next week the second reading is taken from the letter of James, and the gospel of Mark resumes as the gospel proclamation. The gospel text continues the Johannine emphasis on life from the Son of Man by partaking in his very flesh and blood. Furthermore, not only his body but his words are important, for these contain spirit and life. The demand of faith on the part of the Twelve would seem to be the major theme of today's gospel and hence it coincides with the theme of faith in Christ as foundational for any effective sacramental celebration (as mentioned in the theme of the eighteenth Sunday noted above). It is important to note that in last Sunday's gospel Jesus speaks of himself as "the bread of life"; in today's reading the emphasis is on the faith of the Twelve by which they accept Jesus as Lord.

The point here is that just as the will accepts Jesus as Lord it does not do so all by itself, but by acting in union with and under the impulsion of the Father's love. Johannine theology sees that faith is both gift and response to this gift in willing submission to the Lord.

The Old Testament reading from Joshua concerns the choice that was to be made by the people of Israel between their Lord and Savior and other gods whose influence had been spreading. Here, the people are vigorous in their affirmation of faith in the Lord and they proceed not only to state this belief, but they then recount his mighty deeds of salvation, specifically his leading them from the oppression of their sojourn in Egypt. Such a response to God's loving care should be made by the community gathered for the celebration of the eucharist; called by the Father, they come to affirm their faith in God. Especially in the fourth eucharistic prayer, they recount the love of the Father from the dawn of creation through the Exodus and the events of the Old Testament, culminating in the ministry of Jesus and his passage from death to life, the memorial of which is the Christian eucharist. A most appropriate theme for the liturgy this Sunday would be the need for awareness of what we do in celebrating the eucharist and the need for faith, all the while recalling God's deeds for his people.

The alternative theme of the liturgy this Sunday is found in the last paragraph of today's reading from Ephesians where the mystery of the Father's love in Christ is referred to as the mystery of Christ and his Church. This passage is set in the context of the union of husband and wife, which reflects the union of Christ and the Church. As husband and wife are joined in an intimate union, so Christ is joined to his Church, and so believers are joined to their Lord at the celebration of the eucharist.

The rite of blessing and sprinkling with holy water could be introduced this Sunday by reference to our allegiance to Christ and our affirmation of faith in him as the prerequisite for our celebration of the eucharist, or by reference to the mystery of the union of Christ and his Church signified and sacramentalized at the liturgy. Should the presider begin the liturgy with the third penitential rite (c), the use of the seventh set of invocations containing the Johannine terminology of "way" and "truth" would be appropriate to coincide with the gospel theme. The fourth set of invocations, about reconciliation and healing the wounds of sin, would reflect the reading from Ephesians.

The alternative opening prayer, about hearing the word and longing for the Lord more than for the things of this life, and even life itself, coincides with the major theme of the gospel of the day. The theme of the Ephesians reading is reflected in the opening prayer about being joined in unity in mind and heart, and is underscored as well in the prayer over the gifts, about the peace and unity which is Christ's gift to the Church. The most appropriate preface to proclaim would be preface number 1 of Sundays in Ordinary Time, since it speaks of the Church as the chosen race, the royal priesthood, and the holy nation of God's own possession, and of being called from darkness to light. Preface number 8 would also be suitable to reflect the text from Ephesians since it speaks of the unity of Father, Son, and Spirit as a model for Church unity, and the Church as the dwelling place of the Spirit.

TWENTY-SECOND SUNDAY IN ORDINARY TIME

The main focus of attention in the Old Testament reading, the responsorial psalm, and the gospel of Mark proclaimed this Sunday is on being faithful to the covenant of God with his people, the meaning of authentic tradition in the life of the Church, and morality as taught by Jesus. The revelation enshrined in the book of Deuteronomy concerns the obligations placed on those involved in the covenant with Yahweh, where the covenant is understood to require a certain response from those committed to it—Yahweh demanded a response that showed up in their lives and behavior.

In today's gospel reading, Jesus criticizes the way the Scribes and Pharisees "cling to human tradition." He takes these teachers to task because of their concern for conformity to prescribed actions which did not necessarily reflect sincere or authentic piety. For Jesus, what is important is not the minute observance of manmade customs, but rather the internal disposition of our hearts. The teachers of the Old Law had become immersed in a juridicism which stifled true religion and religious practices.

In the reading from Mark, Jesus quotes Isaiah's saying that "lip service" is not enough. True morality, then, is concerned with the dispositions of hearts, and not merely with actions. Jesus' kind of morality offers a greater challenge to men and women than that of the Scribes and Pharisees, for it depends on sincerity of heart, not just doing "the right thing." Actions expressive of authentic devotion were necessary, but if they were done merely to fulfill a legal observance, they would be of little avail.

One theme for the liturgy based on these readings concerns Christian morality as a way of acting from Christlike motives. An alternative theme for this Sunday, from the letter of James, stresses the necessity of doing what the word of the Lord commands, not merely listening to it. What is particularly striking is the part of this text which maintains that concern for the poor and those in sorrow is an essential aspect of religion and is not to be considered as merely an option of faith. A series of liturgies and homilies about the social awareness that should be part of the life of a Christian would be a most appropriate interpretation of this series of readings since the letter of James is read through the twenty-sixth Sunday of the year. Social action and inner-city concern were emphasized in the late 1960s and early 1970s, but there has been some recent slackening of such efforts. The letter of James is quite clear that social concern is at the heart of our faith.

The rite of blessing and sprinkling with holy water could be introduced by mentioning that our faith demands action, not just pious sentiment. Should the third penitential rite (c) be chosen for use this Sunday, invocation number 7, about Jesus showing the way to the Father, and his calling us to reconciliation with one another and with the Father (number 4) would be appropriate to emphasize the main theme of the readings.

For the alternative theme of the day, the eighth set of sample invocations presents the example of Christ as the model of the lives of believers, as they call upon him who cured the sick, forgave sinners, and extended his healing to those in need.

The beginning of the opening prayer is almost identical with the text of the letter of James about every good gift coming from on high. The alternative opening prayer emphasizes this same letter by speaking of faith and the efforts of those who live the Christian life.

The prayer after communion asks that the eucharistic celebration may help us to serve God by serving others.

The fourth eucharistic prayer, with its preface, would be a suitable selection this Sunday because it mentions the mercy of God and his covenant; it also highlights the continuity of the Old and New Testaments by speaking of the revelation of God through the prophets, and of Jesus' ministry to the poor, the imprisoned, and the sorrowing as an example for his followers to imitate.

Being faithful to the Lord's covenant in the practice of the faith and in the conduct of our lives is the theme in numbers 2 and 6 of the prayers over the people. Solemn blessing 3 for Ordinary Time, about growth in faith and perseverance in good works, and numbers 7 and 20 of the prayers over the people, about doing good and sharing the love of God with others, are suitable conclusions to a liturgy based on the second reading.

TWENTY-THIRD SUNDAY IN ORDINARY TIME

The gospel text for this Sunday narrates the cure of a deaf man and contains many typically Markan traits of style and theology. The fact that Jesus raises his eyes to heaven and breathes a sigh may be understood to indicate, in however subtle a way, that the power of God is at work in him. The miracle itself is performed apart from the crowd. But when they realize that the man has been cured, they immediately start to proclaim the news. Jesus, however, bids them "not to tell anyone." This is characteristic of the Markan gospel, where Jesus conceals his Messiahship during his ministry. The cry of the crowd: "He makes the deaf hear and the mute speak," is an allusion to Isaiah's prophecy, foretelling the coming of the Messianic kingdom, when the ". . . eyes of the blind will be opened, the ears of the deaf cleared," as in today's first reading.

In today's gospel, Jesus is shown as the one who not only makes the deaf hear and the dumb speak, but is the proclaimer of the good news of salvation. Furthermore the preaching of this Good News is seen to be the work of the later Church, which continues

Jesus' ministry in preaching the gospel. The Messianic times begun in Christ continue in the present Church as it awaits the kingdom still to come. In the time between the preaching of Jesus and his second coming, the present Church ministers as the herald of his Good News, which proclamation is as effective as flowing water in desert places and making a once barren land fertile and lush (first reading). This regeneration is like the one that Jesus will work in our hearts and minds, for in the preaching of the gospel we too share in a new relationship with God that transcends the Old Covenant. In today's Church, the miracles and deeds of Jesus are not repeated, but his renewal of his people and the world continues through the work of his Church.

The alternative theme of the liturgy of the word this Sunday, taken from the letter of James, is a continuation of the basic theology of the letter wherein a life based on a double standard is reprobated. Places of honor are not to be the source of controversy and conflict, nor should one judge according to the status which society determines. The letter points out that the world's standards are empty and false, and that it is the "poor in the eyes of the world" who are to be heirs of the kingdom of God. Again, one application of this text would be in terms of social awareness and gospel standards as opposed to the trends of modern society, especially where class distinction and race prejudice are concerned.

The introduction to the rite of blessing and sprinkling with holy water could be reworded to invite the community to participate in this eucharist as a participation here and now in the Messianic age begun in Christ. The alternate theme of the scripture readings could also serve to introduce the celebration by stressing our willingness to hear the word of God, especially when it calls into question our very lives and invites us to self-examination and repentance. Should the presider use the third penitential rite (c), the eighth set of invocations, about Christ healing the sick, forgiving sinners, and offering the strength of the eucharist to those in need, coincides with the main theme of the day's liturgy. The message of the alternative theme is emphasized in the fourth set of invocations, about Christ healing the wounds of sin and division, interceding before the Father, and being the source of reconciliation.

The alternative opening prayer speaks of the love of the Father in terms of opening the eyes of believers to appreciate the wonders of his creation. The main theme of the Lord inaugurating the Messianic age in his ministry and spreading his love among the members of the community is at least alluded to in preface number 1 of Sundays in Ordinary Time, about his calling us from darkness to light; preface number 6 speaks of our sharing now in the Messianic age, through hearing and sharing in the good news of his gospel.

In line with the main theme of the day, solemn blessing number 5 of Sundays in Ordinary Time, about the word of God in our hearts, and numbers 20 and 24 of the prayers over the people, about God's blessing and being filled with his Good News, as well as asking the Lord to keep us from harm and firm in the faith, are appropriate selections. In the spirit of the alternative theme of the letter of James, solemn blessing number 3, about growth in faith and persevering in good works, as well as numbers 7 and 20 of the prayers over the people, about doing good and sharing the love of God with others, are suitable conclusions to the liturgy.

TWENTY-FOURTH SUNDAY IN ORDINARY TIME

In today's gospel reading, the evangelist for the first time depicts Jesus as the Messiah and as one who would have to suffer and die. The confession made by Peter that Jesus is the Messiah is followed by Jesus' injunction, typical of the Markan style, to tell no one of his true identity. Peter's confession marks the end of a section of the Markan gospel wherein Jesus has shown again and again that in him the power of God the Father is at work. In the next section of the gospel, Jesus states that, as the Son of Man, he will have to suffer, die, and rise again. He then points out to the crowd and to his own disciples that anyone who wants to follow him will have to imitate his suffering and death in order to share the glory of the resurrection. This statement, unlike Peter's confession that Jesus is the Messiah, is spoken openly so that everyone may know the implications of accepting him as Lord. To be members of the Christian community we must be willing to deny our very selves and take up our crosses to follow the Lord. To lose our human life for the sake of the gospel means, in reality, to save our life for eternity. This prediction of Jesus' passion, death, and resurrection here, as well as in other parts of the New Testament, must be seen against the background of Old Testament prophecies, such as the one in today's first reading from one of the Suffering Servant songs of Isaiah. The servant is Jesus, and the servant followers of Jesus have to accept suffering quite willingly, and be equally willing to give up their lives. Today's responsorial psalm echoes the same message: those who humble themselves and conform to the Lord's will are assured that the Lord will hear their voice when they cry to him, and that he will free their souls from death.

One particular stylistic trait found in today's gospel reading recurs again and again in the rest of the Markan corpus, and that is the use of the word "way." Jesus speaks to his followers as they were "on the way," a term which indicates that his way is one that will lead both himself and them to suffering and death. The liturgy for this and subsequent Sundays could center on what it means to follow Jesus in his way.

The alternative theme of this Sunday is again taken from the epistle of James with its famous statement that "faith without works is dead." This general principle stresses the practice of the faith, and notes that works of charity are an essential part of the work of religion.

In accordance with the main scripture readings of the day, the introduction to the rite of blessing and sprinkling with holy water could be so worded as to show that the way of life of a follower of Christ is the way of suffering and even death in imitation of the passion and death of Jesus. The alternative theme could be introduced with an exhortation to heed the Word of God, especially when its teaching demands a change in the lives of its hearers. Should the presider use the third penitential rite (c), invocations about Christ as the Son of Man, the Lamb of God, and the risen Lord would coincide with the theme of the gospel.

The opening prayer speaks of our serving the Lord with all our heart, and thus coincides with the proclamation of the letter of James; the alternative opening prayer speaks of the Father as the source of strength for people in need, and hence assures the members of the community that in their trial, their strength will come from the Lord their God.

The prayer after communion asks clearly in terms of the gospel of the day that the celebration of the eucharist may influence our thoughts and actions and that the Spirit may guide us on our way to the Father.

For the main theme of the day, preface number 2 of Sunday in Ordinary Time, about Christ's humiliation at his birth and his suffering on the cross, and number 4, about Christ's suffering freeing us from sin, are appropriate selections.

The fourth eucharistic prayer, with its proper preface, would be suitable if the liturgy is focused on Jesus' ministry to the poor and the oppressed as a model of the Christian life of faith and work.

For the main theme of the day, numbers 14 and 17 of the prayers over the people, about the mystery of Christ's redemption as the source of our joy, and his suffering on the cross as our source of new life and hope, are appropriate selections.

Solemn blessing number 3, about persevering in good works and walking in charity and peace, as well as numbers 2, 7, and 20 of the prayers over the people, are suitable choices for a liturgy centered on James' theme that faith without good works is dead.

TWENTY-FIFTH SUNDAY IN ORDINARY TIME

Today's gospel proclamation contains the second prediction of the passion in Mark's gospel. The author also presents in typical Markan fashion the revelation about suffering which Jesus' disciples will have to undergo. This gospel reading begins with Jesus and his disciples coming down from the mountain after his transfiguration, a revelation which Jesus wants to be kept secret. One might expect that at this point Jesus would explain the meaning of the transfiguration. Instead, Jesus teaches his disciples that he must be delivered into the hands of men to be put to death and that he would rise after three days. The disciples did not understand his words, and instead of applying the teaching of Jesus to themselves, they preferred to discuss who was the most important in their little group.

It is at this point that Jesus speaks plainly of what following him would mean. They would have to be the servants of all, to rank as the least of all.

The Old Testament reading from the book of Wisdom is a suitable introduction to this gospel as it speaks of the just man who is beset by his enemies who hate him because he is gentle and trusts in God. The psalm echoes this theme by referring to the Lord who alone upholds life and who is a savior in the face of the fierce men who seek the life of the just.

The letter of James is continued this week with less emphasis on the social demands of the Christian life, and more of a concern that community harmony and peace be hallmarks of the Christian community.

The rite of blessing and sprinkling with holy water could be introduced this week by referring to the Christian way of life. This life involves suffering and mutual service and is not concerned with rank or privilege. For a liturgy whose emphasis is on the letter of James, the introduction to the eucharist could mention our duty to hear the word of God and to live by that word. Should the presider choose the third penitential rite (c) as the introduction to the liturgy, invocation number 7, about Jesus as the Good Shepherd who leads us to everlasting life would be appropriate.

Both the opening prayers are geared more to the instruction found in the reading from James than to the theme of the gospel for they speak of loving one another and coming to perfection in Christ. Sunday preface number 2, about Christ's humiliation at his birth and his suffering on the cross, and number 4, about Christ's suffering freeing us from sin and death, are appropriate selections to coincide with the main theme of today's readings. For the theme of the letter of James, preface number 8 of Sundays in Ordinary Time is a suitable choice as it presents the Church's unity as a reflection of the unity of the Father, Son, and Spirit. Number 14 of the prayers over the people, about the mystery of Christ's redemption as the source of new life and hope, or number 17, about Jesus' sufferings at the hands of evil men, would serve to reiterate the main theme of the day. Solemn blessing number 3 of Sundays in Ordinary Time, about persevering in good works and walking in charity and peace, as well as numbers 2 and 20 of the prayers over the people, are suitable choices to reflect the theme of the epistle of James.

TWENTY-SIXTH SUNDAY IN ORDINARY TIME

While the Old Testament lesson for this Sunday's liturgy serves as an introduction to and a commentary on only part of the gospel proclamation of the day, the issues raised in these readings are especially applicable to the Church in our own day. The issue of the encounter between Moses and the two men who were not members of the seventy elders, but who received the inspiration of the spirit for their mission, is symbolic of the Spirit's activity transcending established institutions.

The gospel text tells of a man who was not of Jesus' first followers, but who performed a good work in his name. The reaction of John was hardly one of openness and understanding. The position that Jesus takes is like that of Moses: the work of God is sometimes carried on by people who are outside the community of Christ's followers. Their deeds are not to be spurned so long as such deeds "are not against" Christ and his people.

All that has been said above can be applied to today's Church. Jesus places the premium not on institutional conformity but on fidelity to the Lord and service in his name. At times, to be a Catholic appeared to mean being confined by the seemingly intransigent attitudes of the Church, and the system seemed to be all that mattered. Yet, as a result of reflection on the Gospel, the system has become more flexible. Authority is now defined and understood in terms of service and ministry to those in need of God's mercy. Centrality in Church administration is now balanced by collegiality on many levels of the Church's mission; the celebration of the eucharist itself admits of differing types of ministry.

The poor have been exalted throughout the letter of James, the last portion of which is read on this Sunday, but there are few denunciations against injustice so strong and forthright as those that occur in today's pericope. James excoriates those who give priority to wealth and to storing up the goods of this world. While the obvious reference here is to those who are rich with money and fine things, each Christian community should take stock of its own priorities in the light of James's epistle.

The rite of blessing and sprinkling with holy water could be introduced this Sunday by referring to that fundamental openness to others which the readings of the day require of believers. The sacramental celebrations of the Church can easily take on an air of exclusiveness unless, as in these readings, Christian communities understand that the mercy of God is also at work in other communities not of this household of the faith. The letter of James is concluded this Sunday, and should the committee choose to take a last look at this epistle, the teaching about riches could be emphasized as one of James' best lessons to the community. Should the presider use the third penitential rite (c), invocation number 7, about Jesus showing us the way to the Father, would fit in well with the main theme of the day.

Both opening prayers speak of the forgiveness of the Lord who helps us to "hurry toward the eternal life."

The fourth eucharistic prayer and its proper preface would be a suitable choice to reflect the theme of the gospel and Old Testament lesson since it speaks of the Father's continual offer of the covenant of his love, and the prayer that the Lord would look favorably on all his people, and "all who seek [him] with a sincere heart."

Solemn blessing number 3 in Ordinary Time, about persevering in good works and walking in charity and peace, as well as numbers 2 and 20 of the prayers over the people, are all suitable choices to reiterate the message of the epistle of James; prayer number 2 speaks of granting the community perfect love for each other and prayer number 20 speaks of the riches of God's grace and our love for all people.

TWENTY-SEVENTH SUNDAY IN ORDINARY TIME

Today's discussions about male-female relationships often revolve around the question of the "liberation" of women, that is, freedom from male dominance or oppression. Today's first reading from the book of Genesis is about man and woman and their relationship with one another and with God. Woman is pictured as having her own excellence; she is a complement to man. Man could not be fulfilled by all the creatures around him, for while in Genesis he was instructed to name the animals, they provided no true companionship for him. Actually, man is fulfilled by living with and personally encountering another person who is capable of union with him, and she is called woman. The point of the Genesis reading is that neither is superior to the other; mutuality is to be the basis of male-female relationships; each complements the other and they are indeed no longer two but one flesh. This "one flesh" is more than a physical union, it is rather an intimate union where the whole person is joined to the other so completely that the two can be called "one" in every way. This reading from the book of Genesis joined with the gospel of Mark on this Sunday is the basic biblical teaching on Christian love and marriage. To fulfill this vocation and the demands of true "love" requires hard work and self-sacrifice, for love is not merely a spontaneous emotion or a warm response. In the words of Genesis it requires a separation and a taking leave before it can be fulfilled in joining with and encountering another. "A man leaves father and mother," the reading says, and he becomes one with his wife. This requires an act of faith in the unknown; it requires separation and leave-taking first, and then meeting and joining in the vocation of Christian marriage. The terms of the discussion for the Christian in marriage involve neither dominance nor unbridled freedom, but sacrifice and mutual trust. Whether one is young or old, married or single, already betrothed or just recently fallen in love, it is nevertheless true that each of us is called to express and live our common vocation of loving maturely, not for self-gain or possession, but to complement others.

The teaching of Jesus in the gospel makes marriage more than a contract. In fact, marriage is a convenant between the two married people and God. At times it means dying to self so that love will more than merely survive. And so the vocation of love, as difficult as it is to fulfill, may be tried and tested, explored and deepened, and from such challenges only grow stronger. The sacrament of marriage is strengthened at the eucharist so that the grace and peace of the risen Lord may reign over all who share the vocation of marriage, and seek to fulfill that vocation in developing and ever-deepening that love.

The alternate theme for the liturgy this Sunday is taken from the letter to the Hebrews, portions of which will be read from this week to the next to last Sunday of the year. The reading for this week contains, as does most of this letter, a profound theology and keen insight into the redemptive work of Christ, his continual intercession for his community, and his high priesthood as the source of our liturgical prayer to and praise of the Father. It was by the power of God in him that Christ accomplished his work; it was through his becoming man and in suffering that the Father exalted him to his position of glory. The author stresses here that Christ who consecrates us to the Father, and we who are consecrated are brothers, and are sons of the same Father; it is Christ our brother who makes intercession for us before our Father in heaven.

The introduction to the rite of blessing and sprinkling with holy water may be reworded in terms of the gospel theme of the day to associate the covenant of marriage with the grace and strength of the eucharist as a sacrament of love and a covenant renewal. Another appropriate introduction to the eucharist for these next weeks would be to reflect on the theme from the letter to the Hebrews, which speaks of our participation in Christ's sacrifice and his continual intercession for the community. Should the presider use the third form (c) of the penitential rite, he could select the fourth set of sample invocations to coincide with the Hebrews reading about Christ as the source of reconciliation and his intercession with the Father.

The alternative opening prayer and the prayer after communion coincide with that part of the reading from Hebrews about Christ's leading the Church on the way of salvation and to the Father.

The main theme of the liturgy of the day is reflected in preface numbers 2, 3, and 6 of Sundays in Ordinary Time. The sufferings of Christ, born of the Virgin, were for our salvation (preface 2); the Father sent his Son to restore us to God's friendship (preface 3), and it is because of the Father's love that the Spirit raised Jesus from the dead to be the foretaste and promise of the paschal feast of heaven (preface 6). The reading from Hebrews refers to Christ's accomplishing our redemption through his suffering and death.

For the main theme of the day, the use of solemn blessing number 4 of Sundays in Ordinary Time, about being freed from anxiety and strengthened in the Father's love, is appropriate; of the prayers over the people, numbers 5 and 6, about remaining faithful to the Father's love and leading lives of fidelity to him, are suitable. For the alternative theme of the reading from Hebrews, the use of solemn blessing number 5, about Christ's intercession leading us to our heavenly inheritance, or number 17 of the prayers over the people, about Christ's suffering as our means of salvation, are suitable choices for the conclusion of the eucharist.

TWENTY-EIGHTH SUNDAY IN ORDINARY TIME

A major principle in the interpretation of a passage of the scriptures is to situate the pericope within its original setting in the community for which it was intended, and to discern the intention of the human author who was the instrument of the composition of the word of God. This is particularly helpful when we realize that while the Bible was written long ago, the setting and situation of the congregations for which it was written were often enough not very different from our own. The letter to the Hebrews, for example, was written to a community that was in danger of falling into apostasy and separation from the foundation of faith and trust in their Lord. The community was drifting from their original faith, and a certain boredom became the temper of the times. Hence, to proclaim today's second reading in this frame of reference brings to light some helpful insights into the author's teaching about the word of the God as revealed in the scriptures.

The community in question was most likely composed of Jewish Christians who were committed to the word of God in the Old Testament but who had to be told, rather to their surprise, that the word and revelation of the Father in both the Old and New Testament scriptures was indeed the very source of their understanding of God and the very substance of his revelation to them. It was important for this community to recall that God's word was living and as incisive as a two-edged sword, and it is equally important that today's Church recall the same fact. We too need to be reminded that the revelation of God is double-edged, for just when we feel comfortable with one of its aspects and feel that we have at least understood and come to terms with its demands, precisely then another aspect of the word begins to cut at us and to penetrate our lives. Hence the scriptures, while at times familiar and filled with language and imagery that can become repetitious, are still challenging, exciting, growth-producing, and life-giving. Their message is ever new as it probes the hearts of today's congregations.

One case in point is this Sunday's gospel reading from Mark. A man comes before Jesus to ask what he must do to be saved. Jesus replies that it is not enough for this man to have kept the commandments, but that he must go beyond the commandments and give up his riches.

One lesson to be learned from this episode is that, whether rich or poor, following Jesus means sharing with others, and thus imitating Christ's love for all people. Charity and justice for all were and are gospel values, and giving from what one has so that others may share in the good things of this life remains a constant gospel demand.

The introduction to the rite of blessing and sprinkling with holy water at the beginning of the eucharist could be reworded this Sunday to invite the community to a deeper faith in the Lord and a willingness to share his love with others, or it might suitably reflect the second reading and invite the congregation to openness to the hearing of the word of God. Should the presider use the third penitential rite (c), invocation number 4, about Jesus who came to call us to reconcile us to one another and to the Father would be appropriate. For a liturgy planned to emphasize today's second reading, the introduction could refer to Jesus who created the heavens and the earth, who is himself the Word of God, and who feeds us with word and sacrament.

The main theme of the day, about placing faith in the Lord and sharing his love with others in works of charity, is reflected in the opening prayer and in the prayer over the gifts. Also, the love of Christ as the motivation for the Christian's faith in God and love for each other is the theme of preface numbers 2, 3, and 6 of the Sundays in Ordinary Time. The same theme is found in solemn blessing 3 of Ordinary Time, and numbers 3, 9, and 23 of the prayers over the people. The alternative theme from Hebrews concerning the word of God as ever new in manifesting the will of the Father for us is reflected indirectly in solemn blessing 5 in Ordinary Time, about the word in our heart and walking in the ways of the Lord, and number 20 of the prayers over the people, about the Good News of salvation and our lives of love for all men.

TWENTY-NINTH SUNDAY IN ORDINARY TIME

The gospel of this Sunday speaks about the very nature of Christianity, and it does so in terms that are most distressing, disturbing, and almost embarrassing, for this passage is about becoming another's servant. A common notion as preached by Jesus and exemplified in his life is one of service, and yet if used in almost any other context most people would abhor the thought that we should be the servant (slave) of another. How often do people in our day spend hours thinking up exalted titles for jobs which appear to be menial? This mania over position was also true at the time the gospels were written, for the people of Jesus' day also abhorred being a member of the servant class since if one was born into servitude, one could never "better" oneself, or rise on the social ladder. With this in mind, Jesus takes James and John to task. They did not want to be left out and did not want to be forgotten when positions of authority were assigned in the kingdom. But Jesus said that seeking after positions of prominence was not the way to salvation; the way to true greatness is "to serve the needs of all."

And yet the meaning of the gospel lies at an even deeper level, for this text concerns not merely a reprimand of Jesus to James and John; it was also a reprimand to the community for which the evangelist Mark wrote, since they themselves were asking for glory without suffering. They wanted to avoid any form of persecution and trial despite the fact that to accept such would be to imitate the Messiah.

The message for the infant Church and for us some 2,000 years later is that to be a member of the Christian community means to accept a new set of standards by which to live. For us today, it is not so much that we endure physical rejection and persecution, but rather that our suffering comes from facing changing mores of society where Christian values are held in little esteem. The suffering which one must now undergo involves living up to the message of Jesus despite the temptations to follow the immoral ways of today's world. For the early Church, the comfort and consolation to face such temptation came from the presence of the risen Lord in the community. His presence in today's Church also gives us the courage to accept the gospel's challenge to the world. Indeed, the main theme of this Sunday's liturgy is that we are a small leaven in the mass of society, that we are to be a sign of contradiction to the nations of the world, that we are a pilgrim Church seeking to revolutionize our world with no other arms than the gospel.

The alternative theme of the liturgy for this Sunday is taken from the continuation of the letter to the Hebrews, which deals with the mediation of God's mercy and grace through Christ our high priest. It is through his mediation that we receive courage, for since he is one of us he can understand the foibles, weaknesses, and limitations of our humanity. The last verse of the reading implies that his understanding and strength come to us each time we celebrate the memorial of his death and resurrection and join in his intercession before the throne of the Father. The introduction to the liturgy could be worded in such a way that the eucharist is understood as a means of purifying our motivation and increasing our willingness to assume the role of being a servant for the spread of the Gospel. Also the invitation to join in this act of common worship could be taken from the letter to the Hebrews, about approaching the throne of the Lord's grace. Should the presider use the third penitential rite (c), invocations reflecting the gospel reading of the day would be number 4, about Jesus as having come to heal the wounds of sin and division, and number 2, about Jesus having come in word and sacrament to strengthen us in holiness.

For the alternative theme from Hebrews, number 4, about Jesus who came to reconcile us to one another and to the Father, and number 7, about Jesus showing the way to the Father, would be suitable.

The opening prayer coincides very well with the main theme of the liturgy of the day since it calls on the Father who is our source of power and inspiration and who strengthens us in serving him. The same theme is reiterated in the prayer over the gifts about God's forgiveness and love which gives us the freedom to serve the Father, and continues in an indirect way in the prayer after communion, about the eucharist as our help to remain faithful to the way of eternal life.

The humility of Jesus as the model of our lives of service is mentioned in preface number 1 of Sundays in Ordinary Time, about his cross and resurrection forming us into his holy people; in preface number 2, about his humble birth of the Virgin, and especially in preface number 4, that by his birth we are reborn and in his suffering we are freed from sin. For the theme of the mediatorship of Christ as our high priest, preface number 3 speaks of Christ as our savior who restored us to friendship with the Father; preface number 7 speaks of our salvation through Jesus, who was "one like ourselves," though free from sin, who restores to us the gifts of grace. For the main theme of the day, the use of solemn blessing number 5 in Ordinary Time, about living according to the word of God and doing what is right and good, and numbers 22 and 23 of the prayers over the people, about doing the

Lord's will in our lives and about remaining close to the Lord in prayer and to each other in love, are appropriate choices for the blessing at the end of the liturgy. For the theme of the letter to the Hebrews, the use of number 1 of the prayers over the people, about being led through Christ to life everlasting, is a most appropriate choice for the final blessing.

THIRTIETH SUNDAY IN ORDINARY TIME

The pericope from the book of Jeremiah that is today's first reading speaks of God's love and healing. For Jeremiah, it was by the power of God that the blind see, the lame walk, and the sorrowing are filled with joy. The gospel tells of the blind Bartimaeus who is cured by Jesus. The center of attention is the blind man who sensed the power of the Messiah more than the rest of the crowd and who trusted that Jesus would be able to cure his illness. Today's readings of both gospel and Old Testament exemplify the power of God at work in Jesus' cures. And yet there is a deeper meaning involved here. The key to understanding these readings is that they are not mere historical episodes in the life and times of the prophet or of Jesus. What they point out is that just as God saved the blind and the lame, and just as Jesus healed the blind man who called upon him, so Christ will heal us. The purpose of the liturgical celebration is for the community to speak its need of healing and express its faith in the power of Christ. The guidance of Jesus to help us walk in his paths is as real for contemporary communities as it was for the lame and blind of the reading from Jeremiah and the blind man in the gospel of Mark. Not just the eyes of the people in scriptural times needed opening to share in the vision of God; also the eyes of every member of the worshiping community need to be opened to see the full meaning of the Christian faith. At the eucharistic assembly, we are assured of the presence of the healing and strengthening power of God who came to cure and to save once in history, who comes now to cure and to save us this day as his people. It is, in fact, the present Church that are the blind, the weak, the lame, the downtrodden, and the poor, who need sight and strength to make us upright Christians and members of the Church of Christ.

The alternative theme of this Sunday's liturgy is a continuation of the letter to the Hebrews which speaks of the office of the high priest as one taken from among men to act on their behalf before the Father in heaven—a high priest who can understand the weaknesses of his community because he himself is a member of that same community. It was precisely in his humanity that Christ became our high priest and mediator with the Father because he was man as well as God.

The introduction to the liturgy this Sunday could be worded to make the community aware of its dependence on God. It is through the mercy and love given through the Son that Christian community exists at all. The alternative theme of the day could serve as a suitable introduction to the eucharist since our prayer is through our high priest to the Father; at the liturgy we receive the love and mercy of the Father through Christ. Should the presider use the third penitential rite (c) at the beginning of the eucharist, invocation number 2, about Jesus coming to us in word and sacrament, and number 6, about Jesus raising us to new life, would be fitting. For the alternative theme, invocation number 7, about Christ as the Good Shepherd, and number 1, about Jesus pleading our cause before the Father, would be appropriate.

Both opening prayers of this liturgy, as well as the prayers over the gifts and after communion, all speak of the eucharist as strengthening our faith, hope, and love, enabling us to serve the Father, and affecting the kind of lives we lead once the celebration has ended.

The ministry of Jesus to those most in need, specifically to the poor, the imprisoned, and those in sorrow, is expressed in the fourth eucharistic prayer with its own preface; using it this Sunday would coincide well with the main theme of the liturgy. The fact of Christ's calling us out of darkness to share in his light is mentioned in preface number 1 of Sundays in Ordinary Time, should the presider use another eucharistic prayer. For the theme of the mediatorship of Christ as our high priest, preface number 3 speaks of Christ as our savior who, though one like us, became our mediator with the Father; preface number 7 speaks of our salvation through Jesus who restores to us the gifts of the Father's grace.

The healing and strengthening power of the eucharist keeping the community in the Father's love, and enriching them in faith, hope, and love, is the theme of the solemn blessing number 4 in Ordinary Time. Also numbers 5 and 23 of the prayers over the people speak of the strength we receive at the eucharist to continue to do the Father's will and to live according to his gospel because of his making us whole by his grace. For the theme of the letter to the Hebrews, the use of number 1 of the prayers over the people, about being led to life everlasting through Christ, is a most appropriate choice for the final blessing.

THIRTY-FIRST SUNDAY IN ORDINARY TIME

The value system of Christianity often enough can be interpreted as odd, paradoxical, and difficult to understand. We believe that life comes from death, that gain comes from loss, that receiving comes from giving, and that Christ had to die and rise again that we might share a new life with him on earth. Faith looks at the world and life, not with the eye of the body, but rather with the interior eye of the soul.

While there is really nothing new or startling in the gospel of this Sunday, for it was in fact all said before in the Old Testament, the paradoxes described above startle us because they are so linked that one is impossible without the other. The paradox is that we show love for God by loving other human beings. The biting question which then arises is "who is my neighbor?" Again and again in the gospels Jesus commands us to extend our love toward all people and tells us that we cannot worship the Father unless we are first reconciled with our neighbor. We plead for forgiveness from God and yet the paradox of the Lord's Prayer is that we must pledge ourselves to forgive others.

The main theme of the liturgy for this Sunday concerns this paradox of faith, and the challenge of the commandment, that love of God is only realized by our love for one another. The alternative theme of today's liturgy is in the reading from the letter to the Hebrews, which speaks of Christ as our one high priest. The author makes use of the imagery and language of the Old Law to interpret the high priesthood of Jesus. Our lives and spirituality depend on him as the one priest of the New Covenant, and our sacrifices join his one sacrifice and act of self-offering before the Father.

The rite of blessing and sprinkling with holy water may be introduced this Sunday by referring to the love of God manifest for us at the liturgy, and our love of neighbor as a result of our faith-celebrations. The alternative theme of the liturgy as our participation now in the high priesthood of Christ would be a suitable introduction to the alternate theme of the day. Should the presider use the third form (c) of the penitential rite, the fourth set of sample invocations, about reconciliation with each other and with the Father, of the end of sin and division, and Christ's intercession before the Father, suitably reflects this alternative theme of the readings.

Both opening prayers speak of our lives of faith and concern for others.

The prayer after communion, true to its nature and form, speaks of the eucharist as the source of Christ's continuing work among us.

Preface number 1 of Sundays in Ordinary Time, about being God's chosen people, and preface number 8, about being God's people, the Body of Christ, and the dwelling place of the Spirit, reflect the main theme of the day. For the alternative theme, preface number 1 speaks specifically about the sacrifice of Christ, and number 7 speaks of Christ as our redeemer and source of all gifts of grace. The sign of peace this Sunday could be introduced by reflecting on the teaching of the gospel about love of God and love for others.

Of the solemn blessings in Ordinary Time, number 3, about being strong in faith and good works, and number 5, about walking in the ways of the Lord, as well as numbers 2 and 20 of the prayers over the people, reflect the main theme of the day, especially since these prayers speak specifically of our love for others.

For the alternative theme of the high priesthood of Christ, solemn blessing number 2 in Ordinary Time, about knowing and loving the Lord, and number 5, about the word of God in our hearts, as well as number 5 of the prayers over the people, about rejoicing in the mercy of God, and number 16, about his care and consolation for his people, are appropriate choices.

THIRTY-SECOND SUNDAY IN ORDINARY TIME

The gospel reading for this Sunday joins two apparently unrelated incidents in the ministry of Jesus: his confrontation with the Scribes whose piety was far from authentic, and his praise of the piety of the widow who gave her small savings for the good of others. Although there were some corrupt leaders, there was still hope for Israel since a poor Jewish widow had true religion at heart. The coins she offered were indeed quite insignificant compared with the value of others' donations, and yet she gave all she had and therefore showed others what true giving should mean. The text of Mark is well introduced by today's Old Testament reading about the widow of Zarephath, who was faithful to the one God of Israel, lived in poverty and obvious dependence on God, and who received the prophet's blessing.

The virtues of the widows in these texts, especially in the light of those to whom they are compared, form the main interest in the liturgy this week. The comparison is not merely on the level of giving, but also on the assurance of the Lord's protection for those who revere his name and teaching. The psalm continues the teaching of these readings by speaking about the Lord giving justice to those to whom it was denied, food to the hungry, liberty to prisoners, sight to the blind, and sustenance to orphans and widows.

The alternative theme of the liturgy this week is from the continuation of the letter to the Hebrews which treats Christ's sacrificial role as the fulfillment of the ceremony of expiation spoken of in Leviticus 16:11–16. Jesus' sacrifice, unlike those of the Old Law, is definitive and final. He does not have to suffer many times, and his sacrifice is not repeated. It is the constant teaching of this letter that there is one perfect sacrifice of Christ once for all. A most fundamental and important aspect of our worship assemblies is that we do not repeat what is the unrepeatable sacrifice of Jesus; rather we enter into his once-for-all redemption for all.

According to the main theme of the liturgy this Sunday, the kingdom of God belongs to those who have purity of intention and true piety; in the alternative theme we learn that the Christian community shares in this kingdom at the eucharistic celebration.

The rite of blessing and sprinkling with holy water could be introduced this week in accord with the main theme of the readings by mentioning the example of the pious widow as one to whom the kingdom belongs. The celebration of the liturgy as our entering into the offering of Christ to the Father could be mentioned as part of this introduction in accord with the theme of the reading from Hebrews. Should the presider use the third penitential rite (c), the main theme of the day is reflected in the first set of sample invocations, about the contrite being healed by the Lord, and Christ calling sinners; for the alternative theme of the day, the fourth set of invocations, about reconciliation, healing sin and division, and Christ's intercession with the Father, is a most suitable choice.

The prayer over the gifts coincides with the theme of the letter to the Hebrews about our liturgy as a proclamation of the once-for-all death of the Lord, while the prayer after communion speaks of the eucharist as our nourishment from these holy gifts and can be taken as a reflection of today's Old Testament lesson about the feeding of the prophet Elijah. Preface number 2 of Sundays in Ordinary Time reflects the main theme of the day in that it presents Christ as our model of humility as he took on our humanity and was born of a woman. For the alternate theme of the day, preface number 1, about the sacrifice of Christ, and number 7, about him as our redeemer and source of all gifts of grace, are appropriate selections. For the major theme of the day, solemn blessing number 5 of Ordinary Time, about walking in the ways of the Lord and knowing what is right and good, as well as numbers 5 and 24 of the prayers over the people, are fitting conclusions to the liturgy where these prayers express the trust in God characteristic of the widow in the first reading. For the alternative theme from the letter to the Hebrews, solemn blessings number 2 and 5, as well as numbers 5, 16, and 18 of the prayers over the people, are appropriate selections for the conclusion of the liturgy.

THIRTY-THIRD SUNDAY IN ORDINARY TIME

Beginning this week, the Sunday readings turn to a more apocalyptic and eschatological theme: the Old Testament reading this week is from the book of Daniel and the gospel text is from Mark 13, a chapter filled with the imagery of Jewish apocalyptic. The same imagery is found at the beginning of the season of Advent, and to show the cyclical nature of the Church year, the next few Sundays deal with the common theme of the end times and the coming of the Lord. The imagery of the scriptures is often difficult to understand and to interpret adequately because many of its references are agrarian in nature and much of it is based on the customs and social institutions of Israel. But the imagery of apocalyptic is especially difficult to understand. At first glance it seems to be a kind of war of the worlds, science fiction. Yet it is, in reality, a form of conveying biblical truth. On one level these texts seem almost embarrassing since they deal with the end of time in a cosmic and symbolic way that seems most fantastic. And yet, at the heart of these readings is much more than a simplistic conflict between good and evil, light and darkness. Indeed, the basis of this kind of imagery is that these extremes must be dealt with continually and that one's allegiance can never be termed "neutral." To be "neutral" or lukewarm is decried in the scriptures, and the imagery here reminds the community that allegiance must be firm and direct, clearly spoken and not hidden. Such imagery is unsettling and uncomfortable, but the judgment mentioned should not be understood as coming at the end of time when an angry God will get his due; rather the judgment is exacted on ourselves when we realize that our Christianity is not what it should be. In the face of a world of sin and lack of faith, what is at the heart of these readings is a conversion that is real and truly lived, not debated or put off until another day. What is important is the "now" of salvation and our determination that we will work to root out sin and evil in our lives, and that we want to be ever faithful to the Lord who will come again in glory.

The alternative theme of the readings this Sunday is from the letter to the Hebrews, where this last passage of this series of readings speaks of our sins being forgiven by the sacrifice of Christ who is now seated at the right hand of the Father. The image of the "right hand" of God is important in the language of apocalyptic; today's psalm speaks of God showing the faithful person "the joys of your right hand forever." The reality of sin-forgiveness and of living our lives in fidelity to the forgiving Lord is an appropriate interpretation of this text in accord with the nature of the Church year, with the season of Advent soon to come.

The rite of blessing and sprinkling with holy water could be suitably introduced this Sunday by referring to the reality of our newness of life through Christ, who has brought us by our common baptism from darkness to light, from sin to forgiveness, from death to life. The alternative theme of the day's liturgy could be mentioned in this introduction in terms of the forgiveness of sins at the eucharist because of the intercession of Christ before the Father. Should the presider use the third penitential rite (c) as the introduction to the liturgy, the second set of suggested invocations about the Lord's coming in glory reflects well the main theme of the day, and the use of the fourth set, about reconciliation and intercession through Christ, reflects the alternative theme of the day.

The opening prayer reflects the main theme of the day about being faithful to the Lord; the prayer over the gifts speaks about the Lord bringing us to life eternal, and the prayer after communion speaks of celebrating this eucharist in memory of Christ who is Lord forever and ever.

For the main theme of this Sunday, preface number 2 of Sundays in Ordinary Time, about eternal life through Christ, and number 4, about our entrance into the heavenly kingdom, would be appropriate, as would preface number 1, about our being freed from sin and death, to reflect the alternative theme of the day. For the main theme, solemn blessing number 4 in Ordinary Time, about the happiness of heaven as well as number 5, about walking in the Lord's ways, would be appropriate choices as would numbers 1, 4, and 16 of the prayers over the people. For the alternate theme of the day, solemn blessings numbers 2 and 5, as well as numbers 5, 16, and 18 of the prayers over the people are appropriate selections.

SUNDAYS OF THE YEAR "C" CYCLE

SECOND SUNDAY IN ORDINARY TIME

Jesus is manifested as the king of all nations at the Epiphany, when the astrologers come to worship him. He is shown as the Son of God at his baptism in the Jordan. In today's gospel, Jesus is manifested in a third way—as one who works signs and wonders by his divine power.

Today's celebration, then, rounds out the theme of Epiphany and Baptism of the Lord, hence, the use of the gospel of John on this Sunday, the one exception to the use of the Lukan gospel throughout the "C" cycle. The responsorial psalm carries on the theme of the manifestation of Jesus' power as it speaks of the Lord's "deeds to all nations." The theme of Jesus' kingly power enunciated in the liturgy of Epiphany is reiterated here.

In today's gospel, Christ manifests his power to the disciples and to his followers, but not to its fullest extent. That supreme manifestation of the Father's love for man in Christ would come when the God-Man died on the cross. This text is significant because it asks believers to look beyond signs and wonders worked by Christ to the One performing them and to respond in faith and trust in the Lord. The scene is typical of the Johannine author for in it Christ's followers are challenged again and again to deepen their conviction and to judge for themselves where their loyalties lie.

Today's Old Testament reading from Isaiah, with its marriage symbolism, has an obvious relationship with the narrative of the wedding feast at Cana. At that wedding feast Jesus begins his ministry which will fulfill the hopes and expectations of the Old Testament, and open a new way of life for all people.

The alternative theme for this Sunday, taken from the reading from first Corinthians, concerns an especially difficult question that arose in the Corinthian church and that arises in the Church today. How is it that some people in the Christian community possess gifts that are greater than the gifts other persons in the same community possess? And yet, all these gifts come from the same Spirit. Paul answers that no matter what the gifts are, or who possesses them, they must always be used for the common good.

The rite of blessing and sprinkling with holy water is certainly the preferred introduction to the Sunday liturgy as it has been designed to replace the other forms of the penitential rite on the Lord's day. However, should the presider prefer to use the third form (c) of the penitential rite, he might wish to use either the second or the seventh sample sets of invocations which reflect typical Johannine themes.

For the composition of the prayer of the faithful, the committee may wish to use as guides sample formula I for Ordinary Time or those noted as "General Formulas." These, however, should serve as no more than helps in the composition of this prayer, which should also reflect the needs and concerns of particular communities.

Since the main theme of the liturgy concerns the revelation of Christ, Sunday preface number 3 or 7 of Sundays in Ordinary Time would be suitable for proclamation since they both speak of our salvation accomplished in Christ.

For the main theme of the liturgy, the third of the solemn blessings in Ordinary Time, about being strengthened in faith, would be a suitable conclusion to the liturgy, as would be number 9 or number 16 of the prayers over the people, which speak of the present community as the people who believe in Christ, and as a community asking for consolation now and life eternal.

The alternative theme of the day is reflected in both forms of the opening prayer since they speak of peace in the community. For the preface this Sunday both the first and the eighth of the Sunday prefaces in Ordinary Time speak of the community of the Church, yet the eighth speaks most directly of the Church and the Body of Christ.

The third invitation to pray the Our Father, about forgiveness of others, would be helpful to continue the message of the reading from first Corinthians.

Of the prayers over the people, number 2, about having perfect love for one another and number 20, about love for all, are appropriate conclusions to the liturgy.

THIRD SUNDAY IN ORDINARY TIME

This is the first Sunday in Ordinary Time to have a pericope from Luke as its gospel reading; this reading is an introduction to the whole Lukan gospel. The quotation from Isaiah as found in the pericope, about Christ's role as the Servant of the Father, sounds the keynote of Luke's message about Christ.

In the first section of the reading, the evangelist confesses that he was not an eyewitness to the events he recounts, but rather relies on such witnesses for his own work in composition and arrangement of the gospel. This disposes of the commonly accepted belief that the evangelists were present at all the scenes they recount. Recent biblical criticism emphasizes rather that the gospel authors had access to already existing material, whether oral or written. The science of interpreting the scriptures is largely concerned with the message the evangelists intended to convey when they edited and adapted this material.

The second part of the gospel reading interprets the ministry of Jesus in the light of the text quoted from Isaiah. The evangelist sees this text as prophetic of Jesus as the Servant of Yahweh, as the preacher of the good news to the poor, liberator of captives, restorer of sight to the blind, and as the one to announce the Lord's favor. One obvious meaning of this text is that today's Church must continue Jesus' ministry to the poor, the imprisoned, and the disabled. Another aspect that might be stressed is the definition of exactly who are those in need. Luke points out that it is not only the physically disabled or physically imprisoned who need to hear the gospel. All of us need to hear the good news preached, for we all need our poverty filled with the Lord's graciousness, our blindness cured by the vision of God's glory, our bondage broken by the Lord's presence with us. Indeed, it is not only the economically downtrodden or the physically oppressed who are in need of the gospel; it is the whole Church that stands in need of this healing word.

The challenge of those planning this liturgy may be to make the more fortunate and affluent community of the faithful aware of its need for God and his love and of his call to help the poor and suffering.

The Old Testament reading from Nehemiah, about Ezra and the scroll of the Law of the Lord, as well as the responsorial psalm, about the word of the Lord as spirit and life, all converge to shed light upon the main theme of the Sunday's liturgy.

The alternative theme for this Sunday continues that of last week's reading from the same chapter of first Corinthians by speaking about the Body of Christ. This text considers the human body in which differing functions are essential for the integrity of the whole, and applies it by analogy to the Church. Thus, the Church is a community of believers whose lives and various abilities work together through the Spirit, who gives the whole body its vitality and causes it to develop.

The rite of blessing and sprinkling with holy water could be introduced by reference to hearing the word of the Lord and to celebrating his healing and strength in the eucharist as the purpose of this assembly.

The alternative theme of the liturgy could be introduced by speaking of the unity in Christ which is ours because we were initiated into and share a common faith and trust in the Lord.

For the main theme of the liturgy of the day, the presider may wish to use invocations which speak of Christ proclaiming the Good News, healing those in need, and strengthening us in the eucharist.

The two forms of the opening prayer closely parallel those for last week since they speak in general terms of unity and peace; the opening prayer itself is the more succinct of the two.

To reiterate today's gospel text, the use of the fourth eucharistic prayer with its own preface would be fitting since this prayer echoes the text from Isaiah quoted in today's gospel: "to the poor he proclaimed the good news of salvation, to prisoners freedom, and to those in sorrow joy."

For the alternative theme, the presider could use either the first or the eighth preface of Sundays in Ordinary Time since both speak of the Church; this is particularly true of the eighth, which mentions the Church specifically as the Body of Christ.

The third invitation to pray the Our Father, about forgiveness of others, would be helpful to continue the message of the gospel, as would a reworded introduction to the sign of peace.

For the conclusion of the liturgy based on the main theme from the gospel and Old Testament readings, the presider could fittingly choose the fifth solemn blessing in Ordinary Time, about being kept from all harm, having the word of the Lord in our hearts, and walking in the Lord's ways.

Of the prayers over the people, number 20, about the Lord bringing the good news of salvation and filling us with love, would be the most appropriate. For the alternative theme, number 2, about having perfect love for one another, and number 23, about being strengthened by the Lord's grace and remaining close to each other in prayer, are appropriate choices.

FOURTH SUNDAY IN ORDINARY TIME

The first reading from the beginning of the book of the prophet Jeremiah, together with the gospel about Jesus' discourse in the synagogue at Nazareth, provide at least two themes around which to plan this Sunday liturgy. The first would be a treatment of the vocation to prophecy in somewhat general terms, and the other would be a consideration of the universality of salvation as a significant theological point made frequently in the Lukan gospel.

The role of the prophet in today's Church and in the world at large has come to be emphasized strongly in recent years and it would be helpful for contemporary congregations to understand what these two readings say about the prophet's gift. According to Jeremiah, the prophet is one who is sent to speak the word of the Lord, not his own word ("tell them all that I command you"), and to interpret the traditional revelation of God for his contemporaries. The prophet cannot rely on the acclaim of the people, for in fact strength can only come from the Lord who promises his continuing support for those whom he has chosen ("I am with you"). These statements, in conjunction with the gospel text, give us two possible views of what prophecy entails. First, there is the not unexpected reaction of others to the message of the prophet's often unpopular teaching. Indeed the gospel states that he is often regarded without honor in his home territory. How often do we as the hearers of the word put up barriers and prejudices so that we in fact do not hear God's word but refer everything to our own predetermined desires? A second element that could also be elaborated concerns the obvious soul-searching demanded of all of us who are called to lead others to know and love Christ by the kind of lives we lead even more forcefully than by the words we speak.

A second major theme from the gospel reading concerns the universality of salvation as offered by the Father since the former barriers of the Law are now transcended in the missionary efforts of the Church. The examples which Luke uses of the widow of Zarephath and Elijah as well as Naaman the Syrian and Elisha are significant since they require reinterpretation in the present Church so that Christians go forth to preach the word far beyond the limits set by the community of the baptized. For the Catholic Christian, this is even more significant as it requires moving from a notion of the Church that can at times be interpreted as "ghetto-like" to an appreciation of the truly Catholic aspects of our tradition, one aspect of which is its universality. In the Creed we confess our belief in "one holy catholic and apostolic church," and yet how often have we used this section to isolate ourselves from others, rather than to remind ourselves of our sense of mission.

The alternative theme from the second reading in this liturgy is found in the continuation of the first letter to the Corinthian church where Paul moves from his instruction on gifts to a more general instruction on love. Since this text is often used in the wedding rite for Christian marriage, this may be a good opportunity for the homilist to point out that love is not to be identified only with the sacrament of marriage, but is an everyday necessity for a truly Christian life which has Christ as its heart and center.

The rite of blessing and sprinkling with holy water would be a most fitting introduction to this liturgy, especially when the introduction is rewritten to reflect the missionary charge which Christians receive at their baptism. Should the presider use the third form (c) of the penitential rite, he may wish to use invocations about Christ bringing salvation (no. 2), showing us the way to the Father (no. 7).

Both forms of the opening prayer speak of God's love for us and our love for one another, the theme of today's first reading. The ending of today's first reading, with its repetition of the word "all," reflects the gospel theme. The alternative opening prayer mentions the Old Testament figures of Abraham and Moses and is a helpful introduction to the proclamation of the text from Jeremiah.

For the alternative theme the presider may wish to use either the seventh or eighth preface of the Sundays in Ordinary Time. The seventh speaks of the Father's great love for us and of our sharing that love in community, while the eighth speaks of the Body of Christ, the Church.

The sign of peace could be emphasized this Sunday to underscore the universality theme of the gospel since this is a sign of our concern for all men and women and not just for the community gathered at this celebration. The prayer after communion takes up this theme by its mention of the growth of the true faith throughout the world.

For the gospel theme of universality, the use of number 9 of the prayers over the people would be appropriate because of its reference to our sharing God's gift of love with others, and spreading it everywhere. For the alternative theme, the presider may fittingly use the third of the solemn blessings in Ordinary Time as well as numbers 2 and 20 of the prayers over the people.

FIFTH SUNDAY IN ORDINARY TIME

Two themes for consideration at this Sunday's liturgy emerge from the Old Testament and gospel readings: one concerns our idea of God and the second concerns our response to God.

From the very first lines of the Old Testament, reading the otherness of God, his supreme holiness, and the unworthiness of humanity is apparent. In this reading, as elsewhere in the Old Testament, God is shown to be the One who is the infinitely-other. In response to the Lord's call, Isaiah declares that he is a man of unclean lips which need purifying. It is only after Isaiah's lips have been cleansed with a burning ember that he is worthy to accept God's mission.

While the New Covenant stresses a greater intimacy of God with his people, the otherness of God still remains, as is shown in today's gospel where Peter says "Leave me, Lord, I am a sinful man." Indeed this mystery of God, his otherness and his transcendence, should not be forgotten in our present theologizing or worship of God. There is much more to the revelation of the scriptures than a certain chumminess which has filtered into some popular writing about Jesus and his relations with us. The scriptures speak of our being cleansed to do the work of the Lord rather than merely asking if "Jesus is running with us." The Lord is on our side all the time, but especially in our worship of the Trinity we must realize that the God upon whom we call for help and salvation is indeed still the totally "other." Just who is this God we worship? This could be the basic theme of this day's liturgy.

The second theme is vocational and concerns the call of Peter, James, and John. What is to be noted here is that the gospel reading, as well as the context which the Old Testament lesson provides for it, shows that this vocation and call to mission should be interpreted as a response to the Lord's revelation of himself. It is in response to this revelation that all vocations should be interpreted.

The alternative theme suggested in the second reading is worth more than passing attention since this text, along with next Sunday's, concerns the teaching of Paul about the resurrection of Christ as the central affirmation of the Christian faith. This reading expresses the most primitive kerygma of the saving events of the death and life of the risen Christ which we now share. It may be noted that today's second reading from first Corinthians, along with the second readings of the next three Sundays, provides a four-week series about Christ's death and resurrection and its relationship to our own death and future life. The committee may wish to plan a four-week series of homilies and liturgies around the mystery of death and our risen life in Christ, along the lines of Paul's letter to the Corinthians.

The rite of blessing and sprinkling with holy water could be reworded so as to stress to us God's revelation of himself to us in faith.

The main theme, the otherness of God, could be adequately underscored should the presider proclaim the fourth eucharistic prayer and its own preface this Sunday.

For the alternative theme from the second reading, the presider may wish to use the first, second, or fourth of the prefaces of the Sundays in Ordinary Time since they speak directly of the cross and resurrection of Christ.

The prayer after communion stresses the gospel theme of Christ helping us to bring his salvation and joy to the whole world.

To continue the theme of the gospel and the Old Testament lesson, the celebrant may wish to use number 8 of the prayers over the people, about the Lord as our creator and ruler, or number 20, about every good gift coming from on high.

For the alternative theme of the liturgy the conclusion to the celebration could be taken from number 1 of the prayers over the people, about life everlasting coming from the Lord, or number 16, about the Lord consoling the community in this life and purifying them to life eternal.

SIXTH SUNDAY IN ORDINARY TIME

The gospel for this Sunday is the Lukan parallel to the Matthean Sermon on the Mount and contains what some commentators have described as some more primitive elements of the gospel tradition as compared with Matthew. Especially significant in reviewing these two texts from Luke and Matthew is the fact that Matthew has reinterpreted much of the original version in terms more "spiritual" than those of the more primitive form. Luke speaks about the "poor," not the "poor in spirit," and goes on to address the hungry, those who weep now, and those who are hated. He parallels these sayings with corresponding statements of "woe" for those who are rich now, those who have their fill of the world's goods, who laugh now, and who are spoken well of now, for they have already received their reward. It is a significant aspect of Lukan theology that he extols those who are the poor and downtrodden since they have fewer obstacles in their way of trying to live the demands of the gospel. It is the Lord alone who fills their poverty, and indeed because of this, they are called blessed.

On the basis of this text the liturgy can take up the Lukan theme of the "poor," that is, those who depend on the Lord rather than on riches or power. Or the liturgy committee can apply this message to the present situation of the Church.

But if the Old Testament reading from Jeremiah is used to provide the background for this proclamation, it would be suitable for the committee to apply this gospel message to the present Church. Indeed, while the physically poor have fewer things in the way of their coming to know the Lord and living according to his truth, this poverty is no guarantee of really knowing him. The New English Bible translation of the beginning of the Matthean version of the sermon: "How blest are those who know their need of God," is at the heart of the matter. Indeed, blessed are those who, whether rich or physically poor, know their need of God's salvation and life. The persons singled out for blessedness in the Lukan text are those who depend on the Lord, who seek to know the Lord's will through his revelation. Jeremiah's warning or curse for those who trust in human beings, and blessing for those who trust in the Lord, provides a fitting introduction to the gospel proclaimed this day and forms a helpful starting point for the homily and theme of the liturgy.

The alternative theme from first Corinthians continues the exploration of the resurrection. Paul here moves to a consideration of the existential implications of Christ's resurrection from the dead. Indeed Christ is the first fruits of those who have fallen asleep, and our destiny is to be with him and share his risen life forever. Depending on the judgment of the planning committee, this reading can be joined with that of last week to form a two-week exploration of the resurrection, or it can be joined with the readings of the following two weeks in treating the theme of Christian death.

The rite of blessing and sprinkling with holy water would be a significant introduction to the liturgy this Sunday since we who have been baptized are nourished by hearing the word of the Lord and by living according to it; we know that the baptized share even now in the risen life of Christ.

Should the presider wish to use the third form (c) of the penitential rite as an introduction to the alternative theme concerning the resurrection, he may suitably select the fifth or sixth set of invocations about the Lord's raising the dead to life, and the present eucharist as a share in the life of Christ.

Both the opening prayer and the alternate speak of living according to God's wisdom and of doing what is right and just, and hence coincide with the major theme of the gospel reading.

Preface number 7 of the Sundays in Ordinary Time, about Christ as our redeemer and the mediator of the gifts of grace through his obedience to the will of the Father, would be a suitable choice to coincide with the theme of living in accord with the Lord's word. On the other hand, the fourth eucharistic prayer with its own preface would be especially helpful since it speaks directly of the "poor" to whom Christ preached the good news of salvation. For the alternative theme of the day, numbers 1, 2, or 4 of the Sunday prefaces would be a suitable selection, as would number 6, about the present eucharist as a foretaste and promise of the paschal feast of heaven.

For the final blessing of the liturgy, the presider may wish to use solemn blessing number 5 in Ordinary Time, about the Lord's word being in our heart and filling the community with lasting joy, to underscore the main gospel theme of the day, or number 6 of the prayers over the people, about following the Lord with greater fidelity. For the theme from first Corinthians, the blessing could be either number 1 or number 16 of the prayers over the people, where the first prayer speaks about everlasting life which the Lord has prepared for us, and the latter speaks of the Lord consoling the community in this life and bringing them to life eternal.

SEVENTH SUNDAY IN ORDINARY TIME

The gospel proclaimed this Sunday is the continuation of last week's Lukan version of the Sermon on the Mount. The crux of the reading comes near the end since it is there that Luke makes it clear that we are to love as we have first been loved, and we are to pardon others as we have first been pardoned through the dying and rising of Christ. While indeed the specific demands enumerated in this text are difficult to follow, the Christian is given both the power and the motivation to live this morality by Christ's first having shown us the true meaning of love. Today's reading can be interpreted as a guide for keeping peace in the Christian community and the world. But it is also clear that the gospel does not demand tranquility at any cost. Thus, while the gospel demands that we love others as the Father has first loved us, Jesus also tells us that we only truly love God when in fact we show that love to others. There is no dichotomy envisioned here, as though one could love God and not our neighbor. This reading is giving instructions on how to live the Christian life and how, by living Christ's command to love others, we show our love for the Father.

It is extremely important that the community assembled for worship realizes that being forgiven as we forgive others is an essential part of the believer's preparation for the reception of the eucharist. Indeed, our acts of worship only make sense when we live in the peace of Christ, and love and serve the Lord by loving and serving each other.

The alternative theme for the day's liturgy comes from the reading from first Corinthians, in which the author continues the resurrection theme of last Sunday's reading by using the Adam/Christ (Second Adam) typology. The community in Corinth was reminded that the "natural" forms the foundation for the "supernatural" in Christ, and that the resurrection is the source of our sharing now in the life Christ came to bring us. The risen Christ is indeed the Second Adam who brings us to real life and undoes the death and destruction brought through the sin of the first Adam. It is because of the sacrifice of the Second Adam that we now bear in our mortal lives the very image and likeness of Christ.

Should the presider prefer to use the third form (c) of the penitential rites, he could select the fifth or sixth set of invocations to introduce the themes of the second reading since these invocations call upon Christ who raised the dead to life and who now gives us a share in his life at the eucharist.

The opening prayer and its alternative speak of the theme of the gospel of the day, that is, of our imitation of Christ in word and in deed. The alternative form begs that our every act may increase our present share in the life offered in Christ.

Preface number 7 for the Sundays in Ordinary Time would be a good selection to continue the theme of the gospel since it describes our salvation as having come through the obedience of Christ and hence our obedience to his word as based on his continual love. For the alternative theme from the second reading, the presider could use the first, fourth, or sixth of the Sunday prefaces in Ordinary Time, especially this last one since it speaks of our share now in the promised paschal feast of heaven.

The use of the second sample introduction to the Lord's Prayer, about forgiving as we are forgiven, is a good selection to continue the gospel theme. This same theme could be developed by expanding the introduction to the sign of peace. The use of solemn blessing 3 in Ordinary Time, about persevering in good works, as well as numbers 6, 9, and 20 of the prayers over the people are all suitable conclusions to a liturgy based on the gospel text.

For the alternative theme, the blessing could be either number 1 or number 16 of the prayers over the people, where the first prayer speaks about the good things that lead to everlasting life, and the second speaks of the Lord consoling the community in this life and bringing them to life eternal.

EIGHTH SUNDAY IN ORDINARY TIME

The gospel reading for this Sunday is the conclusion of the discourse of Jesus that was begun on the sixth Sunday in Ordinary Time in this "C" cycle, the Lukan version of the Sermon on the Mount. This text contains a collection of sayings of Jesus about judging oneself before judging others and realizing that motivation affects the morality of the acts we perform or the words we speak.

The Old Testament lesson declares that it is by speech that people are tested as to "the bent" of their minds. The gospel's admonitions against hypocrisy are strong as in the requirement that one be motivated correctly, not just do the right actions. The responsorial psalm carries through on this theme as it speaks of the just man flourishing like the palm tree, and the Lord as the rock of salvation.

These texts may be applied to the ever-present problem of extrinsicism, where believers do and say all the right things but do not in fact have the proper disposition and motivation. The most telling parts of the gospel speak of self-accusation before accusing another, of self-criticism before criticizing others, of self-scrutiny before passing judgments on others. The right words and deeds may in fact be vitiated because of a lack of true motivation.

The alternative theme of the day's liturgy is found in the ending of the proclamation of the first letter of Paul to the Corinthians. This text also concludes the section of the letter on the resurrection and speaks not only about being freed from death because of the resurrection of Christ, but also of our being freed from sin by Christ's death and risen life. The hymnlike expression of victory over death is a fitting conclusion to this section of the letter with its praise of the Lord's triumphant deeds.

The rite of blessing and sprinkling with holy water is an appropriate introduction to a liturgy based on either of the main scriptural themes of the day. The presider may use the introductory rite to stress the main theme of the day, that is, our being cleansed internally by self-accusation. For the alternative theme, the presider could remind the community of their baptism into the death of Christ which brought them to share his new risen life.

Should the presider use the third form (c) of the penitential rite, the first set of suggested invocations about the Lord's healing the contrite of heart, calling sinners to himself, and interceding for us at the Father's right hand would be an appropriate introduction to the eucharist based on the gospel reading.

The alternative opening prayer, about deepening the life of Christ within us, being witnesses to the gospel, and extending our love for one another, is an appropriate selection to reflect the main theme of the day.

Also to reflect the main theme of the day the presider could profitably use number 1 or number 5 of the Sunday prefaces in Ordinary Time, about the Church as the people called from darkness to light to proclaim the Lord's mighty works and praise the marvels of God's wisdom. For the alternative theme from the second reading, the presider could use the first, fourth, or sixth of these Sunday prefaces, since all refer directly to the paschal mystery and our present share in this new life in Christ.

For the introduction to the Lord's Prayer, reiterating the main theme of the day, the presider could profitably use the third of the suggested invitations to prayer, about being forgiven and in turn forgiving others.

Also, the sign of peace could be introduced in such a way that this gesture becomes a sign of spreading Christ's peace rather than of judging others.

The use of solemn blessing numbers 3 or 5 in Ordinary Time, about walking in charity and peace as well as living with the word of the Lord in our hearts, would be appropriate conclusions to a liturgy based on the main theme of the day.

Of the prayers over the people, numbers 6 and 9, about having a change of heart and sharing the love of God with others, are appropriate selections. For the alternative theme of the day, number 1 or number 16 of the prayers over the people is suitable, where number 1 speaks of the good things that lead to everlasting life, while number 16 speaks of the Lord consoling the community in this life and bringing them to life eternal.

NINTH SUNDAY IN ORDINARY TIME

Beginning with the liturgy this Sunday and extending until the fourteenth Sunday in Ordinary Time, the second reading is taken from the letter of Paul to the Galatians. The whole of this letter can provide the basis for a series of liturgies.

The texts for this Sunday and next are remarkably similar and can be taken as a unit since they speak of the person of Paul himself and of being faithful to the gospel of Christ. The example of Paul's life is used here to indicate the kind of fidelity required of the believer. Part of the background for this insistence on remaining faithful to the revelation of Christ is that there were some in the Galatian church who preached a return to the observances of the Mosaic Law against which Paul fought bitterly. Hence, the whole epistle has come to be understood as a Christian instruction about the place of the law and true Christian freedom. The temptation of "going over to another gospel" by no means ended in the first century, and there is more than a subtle temptation in the present to turn from the demands of Christ's revelation to other systems and practices. The need for continual scrutiny of one's life in the light of the gospel is one possible theme for the liturgy for this Sunday. Coupled with the reading from next Sunday, the example of the life of Paul himself and his fidelity to living and preaching the one gospel of Christ would be a most appropriate theme.

The gospel selection for this Sunday begins another section of the Lukan account and concerns the healing of the centurion's son. The gospels for the next two Sundays are about the raising to life of the son of the widow of Naim and the forgiveness of the woman in sin. These three Sundays could be planned around the theme of the correct understanding of the healing miracles of Jesus and how his healing ministry is carried on in the Church in our day. What is obviously the significant motif in this text is the faith which the centurion placed in the Lord.

Another theme of this gospel, which is reiterated in the Old Testament lesson and the responsorial psalm, is the important Lukan theme of Jesus ministering to a far wider group than that circumscribed by the name "Israel." The great faith of a non-Israelite is stressed here since Jesus admits to never having found such faith among the chosen people. The Old Testament lesson recounts Solomon's prayer asking the Lord to heed the foreigner's requests. The responsorial psalm is the brief Psalm 117 about all nations praising the Lord and all people glorifying him. Furthermore, the response to the psalm is based on Mark's gospel (16:15) about going into the whole world to preach the good news.

In all there would appear to be at least three themes that could provide the basis for the planning of this week's liturgy. The first is from the second reading from Galatians, the second concerns the ministry of healing, and the third concerns the universality of salvation in and through Christ.

For the introductory rite to the liturgy, the blessing and sprinkling with holy water could be introduced by referring to the present community's expression of faith at the eucharist and their receiving from the eucharist the Lord's healing and strength.

For the alternative theme from the second reading, the comment could focus on the believer's remaining faithful to the one gospel of Christ.

For the third form (c) of the penitential rite, the celebrant could introduce the gospel by using the first sample set of invocations.

The opening prayer asks for God's care and protection from danger, a theme general enough to coincide with the theme of healing and the notion of remaining faithful to the one gospel of Christ.

The prayer over the gifts is significant because it states that we who celebrate the eucharist ask that by God's sharing his life with us, we may have our sins forgiven. These could well be sins of infidelity to the gospels or sins against those who do not share our vision of Christianity. For the main theme about healing, the proclamation about Christ found in the second and sixth prefaces in Ordinary Time, about his love for those who sin and his daily offer of a Father's love, are appropriate selections for this Sunday.

For the theme from the second reading, Sunday prefaces number 7 and number 8, about God's faithful love and the mercy he shows to his people even when they sin, show that even when we are unfaithful to the one gospel of Christ we need only return to the Lord in repentance to receive his love and forgiveness. Solemn blessing number 4 in Ordinary Time speaks of healing of a kind other than that mentioned in the gospel; this is the healing that is a result of God's gift of peace. Another choice to reflect this theme of healing is solemn blessing number 2, about the Lord's peace. For the theme of the second reading, the fifth of the solemn blessings speaks about the presence of the word of God in our hearts.

TENTH SUNDAY IN ORDINARY TIME

The main theme of today's liturgy is taken from the gospel reading from Luke. It concerns the healing power of Jesus and is presented in typically Lukan fashion. The universality of Jesus' mission and reign is underscored in that a woman's need is responded to. The Old Testament text sets up this pericope by referring to the prophet's action, but in Jesus it is the new covenant, the reign of God now made manifest through him.

It is most significant that the first reading of today's liturgy concerns a miracle worked by the prophet Elijah, the raising to life of a widow's child.

In the gospel reading, the people, after they see Jesus' miracle, cry out that indeed God has visited his people, just as the widow in the Old Testament reading recognizes Elijah as God's prophet.

The Christian interpretation of such healing stories is not to be left on the level of the physical healings alone. The community gathered for worship should realize that they come to this eucharist to be healed, strengthened, and to have their life renewed through the saving power of God.

The alternative theme of the liturgy comes from the letter of Paul to the Galatians, and here the proclamation of the gospel is again seen in terms of the life and ministry of Paul. The power of the word of God is so strong that it converted Paul the persecutor and helped him to persevere in Christ's service during the rest of his life. The obvious application of this reading is that there is a healing, saving grace in the very act of proclamation of the word. No one of us will experience a conversion as striking as that of Paul, and yet each of us is called upon to be challenged to submit to the Lord in quieter ways, but in ways that are nonetheless real. We too are called to proclaim the Good News of salvation through the way we live and serve God.

The rite of blessing and sprinkling with holy water could be suitably introduced by stating that we come to this celebration as sharers in the eucharist to be strengthened to live in the light of Christ first received at our baptism. The alternative theme of the liturgy could be introduced by noting that the purpose of this assembly is to hear the word of the Lord in the gospel and to live in accordance with it.

Should the presider prefer to use the third form (c) of the penitential rite, the second set of invocations about Jesus who comes in word and sacraments to strengthen us in holiness would be appropriate.

The alternative opening prayer and the prayer after communion both reflect the main theme of the day since the first speaks of those born to new life in Christ and the second speaks of God's healing love.

The proclamation of any of the prefaces for the Sundays in Ordinary Time would reflect the gospel theme of the day concerning the healing power of the risen life of Christ, and yet numbers 1 and 8 refer to the community of believers who "proclaim the Father's mighty works as members of the body of Christ."

The sign of peace could be introduced in a way that would bring out its significance as a rite by which the people show their willingness to accept one another and, by implication, all people everywhere as brothers and sisters in the Lord.

The eucharist as our share now in the consolation and healing power of the Father is seen in the fourth of the solemn blessings in Ordinary Time as well as in numbers 2 and 24 of the prayers over the people. The alternative theme of the liturgy, about being faithful to the gospel of Christ as was St. Paul, is seen in the fifth solemn blessing in Ordinary Time, and in numbers 5, 6, and 9 of the prayers over the people.

ELEVENTH SUNDAY IN ORDINARY TIME

The gospel proclaimed this Sunday is in many ways a summary of the two previous Sunday gospels about healing, curing, and receiving the Lord's grace. At the same time it contains many typically Lukan characteristics, not the least of which is that again the recipient of Jesus' forgiveness is a woman. The woman's sins were great, but so was her love of Jesus, and hence she was forgiven. Her great faith was the cause of her salvation. Jesus' healing power is shown here as it is in other healing stories in the gospels, especially that of the son of the centurion who believed firmly in the Lord. At the end of this section of the gospel there is mention of women being included in Jesus' following. Christ broke with the contemporary culture's antifeminism. After healing this woman by forgiving her sins, Jesus continues on his way, proclaiming the good news of salvation. This good news, and our response to it in faith, brings us forgiveness, grace and strength.

The forgiveness of sins as the result of an effective proclamation and acceptance of God's word is an essential part of the revised Rite of Penance and has always been a firm teaching of the Church. That the preaching of the word is an invitation to real and true conversion to the Lord, and that the eucharist is our present share in the Lord's grace to strengthen and heal us, are important considerations that might be explored this Sunday.

The alternative theme of the liturgy, taken from the letter to the Galatians, marks a shift in the emphasis of the past two weeks, since here we read for the first time of the major theme of the letter—that justification comes from faith alone, not from the mere observance of the law. The justified man does not do good works to make himself just, but being justified, he does good works to show forth his new condition before the Lord and the community.

Hence, there are two major and strong themes to choose from for the liturgy this Sunday; the first concludes a section of the gospel of Luke about healing, and the second introduces what will be the central focus of the readings from Galatians for the next three weeks, although with differing emphases.

For the rite of blessing and sprinkling with holy water, the presider could compose an introduction which speaks of the healing and strengthening aspects of the eucharist and its sin-forgiving orientation, or he could introduce the alternative theme of the day's liturgy by referring to the fact that at this communal act of worship the community comes to symbolize, speak, and proclaim its faith and trust in the Lord.

Should the presider use the third form (c) of the penitential rite, the first set of invocations would fit in with the readings this Sunday.

The opening prayer as well as the prayer over the gifts both reflect the main theme of this Sunday liturgy because of their reference to the Lord as our refuge and strength as well as to the eucharist as food for body and spirit.

The alternative opening prayer speaks of our rejoicing in the faith that draws us together to celebrate these sacred mysteries.

The main theme of the day is seen in most of the prefaces suggested for the Sundays in Ordinary Time; the alternative theme is underscored most clearly in the second and fourth prefaces, about the Lord's giving us eternal life through his rising from the dead.

For the conclusion of the liturgy based on the main theme of the day the choice of solemn blessings 4 or 5 in Ordinary Time, or number 2 of the prayers over the people, would be appropriate. For the alternative theme the presider could profitably use the fourth solemn blessing in Ordinary Time, about the Lord's gifts of faith, hope, and love, as well as number 9 of the prayers over the people, about those who believe in the Lord sharing the gift of his love with others.

TWELFTH SUNDAY IN ORDINARY TIME

The gospel proclamation for this Sunday marks a turning point in the gospel of Luke itself. The confession of Peter is a summation of all that Jesus said and did up to this point in his ministry and bespeaks the insight that Jesus is indeed the Messiah, the long-expected One, whose works and words are an indication of who he is. Jesus confirms his identity as the servant-Messiah who first has to suffer before entering into glory. The present community of faith is asked to make the confession Peter made, while at the same time they are invited to imitate Christ in his suffering and humiliation. The Christian must take up his or her own cross every day, and thus imitate Christ.

The Old Testament reading is the kind of text that was used by the early Church in its interpretation of who Christ was and is. He was, indeed, the suffering servant who was the "only son" and who was "pierced through." Today's liturgy could concentrate on our present imitation of Christ's suffering and humiliation. It should be pointed out that following Christ is not just a way of discipline or a kind of suffering for its own sake, but rather a way of helping us to identify more fully with the life of Christ.

The alternative theme of the liturgy from the epistle to the Galatians speaks of the faith that comes through baptism and which is the cause and source of Christian unity. Paul's point here is that baptism is no private affair to guarantee or to insure faith; it is rather a sign and cause of faith in Christ and a sign and cause of the unity of the community in faith. Paul urges the Galatians to live their baptismal profession by remaining close to one another in a common search for deeper faith. Unity in Christ is more than mere outward observance of ritual. The basis of unity is our baptism into Christ and living our faith from the depth of our being. The eucharist is our source of strength to help us continue to lead our lives according to both the inward and outward demands which baptism places upon us.

For the introduction to the rite of blessing and sprinkling with holy water, the presider may cite our imitation of Christ in suffering and rising with him as having begun at our baptism. The reference to baptism in the second reading and the demands which this sacrament continues to place on the already initiated may also be mentioned. The presider could suitably use the fifth set of invocations of the third form (c) of the penitential rite to reflect the major theme of the day, or the fourth set of invocations to underscore the alternative theme from Galatians.

The opening prayer emphasizes God as the protector of his people (the Church), and asks that they may remain always in the Father's love.

Prefaces numbers 1 and 2 in Ordinary Time refer to the suffering of Christ on the cross and the humiliation of his incarnation. For the alternative theme from Galatians, the eighth preface speaks of the Body of Christ, in which God's people are united.

The Lord's Prayer could be introduced suitably by emphasizing the petition that the Lord's will be done in our lives even when that means suffering for his sake. Or the introduction may refer to our need to foster the unity of the Church, especially by our forgiving others.

Of the prayers over the people, number 17 speaks of Christ's accepting the agony of the cross, and numbers 2 and 20 refer to our love for one another and for all people.

THIRTEENTH SUNDAY IN ORDINARY TIME

Today's gospel reading markes a significant point in the Lukan narrative for it is here that Jesus begins his journey to Jerusalem, where he will freely give his life for our salvation. For the evangelist, Jerusalem becomes a symbol, for it will be the place of Jesus' accomplishing the Father's will in accepting humiliation and death. For Jesus, "To go to Jerusalem," meant to do the Father's will; for us, it means to follow the Lord in his suffering and death.

In this gospel reading, Jesus is determined, resolute, definite, and filled with conviction; the disciples fail to understand what he means to do and give evidence of how difficult they find it to follow him. We ourselves today wish to follow him but like the man in the gospel, there is often something we must do first.

Although we were given faith in Jesus Christ at baptism, there is no easy progression from the font to our final eternal sharing in eternal life. On the way to heaven, believers must not only make choices again and again, they must also ever and again deepen their commitment to the Lord. Hence, the eucharist this Sunday becomes not only the setting for a renewed act of faith; it is the source of our strength as we seek to commit ourselves to the Lord's will.

The alternative theme of this liturgy concerns the important Pauline discussion of freedom and law, liberty and authority. For Paul, we Christians are indeed free; yet we are at the same time restrained by the Gospel's demands. In fact, true Christian freedom means that we are free to do anything so long as it conforms to Christ's love. It means that we should scrutinize our actions so that we are no longer self-motivated, but totally subject to the Lord's will. Paul declares here that while we are indeed freed from the extrinsicism and legalism of the old covenant, we are nonetheless bound to use our freedom to do God's will for the benefit of the community. Christian morality goes beyond the law, beyond the commandments, and lives only for God and neighbor, cost what it will.

For the rite of blessing and sprinkling with holy water, the presider may introduce the liturgy by mentioning that to be strong in our faith and trust in the Father requires sacred moments like these when we not merely repeat our act of faith, but deepen our conviction and resolve to lead lives in conformity with that faith. For the alternative theme, the presider could stress the communal nature of the eucharist and note that freedom is only valid when lived in communion with others, respecting them and caring for them.

For the main theme of the day, the use of the first or second of the Sunday prefaces in Ordinary Time would be suitable because of their emphasis on the paschal mystery of Christ. For the alternative theme of the liturgy the presider could choose the eighth preface, since it describes the unity of the Body of Christ.

The introduction to the Lord's Prayer could be reworded to coincide with the alternative theme by stressing our communal prayer and our asking the Lord's forgiveness for having used our freedom poorly.

For the conclusion of the liturgy, the third solemn blessing in Ordinary Time is appropriate to reflect the main theme about directing our steps to the Lord, as is number 15 of the prayers over the people, about serving the Lord with joy. For the alternative theme, solemn blessing number 5 in Ordinary Time, about walking in God's ways, as well as number 11 of the prayers over the people about readiness to do the Lord's will, are both appropriate selections for a liturgy about the wise use of our freedom.

FOURTEENTH SUNDAY IN ORDINARY TIME

The gospel account of the sending forth of the seventy-two to spread the good news of salvation in Christ is another text containing familiar Lukan emphases, and is one that is particularly applicable to the situation of the present Church. The mission of the seventy-two is recorded by Luke because he is particularly concerned with the continuation of the mission of Christ in the Church. Often cited as the first of the evangelists to develop what could be called a Church consciousness, the author is concerned about how the Church is to continue to live in accord with the commands of Christ. Hence, the actions of preaching, healing, and spreading the Lord's peace are to be interpreted not merely as the duties of first-century ministers, but as essential elements of the Church in any age. This is reiterated in the responsorial psalm, "Let all the earth cry out to God with joy."

Jesus gives the disciples definite directions about what to take on their journey and how to act as representatives. From this we can understand how in every age, the Church must be intent on proclaiming the good news of salvation, even at the cost of its comfort and prestige.

The Church must continue the work of Christ, the preaching, healing, and peace-bearing. Every member of the community—not just those ordained to fill the ranks of bishops, presbyters, and deacons—must participate in this ministry which is shared by all the baptized. The ministry of healing those in need ("cure the sick there") is also a contemporary ministry. While preaching the word brings healing and comfort, we should not so overly intellectualize it that physical healing is neglected. It is doubtless true that the frequency of cures worked in the ministry of Jesus will never be matched in succeeding generations of the Church, but this is no reason to feel that the healing power of Christ is diminished in today's world. Contemporary emphasis on healing, especially in charismatic communities, should not be downplayed, and in fact, the homilist may wish to speak of this as a ministry in the Church.

The spreading of the "peace" of Christ is also an important part of this missionary command, and it too is to be shared by the whole community of the Church. Peace-making and bridge-building between opponents is obviously a continual task for the Church in any age. The alternative theme of the day is taken from today's reading from the letter to the Galatians. Here Paul concludes and summarizes all that went before by citing the cross (and life, death, resurrection, and present glory of Christ) as the center of our faith. The old law has given way to the new covenant, and in this dispensation the cross is the center of the faith. No longer is the law the only way of obeying the will of God; now Christians obey the Lord's will by sharing in the cross of Christ.

The rite of blessing and sprinkling with holy water could be so introduced that it coincides with either theme of the day, by mentioning our common commitment to preaching, healing, and spreading the peace of Christ as a result of our baptism, or by pointing out that our baptism into the death of Christ is our bond of present Church unity.

Should the third penitential rite (c) be used, invocations about Jesus healing the contrite (no. 2), strengthening us in holiness (no. 2), and raising us to new life (no. 6) would be suitable.

Both the opening prayer and its alternative contain references to the obedience of Christ that raised a fallen world and hence refer at least indirectly to the theme of the second reading.

For the selection of a preface to coincide with the alternative theme of the day, the presider may profitably use either the first or fourth preface for the Sundays in Ordinary Time, since number 1 speaks of the people of the Church as a chosen race, a royal priesthood, and number 4 speaks of the suffering, death, and resurrection of Christ.

For the main theme of the day, the fourth eucharistic prayer with its own preface, containing the typically Lukan motif of Jesus preaching the good news to the poor and freeing those in bondage, would be a most suitable selection.

For the conclusion to the liturgy, the main theme is reiterated in numbers 20 and 23 of the prayers over the people, about the good news of salvation as among God's gifts, and of our having true love for each other. For the alternative theme, number 17 of these prayers, about the sufferings of Christ on the cross, is most appropriate.

FIFTEENTH SUNDAY IN ORDINARY TIME

The commandments spoken of in this gospel reading are nothing new since they are taken from the Old Testament, and hence were known very well by the lawyer who asked what he would have to do to inherit eternal life. But the lawyer wants Jesus to be more definite, and so he asks: "Who is my neighbor?" Instead of giving an answer that, as the lawyer hoped, would prescribe some limits to the love of neighbor, Jesus tells the parable of the good Samaritan. The teaching of the parable is that one must continually become a better neighbor to others and spend less and less time determining whether an individual fits into the category of "neighbor." In fact, Jesus never answers the question as it is put to him; rather he speaks of what being a good neighbor to others involves. For the Christian the problem is not "Who is my neighbor?" but "Am I a neighbor to others?"

The main theme of the day's liturgy is to help us strive as best we can to realize that in serving our neighbor we are serving God. This lesson of charity is reiterated in the responsorial psalm which mentions the afflicted, those in pain, the poor, and the lowly.

The alternative theme of the day is taken from the beginning of the letter to the Colossians. The heart of this reading is a hymn to Christ, the Lord of creation. The Church has incorporated it into the Liturgy of the Hours as one of the New Testament canticles for evening prayer. Some scholars say the hymn preexisted the Christ event and has undergone adaptation to fit the early Church's experience of Christ. One interesting aspect of this hymn is that it parallels closely the Jewish prayer of blessing from which the eucharistic anaphora has been derived.

The first part of the hymn is in praise of Christ the creator and the second part speaks of the redemption won in Christ. The same is true for the anaphora, whose origin as a prayer of praise, thanksgiving, glory, and blessing could be emphasized in Western churches, which tended to downplay this aspect of the prayer in favor of isolating other elements which were part of the Last Supper events.

For the rite of blessing and sprinkling with holy water, the presider could rephrase the introduction to stress the communal dimension of faith and the demands which that faith make upon us in terms of serving others; or for the alternative theme, the celebrant could speak in praise of Christ, the foundation of the faith, whose power and might first touched us at our baptism.

Should the celebrant use the third form (c) of the penitential rite, the invocations about Jesus' call to all people to share the peace of the kingdom (no. 2), and his reign as mighty God and Prince of Peace (no. 3), would be fitting.

For the alternative theme of the liturgy, the presider could use the fourth eucharistic prayer and its own preface, about Christ's mission to the world.

For the conclusion of a liturgy centered around the main theme of the day, the presider may choose solemn blessing number 3 in Ordinary Time, about persevering in good works, in charity, and in peace, or numbers 7, 9, or 20 of the prayers over the people, about the community devoting itself to doing good, to sharing love with others, and to loving all people. For the alternative theme of the day, the presider could use the first of the solemn blessings in Ordinary Time, about the Lord keeping us in his care. Of the prayers over the people, number 8 is a fitting choice since it addresses the Lord as our creator and ruler.

SIXTEENTH SUNDAY IN ORDINARY TIME

The Old Testament lesson read this Sunday presents an image of God that is not often associated with the revelation of the God of the Old Covenant, for the appearance to Abraham of the three men is couched in terms more characteristic of friendly visitors than the setting for a divine revelation of the birth of a son to Sarah in her advanced age. The guests eat and drink with their host in a spirit of familiarity and intimacy. The biblical author is telling his readers, in an anthropomorphic way, that what is occurring here is a divine visitation. This spirit of intimacy is reflected in the gospel reading, which shows us Jesus, the Son of God, as a friend of Martha and Mary. As such, he points out to them and to all of us who are his friends and followers, that busy as we may be with our own worldly affairs, the thing that really counts is our love and service of God and neighbor. Mary exemplified her love for Jesus in her way, as Martha did in hers. That Jesus said "Mary has chosen the better portion" does not denigrate Martha's service of the Lord.

The reading from Colossians reminds us of the close connection between the mystery of Christ and the mystery of the Church. Paul speaks of "filling up" what is lacking in the sufferings of Christ for the sake of his body, the Church. When Jesus was on earth he suffered and died for us. He returned to his Father, leaving it to us, the members of his body the Church, to continue his work of love and service to others. We stand in for Christ and do here and now what he would do if he were walking the earth again. The theme of the life of Christ in us and our true life coming from Christ is carried through in the second reading in the liturgy next week, which is from Colossians as well.

The introduction to the rite of blessing and sprinkling with holy water could be rewritten this Sunday to refer to the present eucharist as our meeting with the Lord in the light of the first reading and the gospel—both comprising significant revelations of past salvation history. For the alternative theme of the liturgy the presider may refer to the gathering together of the assembly to worship the Father in order that the Church may become a more accurate reflection of the mystery of Christ.

Should the third form (c) of the penitential rite be used, invocations about Jesus as Prince of Peace (number 3), or Jesus raising us to new life (number 6), would be appropriate.

The opening prayers speak of our cherishing the values of faith, hope, and love and remaining watchful in prayer, themes which coincide with the main theme of the scripture readings this week.

Since the main theme of the liturgy this week concerns God who is revealed in both the Old and New Testaments, the fourth eucharistic prayer and preface, with its praise of God's glory, would be the most suitable choice for the anaphora this Sunday.

For the alternative theme of the scripture readings, Sunday preface number 7 in Ordinary Time speaks of salvation coming through the obedience of Christ, and number 8 praises the Father's wisdom and works.

For the conclusion to the liturgy this Sunday, the presider could choose the fourth solemn blessing in Ordinary Time or the fourth of the prayers over the people to reflect the main theme of the day with their reference to being freed from all anxiety and finding in the Lord the fulfillment of their longing.

For the alternative theme of the liturgy, numbers 2 and 17 of the prayers over the people speak of God's people as being faithful to him, and God's love for them as shown through Christ's suffering on the cross.

SEVENTEENTH SUNDAY IN ORDINARY TIME

Today's gospel reading from Luke contains this evangelist's version of the Lord's Prayer, which in itself provides a significant and appropriate theme for the liturgy this Sunday. The parable of the persistent friend that follows the text of the Lord's Prayer in this reading, together with the Old Testament reading, can be interpreted in the light of the main theme.

The first reading presents Abraham in the curious position of bargaining with God about the coming doom of the city of Sodom, while the gospel parable concerns persistence, even insistence, in prayer. This does not mean that the Christian is to try to coerce God into yielding to our whim and pleasure. Persistence in prayer before God means continuing to find out and follow the Father's will, even when all seems to be going against us. Abraham bargained with the Lord because he knew that God's mercy was boundless. As we today in this assembly pray the Our Father, we too are relying on God's mercy and forgiveness that comes to us in the eucharist.

The alternative theme of today's liturgy is drawn from the continuation of the reading from the letter to the Colossians in which the author elaborates on the theme of new life in Christ bringing the forgiveness of sins. The people of the Church share now in the sacrifice of Christ by sharing in his risen power and glory.

The rite of blessing and sprinkling with holy water could be introduced by referring to the persistence of our prayer in confident hope at the eucharist, or to the eucharist as our renewal now of the covenant made in baptism.

Should the presider use the third form (c) of the penitential rite, invocation number 5, about Jesus raising the dead to life in the Spirit, granting pardon and peace to the sinner, or number 2, about Jesus strengthening us in word and sacrament, would be appropriate.

For the alternative theme of the liturgy this Sunday, the presider can choose from a number of the Sunday prefaces in Ordinary Time: number 1, about the Lord calling us to share his glory; number 4, about our rebirth through him; number 6, about our present life as a foretaste of the life to come; and number 8, about the Body of Christ on earth.

For the main theme of the day's liturgy, the presider could suitably introduce the Lord's Prayer not only as a part of the liturgy but as a model of the prayer of the Christian.

For the conclusion of the liturgy, the presider could choose number 4 of the prayers over the people, about being made holy by the Lord. For the alternative theme of the day, solemn blessing 5 in Ordinary Time, about the Lord's word in our hearts and always walking in his ways, or number 9 of the prayers over the people, about the community of those who believe in the Father, would be appropriate.

EIGHTEENTH SUNDAY IN ORDINARY TIME

The gospel reading for this Sunday takes the believer on a soul-searching journey about value-clarification and getting a perspective on priorities. The text speaks of true treasures, avoiding greed and possessiveness in all its forms. True gospel riches do not come from things that pass away, but from the Lord's free giving—grace, peace, love, joy, forgiveness, and understanding.

The Old Testament lesson from Ecclesiastes contains the familiar statements about "vanity of vanities" and sets an appropriate context for the proclamation of today's gospel. The responsorial psalm this Sunday speaks of opening our hearts to the Lord when we hear his voice. This psalm encourages us to call upon the Lord, who alone is our rock of refuge, for it is he alone whom we worship; we acclaim him as our only God, and pray that any hardness in our hearts will be turned into wills bent to his service.

The alternative theme for the liturgy this Sunday comes from the epistle to the Colossians; the last passage to be read during this "C" cycle is assigned for today. In this lesson the author reiterates a familiar motif, namely, that we are in Christ, that he is the source of our life. This epistle makes us aware of the demands which Christ's teaching places upon us. Truly Christian morality sees fornication, uncleanness, passion, and evil desires as things to be avoided. Further, a believer is to be less concerned about personal salvation than about promoting the unity of the community in Christ.

The rite of blessing and sprinkling with holy water could be introduced this Sunday by referring to our resolve to live out the implications of our baptism. For the alternative theme, this introduction could mention Christ as the basis of morality.

Should the presider choose the third form (c) of the penitential rite, invocation number 6, about Jesus raising us to new life and feeding us with his body and blood, would be suitable.

One aspect of returning to living the gospel's demands after living "on our own" is asking the Lord for forgiveness, and such a petition is part of the opening prayer this Sunday. This is an unusual place for this kind of petition, which is generally found in the prayer over the gifts, or in other places in the rite of the eucharist. The fact that the petition occurs here can help the community appreciate the importance of the eucharist as our communal means of sin-forgiveness and reconciliation with the Father and with each other.

The prayer over the gifts speaks of the alternative theme of the day, that is, about our being made an everlasting gift to the Father, a result of living a Christian moral life.

For the conclusion of the liturgy, the main theme of the day is underscored in the fifth of the solemn blessings in Ordinary Time, about walking in the Lord's ways, as it is in the thirteenth of the prayers over the people, about their seeking the Lord with all their hearts. For the alternative theme of the liturgy, the use of solemn blessing number 3 in Ordinary Time, about persevering in good works, as well as numbers 2, 21, and 24 of the prayers over the people, about having perfect love for one another, about avoiding all evil pleasures, and about being kept from all harm, would be suitable for concluding the liturgy.

NINETEENTH SUNDAY IN ORDINARY TIME

Eschatology, the looking forward to the end time of Christ's second coming, is an important aspect of sacramental theology. The liturgical reforms initiated by the Second Vatican Council look upon the eucharistic celebration not only as the Church's memorial of all that was accomplished in the redemptive acts of Christ in the past, but also as anticipatory of the end time when the Lord will return to bring to completion his work of redemption in the kingdom of the Father. The Church communities celebrating the eucharist are gatherings of people who define themselves in terms of the gospel as pilgrims awaiting their master's return. Although it is impossible to determine the time of the last coming, it is important to be prepared to meet Christ whenever and wherever he calls us to him, as today's reading tell us. The passage, in familiar Lukan style, points out that the kingdom of God is above all earthly riches.

How then are Jesus' followers to live? The gospel tells us that they must always be alert and ready to use every opportunity to do their Master's work, rather than to amass money and power for themselves. To us Christians, God has given great gifts—the grace to know and follow the Master and to live his very life by our sharing in the eucharist. But as the gospel also tells us, when we have been given much, much will be required of us.

And so "as we wait in joyful hope for the coming of our savior Jesus Christ," we must share our good things with others and help them to know and serve the Master until he comes.

The alternative theme for the liturgy is taken from the letter to the Hebrews, portions of which will be read over a period of four weeks, beginning this Sunday. Today's reading explores the implications of faith in God. This faith is by no means only an intellectual assent, for it is characterized as a response of obedience, like that of Abraham and Sarah to the word of the Lord. Even in apparently hopeless situations as in the case of Abraham and Sarah, the believer still puts trust in God's word. But such trust in

God means that there is no assurance of salvation except from the Lord and not from human efforts alone.

The rite of blessing and sprinkling with holy water could be suitably introduced this Sunday by reference to the eucharist as our renewal of the covenant of baptism until the day when the Lord will return to call us all to himself; or the presider could emphasize the faith of Abraham and Sarah as models for the faith which we come to strengthen and foster each Lord's day.

Should the presider use the third form (c) of the penitential rite, he may profitably use the second set of sample invocations, about the Lord's three comings, in the past, in the present liturgical celebration, and in the future.

Both forms of the opening prayer speak of the Lord's leading the Church to its promised inheritance and the life the Lord has promised.

The prayer after communion speaks indirectly of the alternative theme of the day, about remaining faithful to the light of the truth of the Lord.

For the main theme of the liturgy, the presider could choose the sixth preface for the Sundays in Ordinary Time because of its reference to the Spirit as a promise and foretaste of the paschal feast of heaven. For the memorial acclamation in the eucharistic prayer the use of the second form, "Lord Jesus, come in glory," would also reiterate this idea.

For the alternative theme of the liturgy drawn from the reading from Hebrews, the presider could suitably use the fourth eucharistic prayer with its own preface as a moving summary of the history of salvation.

The Lord's Prayer could be introduced by using the fourth sample invitation to prayer to reflect the eschatological notion of the eucharist and the present life of the Christian.

For the conclusion to the liturgy based on the main theme of the gospel, the presider could use the fifth of the solemn blessings in Ordinary Time, about coming into our heavenly inheritance, or numbers 1 or 16 of the prayers over the people, about life everlasting, and the promised life still to come. For the alternative theme of the readings, the presider could fittingly use the third or fourth solemn blessing in Ordinary Time, about being strengthened in faith, or number 2 or 6 of the prayers over the people, about being faithful to the Lord and following him with ever greater fidelity.

TWENTIETH SUNDAY IN ORDINARY TIME

The gospel passage read this Sunday contains what seems to be a strange revelation when Jesus states that he did not come to establish peace on the earth. This is at least a curious statement in the light of recent emphasis by Christian communities on the place and role of peace movements today, the renewed emphasis by the charismatic renewal on peace as a gift of the Spirit, and the restored use of the sign of peace to be exchanged at the eucharist. Yet what must be understood in this reading is that the kind of peace which Christ speaks about here is not the sort of superficial toleration that often pretends that there is no fundamental difference between believers and nonbelievers. The point at issue here is that the word of God invites all people to know, love, and follow Christ. And yet, as long as Christ's followers preach this word by their lives and example, they will meet opposition, persecution, and death.

The Old Testament lesson from Jeremiah presents the fate of the prophet who preached the word of the Lord. The responsorial psalm echoes the cry of those who do God's will and meet persecution: "Lord, come to my aid."

The second reading from the letter to the Hebrews continues the theme begun in last week's reading about faith and trust in the Lord. The author has explored the Old Testament background to the kind of faith demanded of the true believer and here speaks of Christ now seated at the Father's right hand who intercedes for the community of the faithful in their vocation of following him. The message of this reading this week is that believers should not grow slack or abandon the struggle of following the Lord in true faith.

While there are usually two main themes in the liturgy for the Sundays in Ordinary Time, the two themes are closely intertwined this week and can be treated together. Faith demands a response that affects a person's whole life; for comfort and strength in the struggle the believer's only help is the Lord alone. The celebration of the eucharist is most significant for our lives of faith for in it we hear the word proclaimed for instruction and challenge and we receive the very body and blood of the Lord who nourishes us on this life journey in faith.

The introduction to the rite of blessing and sprinkling with holy water could be introduced this Sunday by a comment about baptism as the inauguration, not the final state, of our Christian lives. The eucharist could be mentioned as helping us to live according to the Lord's ways.

Should the presider prefer to use the third form (c) of the penitential rite, the third set of invocations about Jesus reconciling us to one another and to the Father would be fitting.

For the preface to be proclaimed this Sunday, the presider could suitably select the sixth preface for the Sundays in Ordinary Time, about our living in God and how the Holy Spirit gives us the hope of unending joy.

The introduction to the Lord's Prayer can be rewritten to speak of our communal faith in the Lord, and the sign of peace could be introduced in this way as well.

The solemn blessing that would most suitably underscore this same theme is the fourth in Ordinary Time, about the God of all consolation who frees us from all anxiety and who fills us with his gifts of faith, hope, and love. Of the prayers over the people, number 6, about a change of heart and following the Lord with greater fidelity, is most fitting.

TWENTY-FIRST SUNDAY IN ORDINARY TIME

The main theme of this liturgy is reminiscent of the solemnity of the Epiphany when the universality of salvation is emphasized in the adoration of the Child by the astrologers. This theme is also a constant feature of the gospel of Luke as has been seen throughout the various Sunday commentaries, but it is especially obvious in the responsorial psalm this Sunday, which is the same psalm as that used on the ninth Sunday in Ordinary Time. The note of the universality of salvation offered by the Messiah is struck almost immediately in the reading from Isaiah 66, which itself contains some of the imagery now associated with the epiphany of the Lord to the nations.

The gospel speaks of the narrowness of the door through which people will have to pass in order to enter the kingdom, represented here on earth by the Church community. There is a dialectic here between the understanding of the kingdom as open to all and the demands that are made on those seeking entrance into the kingdom. This gospel reading also challenges those of us who are now members of the faith community to live not as those who know not God and his Son, but as people willing to live humbly without concern about who shall be first or who shall be last.

The alternative theme of the day is taken from the continuation of the reading of the letter to the Hebrews, about suffering and how the proper acceptance of discipline can produce peace and justice. What the author is speaking about here is not undergoing discipline merely for the sake of self-assurance, but accepting suffering in total reliance on the Lord, not on oneself. This trust in God leads the believer to maturity in faith.

The introduction to the rite of blessing and sprinkling with holy water could be introduced this Sunday to refer to baptism and the eucharist as the sacraments which assure us of fidelity to God's covenant which he extends to all nations. The alternative theme could be introduced by reference to the acceptance of suffering and our common reliance on the Lord.

Should the presider prefer to use the third form (c) of the penitential rite, he can profitably use the second set of the invocations, which speaks of Jesus who gathers all nations into the peace of God's kingdom.

The end of the alternative opening prayer, about living in this changing world with the assurance of the peace of the kingdom, refers to the main theme of the gospel.

For the alternative theme, the prayer after communion speaks about the healing power of the eucharist.

For the preface to be proclaimed this Sunday, the presider could select the first or eighth preface in Ordinary Time, about characteristics of the Church. For the alternative theme he might choose the second preface in Ordinary Time, about the suffering and glory of Christ, or the sixth preface, about the Spirit's granting us here and now a foretaste of heaven.

For the conclusion of the liturgy, the use of the fourth solemn blessing in Ordinary Time, about consolation in this life, being freed from anxiety, and living in the love of the Father, is a suitable selection for a liturgy based on the theme of the reading from Hebrews. The use of number 5 or number 17 of the prayers over the people, about the Lord strengthening his people and the sufferings of Christ, reiterate this theme. Numbers 9 and 24 of the prayers over the people, about sharing love with others and the Father keeping his trusting children from all harm, reflect the main theme of the day.

TWENTY-SECOND SUNDAY IN ORDINARY TIME

Today's liturgy contains two themes continued from the previous Sunday's liturgy: the one from the gospel is that of the banquet, and the other from the letter to the Hebrews, in which Jesus is shown to be the mediator of the new covenant. The major theme of today may stress that the Lord alone invites us to salvation, and it is only in response to his word that we can be saved. The community of all those who profess faith and trust in him are the ones who are his table-fellows. Jesus' advice about inviting the beggars, the crippled, the blind and the lame to one's banquet is certainly a rebuke to the status-conscious Jewish society of that time. Indeed, the very fact that the Lord Jesus sat at table with tax collectors and sinners was contrary to what many people expected him to do. The lesson to learn is that we are to take care lest we exalt ourselves over the poor, the needy, and the abandoned.

The alternative theme of the day's liturgy comes from the reading from Hebrews, about Christ himself as the mediator of the new covenant. The signs and symbols of the old covenant are used in counterpoint to the revelation of Christ in his person as the only mediator of the covenant of grace and peace. We come near to the new and heavenly Jerusalem by, with, and through him alone. Hence, it is necessary that the believers see beyond things and appearances to the very person of Christ and profess their faith in him alone. This pericope forms a fitting ending to the readings from Hebrews.

The rite of blessing and sprinkling with holy water could be introduced in terms of our common invitation to partake of the eucharistic meal as a means of increasing our strength to live in accord with the gospel's demands, or in terms of partaking in this eucharist of the new covenant where we encounter the person of the living Lord of all.

Should the presider prefer to use the third form (c) of the

penitential rite, number 2, about Jesus strengthening us in holiness, or number 5, about bringing light to those in darkness, would be suitable.

For the main theme the presider could suitably use the sixth preface in Ordinary Time, which refers to the image of the paschal feast of heaven, and for the alternative theme he could well use the second or third of these prefaces which speak about the passion, death, and resurrection of Christ as our source of new life. For the conclusion of the liturgy, the main theme of the readings is underscored in the fourth and fifth solemn blessings in Ordinary Time, about everlasting life and the inheritance of heaven. Numbers 2 and 16 of the prayers over the people also underscore this theme by referring to God's protection of his people and bringing them to the life to come. For the alternative theme of the liturgy, the presider could use the first or second forms of the solemn blessings in Ordinary Time, about the grace and peace of Christ.

TWENTY-THIRD SUNDAY IN ORDINARY TIME

The concept of Christian conversion is seen today as a process of continual renewal. The eucharist has always been considered a prime means of this renewal of initial conversion for by it the Christian community becomes more and more aware of its union with the Lord by the preaching of the word and the proclamation of God's deeds of salvation. Conversion is a process that is not accomplished all-at-once or once-and-for-all, and it is essentially a communal as well as an individual reality. There can be no automatic renewal of the Christian life, but the eucharist does mark an important stage in this growth process.

Today's gospel parables address just such a situation in the lives of believers who have been initiated into the Church but who must continually renew and ratify that initiation. The imagery of the building of a tower and of the king and his army bring out the fact that the Christian life is indeed a lifetime of serving the Lord. Emphasized here is the renewal of commitment so that the Lord's grace will bring the initial decision of faith to perfect fulfillment and completion in the kingdom. The typically Lukan aspects of the gospel are seen in the insistence on renunciation of possessions and turning one's back on anyone and anything that would stand in the way of real conversion. While these features of Lukan theology have been treated in other commentaries in this book, the main theme of the gospel reading as applied to the liturgy this Sunday could consider the implications of growth in faith and renewal in the Christian life.

The alternative theme of this Sunday liturgy is from the rather curious letter of Paul to Philemon. This reading speaks about a specific incident that came to Paul's attention. One application of its message would be to emphasize that Paul did not want the slave's status to prevent his being treated as a beloved brother. The Christian community, even while not being aware of it, or perhaps while not even alluding to it, can also suffer from such a stratification because of the more obvious participation in parish life by some and not by others, or by the obvious external piety of some that others seem not to display.

The liturgy this Sunday could take to task judgments based on such externals and emphasize the virtues of a true Christian community. The offering of the sign of peace to one another should challenge each member of the assembly to weigh his or her intention to share and live in the peace of Christ.

The rite of blessing and sprinkling with holy water could be introduced this Sunday by reference to the eucharist as the means whereby the community is renewed in its conversion to the Lord, or by referring to the demands which this eucharist makes on those who seek to live in accord with others as beloved brothers and sisters.

Should the presider prefer to use the third form (c) of the penitential rite, the second set of invocations, about Christ inviting all peoples to the peace of his kingdom, or the fourth set, about Jesus reconciling us to one another and to the Father, would be suitable.

The opening prayer speaks of being brought to our promised inheritance and hence reiterates one of the gospel's meanings about perseverance in the faith.

For the preface to reflect this main theme, the presider could profitably use the sixth of the Sunday prefaces in Ordinary Time, about our living and moving in God and about Jesus as the promise of the paschal feast of heaven.

The presider might consider using the third eucharistic prayer with its direct reference to the Lord strengthening in faith and love the pilgrim Church on earth. For the alternative theme of this liturgy, about treating each other as brothers and sisters, the presider could select the fourth eucharistic prayer with its own preface because of the reference to the Lord's ministry to the poor, the imprisoned, and those in sorrow.

For the conclusion of the liturgy, the presider could use the fourth of the solemn blessings in Ordinary Time for the main theme of the day since it speaks of being freed from anxiety and looking to life everlasting. The use of number 6 of the prayers over the people, about having a complete change of heart and following the Lord with greater fidelity, would also be suitable. For the alternative theme of the liturgy, the presider could use the third of the solemn blessings in Ordinary Time, about doing good works and walking in charity and peace, or number 9 of the prayers over the people, about sharing God's love with others.

TWENTY-FOURTH SUNDAY IN ORDINARY TIME

The gospel proclamation assigned for this Sunday contains the familiar and significant Lukan parables of the lost sheep, the lost coin, and the errant son. The concern of the shepherd is rewarded, the industry of the widow is exalted, and the forgiveness of the prodigal son by his loving father is extolled here, and all converge is such a way as to describe the God and Father of us all. These are indeed familiar stories and they present very consoling and comforting images of the God whom we worship. But we must also consider the image of the obedient son, who remained at home, did not squander his portion of the fortune, and remained loyal to his father. It is his logical "dollars and cents" approach that is important in the retelling of the story. How often are we the "logical sons" of a loving Father, who bask in the light of a loving parent, but who refuse to show concern for others. How often do we decide for ourselves where and how the mercy of God is to be shown forth; how many times do we catch ourselves condemning others when we ourselves need to be judged for what we have done and what we have failed to do toward our brothers and sisters. If we are moved to judgment rather than forgiveness, then when we gather to celebrate the eucharist, we should ask the

Father to heal us of our uncharitable ways, for this banquet of the Lord is to cure our ills and fill us with the food that brings us back to life.

The alternative theme for the liturgy of the word is taken from the first letter to Timothy, portions of which will be read for the next three Sundays. While the letter concerns pastoral advice from Paul to the leader of a local church community, the three pericopes read in the Sunday liturgy are applicable to the Christian life of the community, not just to the life of those in positions of leadership. Far from being practical hints on church administration, these texts concern the whole Church, the person of Christ, our need to pray, and our vocation to heed and keep his commands. The reading this Sunday speaks of the role and person of Christ as the one who died for our salvation. It is for this reason that Christians gather at the eucharist, to recall his act of redemption and forgiveness and to praise and glorify the Father through him.

The introduction to the rite of blessing with holy water could be reworded to reflect the love of Christ for his Church and the demands which this love places on us to show that love to others, or it could concern our prayer of praise to the Father through Christ who died for our salvation. Should the presider use the third form (c) of the penitential rite, the invocations in number 4 about Jesus, reconciling us to one another and to the Father, and healing the wounds of sin and division would be fitting.

For the alternative theme of the liturgy, the opening prayer with its invitatory about experiencing God's forgiveness in our lives is a most appropriate selection. The alternative form reflects the theme of the reading from first Timothy presenting a very positive image of the Father.

The sixth of the Sunday prefaces in Ordinary Time, about the love of the Father and the Spirit dwelling in us, is an appropriate choice to reiterate the main theme of the day. For the theme of the reading from first Timothy, the presider could choose from the first, seventh, or eighth of these prefaces since they all speak of our salvation through Christ.

The third suggested introduction to the Lord's prayer would be suitable, since it speaks of our forgiving others, a major application of the gospel reading this Sunday.

For the conclusion of the liturgy, the presider may choose the second of the prayers over the people to underscore the main theme of the day about the Lord's love for us and our love for one another. For the alternative theme of the liturgy, he could choose the fifth of the solemn blessings in Ordinary Time, about the Lord's giving us every good gift, or number 8 or 14 of the prayers over the people, about the Father keeping us in his love and about helping us to rejoice in the mystery of his redemption.

TWENTY-FIFTH SUNDAY IN ORDINARY TIME

The gospel reading for this liturgy presents use of the parable as a form of revelation, where the evangelist uses the original story and elaborates on it to fit his own design and purpose. The first story concerns the industrious servant who, by his cleverness, made others indebted to him in order to insure his future. The obvious meaning is to encourage people to be eager in seizing opportunities for the furthering of the kingdom of God.

In the reading of the Old Testament lesson from the prophet Amos about those who trample on the needy, we can see a similarity with today's gospel reading. That is, Christ's followers should seek the riches of the kingdom of God rather than temporal advantage. One cannot serve two masters, especially when one master is money and influence.

The second theme of the liturgy of the word comes from the reading from the first letter to Timothy, about the prayer of petition and its place in the Christian life. The author says that thanksgiving, petition, and intercession for all people, especially for those in authority, are proper Christian intentions for prayer. Prayer, both of praise and of petition, is an essential part of the Christian life, and this liturgy can help focus attention on Christ as our one mediator, from whom all blessings come, and through whom all prayers arise to the Father.

The introduction to the rite of blessing and sprinkling with holy water can refer to the values of the kingdom of God which are proclaimed at these sacred mysteries (gospel theme), or a reference to Christian prayer, not just for oneself, but for all who stand in need of God's mercy and love.

Should the presider prefer to use the third form (c) of the

penitential rite, the invocations in number 2, about Christ inviting all peoples to the peace of his kingdom, and his people in holiness, would be suitable.

The opening prayer reflects the theme of the gospel reading about the values of life eternal. The presider could underscore this same theme by using the second or fourth of the Sunday prefaces in Ordinary Time, about our destiny set in the eternal life prepared by Jesus' death and risen life. For the alternative theme from the second reading, the presider could suitably proclaim the first or eighth of the prefaces for Sundays in Ordinary Time, about the mystery of redemption and our praise of the Lord's mighty works, or the fifth preface, about our daily praise for the marvels of creation and the Lord's creative power.

The presider could use the fourth invitation to pray the Lord's Prayer, about the coming of the kingdom, to fit in with the demands of the gospel to set our hearts on the things of heaven.

The liturgy could be concluded with the fourth of the solemn blessings in Ordinary Time, about the God of all consolation, or numbers 1 or 16 of the prayers over the people, about this life leading to life eternal. For the alternative theme for the second reading, the liturgy could be concluded by using the tenth or twenty-third of the prayers over the people, about asking the Lord for the things we need because of his inviting us to do so, and our remaining close to God in prayer.

TWENTY-SIXTH SUNDAY IN ORDINARY TIME

The gospel proclaimed this Sunday contains at least two important Lukan themes for reflection, one of which has been emphasized in many of the scripture passages of this "C" cycle, and the other of which has not been so stressed. The first theme for reflection this Sunday concerns the final vindication of the poor man Lazarus in contrast to the destiny of the rich man. At death it was Lazarus who was called to the bosom of Abraham while the rich man was the one who had to endure suffering. The ultimate exaltation of the poor man Lazarus fits in with this common Lukan motif. Yet, the element of Lukan theology that has not been stressed thus far in the Sunday Lectionary concerns one's fidelity to the revelation given in the scriptures. In this parable, Jesus is saying in effect that if a person refuses to accept God's teachings, especially as revealed in his Son, then such a person could not be swayed to do so on merely human grounds. All this also implies that extraordinary revelations are not necessary to convince Christ's faithful followers that his word is true.

Today's first reading refers to the rich being "stretched comfortably on their couches," and may also refer to Christian communities who listen to but do not really hear the word as proclaimed and revealed to them. It may well be the case that, like the rich, we rest on cushions of comfortable pews rather than face as honestly as we can the ever-challenging revelation of God.

The alternative theme of the day is taken from first Timothy, and concerns the keeping of God's commands. Although this advice is addressed to a leader of a Christian congregation, it may easily be applied to the whole community. The conclusion of the letter, about the praise of the Lord, is a characteristic of New Testament literature, where exhortation is placed within the context of praise of God.

The rite of blessing and sprinkling with holy water could be introduced this Sunday by referring to the community assembled for worship asking to remain ever-faithful to the revelation of the word, or reference could be made to the eucharist as the renewal of the commitment made at baptism to live in accord with the Lord's commands.

Should the presider use the third form (c) of the penitential rite, invocations about Christ reconciling us to the Father's will (no. 4), or Jesus raising us to new life (no. 6), would be appropriate choices.

Both opening prayers relate to the alternative theme of the day from first Timothy since they speak about forgiveness from the Lord and the power of his love. For the alternative theme from the second reading, the eighth of the prefaces of Sundays in Ordinary Time speaks about the community of the Church being a people made special to the Lord and a community that praises the Lord for his works of creation and redemption through Christ.

Solemn blessing number 4 in Ordinary Time, about being freed from all harm and living in accord with the word and the Lord and his ways, is an appropriate reflection of the main theme from the gospel, as is number 6 of the prayers over the people, about following the Lord with greater fidelity.

318 *Twenty-Sixth Sunday in Ordinary Time C*

The main theme of the liturgy as taken from the gospel of the day concerns the Lord's gift of faith by which believers live. The apostles ask to have their faith increased, and the evangelist casts the Lord's reply in the form of sayings which point out that whatever we do can never be a sufficient repayment for God's gifts to us. We are, therefore, not to take all the credit even when we do good deeds.

The responsorial psalm, which speaks of the man who loves the Lord, and the end of the Habbakuk reading, about the just man's faith, both reflect Jesus' teaching about trust in him. The homilist could explore the dimensions of faith as obedience to and dependence upon the Lord.

The second reading proclaimed this Sunday from the second letter to Timothy inaugurates a series of readings from this New Testament book that continues for four weeks. While these passages are more difficult to apply to the whole congregation than those of first Timothy, many themes are expressed here which can be so applied. Here the author is encouraging the church leader to stir into flame the gift which the Holy Spirit bestowed on him in the laying on of hands. There are indeed many forms of ministry in the Church, and while some have hands imposed on them to mark their task in the Church, nevertheless all the members of the Church share the responsibility for spreading the Lord's word in this world. These texts can form a helpful series of homilies about the differing gifts of the Spirit and the status of the laity in the life of the Church.

For the introduction to the rite of blessing and sprinkling with holy water, the presider could speak of the eucharist as a celebration of the mystery of our faith, or he could introduce the theme of the second reading by mentioning the gifts of the Spirit and the eucharist as sources for renewing our common zeal to do the Lord's work.

Should the presider choose the third form (c) of the penitential rite, invocation number 2, about Jesus who came to gather the nations in place, who grants eternal life to those who believe in his word, or number 7, about Jesus who gives us the consolation of the truth, would be appropriate.

The presider could profitably choose the alternative opening prayer to introduce the main readings of the day since the invitatory speaks of trusting God in faith.

The presider could suitably proclaim the third of the Sunday prefaces in Ordinary Time, about the gift of salvation, for the main theme of the day, or the sixth preface for the alternative theme of the Spirit as the foretaste of the paschal feast of heaven and his showing us the Father's love.

For the conclusion of the liturgy, the use of solemn blessing in Ordinary Time number 3 or number 4, about being strengthened in faith and growing in the gifts of faith, hope and love, or number 9 of the prayers over the people, about those who believe in the Lord, would be suitable selections for the main theme of the gospel reading this Sunday. For the alternative theme of the day, the presider could use the third of the solemn blessings in Ordinary Time, about persevering in good works, or number 23 of the prayers over the people, about remaining close to one another in true love.

TWENTY-EIGHTH SUNDAY IN ORDINARY TIME

The gospel reading of the cleansing of the ten lepers and the solitary stranger returning to give thanks to the Lord is a familiar one and its obvious reference to gratitude is most often emphasized, especially when it is chosen from among the gospel texts for the American festival of Thanksgiving Day. The theme of the universality of salvation in Christ is another aspect of the gospel story that may be emphasized since it is the "foreigner" who returns to the Lord to render him homage. The reference to Samaria at the beginning of the pericope adds to this understanding and the Old Testament lesson about a Syrian returning to give thanks aids this interpretation of the text.

Another aspect of biblical theology found here is that our conventional understanding of "giving thanks" is not what the scriptures mean by giving thanks. The whole host of terms such as praise, glorify, thank, acclaim, confess, and bless all come close, but do not totally define, the reality of what it means to express gratitude. In the scriptures, people give thanks with acclamations, praises, and glorifications which essentially are confessions of faith in the Lord and an acknowledgment of his love for his people. One calls on the Lord as Savior and Lord and then expresses gratitude.

The fact that the former leper returned to Jesus is in itself a confession of faith and an acknowledgment of the Lord's sovereignty in the man's life.

The eucharist is itself a sacrifice of praise and thanksgiving; it is more than just receiving the species of the Lord's body and blood, for it involves our whole personal relation to the Lord in faith.

The theme of the second reading from second Timothy contains some very moving references by Paul to his sufferings for the sake of Christ and includes an early Christian hymn that expresses the mystery of faith. Paul encourages Timothy to be earnest in preaching the word of the Lord even when that preaching results in having to undergo insult and injury for the sake of the Lord. The conclusion of the pericope contains the assurance of God's fidelity even though some believers may be unfaithful. The middle section of the passage acclaims Christ as savior through whom and in whom apparent death becomes life and the endurance of trial leads to reigning with the Lord forever. The assurance of the Lord's grace and peace when bearing witness to the Lord in the midst of trials offers consolation not only to ordained preachers of the word, but to the whole Christian community as well.

The introduction to the rite of blessing and sprinkling with holy water could be rewritten this Sunday to introduce the main theme of the liturgy by mentioning this celebration as a source of healing and cleansing, as a way to give thanks and confess our faith in the Lord. Or for the alternative theme of the day, the presider could speak about the eucharist as a means of strength and courage in the midst of our struggles for the sake of the gospel.

Should the presider use the third form (c) of the penitential rite, the invocations in number 8, about Jesus who healed the sick and forgave sinners, would be appropriate.

The main theme of the liturgy is reflected to some extent in the alternative opening prayer as it speaks of the Lord's guidance, and of our receiving strength from him.

For the main theme of the day, the presider may use preface number 1 of the Sundays in Ordinary Time, about the people of God proclaiming the mighty deeds of redemption, or number 8, praising the Lord's wisdom in his works. For the alternative theme, he may wish to use preface number 2, about the sufferings of Christ as leading to our share in his glory.

For the conclusion of the liturgy this Sunday, the presider could choose the fifth solemn blessing in Ordinary Time, about walking in the Lord's ways, or number 8 of the prayers over the people, about the Lord as our creator and ruler, to coincide with the confession of faith and thanks of the leper who had been cured. For the alternative theme from second Timothy, the presider could choose the fourth of the solemn blessings in Ordinary Time, about the God of all consolation, or number 17 of the prayers over the people, about the love Christ showed us in his accepting the suffering of the cross.

TWENTY-NINTH SUNDAY IN ORDINARY TIME

There are at least two avenues of approach to this Sunday's gospel reading. The first is by way of the widow who by her persistence, and for no other apparent reason, receives a hearing from the judge. For prayer to be fruitful it should be persistent, as well as an honest expression of the faith of the believer.

The other approach, by way of the judge, has been used by some commentators who have associated this figure with the Son of Man who will come to judge the living and the dead. The end of today's pericope, referring to the coming of the Son of Man and whether he will find any faith on earth, would imply the correctness of such a view.

Choosing the first example of the widow's persistence leads almost naturally to a liturgy planned around the strengths and weaknesses of prayer, in common and in private; the choice of the figure of the judge could lead to reflection on the very significant but often misunderstood notion of the coming judgment by the Son of Man.

The alternative theme of the day as taken from the reading from second Timothy concerns the minister's perseverance in preaching God's word and the scriptures as God's revelation to his people. The revival of interest in the more biblical approaches to spirituality cannot but be enhanced by a liturgy whose emphasis is on the place of the word of God in the Christian life, in probing its riches, responding to its call, and inviting Christians to experience the joy of the comfort of the Lord who is present in this living word.

For the rite of blessing and sprinkling with holy water, the presider could introduce the liturgy by speaking about the eucharist as our communal celebration of faith and persistent trust in the Lord, or about the proclamation of the word as an essential part of the celebration of the liturgy.

Should the presider choose to use the third form (c) of the penitential rite, invocations acclaiming Jesus as our intercessor at the Father's right hand (number 1), or as the one who raises the dead to life in the Spirit (number 5) would be suitable.

The invitatory to the alternative opening prayer could be expanded to emphasize the Lord "who bends close to hear our prayer," and hence to underscore the gospel theme of the persistence in prayer.

For the gospel theme about prayer, the presider could profitably choose either the first or the eighth of the Sunday prefaces in Ordinary Time about the Church, the body of Christ, praising the Lord in his works. For the alternative theme, about the preaching of the word and remaining faithful to this ministry, the presider could profitably proclaim the fourth eucharistic prayer which speaks of the ministry of Jesus who brought us the good news of salvation.

For the blessing to conclude the liturgy, the presider could choose solemn blessing number 3 in Ordinary Time or number 23 of the prayers over the people to coincide with the main theme of the gospel, about being strong in faith and remaining close to the Lord in prayer. For the alternative theme of the day, the presider could choose the fifth of the solemn blessings, about the Lord's word filling our hearts with joy, and number 20 of the prayers over the people, about the good news of salvation and being filled with love for all people.

THIRTIETH SUNDAY IN ORDINARY TIME

The gospel proclaimed this Sunday is that of the familiar parable of the Pharisee and the tax collector in which the Pharisee "prays" to the Lord in thanksgiving that he is not like the rest of men, and the tax collector beseeches the Lord to look upon him in mercy as he acknowledges that he is a sinner.

Yet, what is even more important than the words which these two men use in addressing God is their attitude of heart and their real intentions. A person can come before the Lord saying the right things, but in fact may be lacking in integrity and sincerity.

The responsorial psalm and the Old Testament lesson coincide with the gospel proclamation because of their references to the Lord hearing the cry of the poor (psalm response) and the assurance that the prayer of the lowly is heard (Old Testament lesson).

Another aspect of the theology implied in the gospel reading concerns the judgment uttered by the Pharisee. He judged others while neglecting the self-criticism that should have been his prior concern. Again, the application here is an easy one to make, for the Christian community may sometimes be tempted to judge others, while self-evaluation and self-criticism are glossed over.

The alternative theme of the liturgy is found in today's reading from the second letter to Timothy. The author gives a very personal and moving account of his sufferings and his reliance on the Lord for strength and guidance—themes that have appeared in the readings from this epistle during the past three weeks. The Lord alone is Paul's refuge and strength, and it was only because of the Lord's guidance that he was able to carry through the preaching ministry of the word. The end of the reading presents a fitting climax to the letter as it ends in a prayer of praise of the Lord's care for Paul. The theme of the liturgy as taken from this reading could center around the sufferings which Paul endured and the redemptive value of suffering for Christ's followers, or it could concern an exploration of the task of preaching and the ministry of the word as stressed in last Sunday's second reading.

The introduction to the rite of blessing and sprinkling with holy water could be reworded to exhort the community to enter into the eucharist with the attitude of the tax collector in the gospel, or it could be an exhortation to see this eucharist as a sign of the fidelity of the Lord toward his people who are undergoing their present hardships and sufferings.

Should the presider use the third form (c) of the penitential rite, invocation number 8, about Jesus who healed the sick and forgave sinners, or number 6, about raising us to new life, would be suitable.

The invitatory to the alternative opening prayer, about praying in a humble hope for salvation, could be used and even expanded to reflect the gospel proclamation this Sunday.

The prayer over the gifts speaks of the service which renders glory to God. This can very well be understood as referring to our sufferings in this life, thus reflecting the alternative theme of today's liturgy. For the main theme of the day, the use of Sunday preface number 2 in Ordinary Time, about the humility of the Lord as an example for the lives of his followers, would be appropriate, as would use of eucharistic prayer number 4 with its own preface for the alternative theme of the day, proclamation of the good news of salvation.

The introduction to the Lord's Prayer could be rewritten this Sunday to reflect the humility of the tax collector.

For the conclusion of the liturgy, solemn blessing number 3 in Ordinary Time, about the Lord's showing his people how to walk in charity and peace, as well as the tenth of the prayers over the people, about the Lord's blessing his people who hope for his mercy, are appropriate choices. For the alternative theme, solemn blessing number 5, about the Lord's word being set in our heart, is appropriate.

THIRTY-FIRST SUNDAY IN ORDINARY TIME

The gospel text read this Sunday is the familiar story of Zacchaeus, who was "small of stature." The story illustrates that the Lord willed that salvation should extend beyond the boundaries of Judaism. Jesus grants his peace to all who would call upon him, and even further seeks out those in need of his grace, as shown in the case of Zacchaeus whom he selects to be his host. The figure of a tax collector receiving the Lord at home is a variation on the Lukan theme of Jesus' sitting at table with publicans and sinners. This evidence of familiarity, generally reserved for good friends, is now used as an image of the generosity of the Father in dealing with his people through the ministry of Jesus. The Old Testament lesson expands this notion of mercy for all since it speaks of the Lord's grace and favor to all of his creation.

The alternative theme for the liturgy this Sunday is from the second letter to the Thessalonians, portions of which will be read from this Sunday until the thirty-third Sunday in Ordinary Time.

This letter is a most appropriate source for reflection on these Sundays which lead up to the solemnity of Christ the King and the first Sunday of Advent.

The letter mentions the question of the "coming of our Lord Jesus Christ." Paul tells his listeners to be aware that the day of the Lord is now coming and that the Lord is to return to his people. Whether or not Paul expected imminent parousia, the Church today should begin to reflect on themes such as the transitoriness and temporality of all that is, and the reality of a future hidden from us now, but to be revealed in Christ.

The introduction to the rite of blessing and sprinkling with holy water could be reworded to refer to the graciousness and universality of salvation through Christ or to the still-to-come return of the Lord to be ruler and judge of all people.

Should the presider prefer to use the third form (c) of the penitential rite, invocation number 2, about Jesus who came to gather the nations into the peace of God's kingdom, or number 5, about raising the dead to life in the Spirit, would be suitable.

The alternative opening prayer reflects the main theme of the day's liturgy by referring to living the faith we profess and trusting in the promise of life eternal. This is also noted in the prayer after communion, as is customary in these prayers, about the Lord giving us new hope through the eucharist, and bringing us to the joy of his promise.

The use of the fourth eucharistic prayer with its own preface, about the Lord's ministry to all who needed his help and his steadfast love despite man's fickle nature, would be an appropriate selection to coincide with the main theme of the gospel. For the alternative theme of the day from second Thessalonians, the presider could appropriately proclaim the sixth Sunday preface in Ordinary Time, about our share now in a foretaste of the promised paschal feast of heaven.

For the conclusion of the liturgy based on the gospel of the day, it would be appropriate to use solemn blessing number 4 in Ordinary Time, about God granting us consolation and peace.

For the alternative theme from the second reading, the presider could choose the fifth of the solemn blessings in Ordinary Time, which refers to God's filling us with lasting joy, or numbers 1 or 16 of the prayers over the people, about the everlasting life which Christ prepared for us and our receiving now a share in his consolation as we prepare for life eternal.

THIRTY-SECOND SUNDAY IN ORDINARY TIME

The main theme of the liturgy taken from the Old Testament lesson and the gospel reading concerns the debate of Jesus with the members of the Sadducee party over the resurrection, whether or not there is a life to come, and what it will be like. Rather than become embroiled in a senseless controversy, Jesus speaks about this life and the life to come and points out that what will matter in the kingdom is not who is married to whom, but rather that this life to come will be radically new. Christian faith proclaims that when Christ rose from the dead he did not, like Lazarus for example, return to the life he once led on this earth. Images such as a "new state of existence" or "sharing the glory of God" help to indicate that what we are dealing with in our resurrection is not on a par with or a continuation of this physical life we now lead.

The Old Testament lesson points to the gospel reading by its consideration of seven brothers and marriage. One possible pastoral application of this pericope would be to explore what resurrection faith means for the present life of the Christian. How often have believers been led to understand that Christians will share in Jesus' resurrection only at the end of their life. It is true that its fullness is only experienced after this life, but it would be well to lead the community to understand that resurrection faith grants us a share now in the risen life of Christ and that this share aids our perception and appreciation of suffering, agony, and death. To treat the resurrection otherwise is to lessen its importance as a source of real hope now and comfort in present sorrow.

The alternative theme of the day is taken from the reading from second Thessalonians and refers to the present state of the Christian community as situated now between the incarnation and the second coming of Christ. The author encourages the community to stand firm in their faith and to persevere in it. He also encourages prayer for many intentions, and yet underlying them all is a concern to grow in hope until the Lord's coming. This latter theme of hope as based on what has happened in the Christ event and in what is yet to be completed in the second coming could be stressed as a continuation of the theme of last week's liturgy.

The introduction to the rite of blessing and sprinkling with holy water could be reworded to deal with the eucharist as our share now in the risen life of Christ, or it could point out that we come to celebrate our common hope and trust in Christ until he comes again. This second theme from the Thessalonians reading is most significant for any understanding of the eucharist as the sacrament that recalls the past and looks toward the future.

Should the presider prefer to use the third form (c) of the penitential rite, invocation number 5, about Jesus raising the dead to life in the Spirit and his granting pardon and peace to the sinner, is fitting.

The opening prayer underscores the alternative theme of the day's readings as it asks the Lord to protect us from pride so that we may give our lives in service to others. The prayer over the gifts speaks of following the Lord with love, and the prayer after communion asks God to keep us single-minded in his service as a result of the eucharist.

The preface that coincides with the main theme of the day is number 4 for the Sundays in Ordinary Time which refers to our being reborn and rising to everlasting life. The alternative theme of the liturgy is reiterated in the sixth preface, about the Spirit as a promised foretaste of the paschal feast of heaven.

The presider could introduce the Lord's Prayer with the fourth of the sample invitations to prayer, about the coming of the Lord's kingdom which continues the alternative theme.

The fifth solemn blessing in Ordinary Time, about walking in God's ways, and number 23 of the prayers over the people, about being strengthened in faith and persevering in prayer, would be suitable. The main theme of the day is well reflected in solemn blessing number 4, asking for peace now and the everlasting life to come, and the first prayer over the people, about the everlasting life which the Lord prepares for us.

THIRTY-THIRD SUNDAY IN ORDINARY TIME

The second readings in the liturgies for the past two Sundays have both been about the second coming of the Lord and our preparation for that event. This Sunday, however, all the readings of the Lectionary and the whole tenor of prayers of the Sacramentary are focused on the second coming of Christ. This theme will continue from now through the beginning of Advent, and its traces are seen throughout the Advent season. The apocalyptic imagery of today's gospel reading from Luke, about the destruction of the temple, is followed by a warning about false teachers who will attempt to mislead men and women who profess faith in Christ. Christ's followers will be brought to witness on his behalf, and this profession will bring division among families, relatives, and friends. The end of the reading encourages the community to be faithful and patient in endurance. The first reading from the prophet Malachi introduces similar eschatological imagery by speaking of "the day that is coming blazing like an oven." This is the day of the Lord who will judge his people. In the midst of this rather somber liturgy, the responsorial psalms points out that all people and all created things should joyfully welcome the Lord who comes bringing judgment and salvation.

The alternative theme of the liturgy is from the second letter to the Thessalonians and deals with the delay in the second coming of the Lord. Paul urges his community to remain faithful to the Lord by imitating his own perseverance in faith and the ministry.

The introduction to the rite of blessing and sprinkling with holy water could be reworded this Sunday to reflect the theme of the coming of the Lord by mentioning the eucharist as our share now in the sacrament which helps us to persevere until the Lord comes in glory to bring all to the Father. The introduction could refer to the theme of the second reading, about the need of the present Church to persevere and to work for the Lord.

Should the presider prefer to use the third form (c) of the penitential rite, he may find helpful invocations in the second sample form in the Sacramentary, invocations which may be used through the season of Advent.

For the main gospel theme of the day, the presider could profitably proclaim the sixth preface for Sundays in Ordinary Time, about our share now as a foretaste in the paschal feast of heaven. Sunday preface number 7 refers to our salvation through the obedience of Christ.

The presider could suitably introduce the Lord's Prayer with the fourth of the sample invitations, about praying now for the coming of the kingdom of God.

Both the fourth and the fifth of the solemn blessings in Ordinary Time reflect the main theme of the day with their mention of eternal life (no. 4) and our receiving joy from the word of the Lord now until we enter fully into our heavenly inheritance (no. 5).

The first of the prayers over the people, about everlasting life prepared for us, as well as number 16, about receiving consolation now and in the life to come, also fit in with this theme.

For the alternative theme from second Thessalonians, the presider could profitably use the third of the solemn blessings in Ordinary Time, about walking in charity and peace, or the nineteenth of the prayers over the people, about the community being strengthened now with the Lord's blessing.

Chapter Six

Solemnities and Feasts Which Replace
Sunday Observance

FEAST OF THE PRESENTATION OF THE LORD

A liturgical principle regarding Marian festivals which has largely
gone unnoticed in conventional presentations of such feasts and
para-liturgical celebrations is that there was always a close
connection between the evolution and theology of these feasts and
the development of Christology. The recent reform of the Roman
Calendar can be best understood and appreciated when this
principle is kept in mind. In no way has the reformed calendar
replaced or made substitutions for feasts of Mary; yet the revisions
are clearly the result of a rethinking and redirection in Marian
piety. Marian feasts are thus seen always in relation to Christ.
Mary's role in the mystery being celebrated is underscored, but
never to the point of eclipsing the centrality of Christ.

All of this is made evident in the feast of the Presentation of the
Lord, the more ancient and now recovered term for what had
conventionally been called the feast of the Purification of Mary.
That the editors of the Sacramentary wanted to renew this as a
Christological feast is clear not only from its title, but is even more
clear in the Mass formula in the Sacramentary and the scripture
readings assigned for proclamation.

The "Purification of Mary" was the title long used in the
Western Church for what was always celebrated in the East as a
feast of the Savior. Historically, the feast was celebrated in fourth-
century Jerusalem and spread to Constantinople through an edict of
Justinian in the sixth century, and is later found in Rome in the
seventh and eighth centuries. The focal point of the feast
historically was the meeting of the old dispensation and the new,

symbolized and concretized in the temple scene where Simeon recognizes Jesus as the long-awaited light of revelation to the Gentiles. Simeon's proclamation of praise is the acknowledgment that the Messiah had indeed come to save all nations. The prayers of the Mass reflect this theology as the opening prayer speaks of Christ, the "man for us" being presented in the temple; the prayer over the gifts speaks of this Son who offered himself as Lamb without blemish for the sins of all; and the prayer after communion prays that as Simeon welcomed the Messiah so may the present congregation be prepared to meet Christ when he comes to "bring us into life everlasting."

A second element that has become a part of this celebration is the blessing of candles for use at the liturgy, a practice which originated in the seventh and eighth centuries. The present liturgy on this day retains this custom and introduces it with a comment about the presentation of Christ now, forty days after his birth. A processing then follows the blessing and the Mass continues with the Glory to God. There can be no doubt of the historical foundation of this practice and the intent of the present reform in the Roman rite which has renewed this usage. Yet, one element which should be avoided in emphasizing this rite is the tendency to associate this feast with the feast of Christmas. While it has been customary to associate the feast of the Presentation with the close of the Christmas season, there would seem to be little value in emphasizing this any more since the feast of the Baptism of the Lord is now so regarded. Hence in the planning of this celebration, the theology of Christ and acknowledging him as the light of the nations should take priority; any references to Christmas should be eliminated as this would only serve to confuse, rather than to help explain the nature of this day.

The scripture readings for this day speak of the Christological nature of the celebration and should be interpreted clearly in order to underscore the true and significant theology of this feast. The first reading from the prophet Malachi speaks of the one who will come to the temple as the Lord whom they seek. The responsorial psalm praises the Lord as the "king of glory," while the gospel acclamation speaks of this "light of revelation to the nations."

The second reading from the letter to the Hebrews reflects the core of this epistle in its emphasis on the humanity of Christ and his position as merciful and faithful high priest who takes away the sins of the world. He actually shared the human condition of those he came to save.

The gospel proclamation is from Luke and tells how Simeon and Anna recognized the Lord; Simeon had been preserved to see the long-expected one, the "revealing light to the Gentiles."

There are many focal points in this liturgy which could form the basis for the eucharistic celebration this day, but one central element should not be forgotten—the identity of Christ. In the scriptures he comes as intercessor (Hebrews). While it is the child Jesus who is presented in the temple, it is the saving Lord who now intercedes for us and whose function as intercessor is at the heart and core of the letter to the Hebrews. The gospel presents Jesus as the redeemer and revealer whose vocation is to bring light to all.

For the introduction to the liturgy, the presider could profitably use the text in the Sacramentary as it introduces the theology of the day. It should also be noted, however, that this text may be adjusted or newly composed to fit more precisely the pastoral situation of the given congregation.

The blessing of candles replaces any form of "penitential rite" and hence no sample formula is provided here.

The preface for the feast of the Presentation is used on this day. This text reflects well the theology of the feast since it speaks of the Son of God who was presented in the temple and was revealed as the glory of Israel and the light of all peoples.

Solemn blessing number 4 or number 5 in Ordinary Time could be profitably selected as the final blessing for the liturgy this day because of their reference to this life and life everlasting (number 4) and the word of God set in our hearts (number 5).

Of the prayers over the people, number 1 speaks of this life leading to life everlasting, number 14 speaks of our rejoicing in the mystery of redemption, number 20 speaks of the gifts of God from on high, the most important of which is the Son of God and the good news he came to preach, and number 23 speaks of the present Church being strengthened in grace and of our remaining close to God and to each other in prayer and true love.

The common understanding of Joseph as the "silent" one can have many meanings and interpretations, but it is certainly true that the scriptures say little about this foster father of Jesus. Joseph plays a significant part in the infancy narratives of Matthew and Luke, even though these narratives are not reproduced by the other evangelists, Mark and John. In recognition of Joseph's association with Jesus and Mary, the Church celebrates this feast in his honor. Like Mary, Joseph's true importance and significance comes from the part he played in doing the Father's will in the incarnation of Jesus.

The evolution of devotion to Joseph was late in developing in the West and some of the more significant foundations stem only from the fifteenth century and later. These speak of his vocation as foster father of Jesus. It was only in the late fifteenth century that this celebration became a part of the Roman Calendar, and his name was only listed in the Litany of the Saints in the eighteenth century. He became patron of the universal Church by decree of Pius IX in 1870, and in the present reform of the calendar today's celebration is ranked as a solemnity.

Today's celebration is a recollection of Joseph the historical personage, and the life and deeds of this man as model and exemplar for the present believing Church. He is indeed a just man, a wise and loyal servant of God, and a man who had extraordinary concern for his wife and child. While it is easy to romanticize about the earliest days of the life of Jesus and to imagine what Joseph may have done in those early years, such attempts should be avoided in order to get to the heart of the matter—that Joseph's vocation to do the Lord's will is the reason why we so venerate him on this day.

The preface acclaims him as "just," "wise," and "loyal," and one who cherished Mary with a husband's love and watched over Jesus with "fatherly care."

The opening prayer parallels Joseph's care for Christ with the care and service which the present Church should show to its Lord. The prayer over the gifts speaks of the unselfish Joseph as he cared for God's Son.

The planning and celebration of the eucharist this day could involve an appreciation not only of the historical Joseph, but also, and more importantly, of the qualities which this man lived and which all believers are called to live in our own day.

The gospel contains many of the characteristics noted in the Mass formula concerning Joseph, for it was his faithful fulfilling of the law and the will of God in doing as "the angel of the Lord had directed him" that is at the heart of the evangelist's interpretation and portrait of Joseph.

The Old Testament lesson from second Samuel is an accommodation of the father-son motif apparent in the gospel about the incarnation. Here the author traces the lineage of the long-awaited one, "the son of David who will live forever" (responsorial psalm).

The passage from the letter to the Romans, the second reading this day, is centered around the figure of Abraham who became the father of many nations because he trusted in the Lord. It is this second reading that helps us today to understand the figure of Joseph. No longer are we called to the observance of the law which Joseph held dear, for we are first and foremost called to faith and trust in the Lord alone. The new dispensation through Christ is marked by faith, faith which was found in Abraham and Joseph and should mark the lives of those who now follow the Lord. The presider could capitalize on this quality as obedience to the Lord as well as underscore the importance of living up to the words which each of us pledges at our baptism, confirmation, the eucharist, and (for most of the community) at the exchange of marriage vows. What all this implies is a reliance on the constant fidelity of the Lord to us, and our acceptance of our responsibility to continue in obedient witness to Christ.

The celebration of the liturgy follows the regular Sunday pattern of celebration with three readings, a proper preface for the feast, and since there is no solemn blessing proper to Joseph in the Sacramentary, the presider could profitably choose from among the prayers over the people. Number 5 about remaining faithful, number 11 or number 22, about doing the Father's will, or number 24, about putting one's trust in the Lord, his preserving the Church from all harm, and seeking to love him in all things, would be appropriate selections.

The selection of March 25 as the solemnity of the Annunciation to the Virgin Mary that she was to be the mother of God is dependent on the fixing of December 25 as the date of Christmas, the commemoration of the incarnation of the Lord. Since the date of Christmas was not fixed until sometime in the fourth century, the Annunciation was later in evolving than some other Marian feasts, especially that of January 1, which was the most primitive feast in honor of Mary at Rome. (In places where December 25 was not observed as the feast commemorating the incarnation of Christ, and January 6 was the date for this feast, the commemoration of the Annunciation took place on April 7.) The first specific reference to this feast in the liturgical books is found in the Gelasian sacramentaries. By the eighth century it was universally observed in the West. By its nature the celebration's focal point is the mission of the Virgin and not so much her person, for what has always received great emphasis has been her acceptance of the will of God, and her role as instrument and bearer of the word of God. The close association of Christology with the development of a cult of Mary is seen to be operative here as well as in many of the other Marian feasts in the Roman Calendar.

This notion of instrumentality and the mission which the Virgin was to accomplish in her own person is seen in the scripture readings assigned for this day. The first, from the book of Isaiah, a text often used by the Christian Church to trace the origins of the coming Saviour, speaks of the virgin bearing a child and calling him Immanuel.

The responsorial psalm fittingly joins the first and second readings since its refrain is "Here am I, Lord, I come to do your will," which theme is taken up and repeated often in the second reading from the letter to the Hebrews. Christ is the One who came to do the Father's will, and so today's Church is invited to do the Lord's will, since in Christ its sins have been washed away and believers live in the dispensation of grace and freedom.

The gospel proclamation of the announcement to Mary that she would bear the Son of God is significant, not merely because it gives the evangelist's account of the event, but more importantly because of the theological concerns of the evangelist Luke which are evidenced here. The phrase "the Holy Spirit will come upon you" can be easily overlooked, and yet this is more than a promise that the Lord would see to it that God's Spirit would protect the Virgin. Luke is concerned to demonstrate that the present Church, indeed the Church in every generation since the death and resurrection of Jesus, lives in a period of time influenced by the Spirit. It is the Spirit of God who rests on Jesus as he proclaims in Luke 4 that he is the bearer of good news to the poor and oppressed; it is the Spirit of God who inspires Jesus through his ministry to do the Father's will; and it is the same Spirit who inspires the present community of believers to continue to live the gospel of Christ.

One obvious emphasis in planning the liturgy for this feast would be to underscore the role of the Spirit, not only in Mary's life while on earth, but in the lives of each of us as members of the pilgrim Church. Just as the Virgin bore her share of trials and sufferings for the sake of fulfilling her promise that the Lord's will be done through her, so today's Church relies on the Spirit to bring it to perfection and keep it faithful to the demands of the Christian life. The same Spirit who inspired Mary inspires contemporary believers in their journey of faith in this world.

A second note that is underscored by Luke in the gospel, and a more conventional one associated with this feast, is the instrumentality of man and woman in doing God's work. It was Mary's fiat that has caused generations to call her "blessed" among women; it was her fiat that inspires a deep reverence for her person and causes us to call upon her aid as we too seek to be instruments of the mission and work of God in our world. Just as Mary was called to bear the word of God in her very womb, the baptized Christian is called to bear the word of God in his or her very person by the kind of life he or she leads. God still relies on contemporary believers to bring his Son to the world, and while Mary is exalted because of her eminent place in the mission of Christ to the world, each and every member of the Christian community is exalted at baptism as a child of God and charged to bring the good news of Christ to this world.

Both focal points of the gospel, about the presence of the Spirit to aid the present Church as it aided Mary, and Mary's willingness to become the instrument of God's revelation as the first merely human being who lived the vocation of the Church, find ample expression in the Mass formula from the Sacramentary.

The invitatories to the opening prayers ask that we become more like Christ, whereas the alternative opening prayer speaks more clearly of God's exalting a lowly virgin to be his servant in his plan of salvation. The preface proclaims Christ who came to save all humanity by becoming human and the virgin who conceived as a result of "the power of the Holy Spirit."

The solemn blessing (no. 15) on feasts of the Blessed Virgin Mary should be used this day, especially because of its reference to the blessing of God which brings the joys of the Spirit whom we call "Holy."

SOLEMNITY OF JOHN THE BAPTIST

The celebration of the solemnity of John the Baptist traces its origins to the fourth century when it was celebrated in connection with the Epiphany of Christ. Yet it was not long before the feast was placed at the end of June, where it has remained in the calendar of the Western Church. The fact that it was regarded seriously quite early in the Christian Church is attested to by the presence of a complete Mass formula in the earliest of the sacramentaries, the "Leonine." In the present missal, there are two Mass formulas for this day, one for the vigil and the other for the day itself. The first readings for both celebrations reflect the same motifs—the prophet being called from the womb to be God's messenger, and bearing God's word to his people. For the vigil Mass, the text is the familiar passage from Jeremiah about being called at a young age and the fears expressed by this chosen one; yet these fears are allayed by the promise of the Lord's presence and support. This is carried through in the responsorial psalm with the refrain about the Lord being his strength. Divine election evidenced here is confirmed and supported by divine consolation and encouragement.

The life of one so selected is not always easy, for the Lord's ways and word are meant to challenge, not to soothe the spirit of the times. The prophecy uttered by John as the last in a long line of those preparing for the coming of the Lord has a divine guarantee and assurance of success despite contemporary resistance.

The second reading for the vigil Mass is from the first letter of Peter. Salvation which has come in Christ was prepared for and preceded by God's messengers. The gospel acclamation states clearly that John was called to bear witness to the light and to prepare the peoples for the coming event of salvation in Christ.

The gospel proclaimed for the vigil speaks of the announcement to Zechariah and Elizabeth that they would be the parents of one who would be "great in the eyes of the Lord." His mission will be to bring back many of the chosen in Israel, and again, it is the Lord who will support him in this task.

The Mass formula for the vigil alludes to many important elements in the person of John, and yet the note struck in the opening prayer and the prayer after communion about a people following the way of salvation prepared for by John, who led others to the Lamb of God, coincides with the scripture readings as well as with the preface of John the Baptist about John as a prophet.

Of the many descriptions of John, none is more significant than that which sets him at the end of the line of the Old Testament prophets, as the one who made the Lord known when at last he came. John was one who would be close to the Christ event, and yet it was he who would be the first to step aside to allow the Lord himself to assume his role as preacher of the good news. The self-effacement and deference which John evidenced in his life should serve as a model for the contemporary Church. Reliance on the Lord and allowing him to accomplish his ministry, when at times we ourselves would like to be regarded as some sort of messiah, is an important aspect of Christian spirituality. No one will ever replace John's unique role in preparing for Christ's coming, and yet each of us is called upon to make the Lord known to others. The delicate balance between Christian witness and self-satisfaction at doing the Lord's work, as achieved in the person and mission of the Baptizer, could be a fruitful source of reflection for imitation on this feast. Christian ministry is effective ministry when it is Christ who is working while we humbly acknowledge our role as instrument and witness. A constant challenge for all who hear the word of God is to preach God's word and to witness to him, not to themselves.

The first reading for the day's celebration is from the latter part of the prophecy of Isaiah and reflects the kind of call that John received while still in his mother's womb. The author here describes one called from birth to be God's messenger and servant. The responsorial psalm continues this motif since it is taken from the text of Psalm 139, about the Lord's knowing a man from the womb and his scrutinizing all his ways and works. The reading from the Acts of the Apostles is significant for instead of describing some general theory about preparing for Christ and living according to his message, it focuses on a specific baptism of repentance. The constant message of John was his baptism for sin-forgiveness which would be efficacious only until Christ's baptism with the Spirit. And yet John's call to repentance remains a permanent part of the Christian dispensation. Repentance is not only a quality and characteristic of Lent or Advent (the season when John is most central to the liturgy) but rather it is part of the very foundation of Christianity. A major part of John's ministry should become a major factor in every Christian life; to repent and believe in the coming of Christ.

The gospel text proclaimed this day speaks of the naming of John at his circumcision and clearly reiterates his uniqueness since he would not be given his father's name and would be known as one who had the hand of the Lord upon him. Yet, it is the last part of the gospel, about John's staying in the desert until his work began, that is significant since it too reflects the needed preparation and repentance which Christians of every age must undergo as they seek to bear witness to Christ.

The Mass during the day reflects this theme as well since the alternative opening prayer speaks of the voice of John urging repentance and pointing the way to the Lord.

For the conclusion to the liturgy of this feast, the presider could profitably use the third or the fifth of the solemn blessings in Ordinary Time since the third speaks of walking in charity and peace and the fifth speaks of the word of God in our hearts filling us with lasting joy.

Of the prayers over the people, the presider could fittingly choose number 11 or number 22, about doing the Lord's will; number 6, about following the Lord with greater fidelity; or number 24, about receiving the Lord's protection against all harm.

A commemoration of Peter and Paul at the Church of Rome can be dated from the late second century, yet the selection of June 29 for this liturgy goes back as far as the third or fourth century. In any case, it is clear that from early times the Roman Church honored Peter and Paul together and that the sacramentaries contained several Mass formulas for this commemoration. In the fifth century in parts of Gaul, there is evidence of the celebration of this feast on February 22, which date is now the occasion for the celebration of the feast of the Chair of Peter. By the late fifth century there was a great celebration at Rome on June 29 in honor of these men, and the same is true of the church at Constantinople.

Thematically, the liturgy as presented in the revised Sacramentary places great emphasis on the faith of Peter and the preaching of Paul, concretized in Peter's special leadership role in the primitive Church and Paul's vocation as apostle to the Gentiles.

The preface for this day speaks of "Peter, our leader in the faith, and Paul, its fearless preacher." Further on it mentions Peter as raising the Church from the flock of Israel and Paul becoming "the teacher of the world."

The solemn blessing (no. 16) for this feast also speaks in these terms by exalting the "rock of Peter's faith" and the "labors and preaching of St. Paul." Indeed the liturgies for this day can easily center on faith and missionary activity as essential components for the life and activity of the Church in any age. The two figures of Peter and Paul are then merged in the lives and experience of each and every Christian who is called to faith and to bear the gospel message in this world.

Yet there is another level of understanding at work in this feast that can be a fruitful avenue for the planning and celebration of the liturgy, the personal commitment and investment which Peter and Paul were called to make in order to become models of faith and mission. Their central place in the evolution of the Church's life is due to qualities and characteristics that mark the nature of the Church in any age. It is as witness to the risen Christ that Peter is marked for a special role in the Christian community; this theme is seen more clearly in the vigil Mass of the feast.

A second aspect that marked the lives of each of these men as stressed in the scripture readings for the Mass during the day is their maturity in the faith, since far more was required of them than an initial acceptance of the gospel. They had to grow and mature in faith in the face of many trials, yet they still held firm to their initial commitment. Such is also the life of the believer, whose life should be marked by times of renewed conversion and deepening awareness of what his acts of faith mean.

The gospel read at the vigil Mass is taken from the conclusion of John's gospel and is about one of the post-resurrection appearances of Jesus. The fact that Peter is noted elsewhere as among the first to receive the vision of the Lord after the resurrection is elaborated on here with the dialogue about Peter's love for the Lord and his consequent responsibility in the community to feed the flock. Indeed, the role of Peter is here affirmed as special, but the fact that its foundation is a relationship with the Lord is central to understanding this role. It is only because of this relationship that the apostle is called to the duty and obligation of feeding the flock of Christ.

While all are called to differing functions in the Church and these are rather easily defined, each of us is called to an ever-deepening relationship with the Lord which is not so easily identifiable and yet which is the absolutely necessary foundation for any effective building up of the Body of Christ.

The second reading for the vigil casts some of this same light on the figure of Paul since this text from the letter to the Galatians is a rather personal account of his receiving and passing on the revelation of Christ. He too had a special task in the early Church, and his task is easy enough to understand for it was based on a revelation and vision of the Lord that sustained him in his ministry. The underpinnings for any effective preaching and witnessing come from the foundational relationship which one develops and sustains with the Lord.

The Mass formula from the Sacramentary speaks of the prayers and intercession of Peter and Paul, and the prayer over the gifts brings out a hopeful dimension in the eucharistic celebration since it implies that the weaknesses in our own lives of faith can be strengthened by the Lord's grace and power.

The gospel passage read on the day of the feast is the familiar confession of Peter at Caesarea Philippi and his consequent commission to lead the Church on earth. While both factors of confessing faith and receiving the commission to lead the Church are the two essential points in the story, for many the popular interpretation will emphasize immediately Peter's particular role in the Church. Hence, the presider can place the emphasis on the faith of the apostle and then show how we too are called upon to confess that same faith in the Messiah, the Son of the living God.

Our present imitation of Peter is best seen and understood in terms of our lives of faith in Christ. Peter's trust in the Lord may not be fully shared by all religious persons, and yet all of us must search and probe what our faith in Christ truly means. Examples of faith such as Peter's can lead to a deepened understanding of the meaning of this feast. This is treated most vividly in both the first and second readings where both Peter and Paul are singled out for special imprisonment and sufferings for the sake of the faith which they professed.

The opening prayer of the Mass during the day speaks of the Church's faith first coming through Peter and Paul. The alternative opening prayer deserves special notice, for while the second part contains a similar theme, the first section in praise of the Father is a motif not usually found in these prayers. For celebrations both on the evening before and on the feast itself, the proper preface and solemn blessing of Peter and Paul are to be used.

FEAST OF THE TRANSFIGURATION

The commemoration of the Transfiguration of the Lord as a liturgical feast can be traced to the tenth century in the East, where it was a local celebration which was later adopted more universally. In the West, the feast was not observed until the late fifteenth century when Pope Callistus III decreed its celebration throughout the Western Church. It has been retained in the revised Roman Calendar for use throughout the Church and replaces the regular Sunday observance should August 6 fall on the Lord's day. Yet despite this obvious emphasis, there are still some unresolved misgivings that many share about the nature of the commemoration. The difficulty lies primarily in the fact that the revised Lectionary has placed a commemoration of the Transfiguration of Christ at its more proper and traditional place as the gospel reading of the second Sunday of Lent in all three cycles of the Lectionary. Since the gospels presented for the feast have already been commented on in the Lenten observance, further comment on them is not needed here. However, what does give a distinct tone to today's celebration is the fact that the first two readings in the Lectionary are not the same as those used during the Lenten season, and in fact, the first from Daniel 7 is part of the scripture readings for the solemnity of Christ the King in year "B." Hence, what we have here is a liturgical mixture in which the transfigured glory of Jesus in relation to his passion and death is now also seen in its apocalyptic dimensions, as reflected in the first and second readings. Should the planning committee wish to reiterate the understanding of the transfiguration as it relates to the passion and death of Jesus, then the commentaries for the second Sunday of Lent should be consulted. However, should the committee wish to deal with the feast on the second level, one possible starting point would be to consider the apocalyptic imagery of the reading from Daniel as it relates to the event of the transfiguration in relation to the nature of the vision of God which believers share. The reading from second Peter presents a statement about the parousia and the transfiguration. The words, "This is my beloved Son . . . ," can give rise to reflections on who this transfigured Jesus really is.

Hence, despite some rather obscure liturgical origins and the fact that the transfiguration has been treated already in the progress of the liturgical season of Lent, a very fruitful avenue to explore would be the vision of God which men and women of faith have and share. One recent criticism of homilies, and liturgical celebrations in general, is that more often than necessary they lead to "action" steps and things to perform as a result of the emphases of the planning committee. Yet, for any valuable Christian action in response to the word of God, the believer must first come to terms with who this revealing God really is. To discover who this Jesus is, to realize the clouds of mystery that still surround our experience of God, and to comprehend that all is not so apparent even to religious people without contemplation and serious reflection, are all helpful insights for the Christian community.

The liturgy could emphasize that the revelation of Jesus' glory is not an event that happened merely once in the past, but rather that it is a living reality which believers of every age discover and come to experience, for the transfiguration is about who God is as he is in the present. Between Christ's earthly life and his return at the end of time we in the present, particularly at the eucharistic celebration, share in God's glory revealed continually through his Son and our Lord.

The Mass formula from the Sacramentary speaks of being strengthened in faith and listening to the voice of God's Son (opening prayer), and of the true radiance of Christ (prayer after communion). The preface provided for this feast speaks of the transfiguration as strengthening the apostles "for the scandal of the cross."

Blessing number 2 or number 4 would be suitable for the conclusion to the liturgy since each of them emphasizes God's peace and the knowledge and the love of God and his Son.

Should the presider prefer to use one of the prayers over the people, number 18 speaks about our being reborn into a new life through reliving the mystery of the eucharist.

SOLEMNITY OF THE ASSUMPTION

Despite the rather recent declaration of the dogma of the Assumption of the Blessed Virgin Mary, the origin of the feast commemorating her assumption can be traced to fifth-century Palestine, and the selection of August 15 as the date for the celebration dates from the sixth century. The feast became common in Rome in the seventh and eighth centuries and spread to the universal Church in the eighth century. This lag between liturgical observance and a dogmatic declaration merely shows that the liturgy does not celebrate "dogmas"; liturgical celebrations are expressions of piety which grew from popular understandings and sensibilities, and not because of Church decree. The best way to understand the liturgical observance of any feast is to look primarily at its prayers and readings, and not seek to impose on the language and genre of worship the subtleties of dogmatic declaration.

The solemnity of the Assumption is significant historically and in the present as well, because it is indeed not only a feast honoring Mary, but rather a feast of celebration of the lot of all Christians who share her faith in the Lord, and who will one day share with her joy in the kingdom of heaven.

The gospel of the vigil Mass tells how Jesus pointed out that allegiance to God's word is more important than merely taking pride in one's physical descent.

The solemnity of the Assumption can be understood in many ways and under many different aspects, but one way would be to consider it as a feast of the destiny of the Virgin and our eventual destiny with her in the kingdom of God. This is underscored in the second readings for both the vigil Mass and the Mass during the day since they are both from St. Paul's teaching about heaven and life's end, about our present share even now in the reality of the kingdom which Christ has prepared for us.

The question which this feast puts to believers is: how tightly do we grasp the things of this passing world, while having only a slippery hold on the things of life eternal? The values often exalted in this world of money, status, and control should pale for the Christian who reflects on the Virgin Mary, who cherished God's love above all that money could buy. She became the servant of the Lord that all might come to real status as his sons and daughters.

For the planning and celebration of the vigil Mass, the committee might wish to explore the question of where we perceive our destiny to lie, in our hands or in the Lord's hands?

The Mass formula in the Sacramentary refers in the opening prayer to eternal life as the destiny of the believer, and the prayer after communion mentions the eucharist now as a share in the joys of heaven by which we are freed from evil.

The preface for the feast of the Assumption speaks of the pattern of the life of Mary as the model and pattern of the lives of all followers of Jesus in that it refers to the "beginning and pattern of the Church in its perfection" residing in the Virgin, and the Church as finding its "pilgrim way."

The solemn blessing for feasts of the Blessed Virgin Mary is a most fitting conclusion to the liturgy especially because of its reference to being filled with the joys of the Spirit and the "gifts of your eternal home."

The gospel of the Mass during the day, about the visitation of Mary to her cousin Elizabeth and the consequent proclamation of the Magnificat, should lead to reflection on the ordinariness and undramatic nature of the encounter and the simplicity of the prayer uttered by Mary. The values of the kingdom of God are exalted here for it is the poor and lowly who find their strength and life in God their Savior.

The second reading for the Mass during the day continues the theme from Paul about Christ's being raised from the dead as the first fruits of all those who follow and join him in the kingdom. Yet, one aspect that could be explored here is that this share in the resurrection of Christ has already begun in this life and need not wait for its final fulfillment in the eternal kingdom of heaven.

The first reading this feast day is the commonly accommodated text from Revelation about a woman clothed with the sun with the moon beneath her feet. Indeed, the exaltation of one so honored as to be assumed into heaven finds its liturgical emphasis in this text.

To reflect on the humility and simplicity of Mary and her life as a model of serving the Lord is one way of celebrating this feast which honors Mary and all who share even now in her destiny forever with the Lord in the kingdom. The gospel's paradox is seen in exalting the poor, and in the second reading Paul emphasizes not merely Christ's risen life, but also our share in that life.

The opening prayer of the Mass during the day speaks of our final goal and coming into glory as did Mary.

The prayer over the gifts and the prayer after communion speak of Mary's glory and ask that we too may live in God's love.

As was suggested for the liturgy of the vigil Mass, the proper preface of the feast and the solemn blessing of the Blessed Virgin Mary should be used.

FEAST OF THE TRIUMPH OF THE CROSS

The liturgical festival of the exaltation of the cross of Christ can be traced to two historical occurrences in the city of Jerusalem. The first was the dedication of the Constantinian basilica of the Holy Sepulchre on September 14 in the fourth century. The other event was the recovery of the true cross from the Persians in the seventh century, which prompted the declaration of this special feast in honor of the cross.

It is significant that the scripture readings now assigned to the feast avoid any reference to Christ's agony and passion, but offer a positive appreciation of his willing acceptance of death on the cross (second reading) and stress the redeeming value of the cross in relation to salvation history (first reading and gospel texts).

The gospel reading from the Nicodemus dialogue in the third chapter of John reflects the teaching of this evangelist that the Son of Man had to be lifted up and exalted, not as any earthly king, but rather in that as cosmic King of all he would have to be lifted up on the wood of the cross as his throne. For John this is the final and greatest revelation of the glory of the Son of Man; the cross is his greatest act of self-revelation and self-giving for his followers.

The first reading illuminates the gospel text by referring to Moses who raised a bronze serpent on a pole to heal all those who were wounded by the serpents in the desert. Just as the bronze serpent was a symbol of healing and life, so the wood of the cross of Christ symbolizes the healing and strengthening which the Christian receives from the Son of Man lifted up on the cross.

The second reading from the letter to the Philippians is the Christ-hymn in which Christ's self-emptying by taking the form of a slave and his obedient acceptance of suffering on the cross are lauded as pivotal moments in his act of redemption.

Over the years there has been the constant temptation to separate the two events of Christ's ascending the cross and his rising to new life in the resurrection. In fact, the primitive liturgy did not so separate these two events, but rather joined them so that the cross of Christ was not seen as an instrument of suffering and agony. Instead, the cross was and remains an important symbol of the new life itself which has come in Christ. The skull often pictured at the base of the cross in Christian art is the skull of Adam, whose heritage of sin and death has been undone forever by the life which Christ came to bring us through his accepting death on a cross. The imagery of the wood of the tree of the garden in which Adam was tempted and the wood of the cross which Christ ascended is reflected clearly in the preface for this day: "the tree of man's defeat became his tree of victory," a text which is used in the liturgies of many Christian churches and which is derived from an ancient liturgical text. Indeed, the Christian's reflection on Christ's cross need not be a macabre recollection. Rather it can be a very positive understanding of the value of Christ's death and the consequent new life which believers share in and through him.

It is more than an interesting historical note to realize that this feast stems in part from the dedication of the basilica of the Holy Sepulchre in Jerusalem. The Latin rite chapel that adjoins the hill of Calvary in the basilica contains a ceiling decorated with a mosaic depicting the implications of the death of Christ on a cross. This mosaic is of a vine (one would be tempted to use the "true vine" title from John's gospel) which has branches reaching over the whole space symbolizing life, and also parts of this vine motif contain symbols of bread, wine, and foods for the refreshment of all who believe in the value of the wood of the cross. For a graphic example of the nourishment which the Christian receives from the sacrifice of Christ on the cross and the sacrifice of the eucharistic celebration, one would be hard pressed to find a more adequate pictorial expression. Indeed as the gospel acclamation states, "We adore you, Oh Christ, and we praise you, because by your cross you have redeemed the world."

The Mass formula from the Sacramentary and today's readings reflect a mutual understanding of the cross. The opening prayer speaks of Christ's obedience in accepting his suffering on the cross (see the Philippians reading) and both the prayer over the gifts and the prayer after communion speak of the sacrifice of Christ as one with the eucharist, especially in the latter prayer.

Either the preface of the Holy Cross or the first of the prefaces for the Passion of the Lord may be proclaimed this day. The preface of the Cross speaks of salvation coming from the wood of the cross, and the preface of the Passion speaks of the kingship of Christ crucified and his death bringing life to the world.

Solemn blessing number 5, for the Passion of the Lord, or number 17 of the prayers over the people, about the love of Christ as he delivered himself to evil men and suffered the agony of the cross, would be suitable selections.

SOLEMNITY OF ALL SAINTS

While traces of the observance of a feast in honor of all the saints can be found in the East as early as the fourth century, it was only in the seventh century in Rome that such a commemoration was observed on May 13, the date of the dedication of the Pantheon for Christian use. The date was moved to its present November 1 in the eighth century, and the observance became universal in the ninth century.

One overriding theological foundation for the feast is that of the unity of the Church on earth with the communion of the saints and their intercession for the pilgrim Church. The Mass formula for the day is filled with references to the saints who pray for God to forgive our sins (opening prayer), who are concerned to help and save us, (prayer over the gifts), and who pray that we may be delivered "from present evil" (solemn blessing number 18). These men and women, "our brothers and sisters" (preface), give us a pattern and example for our lives (solemn blessing) as we seek to prepare now for the joy of the kingdom (prayer after communion).

The first scripture reading of the feast from the book of Revelation continues this motif since it concerns the elect who are dressed in white singing God's praise before his throne, and who have washed clean their robes in the blood of the Lamb. They are identified as those who have endured the great period of trial and who now stand with the chosen in the kingdom. Hence, they who once shared the fragility of human existence persevered in faith and now intercede before the throne of God for those still in this world.

The second reading from first John speaks of what we are now as God's children, and what we are to be in becoming like him in eternity. Again the association of the present Church and the saints is not seen to be two entirely separate existences; rather the saints remind us of the status to which we are all called in the kingdom.

The gospel reading is the proclamation of the beatitudes from the gospel of Matthew and provides an opportunity for contemporary reflection about the meaning and import of this most central gospel teaching for our day.

While the theme of intercession on behalf of the still pilgrim Church by those now seated in the kingdom is an obvious choice for reflection this day and for the planning of the liturgy, another more general theme could also be selected. The whole idea of sainthood may well be explored this day to help in understanding that the saints have come from the same human stock that we come from. Saints may be defined as those who make the ordinary extraordinary, and the extraordinary credible. In the beatitudes it is the common, almost insignificant people who are to become the most cherished and blessed by God. It is these people whose very ordinary lives often made undramatic biographies who are now called the saints of God. The saint is the individual led by faith and faith's vision to perceive that in the present he or she is called to live the demands of the kingdom. Saints are revealers of who God is to others, and it is because so many remain unofficially recognized by the Church that this feast makes sense. The saints are indeed the ones who have endured a great period of trial and who stand at God's right hand. The saints make us realize that we who are undergoing the trials in this life are called to sanctity. And this kind of sanctity resides in revealing the Lord to others in the everyday situations of life.

SOLEMNITY OF THE IMMACULATE CONCEPTION

The liturgical principle noted above (see feast of the Presentation of the Lord), that the evolution of Marian festivals closely parallels the development of Christology, should be borne in mind when considering this feast. Although the gospel of this feast is the human account of the annunciation to Mary that she was to give birth to the child Jesus, the first two readings speak in more general terms of our situation before God, our present struggle with the forces of evil, and the triumph already accomplished by Christ in whom resides the fullness of every spiritual blessing. The passage from Genesis 3 provides the believer with a significant mythology by which he or she can begin to appreciate and understand the believer's situation in this world of evil and sin. After the fall, mankind was subjected to all the death-dealing and sin-involving forces of the world; their only glimpse of hope (according to this text) is the prophecy that one day the head of the serpent would be crushed. The responsorial psalm follows closely this note of ultimate triumph and salvation since it speaks of God's victory and our praise of him, "for he has done marvelous deeds."

The second reading is the beginning of the letter to the Ephesians where the author, in characteristic style, praises God for the salvation and redemption won through his Son our Lord. It is in Christ that every spiritual blessing has already come and this is seen in Christ's calling each of us adopted sons of his Father. The

Christian has been chosen in Christ and has been granted every spiritual blessing possible. God has triumphed in and through Christ and the still struggling Church can only be confident and comforted by this revelation.

The invitatory to the opening prayer speaks of being freed from sin through Mary's prayers, and the parallel between Mary's sinless state and our being freed from sin and living in this state is seen in both the prayer over the gifts and prayer after communion.

Besides reflecting on Mary as model and example of being free from sin, another way of approaching the feast would be to consider the role of Mary herself in the incarnation, by her willingness to obey the commands of the Lord through the message of the angel. The position of Mary as a model for the Christian has always been an important aspect of the Advent liturgy, and in the revised calendar and Lectionary, her participation in this mystery is emphasized in the liturgies for the fourth Sunday of the season. Yet the occurrence of the feast of the Immaculate Conception early in the season can prepare the Christian to await the liturgical observance of the incarnation at Christmas.

Today's gospel provides a most fitting text for reflection about Mary's obedience to the word of the Lord. As the Church awaits the celebration of Christmas and its annual reflection on the Word become flesh, the Church this day is called upon to evaluate how seriously it takes the Lord's scriptural word and revelation of Christ. Mary's choice to follow the will of the Father was by no means an easy decision, and it was only her constant trust that guided her decision and the living out of her initial choice. The same is true for the life of the follower of Christ, for to choose to be a Christian and to live as Christ's faithful follower involves more than rhetoric and words. It involves the kind of quiet acceptance and pondering of the will of God that marked Mary's life. With this in mind, the second reading from Ephesians provides a fitting selection for this feast as it proclaims to the Church that it is in Christ that every blessing has come and every grace received. On this feast Mary becomes the model of the believer who seeks to live in obedience to the incarnate Word of God.

Chapter Seven

Solemnities of the Lord

TRINITY SUNDAY, SUNDAY AFTER PENTECOST

The difficult theological truth of the Holy Trinity has become one of the most dynamic of liturgical celebrations and feasts; it is by no means merely the province of the theologians. It is a feast about the reality of God in the real lives of believers; it is about the image of God in whom we believe, about an image that is positive and eminently believable.

In the "A" cycle, the first reading from the book of Exodus is about the mediatorship of Moses to whom Yahweh revealed himself as the totally other in the unconsumed yet ominous image of the burning bush. The feast of the Holy Trinity does not reflect this transcendence and otherness of God so much as it reveals the image of Yahweh as a Lord "slow to anger and rich in kindness." Moses speaks of a God who will forgive the sins of his people.

The second reading from second Corinthians does not describe the Lord, but rather dwells on the life of the Trinity in the Christian community. The grace, peace, and fellowship of the Trinity are to be reproduced in the Christian community, and harmony and peace are to be hallmarks of this fellowship.

The gospel completes the picture of the Trinity by presenting the revelation of Jesus to Nicodemus about God's love for the world by sending his own Son to redeem us; faith in him leads to sanctification, not condemnation. The message of the readings is not one of doctrinal speculation, but an assurance of God's presence within the community of the redeemed under the guidance and inspiration of the love of God, the grace of Christ, and the fellowship of the Spirit. Far more important than defining the persons in God is to live according to the Trinity's life-giving qualities.

For the "B" cycle of readings, the implications about belief in the Trinity are stressed. The gospel text is the ending to Matthew's gospel and speaks about the command to go forward teaching all that Jesus taught and to baptize those who believe in him. The Greek word for "Matthew" means "disciple" and so it is entirely fitting that this evangelist should insist in this gospel again and again on making disciples and being better disciples. Undoubtedly the reference to the Father, Son, and Spirit in this text is the reason it was specially chosen for this feast. Whether or not this is a primitive baptismal formula should not concern us so much as the fact that the revelation of God requires more than mere assent or acceptance. It requires mission as an essential part of the Christian religion.

This revelation of who God is (this Sunday is filled with images that reveal the Trinity) begins with the Old Testament text about Moses' discourse about what God has done for his people. This does not mean that Yahweh is the God only of Israel. Rather, Moses is pointing out that God's people are special recipients of his love (and therefore an "elected" people). Today our Christian gatherings for worship are occasions to deepen our awareness of who God is and how he has made us special recipients of his love.

The second reading from chapter 8 of the letter to the Romans speaks of the power of God in adopting us and making us his very own possession.

In the "C" cycle of the Lectionary, two major aspects of God's revelation appear for reflection, proclamation and liturgical planning.

The first concerns the Holy Spirit and is especially helpful for communities who have been led up to the celebration of the solemnity of Pentecost with special programs and preparations, for it concerns the Spirit as the gift of the Father and Son to keep us faithful to the love they have shown us. While there is no longer any octave of Pentecost, and hence, no extension of the Pentecost "season" or "time" as was formerly the case, there is nevertheless every reason to emphasize the power of the Holy Spirit in this liturgy. The Spirit as revealed in the gospel is the Spirit of all truth and the outpouring of the love of the Father and the Son. This Spirit brings no new revelation, but rather confirms the Church in the revelation of the Father and the Son. The intimate unity of the three—Father, Son, and Spirit—is emphasized by referring to Jesus' saying: "All that the Father has belongs to me," and the Spirit is pictured as the one who comes to aid the community to live the truth which the Son came to reveal.

The important role that the Spirit plays in the Christian life is noted again in the second reading where this divine person is shown to be the power of the love of God for us. It is through Christ, in the power of the Spirit we call holy, that we have access to the Father.

The other significant theme that emerges in the liturgy of the word concerns the power of God in creation, seen not merely as a deed of making but rather as a state of keeping all created things in being. We can reason to the necessity of a power to make things, "the maker of heaven and earth," but it is essentially biblical revelation that stresses not merely the act of creation once upon a time, but the force and power of God that continually sustains all things in his love.

The glory of God in creation is poetically expressed in the beautiful hymnlike Psalm 8, used as today's responsorial psalm. The sustaining power of God is personified in the image of Wisdom from the book of Proverbs.

Whatever the theme chosen for this liturgy (and there are many that can be drawn from the readings), it will be the task of the committee to stress the positive and dynamic notion of the divinity. It is often the case that even lifelong Christians have a confused notion of God. To overcome such a situation, a properly prepared and celebrated feast of the Holy Trinity can only help redirect attention to the dynamism and love of God, One-in-three, for his people.

The introduction to the rite of blessing and sprinkling with holy water could stress the idea of the triune God by mentioning our dependence on God's creative work, and the power of the Spirit as that aspect of the divinity that draws the Church together to pray. Should the presider prefer to introduce the liturgy with the third form (c) of the penitential rite, he should bear in mind that the three invocations are of Christ alone and they do not invoke the Father and Spirit directly. Invocations that acclaim Christ as the

Lord who sustains us in our lives of grace and peace and as the redeemer who intercedes for us with the Father in heaven would be appropriate.

The presider could appropriately choose the opening prayer for almost any of the themes of the day, whereas the alternative opening prayer refers to the creative act of God, "the people formed in your image."

The preface of the Holy Trinity contains many of the most primitive images of the Trinity, in expressing the mystery of the Godhead, in revealing the glory of the Son and the Spirit, and in revealing one Lord and God.

If the theme of the liturgy emphasizes the role of the Spirit in man's redemption, the presider could suitably choose the solemn blessing of the Holy Spirit as the conclusion to the liturgy. Should the liturgy emphasize the role of the Trinity in salvation, the first and fifth of the solemn blessings in Ordinary Time, about the Lord keeping us in his care (number 1), or blessing us with all good gifts and filling us with the lasting joy of his word (number 5), are both appropriate.

CORPUS CHRISTI, SUNDAY AFTER TRINITY SUNDAY

According to the directions in the Sacramentary, this solemnity is to be celebrated as a holy day on the Thursday after Trinity Sunday or on the Sunday following Trinity Sunday in places when it is not kept as a holy day; hence its present place in the liturgical cycle is on a Sunday in the revised calendar in the United States. The feast itself dates from the thirteenth century and despite some rather defensive and polemical associations, it was and remains a significant festival. There is a certain tension inherent in reinterpreting some of the extraliturgical aspects of the celebration such as benediction and eucharistic processions, and placing them within a much more theologically and liturgically nuanced framework.

Generations of people who have been brought up on the popular piety which surrounded this day often lament that the processions have become less significant in recent years, and so the liturgical celebration itself has been suggested as the proper focal point for celebration. And yet merely to suggest that the eucharistic celebration itself replace some very significant manifestations of piety may not resolve some of the underlying problems here. What would be far more significant pastorally would be to adapt and apply as much as possible the theology in the readings, prayers and prefaces for this day to the given pastoral situation. Where processions are still part of the order of this day, the planning committee can adapt them in such a way that the liturgical celebration takes priority, and then the procession or other form of devotion can receive a proper orientation. To eliminate completely devotions which many people have found and still find helpful may ultimately do more pastoral harm than trying to adjust some of the elements of this piety to a more complete expression and appreciation of the liturgy of the eucharist.

Proclaimed apart from one another, each of the three readings assigned for the solemnity of Corpus Christi in the "A" cycle could provide a suitable and fitting reflection on what the eucharist is and its place in the life of the Church. The reading from Deuteronomy recalls to the Israelites the favors the Father worked for them in delivering them from bondage, by directing their journeying, and by feeding them on their way to the land of promise. The reading from first Corinthians informs the community that the unity symbolized by the one bread and one cup is a unity that is to be realized in the lives of the assembled community. And the reading from John 6:51–58 is the classic eucharistic interpretation. But one theme which is enunciated in the first reading and which is carried through in the others, and which is most important for the understanding of the eucharist is the word "remember." What Christians do when they celebrate the eucharist is recall the past, reform the present, and look toward the future.

The first reading is about the definitive past, when Yahweh fed his people with manna from on high during their years of wanderings and journeying. The reading from first Corinthians speaks no longer of the past but of the present where we share the one bread and one cup. We are to become the body of Christ in the present, and to imitate the sacrament of his body and blood which we receive. The beginning of the gospel proclamation refers to the bread that the Lord will give, so that anyone who eats this bread, "shall live forever." The orientation here is on the future, the coming of the kingdom, and the bread of the kingdom is the Lord's eschatological gift to those who believe him to be the true bread of life. The eucharist is our community memorial sacrifice, recalling the past deeds of redemption, the present realization of these deeds in the sacraments of the Church, and in the future when we shall all share in the food of heaven in the kingdom of the Father. Whatever the choice of theme for this celebration, the opportunity to focus on the sacrament of the eucharist and its importance for the life of the Church should not be missed by the planning committee.

The readings in the "B" cycle of the Lectionary converge on a number of points, but one which dominates is that of "covenant." The first reading from the Book of Exodus recounts the revelation of God's law, Israel's privileged relationship with him, and their acceptance of the covenant's demands: "We will do everything the Lord has told us." The sacrifice in blood was the symbol of this relationship and the offering of the blood of young bulls continued in Israel to be a "memorial" (see above on the readings of the "A" cycle) of this covenant. The second reading, from the letter to the Hebrews, continues the Old Testament understanding of the covenant and uses this to interpret the sacrifice of Jesus offered once-for-all. The blood of bulls and goats is now superseded by the final offering of Christ for our salvation. We become one with his sacrifice at the eucharist and it is this one perfect offering that is acceptable to the Father.

The gospel proclaimed is from Mark and speaks of the Last Supper of Jesus with his disciples. This meal is continued for the salvation and redemption of all people in every age in the Church. The institution narrative in the eucharistic prayer reflects the synoptic texts by stating that this is a share in the new covenant in the blood of Christ. For planning the liturgy in the "B" cycle, it would be appropriate to stress our present share in the covenant forged in the sacrifice of Christ.

In the "C" cycle of the Lectionary, the comparatively short text from the book of Genesis presents the figure of Melchizedek whose name has been used in the Roman Canon in association with the eucharistic liturgy. "Look with favor on these offerings and accept them as once you accepted the gifts of your servant Abel, the sacrifice of Abraham, our father in faith, and the bread and wine offered by your priest Melchizedek." This rather elusive figure of Old Testament literature is also referred to in the responsorial psalm of this liturgy.

The second reading in the "C" cycle is St. Paul's account of the institution of the Lord's Supper. The instruction given here presents the eschatological aspect of worship for it concludes with a reference to shared eucharist as commemorating the death of the Lord until he comes again in glory.

The gospel reading is the Lukan account of the feeding of the crowds with the multiplied five loaves and two fish. Some of the words and gestures utilized in this text have eucharistic overtones and some exegetes find that the liturgical usage of the early Church influenced the writing of this and similar feeding miracles in the gospels. The Lord provides for his people in a superabundant way because "they all ate, until they had enough. What they had left, over and above, filled twelve baskets." Such is a reference to the Lord's kindness and mercy toward us in caring for us in superabundant ways. The Lord's portion is not "measure for measure" but over and above our need.

The rite of blessing and sprinkling with holy water could introduce this celebration of the eucharist as the meal that renews the covenant made between the believer and the Lord at baptism.

Should the presider prefer to use the third form (c) of the penitential rite, the sixth set of sample invocations would be helpful since it refers to our share in the new life of Christ, to his forgiving our sins, and to the eucharist as our share in the body and blood of Christ.

The opening prayer of the liturgy speaks more directly of the eucharist as food and our present experience of salvation, and the alternative opening prayer speaks of the service which the community is to lavish on others as a result of its participation in the death and risen life of Christ.

The prayer over the gifts speaks of the unity and peace signified in this celebration—a familiar theme of these prayers.

The use of the second preface of the Holy Eucharist would seem to be the more appropriate to reflect the rich imagery of the readings since it mentions the Lamb whose memorial we celebrate at the eucharist, and the eucharist as the action by which the Lord feeds his people and strengthens them in holiness, so that all may walk in one communion of love.

The prayer after communion, as is typical of these prayers, speaks of the eschatological idea of eucharist as our share now in what will one day be shared completely in the kingdom. The use of the third or eighteenth of the prayers over the people, about receiving heavenly gifts at the eucharist (no. 3) and the mystery of the eucharist helping us to lead a new life (no. 18), would seem to be the most appropriate for the celebration of this feast.

SOLEMNITY OF CHRIST THE KING, LAST SUNDAY OF THE YEAR

The celebration of the solemnity of Christ the King is now placed at the end of the Church's celebration of "Ordinary Time" because its emphasis and import more accurately reflect the themes of these last Sundays in Ordinary Time and the first Sundays of Advent. The emphasis on the Lord's established but still to be completed kingship is most significant at this point of the Church year, and its place here is certainly an improvement over its former somewhat arbitrary place at the end of October. The very title "Christ the King" would seem to indicate that we end the liturgical year with more than a note of triumph, power, and glory. It is only fitting that we who proclaim his rule and kingdom week after week should pause this Sunday to acclaim him as the King of Kings and the Lord of Lords. And yet, this is not the essence of this feast.

The readings of the "A" cycle do not proclaim the king of triumph and glory, sovereignty, powerful deeds, and strict authority. The first reading instead gives us our key that the Bible would prefer to speak in terms of the imagery of the shepherd and his flock and not of a super-earthly king and his array of servants. The times may not be the best, says Ezekiel; indeed, they may be "cloudy and dark," but the king whom we acclaim this day imitates the shepherd who seeks out and finds the strays of his flock; he binds up the injured, he heals those in need of healing, and understands the misunderstood. The shepherd is the image of the king we acclaim today, the simple, undramatic servant, not a reigning monarch who insists on rights and privileges.

The second reading speaks of Christ the King as the one who gives life, a new life in God's sight. All were in bondage to sin and death in Adam according to the book of Genesis, but that sin no longer weighs on us because Christ has come to lavish on us a vision of life freed from the corruption of sin and death, a vision of unity and peace granted to us through Christ, who is forever our way to salvation.

The third image is in the gospel, where all of us are invited to participate in Christ's kingship, not by stressing or resting secure in our dignity or even in exercising the power of a monarch. Instead we are asked about how much of a shepherd we still have to become. To be a member of the Church of Christ the King is to be pledged to unity and peace, the same unity and peace which have been granted to us in Christ Jesus. We have been granted all this through him, and on this feast we are to question ourselves as to how much we have extended this to others. But even if we have not shared in or kept to the kingdom's demands, we shall be forgiven in this eucharist and strengthened to begin again to renew the face of this earth according to the image and likeness of the unity and peace of Christ the King who comes as a shepherd to feed the flock of the Church. The gospel presents a very demanding morality and measure for our final judgment. Read in the context set by the first two readings, this kind of life is made possible because of the constant nourishment and care of the shepherd who we acclaim as king.

The first two readings for the liturgy of the word in the "B" cycle present aspects of Christ's sovereignty, glory, and honor as king. In the language of the book of Daniel, all nations, peoples, and languages will come to profess his kingship, another reference here to the apocalyptic imagery of this time of the Church year. The second reading from the book of Revelation contains resonances of this same theme about Christ as the Alpha and Omega and his coming on the clouds of heaven. What also emerges from this text is the beginning of another and more appropriate theme for reflection this Sunday, as Christ is pictured as the first born from the dead, that in his love he washes away the sins of men, and makes of his people a line of kings and priests. Hence, the feast of the kingship of Christ is also a festival of all who share in his kingship through faith.

But the final reading from the gospel of John is also necessary if we are to explore the dimension of kingship that is most important for the Johannine writer. Jesus acknowledges that he is indeed a king, but not in the image and likeness of the worldly kings. He is a king whose realm is not of this world, but which is found wherever his followers witness to the truth. The nature of the kingship that we share as believers is one of imitation of Christ, who revealed his kingship for the final and most important time on the throne of the cross. The Revealer shows that his way, truth, and life end ultimately on the cross, and that for those who witness to him and his kingship, a life of cross-bearing will also be necessary.

The solemnity we celebrate this day is of Christ's kingship and of our share in his lordship, but this share comes from foresaking glory and being servants of one another; of not respecting honors and riches, but in respecting the truth to which our king gave his life as a witness. His mission was not to the powerful, and ours similarly should be to the powerless. The Lord is our king, but the nature of the lordship we share is not dominance, and the form of our respect for this king is in respecting one another in his name.

The gospel reading for the "C" cycle of the Lectionary speaks not of any royal personage arrayed in the finery of this world, but rather of one acclaimed as king by the sign over his head on the throne of a wooden cross. It is paradoxically the thief who recognized in Christ the longed-for Messiah, and it is he who acclaims him as Lord, rather than the religious and political establishment which conspired to put him to death. It is indeed a most paradoxical king whose only throne is wood from a tree, since it was from the tree's fruit that Adam and Eve had to face destruction and death. We no longer share the banished lot of Adam and Eve, but we do share a new life and love through the sacrificial death of the God-Man. The preface of this day speaks of this by referring to Christ as priest offering his life on the altar of the cross.

The second reading presents another paradoxical interpretation, in that Christ as head of the Church is closely identified with the community of the redeemed. Unlike other rulers, he is not distant from his people; in fact they grow ever more fully to participate in his divine life. This image of God in Christ is a most appealing and helpful one since it proclaims the fullness of divinity residing in him, which divinity believers now share through him alone. Again, Christ is indeed proclaimed as king, but the kind of king who draws followers to his Father instead of submitting them to an oppressive bondage of slavery.

Among the many possible interpretations of the readings this Sunday, the two of the sign of the cross as the ultimate sign of the kingship of Christ, and the unity of Christ and his people as the perfect sign of the newness of this kingship are both appropriate emphases for the planning of this liturgy. Conventional understandings and descriptions of kingship and power are transformed in and through the kingship of Christ. This king died that we might live; this king lives with the Father that we might be drawn to him; this king established his kingdom once in history that we might have access to the Father for ever and ever.

The introduction to the rite and blessing with holy water could be in terms of the kingship in which the community first shared at baptism and in which it shares again in the celebration of the eucharist. Being strengthened in the body and blood of the Lord is the way in which we share anew in the kingship of Christ. Should the presider use the third penitential rite (c), the second set of sample invocations reflects well the kingship commemorated this Sunday.

The opening prayer speaks of the lordship of the Lord Jesus whom we gather to acclaim this day, whereas the alternative opening prayer tells of Christ's being brought from death to life. Furthermore, in this prayer he is acclaimed as the cause of the unity and love of all mankind.

The prayer over the gifts mentions the reconciliation offered to mankind through Christ, and the prayer after communion speaks of our share now in what will one day be completed in life everlasting in the joy of his kingdom.

The preface of Christ the King is prescribed for this Sunday and speaks of his kingdom of truth, life, holiness, grace, justice, love, and peace, which are now shared at the eucharist with the Christian community but which need be shared as well with the rest of mankind.

The introduction to the Lord's Prayer could be amplified from the fourth sample invitation to prayer, about the coming of the Lord's kingdom.

The most appropriate solemn blessing for this day is number 3 in Ordinary Time since it speaks of the mercy of God and of walking in charity and peace. An alternative to this would be number 20 of the prayers over the people concerning the richness of God's grace, the good news of salvation, and the task of loving all people.